Gathered
for Life

Gathered for Life

OFFICIAL REPORT

VI Assembly World Council of Churches

Vancouver, Canada
24 July - 10 August
1983

Edited by David Gill

World Council of Churches, Geneva
Wm. B. Eerdmans, Grand Rapids

Published by WCC Publications, Geneva,
in collaboration with Wm. B. Eerdmans Publishing Co.,
Grand Rapids, Michigan, USA
ISBN 2-8254-0779-8 (WCC)
ISBN 0-8028-1987-7 (Eerdmans)

Reports of the Vancouver Assembly are available
in French, German and Spanish

WCC photos: Michael Dominguez, Gideon Musa,
Ron Rice and Peter Williams
Cover design: Michael Dominguez

© 1983 World Council of Churches, 150 route de Ferney,
1211 Geneva 20, Switzerland

Phototypeset by Input Typesetting Ltd, London
Printed in Switzerland

TABLE OF CONTENTS

Preface   vii

Message from the Sixth Assembly   1

1. The Story of an Assembly   5
   1.1 The Task   5
   1.2 The Participants   6
   1.3 From Absent Friends   8
   1.4 So Many Alleluiahs!   9
   1.5 How it Worked   13
   1.6 The Canadian Context   15
   1.7 Related Activities   16
   1.8 A Personal Appraisal   17

2. "Jesus Christ – the Life of the World"   21
   2.1 Theme Presentations   21
   2.2 First Sub-theme: "Life, a Gift of God"   22
   2.3 Second Sub-theme: "Life Confronting and
        Overcoming Death"   23
   2.4 Third Sub-theme: "Life in its Fullness"   24
   2.5 Fourth Sub-theme: "Life in Unity"   25
   2.6 Other Perspectives on the Theme   27
   2.7 The Theme and the Message   27

3. Issues for the Churches and the WCC   30
   3.1 Witnessing in a Divided World   31
   3.2 Taking Steps towards Unity   43
   3.3 Moving towards Participation   52
   3.4 Healing and Sharing Life in Community   62
   3.5 Confronting Threats to Peace and Survival   72
   3.6 Struggling for Justice and Human Dignity   83
   3.7 Learning in Community   93
   3.8 Communicating Credibly   103

4. Reviewing the Past: Charting the Future   112
   4.1 Reports and Responses   112
   4.2 The WCC and its Member Churches   115

4.3 Relations with the Roman Catholic Church 117
4.4 Christian World Communions 122
4.5 Nominations, Elections 123
4.6 Programme Guidelines and Finance 127

5. World Affairs in Ecumenical Perspective 129
   5.1 Statement on Peace and Justice 130
   5.2 Statement on Human Rights 138
   5.3 Statement on the International Food Disorder 144
   5.4 Statement on the Middle East 147
   5.5 Statement on Southern Africa 151
   5.6 Statement on Central America 156
   5.7 Resolution on Afghanistan 161
   5.8 Resolution on Cyprus 162
   5.9 Resolution on the Pacific 163
   5.10 Resolution on the Rights of the Aboriginal
        Peoples of Canada 164
   5.11 Minutes on Public Issues of Continuing Concern
        to the WCC 165
        Armenian Genocide 165
        US Military Bases in the Philippines 166
        Situation in Sri Lanka 166
        Situation in Lesotho 167

APPENDICES
    I. Assembly Programme 171
   II. Report of the Moderator of the Central Committee 175
  III. Report of the General Secretary 193
   IV. Messages 210
    V. Presentations on the Assembly Theme 213
       1. By Theodore Stylianopoulos 213
       2. By Allan Boesak 222
   VI. Assembly Committees and Issue Groups 230
  VII. Report of the Assembly's Finance Committee 240
 VIII. Report of the Assembly's Programme Guidelines
       Committee 247
   IX. The Presidents and Members of the Central
       Committee 261
    X. Member Churches of the WCC 266
   XI. Assembly Participants 279
  XII. Constitution and Rules 324

ACKNOWLEDGMENTS 348

INDEX 349

As this broken bread was
scattered upon the
mountains, and being
gathered together became
one, so may your Church
be gathered together from
the ends of the earth into
your kingdom; for yours is
the glory and the power,
through Jesus Christ, for
ever and ever.

From the Didache,
second century

PREFACE

I heartily commend this Official Report of the Sixth Assembly of the World Council of Churches which met in Vancouver, Canada, from 24 July to 10 August 1983.

The report provides a record of what happened during those exciting and hectic days spent on the beautiful campus of the University of British Columbia in Vancouver. There representatives of the over three hundred member churches of the World Council came together to celebrate the theme: "Jesus Christ – the Life of the World". Along with many others they deliberated on the implications of the theme, and they wrestled with the issues facing the churches of the world, arising out of the work of the Council since the Fifth Assembly in Nairobi in 1975. They grappled with the burning concerns of people around the globe where life is threatened and death reigns. And they sought to discern the tasks to be undertaken by the churches and the Council in the coming years.

Readers are given a flavour of the Assembly through the lively narrative of what happened and a personal appraisal of the event by the Rev. David Gill, General Secretary of the Uniting Church of Australia, who has had a long association with the Council and had played a significant role in preparing the Nairobi Assembly. David Gill has given a faithful and coherent account of the varied ways in which the theme was presented and discussed, and has succinctly introduced the many reports, statements and resolutions which the Assembly adopted or commended to the churches for study and appropriate action.

The reports of the Moderator of the Central Committee and the General Secretary, as well as the two main addresses on the Assembly theme are given here in full as appendices. The other addresses are not included, mainly for reasons of space; but some of them have appeared in the October 1983 issue of *The Ecumenical Review*.

We are deeply grateful to David Gill for editing the English version of the Official Report with such skill and speed. We are also grateful to the German editor, Dr Walter Müller-Römheld, the French editors Prof. Jean-Marc Chappuis and Père René Beaupère, and the Spanish editor Dr Julio Barreiro.

It is our fervent hope that this report will be widely read and used in the churches. It represents where we have reached in our pilgrimage as the people of God gathered together in the World Council of Churches over these thirty-five tumultuous years in the world's history. It shows where we are as we seek to witness to "Jesus Christ – the Life of the World" in these dangerous times.

The Assembly, through the report of its Programme Guidelines Committee, perceived that the period before us must be one in which we grow more and more into Christ and therefore towards unity, justice and peace, vital and coherent theology, new dimensions of our self-understanding as churches, and a community of confessing and learning. In the same spirit, the Message of the Assembly has called the churches, in "life together", to renew our commitment to unity, mission and evangelism, justice and peace. Indeed, life in Christ means commitment to him and to God's purpose of good for humanity and for creation and to grow in him who is the head of the body, the Church, and who fills all in all with his life.

Geneva, 10 October 1983 PHILIP POTTER
General Secretary

MESSAGE FROM THE
SIXTH ASSEMBLY OF THE
WORLD COUNCIL OF CHURCHES

LIFE TOGETHER

Greetings in the name of Jesus Christ, from the Sixth Assembly of
the World Council of Churches in Vancouver, Canada. We represent
four hundred million people of three hundred member churches.
Among us women, young people and persons with disabilities are
participating in larger numbers than before. Thank you for your
supporting prayers. We are filled with praise to God for the grace
given to us since our last meeting. In many places churches have
grown in numbers and depth of commitment. We rejoice in courage
and faith shown in adversity. We are humbled by those newly called
to be martyrs. The Holy Spirit has poured out these and many other
gifts, so that we meet with thanksgiving.

This meeting comes in a succession which began at Amsterdam
in 1948 with the commitment to stay together. Since then we have
been called to grow together and to struggle together. Here under
the theme "Jesus Christ – the Life of the World" we are called to
live together. In the Assembly we taste that life. Our worship in a
great tent which reminds us of the pilgrim people; the presence of
Canadian Indians which has challenged us; our moving prayer and
praise in many languages but one spirit of devotion; our struggles
to face divisive issues; the songs of children – all are part of life
together in the Christian family. The significant participation of
guests from other faiths and of thousands of visitors speaks to us of
the wider human community.

This engagement together in Vancouver underlines how critical
this moment is in the life of the world, like the turning of a page
of history. We hear the cries of millions who face a daily struggle
for survival, who are crushed by military power or the propaganda
of the powerful. We see the camps of refugees and the tears of all
who suffer inhuman loss. We sense the fear of rich groups and

nations and the hopelessness of many in the world rich in things who live in great emptiness of spirit. There is a great divide between North and South, between East and West. Our world – God's world – has to choose between "life and death, blessing and curse".

This critical choice compels us to proclaim anew that life is God's gift. Life in all its fullness reflects the loving communion of God, Father, Son and Holy Spirit. This is the pattern for our life, a gift filled with wonder and glory, priceless, fragile and irreplaceable. Only when we respond in a loving relationship with God, with one another and with the natural world can there be life in its fullness. The misery and chaos of the world result from the rejection of God's design for us. Constantly, in public and private, fellowship is broken, life is mutilated and we live alone. In the life of Jesus we meet the very life of God, face to face. He experienced our life, our birth and childhood, our tiredness, our laughter and tears. He shared food with the hungry, love with the rejected, healing with the sick, forgiveness with the penitent. He lived in solidarity with the poor and oppressed and at the end gave his life for others. In the mystery of the Eucharist the resurrected Lord empowers us to live this way of giving and receiving. "Unless a grain of wheat falls into the earth and dies, it remains alone; but if it dies it bears much fruit" (John 12:24). Only the converting power of the Holy Spirit enables this way of life to be formed in us. Such a transformation is costly and means the willingness to risk even death in our Kingdom pilgrimage.

On that road we acknowledge our unfaithfulness. The division of the Church at central points of its life, our failure to witness with courage and imagination, our clinging to old prejudice, our share in the injustice of the world – all this tells us that we are disobedient. Yet God's graciousness amazes us, for we are still called to be God's people, the house of living stones built on Christ the foundation. One sign of this grace is the ecumenical movement in which no member or church stands alone.

The Assembly therefore renews its commitment to the ecumenical vision. The Lord prays for the unity of his people as a sign by which the world may be brought to faith, renewal and unity. We take slow, stumbling steps on the way to the visible unity of the Church but we are sure the direction is essential to our faithfulness. Since the Nairobi Assembly there has been movement in many places, new united churches, acts of common witness, local ecumenical projects. There is new theological convergence which could enable decisive steps towards one eucharistic fellowship. We especially thank God for the hope given to us by the "Baptism, Eucharist and Ministry" document and seek widespread response to it.

We renew our commitment to mission and evangelism. By this we mean that deep identification with others in which we can tell the good news that Jesus Christ, God and Saviour, is the Life of the World. We cannot impose faith by our eloquence. We can nourish it with patience and caring so that the Holy Spirit, God the Evangelist, may give us the words to speak. Our proclamation has to be translated into every language and culture. Whatever our context among people of living faiths and no faith, we remember that God's love is for everyone, without exception. All are invited to the banquet. Jesus Christ, the living bread, calls everyone who is hungry, and his food is unlimited.

We renew our commitment to justice and peace. Since Jesus Christ healed and challenged the whole of life, so we are called to serve the life of all. We see God's good gift battered by the powers of death. Injustice denies God's gifts of unity, sharing and responsibility. When nations, groups and systems hold the power of deciding other people's lives, they love that power. God's way is to share power, to give it to every person. Injustice corrupts the powerful and disfigures the powerless. Poverty, continual and hopeless, is the fate of millions; stolen land is a cause of bitterness and war; the diversity of race becomes the evil imprisonment of racism. We urgently need a new international economic order in which power is shared, not grasped. We are committed to work for it. But the question comes back to us, what of the Church? Do we yet share power freely? Do we cling to the wealth of the Church? Do we claim the powerful as friends and remain deaf to the powerless? We have tasks near home.

Injustice, flagrant, constant and oppressive, leads to violence. Today life is threatened by war, the increase in armaments of all sorts, and particularly the nuclear arms race. Science and technology, which can do so much to feed, clothe and house all people, can today be used to terminate the life of the earth. The arms race everywhere consumes great resources that are desperately needed to support human life. Those who threaten with military might are dealing in the politics of death. It is a time of crisis for us all. We stand in solidarity across the world to call persistently, in every forum, for a halt to the arms race. The life which is God's good gift must be guarded when national security becomes the excuse for arrogant militarism. The tree of peace has justice for its roots.

Life is given. We receive God's gift with constant thankfulness. At the Assembly's opening worship a mother held up her baby at the Lord's Table. It was a sign of hope and of continuity of life. Sometimes we are almost overcome by the smallness and insignificance of our lives; then we feel helpless. But as we feed upon the bread of life in worship we know again and again God's saving act in Christ in our own lives. We are astounded and surprised that the eternal purpose of God is persistently entrusted to ordinary people. That is the risk God takes. The forces of death are strong. The gift of life in Christ is stronger. We commit ourselves to live that life, with all its risks and joys, and therefore dare to cry, with all the host of heaven: "O death, where is your victory?" Christ is risen. He is risen indeed.

Assembly participants flocked to the worship tent several times a day

I. THE STORY OF AN ASSEMBLY

The Fifth Assembly of the World Council of Churches was drawing to a close, in December 1975, when the well-known anthropologist Margaret Mead managed to get a microphone.

She surveyed the gathered throng. Two-and-a-half thousand people, of many cultures and denominational labels, speaking hundreds of different languages. People ranging from a Ghanaian High Court Judge to a Memphis used-car salesman, from the Archbishop of Canterbury to a tribesman from northern Kenya who had walked for three days just to watch, and listen, and pray. And she delivered herself of a professional opinion on it all.

"You people", said Dr Mead, "are a sociological impossibility. You have absolutely nothing in common – except your extraordinary conviction that Jesus Christ is the Saviour of the world."

Every WCC Assembly reasserts the power of that extraordinary conviction. Alongside it are the many lesser convictions the churches carry in the baggage brought with them on their ecumenical journey. That dynamic interplay of convictions about the faith and perspectives on the world is what made the Sixth Assembly in Vancouver, like each of its predecessors, such an inspiring, bewildering, sometimes infuriating, always fascinating, encounter of hearts and minds.

1.1 The task

The Vancouver gathering began long before the opening day of the Assembly itself – 24 July 1983. During the previous 18 months 79 ecumenical teams visited most member churches, to begin with them the process of preparing for what would happen at Vancouver. Most delegates were involved in one or more preparatory meetings on regional, sub-regional or national level. Churches, congregations, Christian groups and theological seminaries studied the biblical and theological material and read the various papers and books published in preparation for the Assembly. More than ever before, it was hoped, the delegates who came to Vancouver would come as representatives of their various churches and communities throughout the world.

There are three general features to any Assembly of the World Council of Churches.

First, as the most representative gathering of the member churches, the Assembly is the occasion to reaffirm and celebrate the covenant the churches have made with one another. According to its constitution, the WCC is "a fellowship of churches which confess Jesus Christ as God and Saviour". The Assembly, therefore, is the time for the churches to renew their confession of Jesus Christ in the light of the challenges of the present day. The main theme of the Sixth Assembly, "Jesus Christ – the Life of the World", provided a focus for this common act of confessing the faith. In smaller or larger groupings, the Assembly reflected on the main theme, joined in Bible study and worship, and celebrated the unity of God's people through its common witness to Jesus Christ the Life of the World.

Secondly, the World Council of Churches has been constituted in order to serve the common calling of its member churches in the areas of unity and mission, service and renewal. The main activities of the WCC must promote these basic goals. An Assembly is the occasion when the member churches receive an account of the work the Council has done, together with them and on their behalf, during the period since the preceding Assembly. It will examine the results, and formulate recommendations both to the WCC and to member churches on further action to be taken. For the purpose of the discussion at Vancouver, the activities of the WCC were grouped around eight Issues which reflected the major areas of concentration adopted by the Central Committee following the last Assembly at Nairobi.

Finally, the Assembly is the highest constitutional decision-making and governing body of the WCC. It considers the report of the Central Committee which has directed and supervised the work of the WCC since the previous Assembly. It chooses from among the delegates the members of the new Central Committee, as well as the members of the Presidium of the Council, who together will carry the responsibility in the years following the Assembly. It also receives and acts upon policy recommendations in the area of programme guidelines, finance, and public responsibility.

While these three features interacted throughout the period of the Sixth Assembly, the three tasks corresponded roughly with the three weeks during which the Assembly met.

1.2   The participants

More than 4,500 people a day, on average, found themselves taking part one way or another in the Assembly. They wore many labels:
– 6 retiring Presidents;

- 24 from the retiring Central Committee;
- 847 voting Delegates from WCC member churches (63 places were not taken up);
- 23 Delegated Representatives from the associate member churches;
- 32 Delegated Observers from the Roman Catholic Church and a few other non-member churches with which the WCC has a working relationship;
- 84 Advisers, invited by the Central Committee, because of their particular expertise, to assist the Assembly in its work;
- 90 Delegated Representatives of the associate councils of the WCC and of the Commission for World Mission and Evangelism; of world ecumenical organizations which collaborate with the WCC; and of Christian World Communions;
- 38 Guests, invited in a personal capacity;
- 87 Observers representing other councils of churches, ecumenical or international organizations, churches or religious bodies;
- 7 Guest representatives of the Canadian churches;
- 159 Stewards, aged between 18 and 30, from 82 different countries;
- 168 members of the WCC staff, plus 194 coopted staff including interpreters and translators;
- nearly 850 members of the press: journalists, radio and television reporters, technicians, etc.

In addition, there were members of the Vancouver Planning Committee and volunteers responsible for all aspects of local arrangements. Seven hundred Accredited Visitors were accompanied by several hundred daily visitors. Three related events provided additional opportunities for participation: some 150 persons had enrolled in the Special Summer Session at the Vancouver School of Theology; over 200 theological students followed their own programme which was interwoven with the Assembly; and over 600 interested church members shared an intensive one-week programme in nearby Bellingham, with visits to the Assembly and watching the proceedings on the TV.

Of the delegates 30.46% were women (Nairobi had 22%; Uppsala 9%), 13.46% were under 30 years of age (Nairobi 9%; Uppsala 4% under 35) and 46.3% were lay people (Nairobi 42%; Uppsala 25%). Only about 20% had been to a WCC Assembly before (Nairobi had the same high proportion of new blood to old). The regional breakdown was North America (158), Western Europe (152), Eastern Europe (142), Africa (131), Asia (114), Middle East (53), Latin America (30), Caribbean (19), Australia, New Zealand (26) and the Pacific (22).

Denominationally, the delegates hailed from Reformed (176), Lutheran (122), Eastern Orthodox (125), Anglican (89), Methodist (95), United (82), Oriental Orthodox (44), Baptist (38), Moravian (11), Disciples (13), Old Catholic (8), Independent (6), Pentecostal (11), Kimbanguist (6), Mar Thoma (3), Menonnite (2), Brethren (2) and other (14) churches.

"A glorious patchwork" was the image one participant used to describe it all. Not only the diversity of member churches, but also the diversity of the human family within and beyond the churches, was striking for all to behold. Fifteen guests of other faiths were active participants; five of them addressed the Assembly at one point. A small but significant group of disabled persons took part. Headsets provided simultaneous interpretation not only in the World Council's five working languages (English, French, German, Spanish, Russian) but for the first time in Greek as well. Those seated near the podium could see sign language being used to communicate what was going on to a small group of deaf participants. Even the platoon of amiable (well, more or less), placard-waving protesters did its bit to contribute to the ethos of extraordinary diversity that marked the Sixth Assembly.

The accredited press representatives and broadcasters covered the Assembly, worship services, debates in plenary sessions and some of the smaller groups, and press conferences were broadcast live by cable television and satellite link across North America. Never before had any church meeting, let alone a WCC Assembly, been made so accessible to so many.

1.3   From absent friends

Of all the greetings reported by the General Secretary throughout the Assembly, none received more attention than the message of the WCC's first General Secretary and current Honorary President, Dr W. A. Visser 't Hooft. Neither he nor his successor, Dr Eugene Carson Blake, was able to travel to Vancouver. Dr Visser 't Hooft recalled the basic motivation of the ecumenical movement, and assured the Assembly of his thoughts and prayers (for full message, see Appendix IV).

A message from Pope John Paul II was conveyed by the Most Rev. James Carney, Archbishop of Vancouver. The Pope commended the theme of the Assembly, and assured the participants of his "deep pastoral interest and closeness in prayer" (for the full text of the message, see Appendix IV).

A great many other messages were received from heads of member churches, partner ecumenical bodies and other religious groups, international non-governmental organizations, and host organizations within Canada.

1.4 So many alleluias and kyries

Ms Jean Skuse, a Vice-Moderator of the retiring Central Committee, dropped in on a staff party the night the marathon ended. With weary exhilaration she named one thing she would never forget about the Sixth Assembly: "I have never sung so many alleluias or kyries before in my life!" Msgr Basil Meeking, of the Vatican's Secretariat for Promoting Christian Unity, called Vancouver "the praying Assembly".

"The Spirit has taken possession of a large part of this Assembly," commented the British broadcast journalist Ms Pauline Webb: "not all of it, I confess, but a sufficient slice of it to have infected a new generation of ecumenical enthusiasts for whom life after this Assembly will never be quite the same again." At the heart of that inspiration was the Assembly's worship, centred on a huge gold and white tent set up on the lawns at the University of British Columbia. That canvas cathedral became the abiding symbol of the Sixth Assembly.

Careful preparation had produced an Assembly worship book containing an order for daily worship (each morning at 8.15), liturgical material on the four sub-themes, prayers for various occasions and a selection of musical acclamations and hymns to supplement the WCC hymn book *Cantate Domino*. A team of highly competent animators ensured every act of worship was carefully prepared and well led, and a choir of local volunteers made the singing worthy of a Welsh mining town or a Pacific Island congregation. Long before the Assembly convened, a small group had been praying for it – and for the participants by name – in St Andrew's Chapel, next to the tent, and during the Assembly that chapel was reserved as a place of silent prayer.

In addition to the morning worship there were daily eucharistic celebrations following various traditions, midday preaching services, evening prayers led by people from neighbouring congregations and seven major liturgical events.

The opening service, on the morning of Sunday 24 July, led by the officers of the Council, was a joyful, colourful celebration of life and the Word of Life, Jesus Christ. Pennants naming the 301 churches belonging to the WCC were put up around three sides of the tent, where they remained for the duration of the Assembly. At one point, symbols of life from various cultures were brought to the altar. One, a small African baby, was brought and handed to the tall WCC General Secretary Philip Potter, who rocked her gently in his arms – evoking unscripted applause from the congregation. There were prayers of gratitude, prayers for the poor and hungry, prayers for the overcoming of all hatred and division. "Make us one by the power of your Spirit", came the response in many languages. Preaching on a text from 1 John 1, Ms Pauline Webb spoke of the author's personal testimony as of one who had found life, "real life, abundant life, unending life in encountering Jesus Christ" (for the full text of the sermon, see *The Ecumenical Review*, Vol. 35, No. 4, October 1983).

That afternoon the Assembly received a memorable welcome from its Canadian hosts, when 15,000 people filled Vancouver's Pacific Coliseum for a 2¼ hour pageant tracing the scriptural basis of Christian faith. The biblical drama – from creation, through crucifixion and resurrection, to the promise of the holy city – was interpreted through readings, liturgical dance, and music from a 750-voice choir. The Canadian Governor General urged the Assembly to act boldly, to influence those responsible for temporal affairs. Keynote speaker was Dr Jean Vanier, founder of l'Arche homes for handicapped people. Switching between English and French without benefit of notes, dressed simply in slacks and windbreaker, Dr Vanier evoked the Beatitudes as the Church's charter. He called for a church "audacious enough to announce the wonderful news that God is present in our world and that the kingdom of God is today present, hidden in the weak and the rejected and the poor".

It was an uplifting start – but at least one editor managed to ignore the uplift. Delegates were bemused, next morning, to find a local newspaper picturing a handful of anti-WCC protestors and headlining its story "Rage greets opening of WCC Assembly"!

On Saturday 30 July, in the evening, there was a service of preparation and anticipation for holy communion. Catholicos Karekin II preached on Jesus' charge to the disciples after he found them sleeping in Gethsemane. Baptismal vows were renewed. With the ancient hymn "Let all mortal flesh keep silence", participants moved into darkness to continue preparing themselves for the event next day that for many would mark the high point of the Sixth Assembly.

It was another milestone on the long pilgrimage of the ecumenical movement. On Sunday 31 July, under sunny skies, the tent was packed for a celebration of the eucharist, using what has entered ecumenical shorthand as "the Lima Liturgy" – a liturgical expression of the convergence in faith achieved on baptism, eucharist and ministry. Archbishop of Canterbury Robert Runcie presided. Celebrating with him were a Lutheran pastor from Denmark, a Reformed from Indonesia, a Methodist from Benin, a Baptist from Hungary, a Moravian from Jamaica and a minister of the United Church of Canada. Flanked by the two women among them, Archbishop Runcie repeated the biblical words recalling Jesus' institution of the eucharist, and then the congregation sang (in English, to a melody composed by an Argentinian): "Your death, Lord Jesus, we proclaim! Your resurrection we celebrate! Your coming in glory we await!" Prayers were led and lessons read by an even broader spectrum of people including Roman Catholics and Eastern and Oriental Orthodox. Bishop Jesudason, Moderator of the Church of South India, preached, and the bread and wine were distributed by about 60 two-person teams. It was a charismatic moment for the World Council of Churches, a tantalizing foretaste of that which drives the ecumenical movement on.

August 6 marks the anniversary of the destruction of Hiroshima – and the festival, in many churches, of the transfiguration of Christ. The Assembly marked this coincidence of dates with a public witness for justice and peace. It began in the early evening of Friday 5th, moved to the tent and turned into an act of worship led by Sweden's Archbishop Olof Sundby. General Secretary Dr Philip Potter preached on the Transfiguration (Matt. 17:1–8), drawing out its implications for the Church's witness for peace and justice. He said:

> We who are gathered at this Assembly as the company of believers in Christ have been confessing our faith in Christ, the Son of the living God, as the life of the world. We confess that he took on our human form (*morphe*), that is, what we are in and for ourselves as made in God's image. We come making this confession also as members of the human race in all its agony and despair, in its deformed and distorted character. We represent all that went into the decision regarding the bombing of Hiroshima and Nagasaki; and also its effects in death and destruction. Our worship here, our testimonies, have enabled us to glimpse again the transformed, transfigured being of Christ the bringer of peace and righteousness, justice. He, the transfigured one, is our peace and justice and only in him and through him can we take an unequivocal stand for peace and justice, as peacemakers and as those who hunger and thirst for righteousness, justice, and keep on seeking it.

The vigil was maintained throughout the night. Thousands were still there at midnight, when Bishop Desmond Tutu of South Africa appeared at the Assembly for the first time and received a standing ovation. "If God be for us, who can be against us!" said the man who for so many symbolizes the Church's struggle for justice and reconciliation. Standing amidst so many of God's children, he reflected: "It is one of the most wonderful things to belong to the

Church of God." What had begun on a note of deep concern ended next morning with a solemn celebration of Christian hope, when the vigil made way for a celebration of the eucharist in praise of the transfigured Lord. Archbishop Iakovos, head of the Greek Orthodox Archdiocese of North and South America, presided, using the Divine Liturgy of St John Chrysostom.

The closing service, on Wednesday 10 August, included an affirmation based on the Assembly's Message, the induction of new Presidents and Central Committee members into their responsibilities and an act of commitment to the Lord of life. It ended with the hymn that for decades has been the marching song of the World Council of Churches: "Yours be the glory, yours O risen friend! You have won for ever, victory without end!" ·

Your editor has been at three WCC Assemblies and countless other ecumenical corroborees during the past fifteen years. Vancouver towers above them all for the quality of its liturgical life. What was the secret?

Partly it was sound planning by people who knew what they were doing. Partly it was the use of symbols, both traditional and contemporary, that cut through barriers of language, culture and denomination. Partly it was the skilled combination of carefully sculpted form and charismatic freedom. But there were three other factors that have deep significance, and not only for the WCC.

First, planners this time around managed to avoid an instrumental view of worship which is one of Protestantism's besetting sins and has warped the liturgical life of many recent ecumenical gatherings. Prayers were offerings to the divine Mystery – not efforts to moralize at the congregation about the condition of the world and what we should all be doing to fix it. Hymns were acts of praise – not devices for extracting certain desired responses from the singers. Worship was an end in itself, not a means for achieving something else. God was worshipped, not used.

Second, Vancouver revealed that the focus on *Baptism, Eucharist and Ministry* (BEM) is producing something far more important than a cerebral theological encounter. What came through at the Assembly was a widespread desire to reappropriate the riches of sacramental spirituality. Delegates went away sensing that the much-discussed "reception" of the BEM convergence would be less a matter of what people may say to each other at committee tables than of what they may discover afresh, together, at the Holy Table.

Third, an Assembly always echoes what is happening, often unarticulated, in the member churches. Why people kept flocking to that tent merits careful reflection, in terms of what it says about the spiritual ethos of the churches in the Year of Grace 1983. One thing it says, perhaps, is that many Christians are recovering confidence in worship – a confidence that took quite a battering, in some churches, during the stormy sixties and seventies. Another is that churches (and their ecumenical movement) that are managing to get their worship right can look forward to a great many other things beginning to fall into place as well.

1.5   How it worked

A heavy load of *plenary sessions* marked the first and third weeks of the Assembly.

Four plenaries were set aside for opening business, including the reports of the Moderator of the Central Committee and the General Secretary. Moderator Scott's address was the first, and he outlined the work of the Council since Nairobi (for the full text see Appendix II). General Secretary Potter followed, providing a biblical and theological framework for the Council's work and witness, which was picked up again and again by groups discussing issues and concerns in the course of the Assembly (see Appendix III).

Five other plenary sessions in the first week were used for presentations on the main theme and the four sub-themes. The play "Voyage" by Rex Deverell occupied another plenary to present a succinct, self-critical but humorous history of Canada and its churches. A further plenary session reminded participants that they were meeting on the rim of the vast Pacific basin: Dr Sione Havea of Tonga, supported by representatives of the island churches, gave the Assembly a lesson in the delicate art of doing "coconut theology".

The second week saw a concentration of work into smaller groupings. There were five categories.

First, the Assembly broke into some 65 *Small Groups*, each comprising about twenty persons. These served as a "home base", a place where participants could belong, experience fellowship and share with one another their different backgrounds and traditions. As at Nairobi in 1975, many found these Small Groups to be intensely rewarding. For a few, also echoing Nairobi, they failed completely. During the first week, the Small Groups concentrated on the theme and sub-theme presentations, channelling their insights to larger groupings known as *Clusters* which in turn reported to the plenary and provided grist for the mill of the Message Committee.

In the event, the Cluster reports were very diffuse, producing a debate that ranged far and wide but not doing much to focus the Assembly's understanding of the theme. During the second week, the Small Groups were encouraged to work at Bible study, to accompany the Assembly's thinking on issues, to reflect on some of the special events such as the witness for justice and peace – or simply to do their own thing. Many of the Groups made use of a series of study outlines on "Biblical Images of Life".

Issue Groups (similar to what earlier Assemblies knew as Sections) laboured during the second week. There were eight, charged with reflecting on current ecumenical issues which had engaged the churches in the years since Nairobi. Each Issue Group comprised over 120 people. They met eight times, in smaller groups and in plenary, and then submitted their reports to the whole Assembly. Some of these reports, it must be said, will win no prizes for the quality of their theological or social analyses, not to mention their prose. With the exception of the document "Taking Steps Towards Unity", all show signs of the time pressure under which Issue Groups worked. The pressure was even greater when the delegates in plenary session, already behind with their agenda, had to deal with the reports in rapid-fire succession.

There were four *Programme Hearings* – one for each of the WCC's three Programme Units and one for the cluster of activities grouped directly under the General Secretariat. They were the points where the delegates addressed themselves to the official report *Nairobi to Vancouver* and commented on programmes and priorities for the future work of the World Council.

About 300 delegates were elected on to *Committees*, mostly to prepare for decisions to be taken by the Assembly in its business sessions. They comprised:

– *Nominations Committee* proposed names from among the delegates for the new Central Committee, and submitted names for the new Presidium.
– *Credentials Committee* recommended action on problems arising from changes in the composition of delegates or any confusion about representation.
– *Finance Committee* considered the World Council's general financial situation and recommended action the Assembly should take in that regard.
– *Programme Guidelines Committee* proposed formal action on the official report, *Nairobi to Vancouver*; took careful note of proposals for future programmes that emerged at various points during the Assembly; and recommended general guidelines for the activities of the WCC during the period following the Assembly.
– *Two Policy Reference Committees* – Policy Reference Committee I dealt with the reports of the Moderator and General Secretary, issues of relationships with the Roman Catholic Church (Fifth Report of the Joint-Working Group), with Christian World Communions and with regional ecumenical organizations. Policy Reference Committee II prepared statements on public issues.

- *Worship Committee* was responsible for guiding the Assembly's daily worship life and for the preparation of the special services.
- *Message Committee* prepared a message formulating the Assembly's reponse to its theme.
- *Assembly Business Committee*, composed of WCC Presidents, Officers, Moderators of Issue Groups and Committees and other elected persons, served as steering committee for the Assembly's work as a whole.
- *Press and Broadcasting Committee* dealt with problems in the area of the Assembly's relations with the mass media.

Three programme sessions were set aside for regional meetings, when participants from each region could meet one another, clarify common concerns and plan the follow-up of the Assembly in their own churches.

The Assembly's closing days were spent in plenary sessions, dealing with reports from Committees and Issue Groups. After protracted debates over the composition of the new Central Committee and the numerous resolutions on public issues, the agenda never quite recovered. Even with a fast sprint through business on the last afternoon and an additional session running into the evening of Wednesday 10 August, the Assembly found it necessary to refer several important matters to the following day's meeting of the new Central Committee.

1.6 The Canadian context

Canada's cultures and concerns made a strong impact on the Sixth Assembly.

A native arbour, "a sacred meditative area among the trees", was set aside on the campus of the University of British Columbia. A sacred flame burned nearby for the duration of the Assembly. Appropriately, it was lighted by an elder of the Musqueam tribe, on whose lands the university now stands. A 15-metre high totem pole, carved by Native inmates of Agassiz Mountain Prison to symbolize humanity's spiritual quest through the ages, was raised on the campus during the Assembly. It will find a permanent home in Geneva. Through plenary presentations and public forums, participants became aware of the thinking of Native Canadians particularly concerning land claims.

A host programme, organized by the Vancouver Planning Committee, meant that some participants were able to stay with local families for a few days before the Assembly began or following its close. August 7 – Visitation Sunday – saw many Assembly people worshipping with local congregations in the Vancouver area, on

Vancouver Island and in Seattle, Washington (USA). Canada Post issued a special stamp, with a cross motif, to mark the Assembly.

Then there were the Canadian volunteers, thousands of them. They did everything from driving buses to sewing tote bags in which participants bagged around their ecumenical documents (the stitching must have been strong: these bags held together even as the Assembly chewed its way through fourteen tons of paper). They sang in choirs, prepared banners, helped with registrations, even presented everyone with cushions to soften the Assembly's impact on sensitive ecumenical posteriors.

The Vancouver Planning Committee had done an excellent job. The Committee richly deserved the standing ovation given by the Assembly to its friendly, unobtrusively efficient hosts.

1.7   Related activities

Two pre-Assembly events had a significant impact on the Sixth Assembly. About 300 participants, including some men, took part in a four-day women's meeting. Some 200 young people met as youth participants. These programmes enabled them, among other things, to become familiar with Assembly programme and procedures. Both events helped foster a sense of corporate identity and confidence in these two important minority (in delegation terms, anyway) groups.

Ploughshares, a coffee house where peace and justice concerns were aired throughout the Assembly, operated out of one of the campus buildings. The Well was a focal point for women's concerns. An Asian art exhibition, supervised by Japan's Mr Yushi Nomura, contained more than 50 works from seven countries. Special interest groups were free to present their particular concerns in the Agora, a market place of ideas and convictions. Groups represented there ranged from Canada's Boy Scouts through the United Nations Association to an organization advocating creation science – some sixty in all. There was a film festival, a children's art exhibition on the Assembly theme, a display of liturgical art sponsored by the Canadian Conference of Catholic Bishops – and more.

This public programme, organized by the Vancouver Planning Committee, and the Visitors' Programme, set up by the WCC for the droves of accredited and daily visitors, offered an extraordinary range of Assembly-related events on campus and in downtown Vancouver. It was a feast of opportunities to meet church leaders and hear significant voices from around the world. Some delegates must have been sorely tempted to play truant from their programme in order to share the excitement of the visitors.

In the midst of the mayhem, the happily harassed staff of the WCC bookshop were doing a roaring trade.

Special interest groups responded to the Assembly in different ways. One of the most striking reactions came from "Evangelicals" who, towards the end of the Assembly, put their names to an open letter saying Vancouver's spiritual and biblical orientation had "challenged stereotypes some of us (evangelicals) have had of the WCC". The letter took a strong line against fringe groups that had picketed delegates and distributed "scurrilous" literature. While offering some criticisms of the Sixth Assembly, the letter called for active participation in the ecumenical movement and challenged "that all too popular evangelical heresy – that the way to renew the body of Christ is to separate from it and relentlessly criticize it".

Finally there was *Canvas*, the very professional daily newspaper of the Assembly without which nobody could have begun to have an overview of all that went on in this action-packed gathering.

1.8   A personal appraisal

One should not rush to judgment on the Sixth Assembly. For one thing, it will take time to evaluate what really happened during those eighteen frenzied days and nights. For another, the significance of any Assembly derives in part from what flows from it. Uppsala, for example, earned renown as the great racism and development Assembly – partly because of what the delegates said and did, but partly too because of programmes the Central Committee initiated at their behest.

It will be some time before the verdict is in on Vancouver. Even so, the churches may find it helpful to have a few comments to aid them in that evaluation.

First, some media reporting makes it necessary to point out a few things the Sixth Assembly was *not*.

It was *not* an exercise in super-power politics. Press coverage, generally, appears to have been fair. Some journalists, however, managed to ignore theology, the Bible, the tent, even Christian witness and unity, to present the Assembly solely as an encounter over social and political issues. A few, even more narrowly blinkered, tried to interpret the whole exercise in the light of current wrangles between Washington and Moscow. Pressing the Assembly into that ideological mould meant distorting it beyond all recognition.

It was *not* a retreat from the passion for justice and peace that has always been part of the World Council's witness and that was emphasized so strongly at the two previous Assemblies. Delegates read their Bibles, said their prayers and rejoiced in the eucharistic celebrations. They also, however, faced with courage the world's anguish and took a remarkably strong line on questions of peace and human rights. Significantly, Vancouver showed no desire whatever to back away from that symbol of ecumenical social engagement, the Programme to Combat Racism.

It was *not* merely a rerun of previous Assemblies. Even apart from its memorable liturgical life, Vancouver marked significant progress over the Nairobi gathering eight years earlier. Leadership by women, prominent as never before, was welcomed for the obvious competence of those providing it. An extraordinarily diverse set of testimonies, short addresses and responses was crammed into the theme and sub-theme presentations. Venue and local preparations were superb. Thousands – official participants, visitors and general public – went away informed, excited and committed to a World Council that until then had been merely a name. And the spiritual ethos of the member churches in 1983 was intuited, reflected and in some important respects challenged.

One must also concede, however, that the Sixth Assembly was not quite Pentecost!

Hassles over nominations for the new Central Committee, and a preoccupation with categories rather than competence, did not show forth the WCC at its sparkling best. People seemed to overlook the fact that those appointed to the Central Committee are there to represent the Assembly as a whole, not one or another of its composite parts. Perhaps there are now so many categories to be juggled – confessional, regional, national, lay/clerical, age, gender, etc. – that they have begun to cancel each other out and render the entire nominations procedure in need of review. Maybe delegates need to feel more clearly that they have other, equally tangible ways of asserting their "ownership" of their Council.

The quality of the work done by most of the Issue Groups left a lot to be desired. Planners had stressed that this was to be a participatory Assembly, drawing on the gifts and experience of delegates and generally foregoing the substantial addresses by leading figures that have helped shape previous Assemblies. The attempt was worth making. Whether it is worth repeating, if the price includes a mediocrity in the written output "commended to the churches for study and appropriate action", is another question.

A related problem is the relative inexperience of many delegates. Eighty per cent, at both Nairobi and Vancouver, had never played the game before, and at times it showed. If future Assemblies are not to be condemned to reinventing the wheel every seven or eight years, the WCC will need to ensure that they have built into them an adequate ecumenical memory.

Finally there was the demon of time which produced inadequate plenary debates on some major issues, an inability to complete the Assembly's business – and high frustration on all sides. Every Assembly, of course, faces almost irresistible pressure to swallow more than it can reasonably be expected to chew, but the Vancouver experience points to the need for a sharp reduction in the number of Issue Group reports and statements on public issues put to an Assembly in plenary session.

And if somebody could find a way of discouraging delegates who come determined to deliver set speeches – and proceed to do so, undeterred by considerations of time or relevance – that would be wonderful!

★ ★ ★

What then are we to make of the Vancouver event?

The significance of the Sixth Assembly lies not with its particular strengths or weaknesses, not with things that were said or decisions made. It lies with the nuances – the deep gratitude for the Church and yearning for its unity, the hunger for peace and the hands outstretched towards all people everywhere, the rediscovery of old certainties, the taste of bread and wine, the dream of a renewed Church for a renewed world . . . Those nuances, taken together, point to a healing of a spiritual schizophrenia that too long has run through our churches, our ccumenism, our own souls. That midnight scene in the tent, when thousands keeping vigil for justice and peace offered their heartfelt praise to the Lord of life, said it all.

For this was an Assembly of reintegration. At Vancouver, Amsterdam and Uppsala appeared to have come to terms with each other.

The Rev. Dr Theodore
Stylianopoulos, USA

The Rev. Dr Allan Boesak
South Africa

The University of British Columbia's gymnasium was converted into a plenary hall
for the Assembly

2. "JESUS CHRIST – THE LIFE OF THE WORLD"

The theme of the Assembly was woven through its worship. Five plenary presentations on the theme and the four sub-themes took place during the first week. At the same time, participants worked away in their small groups on the meaning of this great claim about the man the Church calls Lord.

2.1 Theme presentations

Dame Nita Barrow (Methodist), of Barbados, introduced the first presentation. Undeterred by a slide projector that refused to project, she recalled some of the key biblical images of life. These were set in the context of the world's present experience of life and joy, and of death and ugliness; and the question was posed: who is he who had died and risen for the life of the world?

Professor Theodore Stylianopoulos, USA (representing the Ecumenical Patriarchate), led off with an address that developed the Christological affirmation of the Prologue to St John's Gospel. The Assembly theme, he said, was a call to Christians for radical repentance and spiritual renewal; it urged us to walk together towards unity, common witness and prophetic action. It called upon us to be ready to die for others in Christ's name. In the light of the Incarnation there could be no distinction between the "vertical" and "horizontal" dimensions of Christian life (for full text, see Appendix V).

Jesus Christ is the same yesterday, today and forever. Yet through the centuries and across the nations his people have seen him from different perspectives and spoken of him with different accents. The second speaker provided a perspective that was at once dramatically contemporary and as old as the faith itself.

Dr Allan Boesak, of the Dutch Reformed Mission Church in South Africa, referred to the theme's affirmation as the Church's "quiet, subversive piety" which refuses to believe that the power of oppression, death and destruction has the last word. This faith in the living One, this refusal to bow down to the false gods of death, is the strength of the Church. In the face of humanity's hunger for peace, its yearning for justice, Christians are called to a kind of worship that encompasses the whole of life so that every prayer for liberation, every action for human dignity, every protest against the sinful realities of this world becomes an offering to God for the sake of his kingdom (for full text, see Appendix V).

The standing ovation that followed provided the first hint that delegates to the Sixth Assembly were in no mood to retreat from commitments made by their predecessors at the previous Assemblies. Those commitments had stemmed not from passing fads but from the very heart of the Gospel. The centrality of God's act in Christ was joyfully recalled, yet again, as participants were summoned to an Act of Commitment with which the plenary closed:

> Come, let us worship and fall down before Christ, who is one of the Holy Trinity, the only begotten Son and immortal Word of God, glorified with the Father and the Holy Spirit. For our salvation he was incarnate and crucified in the flesh and gave himself up for the life of the world. By his death he destroyed death. Come you faithful, let us praise and glorify the risen Christ our God. Giver of Life, he has filled all things with joy in coming to save the world.

2.2   First sub-theme: "Life, a gift of God"

Life is inherited by all creation. The Church affirms this life as God-given through Christ, to be nurtured among all people and in all creation – yet Christians must confess that they share in the neglect and violation of life in all its forms. The first sub-theme highlighted the need to understand anew and proclaim afresh God's purpose for the world, and to exercise a more responsible stewardship of the world's resources and develop a greater reverence for life.

Archbishop John Vikström, of the Church of Finland, provided a biblical context. He spoke of God as the personal power, the love, which calls everything into being, and of the rebellion that leads us away from God, from one another, from our own true selves, from a proper relationship with nature. The world has been occupied by a foreign power – but the lawful king has come, incognito, to this his occupied world. "We who have gathered at this Assembly are members of this resistance movement. At times we may find it hard to recognize both ourselves and others as Christians – and sometimes we may have difficulty in recognizing our disguised king, Jesus Christ. But we wish to give each other support, to be more closely united in order to fight for our Lord and his kingdom, inspired with the hope that this kingdom will indeed come." For by him is creation set free and renewed.

By him, yes. But by us? Dr John Francis, a nuclear physicist and member of the Church of Scotland, drew attention to the way every scientific advance brings with it new threats as well as new possibilities. Scientists do not hold back on discoveries, but more and more they are anxious to inform a wider public about the consequences of what they discover. The challenge to the churches is to become vigorously involved in dialogue with them, so that the power of science and technology may be harnessed in the cause of peace, the feeding of the hungry and the healing of the sick.

Very different perspectives were provided by two short testimonies. Ms Sithembiso Nyoni, an Anglican from Zimbabwe, told of her experience of motherhood and her hopes and fears for her children. "Am I producing future soldiers? Will they belong to the deprived 80% – no jobs, no land, no hope? What is the destiny of my children under all these dangers?" Mr Roderick Robinson, an hereditary chief of the Nishga tribe, recounted his tribe's struggle for recognition by the Canadian government of its title to God-given lands.

Then followed brief comments by guests from other faiths: Mr Masuo Nezo (Buddhist, Japan), Shri Shrivatsa Goswami (Hindu, India), Sheikh Yusufkhan Shakirov (Muslim, USSR) and Rabbi Marc Tannenbaum (Jewish, USA). Finally the main theme was evoked by dancer Ms Shobana Jeyasingh, of India. Using the classical Bharathanatyam dance mode from South India, she dramatized the incident of Jesus' meeting the Samaritan woman at the well.

2.3 Second sub-theme: "Life confronting and overcoming death"

Christ is risen from the dead. We affirm this risen life in the midst of sinful forces which work death and destruction. The Church is called to make manifest God's forgiving and compassionate love for humanity and to struggle against the forces of death. As presentations on the second sub-theme made painfully clear, we ourselves are party to these destructive forces. Yet we are called to witness to the victory of Christ and to the freedom from death that he has won for us.

It was with a reference to a moving Easter service in 1973 that the Rev. Hyung Kyu Park, former Moderator of the Presbyterian Church in the Republic of Korea, began his account of the attempts by Korean Christians to witness to the Lord of life in a seemingly hopeless situation, a long, dark night of death under a repressive military regime. Listen to the dialogue between the rich young ruler and Jesus, he urged Christians in the first world. Those engaged in the Korean struggle had discovered Christ anew as the source of life, hope and joy. "Because he lived as the powerless, he became the power of the people. Because he died on the cross, God-forsaken, he became the Lord of the world. Because he died, he became the life of the world. And he has been resurrected from the dead."

Ms Frieda Haddad, of the Greek Orthodox Patriarchate of Antioch and All the East, told of singing the Divine Liturgy on Easter morning in Lebanon while shellfire shook the church building. Pondering the deep mystery of God's immersion in human suffering, she spoke of "the purifying fire of boundary situations" in which all that is non-essential in us disappears and the power of the resurrection is experienced afresh.

Dr Anezka Ebertova, of the Hussite Church, Czechoslovakia, added the experience of millions in Europe. The quest for justice and peace, she said, is a struggle against one common enemy: the sin of human selfishness, greed, lust for power, and indifference to the needs of others, both within the heart and in the social structures into which it is projected. Australian medical doctor and anti-war activist Dr Helen Caldicott graphically described the effects of nuclear war, which she termed the ultimate moral and religious issue of our time. "We hold God's creation in the palm of our hand. This generation will either decide actively to save it, or by passive complicity destroy it."

Ugandan Anglican Bishop Misaeri Kauma spoke of the violence that has engulfed his country before and after independence. Solutions must be found through the traditional African way of talking things over, he said, and through arms reduction and by addressing the problem of poverty. Ms Domitila Barrios de Chungara, the wife of a Bolivian tin miner, related the story of a hunger strike in which she was involved, and shared the experience of living in a country that has had 188 coups d'etat in its 158 years. The hunger strike did succeed in this case.

2.4   Third sub-theme: "Life in its fullness"

Christ promises life in its fullness – life new and eternal. Sharing here and now in the risen life of Christ, the Church is called to proclaim and embody this gospel of full life for all the world.

That entails, among other things, challenging false gospels and their illusory promises. For Dr Dorothee Sölle, the great illusion of our age finds expression in the materialism of the affluent nations: "life without a soul lived in a world which calculates everything in terms of what it's worth . . . We are empty and at the same time surfeited with superfluous goods and products." Material wealth and fullness of life are incompatible, argued the German writer and theologian who currently teaches in the USA. By participating in structures that impoverish millions of people, the world's wealthy not only make fullness of life impossible for themselves; they also strip the poor of life's goodness. For the poor too she had hard words. She warned them not to pursue the same dead-end track: "Do not follow our example. Claim back what we have stolen from you, but do not follow us. Otherwise . . . you will have sorrowfully to bid farewell to Christ. Do not pursue the idea of fullness of life as we have developed it in the Western world. It is a delusion. It separates us from God, it makes us rich . . . and dead." Militarism and the arms race are the inevitable by-products of this idolatry of things; for those who make money their god are bound to make "security" their state ideology and armaments a political priority. Look instead, she urged, to Isaiah 58:6–12, with its picture of the richness of life of the fulfilled human person.

Echoing the same message from a quite different background was Mother Euphrasia, the superior of a monastic community of the Romanian Orthodox Church. Reflecting on her experience, she called monastic vows a challenge to the false gods of wealth, pleasure and pride. She saw the monastic experience offering an answer to all who today are seeking an authentic life-style. Existence with and for others is what gives life its fullness, and prayer is an integral part of that existence. "People today are secularized and they run away from prayer because they are afraid to look into their inner lives, which are very often fragmented and disintegrated. Prayer restores the human spirit to a state of fellowship and love. It makes an individual into a person . . . like a sunflower turned to the sun, the source of (its) life and identity."

Veteran Pentecostal ecumenist Dr David DuPlessis led a panel of responders to the presentation on the sub-theme. Noting that "all Bible-believing churches accept Jesus Christ as the head", he said: "If there is only one head, there can be only one body. Clearly the salvation of humanity depends on our unity." Other responses were offered by Mr Keith Branch (Anglican, Guyana), Dr Peter Kuzmic (Pentecostal, Yugoslavia), Ms Maria Teresa Porcile Santiso (Roman Catholic, Uruguay) and Ms Helen Hempfling (Disciples of Christ, USA).

2.5 Fourth sub-theme: "Life in unity"
Christ prays that we may all be one. We affirm that God's purpose is to restore all things into unity in Christ. The Church is called to be a sign of that unity which binds together all generations and all peoples.

At the centre of the Church's life is the eucharist, the sacrament of unity and peace. Protopresbyter Vitaly Borovoy, of the Russian Orthodox Church, expounded the significance of the Supper of

Love for the Church's faith, self-understanding, corporate life and social witness. From the teaching of the ancient Church he drew some very contemporary implications. "If the bread of the eucharist is the bread of eternal life and in breaking it we enter into communion with Christ and each other, it is only natural that we should fight against hunger, poverty, illnesses, and other manifestations of social injustices with regard to other people, who are all brothers and sisters," he said. "If we are called to live out this unity, then any hostility, discrimination and division of people due to racial, national, ethnic, language or cultural characteristics, sex, social status or educational background are incompatible with Christian faith and membership in the Church." The eucharist makes imperative not only unity among Christians but also their dialogue with people of other faiths and engagement in the quest for world peace.

With the aid of a film on Andrei Rublov's famous fifteenth century icon of the Trinity, the Assembly was led in meditation on the triune God as the ultimate ground for both the unity of the Church and the renewal of human community.

Dr Jan Pronk, youth consultant at the 1968 Uppsala Assembly and currently Deputy Secretary General of UNCTAD, spoke of the sub-theme's economic implications. Life in unity means work and bread for all, he said. What we see in the 1980s, however, is less work and less bread for more people, with the prospect of at least a billion people living below any decent level of existence at the turn of the century. Tragically, the international economic crisis is parallelled by a crisis in decision-making due to the short-term horizons of decision-makers and an inclination to shift burdens on to the shoulders of weaker groups. The super-powers are preoccupied with strengthening their spheres of influence rather than solving global problems. Urging the churches to play a role in building a new international economic order, he stressed the importance of grassroots involvement in such decision-making. "Life in unity should not only be seen as the aim of a process, as its final outcome. It should also characterize the process itself."

Another speaker was the Rev. Daniel N'toni N'zinga, a Baptist pastor who heads the Angolan Council of Churches. He referred to Southern Africa's experience of the forces that militated against life in unity. Metropolitan Chrysostomos of Myra (Ecumenical Patriarchate) led the plenary in the Eastern Orthodox liturgical blessing and distribution of bread, highlighting again the link between the Church's eucharist and the world's hunger.

2.6 Other perspectives on the theme

Reports from the Clusters indicated some of the theme-related discussion that had gone on in Small Groups.

At the end of the first session of Cluster reports, Brother Roger of the Taizé Community in France reflected on the theme's relevance for the younger generation. So many of the young, he said, have been scarred by broken relationships and had lost the confident trust that is essential for life. They yearn to find places of struggle and contemplation that anticipate forgiveness, communion and reconciliation. The resources of the ecumenical movement should be focused on a pastoral concern to enable each person to reconcile, in him- or herself, "the irreplaceable treasures of the Orthodox churches, with the specific gifts of the Protestant churches, with all the charisms of the Catholic Church".

Concluding the second session of Cluster reports, Prof. Krister Stendahl suggested that what had been new in the theological reflection was a fresh awareness of the issue of power. Matthew 5:23–26 speaks of reconciliation before the altar of God. These days had held out the prospect of being able to go back to the altar with the gift of the Church's theology purified of the power game by the gift of participation. The one who enables this, the vine dresser, he said, is God.

2.7 The theme and the Message

The Message of the Vancouver Assembly was an attempt to convey to the churches, in succinct form, what their delegates had learned, glimpsed, dreamt during their worship and work together. It summarized, in particular, what the affirmation of Jesus Christ as the life of the world came to mean to the participants.

The Very Rev. Lois Wilson (United Church, Canada), Moderator of the Message Committee, first invited written comments on an initial draft and then presented a revised version for consideration in plenary session. Responses to it were generally positive.

Dr Adebisi Sowunmi (Anglican, Nigeria) felt, however, that the statement was lopsided because it had singled out nuclear war as the major threat to peace. Two other major threats – racial discrimination and the unjust accumulation of wealth – had surfaced repeatedly during the Assembly and should be mentioned in the Message. Dr David Russell (Baptist, UK) asked for a clearer statement on the uniqueness of Jesus Christ and the distinctive calling of the Church. Bishop Per Lønning, of the Church of Norway, wanted references to nuclear armaments broadened to include all weapons of mass destruction. The call to evangelism should be strengthened, said the Rev. Dr William Klempa (Presbyterian, Canada). Ms Lois Quam of the American Lutheran Church found what was said about science and technology too simplistic. Ms Nancy Peirera (Methodist, Brazil), while agreeing that injustice corrupts the powerful and powerless alike, pointed out that it does so in very different ways.

The Message, subject to amendments the Committee would make in the light of the discussion, was adopted (see pp. 1–4).

The opening worship: from left to right, Archbishop Edward W. Scott, Moderator of the Central Committee; Dr Philip Potter, WCC General Secretary; and Ms Pauline Webb, Central Committee member and preacher for the occasion

Dramatization of the eight Issues made the point that beyond the eight abstractions stand millions of flesh-and-blood human beings

3. ISSUES FOR THE CHURCHES AND THE WCC

In the place of what previous Assemblies knew as Sections, Vancouver had Issue Groups. There were eight, each representing an area of urgent concern for the Church arising out of the programmes carried out by the Council on the basis of the mandate from Nairobi. These were an attempt to bring out – and to build on – the insights gained for the churches and the future work of the Council through following the four major areas of programme concentration identified by the Central Committee in 1976:
1) the expression and communication of our faith in the triune God;
2) the search for a just, participatory and sustainable society;
3) the unity of the Church and its relation to the unity of humankind;
4) education and renewal in search of true community.

Armenian Catholios Karekin II, a Vice-Moderator of the Central Committee, introduced this part of the agenda at the beginning of the second week. Each Issue Group was expected to provide a succinct report surveying its topic, restating any ecumenical convictions already reached, acknowledging such divergences as might still remain, and offering recommendations for action by the churches and for the WCC. Delegates should ensure that their own deeply held convictions find expression in the discussions, the Catholicos said, to guard the Issue Groups against a purely academic, technical approach. Staff wearing larger than life-size masks and appropriate costumes then dramatized the eight Issues, making the point that beyond the eight abstractions stand millions of flesh-and-blood human beings.

Towards the end of the Assembly the moderators of Issue Groups presented their reports. These were considered by the plenary meeting in deliberative sessions, a procedure followed by the Assembly "when the matters before it are of such a theological or general policy nature that detailed amendment is impracticable" (Rule XIV,6). According to that procedure, delegates had two options after they had debated each report. It could be bounced back to the Issue Group for reconsideration and revision, or approved in substance by the Assembly (subject to amendments in the light of points made in the debate) and commended by it to the churches for study and appropriate action.

The reports of the Issue Groups are printed here in their final form, each prefaced by a brief summary of the related debate in the plenary.

3.1 WITNESSING IN A DIVIDED WORLD

Rev. Inoke Nabulivou (Methodist, Fiji), Moderator of the first Issue Group, and Rev. Dr James Veitch (Presbyterian, New Zealand), presented its report.

Several speakers criticized the document as lacking input from recent WCC work on mission and evangelism. Rev. Kim Crutchfield (International Evangelical Church, USA) wanted a clearer statement on the role of Christ, and others were uneasy that some paragraphs might be construed as "universalism". Mr Bassam Tabshouri (Greek Orthodox Patriarchate of Antioch and All the East) found it too negative in speaking of the work of missionaries, and Dr Adebisi Sowunmi (Anglican, Nigeria) spoke of the need to challenge un-Christian aspects of local cultures. Applause greeted an appeal from Bishop Ole Borgen (Methodist, Sweden) for a more scriptural approach, and Bishop Per Lønning of the Church of Norway successfully moved that the report be sent back to the Issue Group for reworking.

A revised version reached the plenary on the last day of the Assembly, but the pressure of time on an already overcrowded agenda made this one of several pieces of unfinished business that were referred to the new Central Committee. Acting for the Assembly, the Central Committee subsequently agreed that the substance of the revised report should be approved and commended to the churches for study and suitable action.

Introduction

1. The starting point for our thinking is Jesus Christ. He taught and prayed, proclaimed and healed, lived for God and neighbour; he accepted people, forgave and renewed, and brought change into the lives of those who were open to hear him.

2. To be a witness means to live the life of Christ in the place where we are; it means listening and seeking to understand the faith and perspectives of our neighbours, it means speaking about Jesus the Christ as the Life of the World.

3. Christians are called to witness to Christ in all ages; in each generation we are called to examine the nature of our witness. In discussing this theme we have dealt with five areas in which the

World Council of Churches has been engaged during the period since Nairobi. The following is our report.

Culture: the context for our witnessing

4. The question of the nature of the relationship between the Gospel and culture has been with us for some time, but the issue of culture has arisen in a fresh way because we are coming (a) to a deeper understanding of the meaning and function of culture and of its plurality, (b) to a better understanding of the ways in which the Gospel has interacted with cultures, and (c) to a clearer realization of the problems that have been caused by ignoring or denigrating the receptor cultures during the Western missionary era that often went hand in hand with Western colonial expansion.

5. Culture is what holds a community together, giving a common framework of meaning. It is preserved in language, thought patterns, ways of life, attitudes, symbols and presuppositions, and is celebrated in art, music, drama, literature and the like. It constitutes the collective memory of the people and the collective heritage which will be handed down to generations still to come.

6. While we affirm and celebrate cultures as expressing the plural wonder of God's creation, we recognize that not all aspects of every culture are necessarily good. There are aspects within each culture which deny life and oppress people. Also emerging in our time are certain forms of religious culture and sub-cultures which are demonic because they manipulate people and project a world-view and values which are life-denying rather than life-affirming.

7. Given on the one hand the richness and variety of cultures, and on the other the conflict between life-affirming and life-denying aspects within each culture, we need to look again at the whole issue of Christ and culture in the present historical situation.

8. In making this suggestion, we have, amongst others, two particular historical instances of the encounter of the Gospel with culture that we will draw upon.

9. Christ transcends all cultural settings. In confronting and being confronted by the world, into which the Gospel came, Christianity shed some of its Jewish-Hellenistic characteristics, while acquiring characteristics from its receptor cultures. In so doing it sometimes accepted certain elements as they were, at other times transforming them, and at yet other times rejecting elements that were considered to be inimical to the Gospel. This process continued as the Christian message spread throughout Europe and into parts of the Eastern world.

10. The later missionary enterprise which carried the Christian message to the Americas, Africa, Asia and the Pacific, raised a new

problem in understanding the relationship between the Gospel and culture. This missionary movement brought the Gospel to all parts of the world. There have always been people who like Paul became a Jew to the Jews and a Greek to the Greeks. Confronted by cultures whose world-view, thought-forms and artistic expressions were strange, "Western" missionaries however, by and large denigrated these cultures as pagan and heathen and as inimical to the Gospel. As they did this, many missionaries did not realize that the Gospel they preached was already influenced by centuries-old interaction with many and different cultures and that they were at this point imposing a culturally-bound Christian proclamation on other people. Neither did they realize that they were in fact inhibiting the Gospel from taking root in the cultural soil into which it had come.

11. However, we now have indigenous or local expressions of the Christian faith in many parts of the world, which present more manifestations of diverse forms of Christianity. The Gospel message becomes a transforming power within the life of a community when it is expressed in the cultural forms in which the community understands itself.

12. Therefore, in the search for a theological understanding of culture we are working towards a new ecumenical agenda in which various cultural expressions of the Christian faith may be in conversation with each other. In this encounter the theology, missionary perspectives and historical experiences of many churches, from the most diverse traditions (for example Orthodox and Roman Catholic churches) offer fresh possibilities. So too do the contributions made by women and young people in this search for a new ecumenical agenda.

13. With this background in mind we need to take specific steps:

a) In the search for a theological understanding of culture, we can do the following: share a rich diversity of manifestations of the Christian faith; discover the unity that binds these together; and affirm together the Christological centre and Trinitarian source of our faith in all of its varied expressions.

b) We need to be aware of the possibility of our witness to the Gospel becoming captive to any culture, recognizing the fact that all cultures are judged by the Gospel.

c) In contemporary societies there is an evolution of a new culture due in part to modernization and technology. There is a search for a culture that will preserve human values and build community. We need to reassess the role played by, in particular, secular and religious ideologies in the formation of culture, and the relationship between this process and the demands of the Gospel and our witness to it.

d) While we recognize the emergence of Christian communities within minority groups that affirm their cultural identity, we should pay special attention to the fact that many of these are in danger of being destroyed because they are seen as a threat to a dominant culture.

e) We need to look again at the whole matter of witnessing to the Gospel across cultural boundaries, realizing that listening to and learning from the receptor culture is an essential part of the proclamation of the Christian message.

Worship: the perspective and the power with which we witness

14. Gathered in this Assembly as members of churches from different confessions, continents and cultures, we were reminded again that we are receivers first. As receivers of God's love we are expected to share in witnessing to our neighbours in everyday life, what we receive in the worshipping community. If we do not we shall not go on receiving. Our witness to Jesus Christ as the life of the world is our response to the liberating and uniting work of God's Spirit that we experience despite the divisions of our world.

15. During the various meetings at this Assembly we expressed the urgent need for justice, equality, and solidarity with the poor. But do we really share, or do we in the end prefer ourselves?

16. The basic question is, who can free us from this captivity to ourselves? According to the apostolic experience, only a living fellowship with Christ – as received in prayer and worship – can free us from our personal interests and concerns and renew the spirit of sacrifice and courage so that we may fight for justice even when situations appear hopeless.

17. We have appreciated the central role daily worship has played in this Assembly. It renewed the fellowship of the Spirit and gave us spiritual strength to cope with the different challenges and even frustrations with which we were confronted.

18. Worship is the central act of the life and mission, witness and service of the Church. It is a way in which women and men, rich and poor, able and disabled, share in God's grace and seek forgiveness. It is a liturgical, sacramental and public realization of the unique act of Jesus Christ for the life of the world. The evangelistic, redeeming power of worship lies in the very fact of the "announcement of the death of the Lord until he comes" (1 Cor. 11:26).

19. Worship should be the central act of the life of the Church; however, we heard about a widespread tiredness towards Sunday worship. Where this is true, worship does not have the public witnessing character it should.

20. What are the reasons behind this? Besides a general lack of spiritual enthusiasm in our congregations, people may find worship boring because:

a) there is a language barrier which makes meaningful participation impossible for many;

b) it is formal and does not provide scope for meaningful and spontaneous participation by the congregation;

c) there is often a lack of real fellowship;

d) worship does not bring the anxieties of the people before God; rather it seems to be irrelevant for the daily life of believers and the surrounding human community.

21. How can we overcome this dilemma? We heard about encouraging examples of a cross–fertilization between different liturgical traditions arising out of mutual visits to worship with members of another confession. Some churches are experiencing liturgical renewal. Old liturgies are being reintroduced into the liturgical life of some churches and new forms of worship are being created. The dimension of witness in worship is often emphasized in services for young people, and for parents and children. Worshipping together as families is commended as a fruitful way of sharing the Christian faith. Active participation from all members of the worshipping community is to be encouraged. We also need to pray for each other.

22. Confessing the apostolic creed in our worship we affirm our belief in the community of saints. Thus we are reminded that we live together with the martyrs of all times. Christians who give their lives for the sake of the kingdom are martyrs. We remember them in our worship as encouraging examples. They are symbols of the total Church. They give us inspiration as to how "worship and work must be one". We have learned that the unity between worship and daily Christian life needs urgently to be recovered.

23. For the sake of the witnessing vocation of the Church we need to find a true rhythm of Christian involvement in the world. The Church is gathered for worship and scattered for everyday life. Whilst in some situations in the witnessing dimension of worship there must be a "liturgy after the liturgy", service to the world as praise to God, in other contexts it must be stressed that there is no Christian service to the world unless it is rooted in the service of worship.

Special areas of concern – witnessing among children

24. The child is a living parable of the way the kingdom is to be received and appreciated. The Bible speaks of God's special concern for "little ones":

> Let the children come to me, and do not hinder them; for to such
> belongs the kingdom of heaven (Matt. 19:14, RSV).

On another occasion Jesus and the disciples were discussing the
question: "Who is the greatest in the kingdom of heaven?" – when
Jesus called to him a child and said:

> Truly I say to you unless you turn and become like children, you will
> never enter the kingdom of heaven. Whoever humbles himself or
> herself like this child, that person is the greatest in the kingdom of
> heaven (Matt. 18:3–4, RSV).

25. The population of the world is growing rapidly. In some
places children constitute the majority of the population, and they
raise questions for the adults. In Jesus' encounter with children we
see the gospel at work. Forgiveness and love are given and received
with a freedom or openness adults quickly lose. Children, because
they are powerless and vulnerable, respond to God's love in warm,
accepting ways. However, children are not idealized by the Bible.
They stand in need of the grace and love of God. And yet Jesus
proclaimed, "theirs is the kingdom". Their very vulnerability and
powerlessness demand that we so speak for them and stand with
them, that we use their needs and situations as a yardstick for our
churches' thinking, programmes and priorities.

26. Stories about children can help focus the global issues we
face and place question marks against our priorities and attitudes.
Through them we can begin to understand the Gospel in a new
way. Tonight and every night, thousands of children will sleep on
the streets of our cities and in the open. Thousands of malnourished
children will eventually become mentally retarded adults unable to
participate as fully in their society as they may have done if they had
been given adequate food. Thousands of children are left homeless,
orphaned and mutilated by war. Young teenagers throw rocks and
carry weapons, caught up in the cruelty and hatred of war created
by an adult world.

27. Our environment is polluted, damaged and threatened. "Jelly
babies" and deformed children are born in the Pacific Islands because
of nuclear testing. A child refuses to think of the future and loses
dreams of hope because of a belief that the world will be destroyed
by nuclear war before school is finished. Thousands of children die
unnecessarily each day from curable and preventable diseases.

28. The attitudes and priorities of our adult society are questioned
by what happens to children in our world.

29. The baptism or dedication of a child in a parish is a time of
celebration and rejoicing. However, children are often not included
in worship, sometimes not able to participate in the eucharist. A

child at 14 joins an occult sect asserting that she has found meaning and value in that group and not in the Church. The parents and the Church are deeply disappointed and puzzled by her action. Some children feel they do not belong to the Church and that they have no real place in it. Many children will never hear the gospel as their parents are indifferent to the Christian faith or have no faith at all.

30. These stories raise important issues for the churches in relation to our witness in a real and divided world.

31. "Do not hinder the children," says Jesus. Everything we do in the name of Jesus Christ needs to be seen in the light of this demand. There is, therefore, an urgent need for the churches through the WCC to take up the challenge that our children pose for us.

Special areas of concern: witnessing among the poor

32. The Church is called to witness to the Good News of the life, death and resurrection of Jesus Christ, to a world where there is a frightening and growing gap between rich and poor nations and between rich and poor within nations. Poverty exists on an unprecedented global scale. In a world which is today torn by conflicting ideologies, the poor are most apt to be ignored and forgotten. An increasing number of people find themselves marginalized, second-class citizens unable to control their own destiny and resigned to being and remaining poor. Children, the disabled, and women are among those who suffer most seriously the cruelty and despair of poverty. Racism, exploitation, militarization, and the resources expended in the arms race are different ways in which poverty is promoted and increased. Poverty is treated as a problem, rather than as a scandal calling for radical action to attack its causes and roots in human sinfulness and an unwillingness to share.

33. The Christian Gospel of salvation is good news to all people, but especially to the poor (cf. Luke 7:22). To them, as to all, is addressed the offer of God's forgiveness, the call to repentance, and the vision of a new heaven and a new earth. The message of the prophets is that God in no way assumes a neutral position between the rich and the poor. God is on the side of the poor and champions their cause for justice and fullness of life. They are blessed not because they are poor but because in their poverty Christ has come to offer them the gift of the kingdom. The poor have possibilities of a new awareness of the riches that are in Christ and therefore have much to give.

34. In not sharing the good news of the Gospel there has been a double injustice: the poor are victims of social, economic and political oppression and often have been deprived of the knowledge

of God's special love for them and the energizing liberation which
such knowledge brings. In the parable of the last judgment (Matt.
25:30ff.) Jesus identifies himself with the hungry, the homeless, the
naked, the sick and prisoners. This demands of us as Christians a
corresponding allegiance. If we are to follow Christ then we must
care for the poor and seek to reverse their situation.

35. The Church's call to witness in the life of the poor is therefore
a call for the people of God to rethink its priorities in its missions
and its programmes, and it is a challenge to its lifestyle on both a
corporate and an individual level. A more simple lifestyle and even
a life of poverty is laid on the Church and Christians as a witness
to the poverty of Christ "who though he was rich for our sake
became poor" (2 Cor. 8:9). Christians and churches, of course, find
themselves in very different circumstances, some rich and others
poor. To all, the call to share the good news with the poor comes
as a priority and a specific challenge. The Gospel must be proclaimed
in both word and deed; word without service is empty and service
without the word is without power. The churches today are learning
afresh, through the call to witness to the poor, to overcome the old
dichotomy between evangelism and social action. In Jesus' announcement of the kingdom the spiritual and material Gospel belong
together.

36. As the Church witnesses to the Gospel, it needs to reflect
faithfully the totality and universality of God's mission in a world
divided into rich and poor, different ideological camps, male and
female, young and old, slave and free, able and disabled. In its
witness to the poor and the oppressed it can and must be the voice
of those who are often rendered voiceless. God's own upholding of
the right of the poor, the outcast, the widows and the orphan is a
rebuke to complacent Christians and churches, and a summons to
repentance and a new commitment to the cause of justice. To claim
to witness to the poor and to side with them without working to
change the conditions which make for poverty is hypocritical. The
churches must struggle to put in place a new international order for
a more just world and be willing to change their own structures in
response. It must call on those who have power to use their power
to make human life more human.

37. As the Church ministers to those who are affluent, it must
call them to repentance and declare to them the good news of
liberation from enslavement to worldly possessions. There is a
poverty in the human condition which riches cannot mask and the
Church has a ministry of testifying to the Christ who can liberate
people from all their need. We must help our church members
understand that affluence has a way of sometimes impoverishing,

separating and blinding the rich so that they do not see the poor (Luke 16:19–31). Those who concentrate on riches, such as the rich farmer in Jesus' parable, are in danger of losing their souls. Thus the New Testament writers warn against the dangers of wealth, particularly the apostle James who delivers stern warnings to the rich (5:1–3) and censures them for exploiting the poor (5:4–6).

38. All Christians and churches have the duty, as part of their prophetic mission, to denounce the concentration of goods in the hands of a few, the adherence to the values of high consumption and the investment in death represented by the arms race which is one of the principal causes for the growing gap between the rich and the poor and the consequent failure to invest for the alleviation of poverty. Churches which have are called to share with churches which have not, and within the churches there must be a sharing so that the apostolic standard "there was not a needy person among them" (Acts 4:34) may be realized.

39. We rejoice that the churches are growing today among the poor of the earth and that new insights and perspectives on the Gospel are coming to the whole Church from communities of the poor. They are discovering and making known dimensions of the Gospel which have long been neglected and forgotten by the Church. The richness and freshness of their experience is an inspiration, blessing and challenge to the established churches. The centres of missionary expansion are moving from the North to the South as the poor have become not just the subjects but also the bearers of the good news; when people discover Christ they discover for themselves a liberating initiative and a new ethos towards the fullness of life. In the words of the Melbourne affirmation: "God is working through the poor of the earth to awaken the consciousness of humanity to his call for repentance, for justice and for love."

Special areas of concern: witnessing among people of living faiths

40. We live as people and as Christians in a religiously and ideologically pluralistic world. Christians from all parts of the oikumene raise questions about living alongside of, and witnessing to, neighbours of other faiths and diverse ideological commitments who have their own specific testimonies to offer. In such situations witness is not a one-way process: "from us to them". There is also a witness from "them to us", except in certain cases of martyrdom, the witness up to death, which could be understood as an extreme example of one-way testimony. However, in most normal circumstances, we, as human beings, are caught up in a search for reality and fulfilment, seeking to be understood and to understand and thus

discover meaning for living. Of all the things we do as Christians, witnessing among peoples of living faiths and ideologies causes the most difficulty and confusion. In this task we are hesitant learners, and need to acquire sensitivity not only to the peoples of other faiths and ideologies, but also to Christians caught up in situations of witness and dialogue in different parts of the world.

41. In our discussions and reflections on the question of witnessing to Christ among people of other faiths we have heard encouraging reports of many examples of dialogue in local situations. But we have also become aware of some matters which remain to be explored in the years that lie ahead. We note amongst other things the following:

a) We wish to place on record our appreciation to our friends from other faiths who have been present with us in this Sixth Assembly. We value their contribution, and their presence has raised for us questions about the special nature of the witness Christians bring to the world community.

b) While affirming the uniqueness of the birth, life, death, and resurrection of Jesus, to which we bear witness, we recognize God's creative work in the seeking for religious truth among people of other faiths.

c) We acknowledge the experience of common action and cooperation between Christians and persons of other faiths and the urgency of working together, especially in areas concerning the poor, basic human dignity, justice and peace, economic reconstruction, and the eradication of hunger and disease.

42. We see, however, the need to distinguish between witness and dialogue, whilst at the same time affirming their inter-relatedness.

43. Witness may be described at those acts and words by which a Christian or community gives testimony to Christ and invites others to make their response to him. In witness we expect to share the good news of Jesus and be challenged in relation to our understanding of, and our obedience to that good news.

44. Dialogue may be described as that encounter where people holding different claims about ultimate reality can meet and explore these claims in a context of mutual respect. From dialogue we expect to discern more about how God is active in our world, and to appreciate for their own sake the insights and experiences people of other faiths have of ultimate reality.

45. Dialogue is not a device for nor a denial of Christian witness. It is rather a mutual venture to bear witness to each other and the world, in relation to different perceptions of ultimate reality.

46. While distinctions can be made between dialogue, cooperation and mutual witness in the real experience of living in a religiously

and ideologically pluralistic situation they in practice intermingle and are closely inter-related.

47. All these must be seen in the context of shared responsibility for a common future, based on mutual respect, equal rights, and equal obligations.

48 There are still many questions remaining for further studies:

a) When witnessing among people of living faiths, an account must be taken of the influence of the dominant ideologies on religious belief and practices present and active in the particular cultural context.

b) An important concern is the degree to which Christians of different confessions can work towards sharing a common understanding of what it means to be human, an understanding of what it means to be the Church, and how these concerns relate to the witness of the Christian community and the involvement of Christians in dialogue with people of living faiths and ideologies.

c) Meeting in Vancouver and hearing about the religious life of the Native peoples has focused attention on the need to give a higher profile to dialogue with people from traditional religions.

d) The question of shared worship or prayer with people from other faiths needs to be explored.

e) Another of the religious phenomena of our day is the influence of various kinds of new religious movements. We need to discover more about these.

In all these explorations of faith it is important to involve women and young people. Their self-understanding of their role in the faith community will deepen and widen the theological quest.

49. We are encouraged by the insights and experience which have been gradually built up through various meetings between Christians and people of other living faiths. We look forward to the fruits of further encounters. In the next seven years we anticipate theological reflection on the nature of witness and dialogue which will encourage the life of the Christian community in many different parts of the world.

50. *Recommendations to member churches*:

a) That member churches be encouraged to engage actively in their calling to witness to their faith: towards that end they are encouraged to translate and distribute widely the document *Mission and Evangelism: an Ecumenical Affirmation*.

b) That member churches be encouraged to visit each other at local parish level in order to share in each other's worship and build up partner relationships with different liturgical traditions.

c) That member churches be asked to study the report of the Melbourne conference, especially the section on the poor, and to continue or to initiate programmes of action based on this.
d) That member churches be encouraged to translate, distribute and study the *Guidelines on Dialogue*.
e) That member churches be encouraged to share with one another their experiences of witness and dialogue among peoples of living faiths, and among people of no religion, through the World Council of Churches.
f) That member churches initiate studies on Gospel and culture in cooperation with regional councils of churches and the World Council of Churches.

Archbishop of Canterbury Robert Runcie presided at the Lima liturgy on 31 July. Assisting were, from left to right, Rev. Livingston Thompson (Moravian), Jamaica; Rev. Harry Henry (Methodist), Benin; Rev. Elisabeth Lidell (Lutheran), Denmark; Rev. Caroline Pattiasina-Toreh (Reformed), Indonesia; Bishop I. Jesudasan (United), India; and Rev. Robert Wallace (United), Canada

3.2   TAKING STEPS TOWARDS UNITY

Metropolitan John of Helsinki (Orthodox, Finland) Moderator of Issue Group 2, and Dr Paul Crow (Disciples, USA), presented the report.
    Archbishop Robert Runcie (Church of England) said that the churches were greatly indebted to the WCC for the work reflected in this report. He applauded its understanding of the relation between Church unity and the renewal of human community, the World Council's essential role in bilateral church-to-church conversations and the reception process foreseen for the Baptism, Eucharist and Ministry (BEM) text. Bishop Gunnar Lislerud, of the Church of Norway, urged that the reception of BEM be delayed no longer than necessary; during the reception period Faith and Order should not be overloaded with other responsibilities. Dr Dorothea Vorlaender (EKD, Federal Republic of Germany) expressed some concern lest the Lutheran emphasis on the preached word be neglected with the BEM emphasis on the eucharist. The document should be careful about advocating "the Lima Liturgy", said Rev. Michel Bertrand (Reformed, France), for neither the Assembly nor the churches have had an opportunity to discuss it. Metropolitan Chrysostomos of Myra (Ecumenical Patriarchate, Turkey) found it an excellent, well-balanced report. Concern was expressed by Dr Margaret Sonnenday (Methodist, USA) that there should be an explicit commitment to follow up the study on the Community of Women and Men in the Church, as an aspect of the relation between Christian unity and human community. Archbishop Michael Peers (Anglican, Canada) evoked the principle of lex orandi, lex credendi: not only does doctrine influence how we pray, but common worship and shared witness help shape doctrinal consensus.
    Dr Crow, responding, said that the BEM text understood the eucharist as both proclaimed word and celebrated supper. The reference to the Lima liturgy was not to suggest that it had become a normative liturgical text, but to draw the churches' attention to our experience and excitement in using it at Vancouver. The officers of the Issue Group, in polishing the text, would take into account other comments that had been made.
    The substance of the report was approved and commended to the churches for study and appropriate action.

I.   The goal: Church unity as a credible sign and witness

1.   Our central ecumenical goal is acknowledged in the World Council of Churches' first purpose and function: "To call the churches to the goal of visible unity in one faith and in one eucharistic fellowship expressed in worship and in common life in Christ, and to advance towards that unity in order that the world may believe." This single vision unites our two profoundest ecumenical concerns: the unity and renewal of the Church and the healing and destiny of

the human community. Church unity is vital to the health of the Church and to the future of the human family. Moreover, it is a response of obedience to God's will and an offering of praise to God's glory.

2. Earlier gatherings have perceived and stressed various aspects of this vision. The churches at Amsterdam (1948) said: "We intend to stay together" in their journey towards that goal. The Evanston Assembly (1954) discerned in Jesus Christ the only hope which can motivate such a journey. New Delhi (1961) emphasized that this unity means "all in each place as one fully committed fellowship". Montreal (1963) spoke of the primary source of such unity: "the Tradition of the Gospel testified in scripture, transmitted in and by the Church through the power of the Holy Spirit". Uppsala (1968) lifted up the catholicity and diversity of true unity.

3. Nairobi (1975) attempted to gather up many of these themes in a way which emphasizes the universality of the goal:

> The one Church is to be envisioned as a conciliar fellowship of local churches which are themselves truly united. In this conciliar fellowship, each local church possesses, in communion with the others, the fullness of catholicity, witnesses to the same apostolic faith, and therefore recognizes the others as belonging to the same Church of Christ and guided by the same Spirit . . . They are bound together because they have received the same baptism and share in the same eucharist; they recognize each other's members and ministries. They are one in their common commitment to confess the Gospel of Christ by proclamation and service to the world. To this end, each church aims at maintaining sustained and sustaining relationships with her sister churches, expressed in conciliar gatherings whenever required for the fulfillment of their common calling.

This view of the goal clearly will and should be further developed.

4. It is the implication of such Church unity for the destiny of the human community – an implication clearly contained in earlier statements but not so clearly expressed – which has impressed this Vancouver Assembly. Peace and justice, on the one hand, baptism, eucharist and ministry, on the other, have claimed our attention. They belong together. Indeed the aspect of Christian unity which has been most striking to us here in Vancouver is that of a *eucharistic vision*. Christ – the life of the world – unites heaven and earth, God and world, spiritual and secular. His body and blood, given us in the elements of bread and wine, integrate liturgy and diaconate, proclamation and acts of healing. "The remembrance of Christ is the very content of the preached word as it is of the eucharistic meal, each reinforces the other. The celebration of the eucharist properly includes the proclamation of the word" (BEM, Eucharist,

12). Our eucharistic vision thus encompasses the whole reality of Christian worship, life and witness, and tends – when truly discovered – to shed new light on Christian unity in its full richness of diversity. It also sharpens the pain of our present division at the table of the Lord; but in bringing forth the organic unity of Christian commitment and of its unique source in the incarnate self-sacrifice of Christ, the *eucharistic vision* provides us with new and inspiring guidance on our journey towards a full and credible realization of our given unity.

II. Marks of such a witnessing unity

5. Such a strong Church unity, affirmed in words, lived in deeds, relevant and credible to the problems of human community, would properly have at least three marks which the divided churches do not yet fully share.

6. First, the churches would share a common understanding of the apostolic faith, and be able to confess this Message together in ways understandable, reconciling and liberating to their contemporaries. Living this apostolic faith together, the churches help the world to realize God's design for creation.

7. Second, confessing the apostolic faith together, the churches would share a full mutual recognition of baptism, the eucharist and ministry, and be able through their visible communion to let the healing and uniting power of these gifts become more evident amidst the divisions of humankind.

8. Third, the churches would agree on common ways of decision-making and ways of teaching authoritatively, and be able to demonstrate qualities of communion, participation and corporate responsibility which could shed healing light in a world of conflict.

9. Such a unity – overcoming church division, binding us together in the face of racism, sexism, injustice – would be a witnessing unity, a credible sign of the new creation.

III. Steps we can take now towards this goal

10. While it is important to reflect further upon the goal of Church unity, the essential need now is for actions which advance towards the goal as we have seen it already in the WCC. In the light of our vision of the goal, four steps seem to us especially promising in the years immediately ahead.

A. We can encourage the process of reception of "Baptism, Eucharist and Ministry" by the churches

11. "Baptism, Eucharist and Ministry" is at one and the same time a challenge and an opportunity for the churches. For the first

time the various traditions are challenged to face each other not simply on the basis of their own identities, but in the presence of a common attempt to express a convergent statement of the apostolic faith. This text is grounded in that "Tradition of the Gospel" of which Montreal spoke. Confronted with this text, the churches are called to express in what measure they can recognize *together* the same apostolic faith. The document invites our churches to make the journey from isolated identities towards fuller fellowship. We receive this invitation with real excitement, but also with a realization that despite its achievements, "Baptism, Eucharist and Ministry" falls short of convergence on some important issues. The pain which this causes will be felt on our journey.

12. The terminology we must use in this process of reception differs in various churches, and it is not possible or proper for the WCC to prescribe official definitions. But it may be helpful to suggest the following:

13. In speaking of "Baptism, Eucharist and Ministry" as a "convergent statement", we do not imply that full agreement has already been reached. Rather, we speak of a statement which arises out of diverse ways of expressing the same faith, but which points to a common life and understanding not yet fully attained or expressed. Nevertheless, this unity remains the goal of the ecumenical task. These expressions "bend towards each other". These convergences give assurance that despite a diversity of traditions the churches have much in common in their understanding of the faith. The "Baptism, Eucharist and Ministry" text, however, is not yet a "consensus statement", meaning by that term "that experience of life and articulation of faith necessary to realize and maintain the Church's visible unity" (BEM Preface, ix).

14. It is also important to distinguish the "process of reception" and the "official response". The "official response", which is requested at a relatively early date, is intended to initiate a process of study and communication in which each church will attempt to provide an answer to the four preface questions, answers which are not simply the response of individuals or groups within the church but which, in some sense, understood by the church itself, are given on behalf of the church. This "official response" is explicitly not understood to be the church's ultimate decisions about "Baptism, Eucharist and Ministry", but rather the initial step in a longer process of reception. This "process of reception" is something which each church will have to understand in terms of its own tradition; it refers generally, however, to the long-range process by which the churches seek to recognize the one apostolic faith in and through the words of the text and freshly to lay hold of the new life which

that faith promises. This process is thus often spoken of as a "spiritual process of reception", and it will require much time and wide participation at various levels of the life of the church: congregations, theological faculties and ecumenical commissions, and ecclesiastical authorities. Additional ecumenical consultations may be helpful. We emphasize the importance of this "spiritual process of reception". The measure of our participation in this spiritual pilgrimage is at the same time an indication of the quality of our reception. It is clear that the meaning of the term "reception", since it is now used with respect to churches in a divided situation, varies somewhat from, but does not contradict, the usage of the early centuries.

15. We recognize that some churches will need more time than others to submit their official response. Therefore, this Assembly ᷍recommends the following timetable:

31 December 1984   All churches are requested to report briefly to Faith and Order by this date on how the process of official response and reception is being pursued.

31 December 1985   Desired date for official responses.

1987 or 1988   Fifth World Conference on Faith and Order.

16. Since it is essential that the process of reception enable the involvement and active participation of members at all levels of church life, we recommend that the churches consider the following:
– "Baptism, Eucharist and Ministry" has already been translated into over a dozen languages. It is hoped that this process will continue to enable it to reach the widest possible audience. When possible, such translations should be undertaken by ecumenical teams.
– The WCC has already produced a study guide and other materials to help facilitate congregational study. The adaptation of these materials to local situations and/or the production of other study material will greatly facilitate a more effective study of the document by a large number of church people.
– The celebration of the liturgy based on the guidelines already incorporated into the document has been a memorable and deeply moving event for many of us at Vancouver. This experience encourages us to underline the importance of the request that the official response should also deal with "the guidance your church can take from this text for its worship life" (BEM preface).
– As part of the spiritual process of reception, member churches should continuously remember the reception process before God in prayer and meditation, with penitence, thanksgiving, joy and

hope that they will be able to find within it the faith of the Church through the ages.

17. This convergent text should be seen in relation to other parts of the one ecumenical movement: (a) bilateral church conversations, (b) church union negotiations, (c) national and regional councils of churches, (d) local ecumenical projects. We must remember that each of these is important for the movement towards unity of the Church: indeeed, properly understood, they are complementary and enrich each other.

B. We can clarify the meaning of "a common understanding of the apostolic faith".

18. Reception of "Baptism, Eucharist and Ministry" clearly implies this further step, for *what* the churches are asked to receive in this text is not simply a document, but *in* this document the apostolic faith from which it comes, and to which it bears witness. Nairobi (1975) strongly recommended that: ". . . the churches . . . undertake a common effort to receive, reappropriate and confess together, as contemporary occasion requires, the Christian truth and faith, delivered through the apostles and handed down through the centuries. Such common action, arising from free and inclusive discussion under the commonly acknowledged authority of God's word, must aim both to clarify and to embody the unity and the diversity which are proper to the Church's life and mission."

19. As this effort has begun to take shape – its first fruits are still several years ahead of us – it has become clear that any common attempt by the churches to express that faith which unites all contemporary churches and all believers of all ages with the apostolic Church would need to be conceived along three lines: first, a common recognition of the apostolic faith as expressed in creeds of the undivided Church such as the Apostolic Symbol and especially the Nicene Creed; second, a common explication of the faith so recognized in terms understandable today; and third, a common confession by the churches today of that same apostolic faith in relation to the contemporary challenges to the Gospel.

20. Such an achievement is obviously beyond the reach of any commission document or WCC action. It could only be an event, given by God and received by the churches themselves – perhaps such an event as the Nairobi description of conciliar fellowship envisioned. Nevertheless, such an event can be hoped and prayed for, and the project "Towards the Common Expression of the Apostolic Faith Today" offers a beginning towards such an event. It will be impossible to take this common step if in this study of the apostolic faith we do not give special attention to the nature and

mystery of the Church of God, since the confession of the one, holy, catholic and apostolic Church belongs to the apostolic faith.

C. *We can help our churches to explore and express more clearly the relation between the unity of the Church, the eucharistic fellowship of believers, and the transformation of human community.*

21. At this Assembly we have sensed a tension between some of those who are concerned with the unity of the Church and others concerned with the desperate need for justice, peace and reconciliation in the human community. For some, the search for a unity in one faith and one eucharistic fellowship seems, at best secondary, at worst irrelevant to the struggles for peace, justice and human dignity; for others the Church's political involvement against the evils of history seems, at best, secondary, at worst detrimental to its role as eucharistic community and witness to the Gospel.

22. As Christians we want to affirm there can be no such division between unity and human renewal, either in the Church or in the agenda of the WCC. Indeed the "Baptism, Eucharist and Ministry" text has underlined for us that baptism, eucharist and ministry are healing and uniting signs of a Church living and working for a renewed and reconciled humankind.

> As they grow in the Christian life of faith, baptized believers demonstrate that humanity can be regenerated and liberated . . . Likewise, they acknowledge that baptism, as a baptism into Christ's death, has ethical implications which not only call for personal sanctification, but also motivate Christians to strive for the realization of the will of God in all realms of life (Rom. 6:9ff; Gal. 3:27–28; 1 Pet. 2:21, 4:6).

23. In the same way, the text on the eucharist expressly endorses a kind of eucharistic life-style in the midst of all struggles for justice, peace and freedom in today's world:

> The eucharist embraces all aspects of life. It is a representative act of thanksgiving and offering on behalf of the whole world . . . All kinds of injustice, racism, separation and lack of freedom are radically challenged when we share in the body and blood of Christ. Through the eucharist the all-renewing grace of God penetrates and restores human personality and dignity.

24. Similarly, through the study on the Community of Women and Men in the Church, many have discovered that life in unity must carry with it the overcoming of division between the sexes, and have begun to envision what profound changes must take place in the life of the Church and the world. The participants at the Sheffield conference on the Community of Women and Men in the Church emphasized that one form of oppression is interwoven with

others. The inter-relatedness of racism, classism and sexism calls for a combined struggle since no one form of renewal will, by itself, accomplish a renewal of ecclesial community. Such insights should be deepened and built upon with the study on the Unity of the Church and the Renewal of Human Community. Further, the specific challenges contained in the Sheffield recommendations should be taken up in the process of response to "Baptism, Eucharist and Ministry", the work on confessing the apostolic faith, and the quest for common ways of decision-making and teaching authoritatively.

25. As we have explored together the relation between God's Church and God's world, we have been struck by Uppsala's affirmation that "the Church is bold in speaking of itself as the sign of the coming unity of humankind". At Vancouver we have been challenged to deepen our understanding of what we mean when we make such a bold claim. Thus we propose that the Faith and Order Commission make a theological exploration of the Church as "sign" a central part of its programme on the Unity of the Church and the Renewal of Human Community. This recommendation implies our conviction that the Church is called to be a prophetic "sign", a prophetic.community through which and by which the transformation of the world can take place. It is only a church which goes out from its eucharistic centre, strengthened by word and sacrament and thus strengthened in its own identity, resolved to become what it is, that it can take the world on to its agenda. There never will be a time when the world, with all its political, social and economic issues, ceases to be the agenda of the Church. At the same time, the Church can go out to the edges of society, not fearful of being distorted or confused by the world's agenda, but confident and capable of recognizing that God is already there.

D. We can further the churches' common quest for agreement on common ways of decision-making and teaching authoritatively.

26. The ways in which the churches respond to "Baptism, Eucharist and Ministry", and the ways in which they engage in a longer process of reception, provide an ecumenical context within which the churches can learn to understand and encounter each other's ways of making decisions about church teaching. The significance of this opportunity needs to be emphasized, for common agreement about ways of teaching and decision-making is one of the fundamental marks of Church unity. Earlier ecumenical studies of how the Church teaches authoritatively today need to be taken up again in this new context.

IV. Towards a Fifth World Conference on Faith and Order

27. It is more than twenty years since the churches have had an opportunity to survey and appraise the advances towards Church unity in a comprehensive conference on Faith and Order. Earlier conferences – Lausanne 1927, Edinburgh 1937, Lund 1952, Montreal 1963 – each marked an important ecumenical milestone.

28. Such a conference is essential in ˙gathering up the fruits especially of our work on "Baptism, Eucharist and the Ministry", on the common expression of the apostolic faith, on common ways of teaching and decision-making, and on the unity of the Church and the renewal of the human community. Significant roles in this conference should be given to representatives of bilateral dialogues, united and uniting churches, Christian World Communions, national and regional councils of churches. The task of such a conference should be more than simply to survey the ecumenical situation. It should be asked to help the churches evaluate the implications of these various steps towards unity for their ecumenical task and relationships. The "Baptism, Eucharist and Ministry" project has begun to teach the WCC how to formulate and lay an ecumenical question before the churches, and the churches are showing genuine readiness for creative response to such initiatives. Thus we recommend that this Assembly endorse the calling of a Fifth World Conference on Faith and Order in 1987 or 1988, and urge the Faith and Order Secretariat to submit specific plans for its approval to the Central Committee in 1984.

V. The World Council of Churches within the one ecumenical movement

29. It is the goal of the ecumenical movement to serve the cause of the visible unity of the one, holy, catholic and apostolic Church. The ecumenical movement is more than the World Council of Churches, and it is not limited to any one Christian World Communion or church. In response to the promptings of the Holy Spirit, it encompasses a worldwide variety of forms of expression: Christian churches, including united and uniting churches, councils, bilateral and multilateral dialogues and other networks, proclaiming together in word and deed that Jesus Christ is the life of the world.

30. The World Council of Churches is a privileged instrument of the ecumenical movement. Visible Church unity and dynamic Church mission constitute the inter-related central core of the World Council's permanent agenda. Our God-given unity and our world-directed mission should never be severed from each other. This is the revealed will of the crucified and risen Christ whom we worship and serve as Lord and Saviour. "That they may all be one" is the

source of our unity; "that the world may believe" is the motive to,
our mission (John 17:21).

31. The fellowship of churches which constitutes the World
Council of Churches is a preliminary expression of that unity which
is God's will and gift for which Christians pray and work. It
provides a forum for intensive encounter and exchange of Christian
experiences, theological convictions and spiritual insights, as well as
an ecumenical framework for the ever more inclusive cooperation
of its member churches in common witness and service to the
world. While the World Council of Churches is an expression of the
ecumenical movement, the real agents of that movement are the
Christian churches themselves.

32. We gratefully confess that we have experienced this anew in
Vancouver. At this Assembly we have been especially blessed as
our theology has climaxed in doxology, our doctrinal convergences
in our praise and adoration of the triune God. Celebrating the Lima
eucharistic liturgy together could become a most powerful step in
the spiritual process of receiving the teachings of the ecumenical
text which lies at its base. What we believe truly governs how
we pray and work, even as prayer and action help deepen our
understanding of faith. May our growing doctrinal agreements
within the fellowship of the World Council of Churches enable both
more profound united worship and more effective common witness.
Jesus Christ who is the head of the body, the Church, is Lord and
Life given to all creation (Col. 1:18–20).

3.3   MOVING TOWARDS PARTICIPATION

*Ms Nicole Fischer (Reformed, Switzerland) introduced the report, as
Moderator of the third Issue Group. Stressing that participation has to be
lived, not learned, she asked different groups in the Assembly to stand –
laity, women, young people, other participants, the disabled and children.
Switching from French to English ("a minority's effort to accommodate the
majority!"), she suggested ways of making the Church more truly "a
fellowship of participation".*

*Several speakers commented on the role of women in the Church,
including the question of ordination. Ms Liv Nordhaug (Church of
Norway) said barriers to participation include not only those listed in the
document – illiteracy, unjust power structures, discrimination, etc. – but
also such personal barriers as indifference and fear of criticism. An inner
liberation is needed. Rev. Alida Anje In 't Veld, of the Remonstrant
Brotherhood in the Netherlands, asked that the document address the issue*

Native inmates of Agassiz Mountain Prison, near Vancouver, carved a 15-metre high totem pole for the Assembly, which was raised at the Vancouver School of Theology. After the Assembly it was transported to Geneva

*of homosexuals' involvement in the Church, particularly in the ordained
ministry. Ms Gillian Morton (Church of Scotland) drew attention to some
inadvertent elitism in a section on the roles of clergy and laity. The WCC
must help the churches give more support to people's movements, said Dr
Jone Bos of the Netherlands Reformed Church.*

*Subject to minor amendments following the debate, the substance of the
report was approved and commended to the churches for study and appropriate action.*

Introduction
Life is a gift of God. It is given to us by God, and we are called to
life in its fullness. Such full life becomes possible only through
participation.

In Jesus we have a model of participation. Here, as in all things,
he is the way, and he shows us the way. He demands that we be
born anew through the word of God to become new people who
are truly human. To be thus truly human is to cease to be oppressors,
or racists, or sexists. It is to live in solidarity with the poor and the
marginalized, even as Jesus did. Through our baptism and in the
eucharist we participate in God's creation, in the Church which is
the body of Christ, and in God's own life which is the source of all
our joy and hope.

The challenge before us and our churches is to be obedient to our
faith, that we really become a priesthood of all believers and living
stones of the whole house, dedicated to God, sharing his gifts with
the whole humankind (1 Pet. 2:4–5). That is what it means to be
involved in a fellowship of participation.

Real participation means becoming truly human. It implies involvement and encounter with others, sharing with others, working
together, making decisions and living together as people of God.

I.   General factors that impede participation
While we acknowledge that the WCC and some of our churches
have taken steps to make participation a reality, there are still inside
and outside the churches many factors which impede the full participation of all persons and we have to find ways to overcome these
barriers to full participation.

1. Illiteracy and lack of formal education prevent many people
from voicing their needs and wishes. Hunger, malnutrition and lack
of adequate medical care also impede full participation.

2. Unjust power structures in and outside the Church often enable
a few to dominate the many.

3. Economic, political and religious domination by external
forces and military intervention are also barriers to participation.

4. Changes in society, institutions and in the international order give rise to fears and suspicion, and make it difficult for both the powerful and the oppressed to participate in the creation of a new order.

5. Discrimination in terms of race, sex, religion and class is another factor which works against participation.

The experience of this group and the preparation of the report are good examples of how time pressure and respect for deadlines impede true participation.

In addition to such general factors there are others which specifically affect special groups in their search for full participation.

II.   Factors related to special groups

Laity
The Church, the body of Christ, has been entrusted with the mission of calling the whole of humanity to become God's people. This mission to the world should be undertaken by the whole people of God (laos), the ordained and laity, in a fellowship of participation (koinonia). This involves the effective utilization of the diverse gifts and ministries of the whole laos.

But participation by laity becomes impossible: (1) when the laity is excluded from the decision-making structures of the Church; (2) when the laity is not effectively equipped or encouraged for ministry in the world. We affirm that the laity has a special opportunity to share and interpret the Gospel creatively and sensitively in the home, in the community, and in all areas of daily work, especially in the field of science, technology and politics.

Women
Women constitute the largest part of congregations around the world, but the structures of power within and outside the churches inhibit their growth and full participation.

Their own lack of confidence and their general aversion to manipulative power tactics sometimes mean that women miss opportunities to participate.

Tradition, cultural patterns, the domination of imported theologies, and traditional male interpretations of the Bible make the situation even more difficult for women.

Jesus Christ gave important roles to women, and they were the first witnesses of his resurrection. But the Church he founded, through the centuries marginalized women. Networks of women's organizations inside and outside the Church are however a hopeful sign in our day.

Young people, the ageing, and children
These three groups are denied full participation in Church and society on the basis of age.

Young people who are an integral part of the people of God have special gifts to offer: enthusiasm, fresh ways of looking at life, the willingness to challenge structures. They are, however, often perceived as lacking in experience and an understanding of how the Church functions. Tradition too is interpreted in such a way as to give older generations an unfair advantage. This leads to mutual misunderstanding, frustration on the part of youth and sometimes their rejection of the Church. Opportunities which exist for dialogue need to be encouraged.

The ageing, through their experience and understanding, can enrich the life of both Church and society, sharing their gifts with the whole community. They constitute approximately one-third of the world's population. Statistics show that their number will increase over the years.

This phase of life should not be seen only in terms of chronological age; the various life-contexts, socio-economic as well as health conditions, influence greatly the ageing of people. Often the ageing are seen as useless, denied the rights to participate and condemned to loneliness and neglect. Sometimes, however, the Church and society permit and encourage them to hold on to power and control for too long, denying opportunities to young people, and giving rise to conflict! The churches have to discover better strategies in this area which would provide for participation and not perpetuate control.

The Church should not accept the "generation gap" which is a breach of the unity we seek, but should work for better relations between generations at all levels and in all areas.

Children bring a special quality to the family of God and are held up many times in the Gospels as examples of Christian behaviour. Their spontaneity and simple trust are special gifts. We, however, exclude them from full participation in the Church because of their inability to comprehend faith rationally and to make "adult" decisions, even when these decisions affect their lives in community. In some societies they are seen as non-producers and therefore marginal, while in others they have been forced, through poverty and injustice, to work for a living, even into prostitution. They increasingly suffer physical and mental abuse. Children and women represent the highest numbers of refugees around the world. Also, in many societies children suffer greatly as family growth is complicated by depressive economic factors. Children who embody so much of the future hope of both Church and society need to be given their rightful place in the community of both.

Persons with disabilities
We are all created in the image of God; all of us, including persons with disabilities, are living stones of the house which God is building, which is the Church. Persons with disabilities cannot be isolated; they are part of the house (oikos), and essential for the wholeness of the life and the worth of the Church. The 10% of the world's population who belong to the group of people who have hearing, seeing, speaking, behavioural, mobility, mental and other disabilities, are an integral part of the Church and the society.

We recognize the positive steps the WCC and some Churches have taken to create an awareness with regard to the needs of persons with disabilities. A good beginning has been made, but there is much more to do, as expressed in the recommendations, so that each local church may become a genuine healing and caring community and the gifts of each one are recognized and accepted as contributing to the total fellowship.

People's participation in the political process
People's participation is impeded on all levels by the factors mentioned at the beginning of this report.

The problems differ from one political system to another. In many political systems bureaucracy tends to stifle the creativity and initiatives of the majority of people, as is illustrated in the discussion of the problems of environment, armament and hunger. In South Africa and Namibia legalized racism prevents the vast majority of the people from participating in the crucial decisions affecting their lives.

But all over the world people's movements and groups have begun to fight for self-determination and full participation in the decisions which affect their destiny. The churches should support such initiatives. On the international level they should make concerted efforts, in cooperation with the WCC, to open for the people possibilities of participation. The programme of the WCC on Transnational Corporations (TNCs) is part of such efforts.

III. Recommendations to the member churches
God has blessed the members of the Church with rich and various gifts. Only when these gifts are developed and allowed to function will the Church become what God wants it to be.

a) Recommendations on laity

1. Churches should encourage and ensure the full participation of the laity at all levels of the Church's structures and recognize the particular gifts of all Church members.

2. Churches are encouraged to re-examine their own programmes in order to ensure that they provide for appropriate instruments for equipping laity for ministry in the world.

3. The churches should examine their relationship to the variety of movements and groups which have sprung up to deal with the numerous issues which the laity especially have identified as being central to the witness of the churches today.

b) Recommendations on women

1. Churches must evolve clear criteria to ensure that the structure provides a working mechanism for the participation of women.

2. In times of budget cuts, women and youth programmes must not suffer; they should be given financial priority.

3. In future team visits 50% of the participants should be women.

4. Member churches should, through skills training especially in relation to advocacy roles, provide greater opportunities for women to participate. They should encourage women to participate in vital justice and peace issues and keep contact and maintain cooperation with these groups.

5. The Orthodox churches should take the initiative to provide simple study material and information on the Orthodox Church and the role of women, for the benefit of non-Orthodox women and men. This information would greatly strengthen the understanding and sisterhood between women of different confessions. The WCC should assist in this exercise.

6. While the position of Orthodox women needs to be respected, the ordination of women must still be kept actively on the ecumenical agenda.

c) Recommendations on young people

1. National and regional ecumenism is at a low ebb in many places. Churches are asked to make a much greater effort to build up ecumenical groups in order to give visibility to Church unity.

2. In 1985, the International Youth Year, churches are asked to arrange programmes that will focus on youth, the witness by youth and unity among young people, bearing in mind the theme for the year: "Participation, Development, Peace".

3. It is recommended that churches give better opportunity for young people to develop leadership skills, and allow them more opportunity to move towards the centre of the work of the WCC.

This should include representing their churches at WCC programmes, meetings and committees.

4. The churches and ecumenical youth should organize their work more closely with campus ministries and university chaplaincies in order to strengthen ecumenism among students and their involvement in the WCC.

d) Recommendations on the ageing

Those who are 60 and over form the fastest growing section of the world's population (estimated to be 1,121 million in the year 2025 as compared to 214 million in 1950, of which 800 million will be living in developing countries). In some countries the age of retirement has been brought down to 55. This rapidly changing situation creates new opportunities as well as new obligations for the churches and the society at large.

Churches should give special emphasis:

1) to the need to enable ageing people to make their experience, skills and wisdom available to the whole community;
2) to the training of theological students for providing pastoral care to the aged;
3) to study in depth, biblically and theologically, the teaching on death to be given to the elderly, and to all others;
4) to the need for congregations to be caring communities;
5) to develop ways of integration between the different generations, making use of their special skills and experience.

e) Recommendations on children

On participation in the Church

Churches should be encouraged:

1) to have children participating in discussions on the issues of "Baptism, Eucharist, Ministry";
2) to include the concern for children's participation in the life of the Church in the training programmes for ministers and lay workers.
3) to review Church structures, worship and related activities in order to give room for the participation of children;
4) to consider the part of children in decision-making, *at least* when programmes are established for them in churches.
5) to develop supportive ministries for families and children subjected to abuse and violence in the family.

On participation in society

1. Churches should help develop the gifts of children for the life of the whole community.

2. In poor countries churches should develop a ministry addressed to the social and economic needs of children as well as to their spiritual needs.

f) Recommendations on the disabled
Churches are urged to:
1) initiate and pursue study/action programmes leading to preventing disabilities from whatever causes – environmental, nutritional, accidental, or as a result of unjust social, economic and political situations – rehabilitating those in need, using the resources and means available locally;
2) concretely affirm that all persons with disabilities are living stones in the house of God, by including them in the decision-making bodies of the churches at all levels;
3) examine with congregations the factors which hinder the integration and participation of persons with disabilities and take concrete steps to remove them (including the architectural barriers);
4) encourage and facilitate mutual support among families with one or more disabled members, collaborating with existing services where available, and creating such services where necessary;
5) introduce special courses related to persons with disabilities in the theological training programmes;
6) take the initiative to introduce educational programmes in the regular schools to help foster better relations between the children with disabilities and other children;
7) conduct surveys to identify all the people with disabilities in their congregations as a first step towards their integration in the life of the Church (as far as possible this should be an ecumenical effort);
8) offer the sacraments to people with physical and mental disabilities (we are convinced that the disabled people can also have a spiritual understanding of the sacrament and that they are able to participate in their own way in the spiritual life of the Church and the congregation);
9) reconsider how the disabled may have access to ordained ministry;
10) accept persons with disabilities as students and teachers in theological and training schools and colleges.

g) Recommendations on people's participation
The churches are asked to support people's movements and development groups and share their experiences with them.

The closing worship

3.4   HEALING AND SHARING LIFE IN COMMUNITY

Bishop Johannes Hempel (BEK, German Democratic Republic), Moderator of the Issue Group, Bishop Aram Keshishian (Armenian, Lebanon) and the rapporteurs of the Issue Group presented the report.

They indicated that some changes would be made to the text in the light of written comments already received. There was little time, however, for any significant debate in the plenary.

On the understanding that the Issue Group's officers would make further minor amendments, the Assembly approved the substance of the report and commended it to the churches for study and action.

Theological foundation

1. Sharing is rooted in the very nature of the triune God as a "community of sharing" characterized by dynamic and creative mutuality. Christ is the concrete expression in time and space of God's *economia* of sharing. In Christ, God enters with us into an existential relationship of sharing and healing. The cross is the expression of Christ's complete sharing of himself. Hence, the Church as the living body of Christ, by its very nature and mission, is a *koinonia* of sharing and healing.

2. The Church's conscious sharing and healing begins in the eucharist. It is the sign and locus of the Church's ministry of sharing and healing. The eucharist is essentially the self-giving of God in Christ to the world. It is both a reassurance and an imperative. As we share in Christ's broken body, so we become bread for the world to *be* broken and shared – what we are and what we possess. This implies cross, *kenosis*, which disturbs us creatively.

3. The "liturgy after the liturgy" is *diakonia*. Diakonia as the Church's ministry of sharing, healing and reconciliation is of the very nature of the Church. It demands of individuals and churches a giving which comes not out of what they have, but what they are. This exposes them to the risk of insecurity and the cost of justice and freedom. Diakonia constantly has to challenge the frozen, static, self-centred structures of the Church and transform them into living instruments of the sharing and healing ministry of the Church. Diakonia cannot be confined within the institutional framework. It should transcend the established structures and boundaries of the institutional Church and become the sharing and healing action of the Holy Spirit through the community of God's people in and for the world.

4. The Church's sharing and healing ministry originates from the very life and mission of Christ himself. Sharing and healing begin at a personal level, but they become societal both on local and

ecumenical levels. They demand right and direct relationships, based on love and justice, with self, with neighbour and with God. Sharing and healing are sacramental in origin and communal in scope. They are closely inter-related.

5. It is vitally important that sharing and healing in community be approached holistically. Since they embrace the whole human person and all life, the totality of community life in all its aspects and dimensions – physical, material, mental, spiritual etc. – sharing and healing are not just a process of giving and receiving but committed participation, conscious self-giving. It is essentially the community-building process.

The ministry of sharing

6. After the Fifth Assembly at Nairobi, the WCC Central Committee launched a study programme on the Ecumenical Sharing of Resources. In 1980 the Central Committee adopted a "Message to the Churches" and commended the study guide *Empty Hands* to the churches. The insights gained in the study have challenged the WCC and the churches to review their understanding of and involvement in the sharing of resources. All the resources held by the churches are given to them in trust by God. The ministry of sharing is a challenge to the churches to practise what they are called to be: sharing communities which seek to do justice, taking the side of all those who are denied their share in the fullness of life that God has promised.

Spiritual and human resources

7. In the Church we have been given a wealth of spiritual and human resources. This Assembly, in its worship, fellowship and many personal exchanges, has helped us to realize how very much there is within the body of Christ which we must both receive and give.

7.1 All Christians may be enriched by sharing in patterns of Christian life and devotion which are different from their own. We have much to learn from one another's spirituality, in prayer, life-style, suffering and struggle.

7.2 In the global village which we are, Christians should visit one another more often. We welcome and encourage new forms of multilateral sharing of personnel in world mission, in the healing and sharing ministry of the churches. We see such sharing as a strengthening of witness and a sign of the universality of the Church of Christ.

Material resources

8. The sharing of material resources must be seen in its proper context, that of Christian stewardship. All churches have a claim on each other's resources, and a responsibility to challenge and help one another to use each other's resources properly. Material wealth should not confer power on those who have, reducing others to dependence. On the contrary, sharing among the churches should point towards justice and the renewal of the human community.

8.1 There is a great need for a new theological understanding of sharing material resources based on justice and solidarity with the poor. Education and dialogue are necessary to help the churches and their agencies understand and put into practice the true meaning of such sharing.

8.2 Christian stewardship implies that the churches develop mutual trust and hold each other accountable for the resources God has put into their hands.

8.3 Churches in rich countries have to learn how to receive from materially poor churches, even as the latter must learn how to be givers.

8.4 We must seek models of sharing material resources. The donor-receiver type of relationship must give way to relationships which facilitate the sharing of decision-making and power. This means that priorities for the allocation of funds be set by the local communities and that more funds be made available without specific designation. Bilateral or confessional patterns of sharing should be challenged so that the churches may grow towards greater ecumenical sharing on local, regional and international levels. Their agencies for mission and development should be together involved in such efforts.

The healing ministry of the Church

9. Considerable importance was attached to the contribution of the Christian Medical Commission (CMC) since the Fifth Assembly in Nairobi, especially to its new definition of health that encompasses the individual as well as his/her relationship to society, the environment and God.

Love, justice and health

10. The Church exists in the midst of the world where brokenness and lack of harmony find their expression not only in sickness and conflicts but also in the marginalization and oppression that many people endure due to economic, racial, political and cultural reasons. This situation is a challenge to the Church to carry out its healing

ministry in a holistic way, and in a praxis renewed by the power of Christ's love – which is the basis of the ministry.

10.1 Many nations, with only limited resources, must order their national priorities accordingly; others, with adequate resources, have not justly managed their priorities. In all cases the question of justice in the distribution of these resources is of paramount importance. In so many countries only a privileged few have access to such health care. Where the doctrine of national security based on the force of arms prevails, the possibilities of meeting basic health care needs decrease. In such cases the urban and rural poor always lose out. While the emphasis on distributive justice is vital for developing countries, many industrialized and affluent states also have the problem of unjust distribution of resources. The urban poor living alongside health care institutions of high excellence still suffer from malnutrition and appalling health conditions. The Church expresses its concern over the growing hunger and malnutrition in *all* regions, and recognizes the need to tackle the complex questions surrounding the local and global supply of food.

10.2 It was strongly affirmed that the churches have an important role to play to bring about change both locally and abroad, through their own health policies and programmes, as well as through their governments' national and international health policies. The role of transnational corporations needs to be carefully analyzed in the context of justice and health – both their operations in the developing countries and their impact on the societies of industrialized and affluent countries.

The churches' health care programmes

11. The churches must continue to emphasize and explore primary health care as one of the ways to overcome the injustice of the present system of distribution of health resources. This emphasis does not rule out the need to maintain and use institutional services which, however, must be humanized. The study of traditional healing practices and of the contribution of traditional healers should be a part of this effort.

11.1 The role of spiritual healing as well as the healing ministry of the congregation calls for further study. Pastoral counselling is an integral part of the holistic approach to healing. A congregation can only become a healing community when it provides the opportunity to its members to participate fully in every aspect of its life and healing mission.

11.2 The key to the success of health care is *people* who are well trained and motivated. Therefore, the involvement of churches in health care must be pursued at several levels: *policy* – direction and objectives guided by the concern for outgoing love and justice; *planning* – identification of priorities, resources and technologies; *service* – functioning, management, motivation; *training* – recruitment, education, deployment, course content. Such an approach to health care can provide a basis for church-government collaboration. The churches are called to play a major role in terms or reorienting the health policy of their governments, both at home and abroad, towards a more community-based and just health care programme.

11.3 The selection of priority areas in response to local needs must begin with a broad concern for both rural and urban poor and the populations most at risk, children, and women in their child-bearing years. It must also include a concern for the role of women as providers of care, as food providers, and as those with special health needs.

Human values and ethical issues

12. The churches must emphasize the humanization of health care and the participation and responsibility of every individual in the health care of the community as well as in his/her own. This must be accompanied by a vigorous approach to some of the ethical issues which face society and the Church.

12.1 Medical technological advances should be viewed in their proper perspective, as gifts of God, in order to avoid the dehumanizing idolatry of science. Such idolatry can result in the loss of many human values and the Christian understanding of health, disease and death, and encourage the persisting belief that disease is a simple dysfunction of body organs or the result of unfortunate accidents which scientific medicine can prevent or cure.

Disability and ageing

13. The all-inclusive nature of this topic is seen in this fact: 450 million people, 85% of them in the third world, are disabled; and *all* of us are ageing and, in a sense, are dying. Disability may be caused by accidents, disease, hereditary and congenital disorders, torture, hunger and wars. Underlying many of these are the conditions of economic and social injustice and poverty with which so many must live. This presents to both society and Church a challenge that cannot be ignored, because disability cuts across every cultural, social and economic stratum. That challenge begins to be answered with a preventive approach to both the root causes and the immediate causes of disability.

13.1 In the past, persons with disabilities, as well as the elderly and the dying, were often cut off from meaningful participation in family life, denied opportunities for education or self-expression, or simply shut away in institutions. They were obliged to exist with little or no emotional or spiritual support from either society or Church. The consequences in dehumanization, loneliness, deprivation, fear, guilt and economic dislocation have been beyond description.

13.2 It is not only those who are disabled, ageing and dying, who must face their mortality and come to terms with it; all of us must. By learning to accept ourselves, we will be able to accept others. By the grace of God we will be able to accept and love each other as Christ has loved us. Generally the Church has been slow to take a leadership role in helping the disabled, ageing and dying. Only recently are we beginning to recognize this neglect and rejection.

Alcoholism and drug abuse

14. Statistics point out that alcoholism, drug abuse and smoking are increasing alarmingly in every nation, creating a problem that cannot be ignored. Behind these statistics are human lives experiencing the devastating effects of alcohol, smoking and drug abuse which debilitate persons and bring disease and death to themselves and to others.

14.1 Addiction to any of these undermines the physical, mental and spiritual competence of individuals. The Church has the responsibility to face these problems that enslave so many people. Not surprisingly perhaps, alcoholism, smoking and drug abuse are also prevalent among the leadership of some of our own churches.

14.2 Young people as well as many ethnic/racial minorities are among those most heavily affected and they continue to be a principal target of the promotional efforts which seek to increase the sales and profitability of these substances. The root causes of this appalling global problem may be found in the social and economic conditions which lead to stress, fear, unemployment, isolation, loneliness, dissatisfaction and in the need to be socially accepted.

14.3 The economic and political forces behind the traffic of alcohol and drugs are powerful indeed, touching countries around the world. Efforts to restrict, control or legislate that traffic have met strong resistance not least because of the financial implications of decreased production and consumption. If this trend is to be reversed, and if the next generation is to be preserved from even greater dependence on alcohol, tobacco and drugs, the churches must join with other concerned social groups in a vigorous action programme. That effort will demand a deeper understanding of the root causes behind the problem in both rich and poor countries. It will also demand a new approach to the pastoral ministry among those afflicted. Such an effort will call for specific training for church workers and educational programmes at the congregational level.

Community of women and men in the Church

15. The broad definition of health which includes harmony in community contributes to a better understanding of the relationship of men and women in society, and makes clear that harmonious relations between men and women promote health.

16. We urge that the unique gifts of the male and the female be conserved for the life of the Church. At the same time we recognize the value for the Church in the development of new roles for men and women.

17. The fact of the changing roles is familiar enough. The passive acceptance of an oppressed role could be a major block to creative change. On the other hand a common commitment to engage together in dealing with social problems (such as threats to peace, the ecological crisis, etc.) may assist in achieving a more equitable community of women and men. It is noted that in most situations male dominance remains the mode of social organization, though its manifestation differs from one culture to another.

18. Parental responsibility seems to us to be a focal point in gauging the significance of change in the role of men and women. Much of the uneasiness about the changing roles is expressed in terms of the nurture of children and the role of the mother and the father as a nurturing parent and care-giver. We believe that the churches must give careful attention to the study and understanding of this area of change, and of the biblical principles that justify a desire for change. It is clear that Jesus' ministry broke new ground in the matter of changing roles, as in the case of the Samaritan woman.

19. While we reflect on the family we must also reflect upon the tensions that arise as more societies move from the extended and even the nuclear family pattern; the exploitative labour conditions in many parts of the world that separate families; the increase in the incidence of divorce and the rise of single-parent families, now common in almost all cultures; and those persons in society who remain or become single in different periods of their life. All these situations demand the attention of the churches and challenge them to create conditions of healing, sharing and wholeness.

Recommendations

The participants in Issue 4 recommend:

20. That the churches be encouraged to pursue theological studies to promote a greater understanding of the common imperative for

healing and sharing, and the implications of that understanding for the ministry of the Church.

21. That the churches initiate new models of *diakonia*, rooted in the local congregation as it is confronted by increasing brokenness as a result of poverty, unemployment, marginalization and consumerism.

22. That the churches develop sharing and exchange with Christians across the world, through, for example, congregational or pastoral exchanges, "twinning" arrangements between local churches, and exchanges of people in all walks of Christian life and vocation.

23. That the churches join in the efforts of the WCC to build up the new resource sharing system as a model of ecumenical action, beyond confessional limits and in a spirit of equality and mutuality, while providing full information on their involvement in the sharing of resources so that all can learn from one another's rich experience. The WCC should facilitate such flow of information.

24. That the churches increase their financial support to the 2% Appeal and to the Ecumenical Church Loan Fund (ECLOF), and review their investment policy to increase their support for the Ecumenical Development Cooperative Society (EDCS) from their investment funds.

25. That the churches, at both national and international levels, monitor the policies of governments and international negotiations and agreements, as they relate to the sharing of the earth's resources, with a view to establishing a just and participatory sharing and distribution of the resources of the world.

26. That, as the churches continue to develop their healing ministry, they (a) further reflect on the nature of the healing ministry of the Church and congregation, (b) actively consider different and alternative expressions of a holistic healing ministry which conform to a spirit of justice and accepting love, (c) maintain the capacity to respond to urgent and special needs as they arise, and (d) communicate and coordinate within and among themselves on all these issues.

27. That the churches be encouraged to examine for themselves and with each other the difficult questions emerging in areas of human values and ethics, including those related to biomedical technology, as well as abortion, euthanasia, and genetic engineering, noting especially the pastoral responsibility of the churches everywhere for all those whose lives are affected by these.

28. That the churches be encouraged to examine and study for themselves and with one another the question of homosexuality, with special stress on the pastoral responsibility of the churches everywhere for those who are homosexual.

29. That the churches recognize and use the gifts of young and old alike, involving in the total ministry of the Church the ageing and those who have disabilities, to the building up of the body of Christ; and affirm that a person with a disability is able to be a leader in the Church, that ordination of such is not only possible but can be a healing symbol of our acceptance. Beyond symbolic acceptance, church placement structures should enable ordained people with disabilities to serve in parishes and should support congregations in working with the unique needs and gifts of clergy with disabilities.

30. That the churches accept the normal and rightful place of the disabled and ageing among us, and work actively to identify and overcome personal and non-accepting barriers, provide for barrier-free transportation and architecture, and assure adequate aids for communicating during worship; and ensure the provision of loving and adequate care of the very elderly, the infirm and the dying. In particular, the churches must recognize their responsibility to prepare human persons for dying as well as living, on the basis and in the hope of our life in Jesus Christ.

31. That the churches give guidance in personal Christian life-style in order to counter the temptations of alcohol, tobacco and addictive drugs, especially in the case of young people and ethnic/racial minority groups; while pursuing the analysis of and the struggle against the social, political and economic conditions which underlie this global problem, involving young and minority people themselves in the ministry.

32. That the churches be challenged to exert influence over their governments for the control and restriction of the production and marketing of alcohol, tobacco and addictive substances, pursuing at the same time a study of the economic and political implications of such control.

33. That local congregations be urged to offer continuing support to single persons and families, and seek to meet the special needs of single-parent families.

34. That the churches continue to explore appropriate models of response to the changing roles of women and men within society, work, church and family life, bearing in mind the effects of econ-omic and political stress as well as regional and cultural differences; and that, recognizing the sensitivity in many churches with regard to the question of the ordination of women, while acknowledging the need for healing and sharing in this context of our brokenness, the churches continue to pursue a consultative process among them-selves on this matter.

August 6, the anniversary of the destruction of Hiroshima, was marked by a public witness for justice and peace

3.5   CONFRONTING THREATS
TO PEACE AND SURVIVAL

Metropolitan Paulos Mar Gregorios (Orthodox Syrian Church of the East, India) presented the report as Moderator of the Issue Group. He indicated that a section on theology and the foundations of peace had been dropped for reasons of space; even so the document exceeded the prescribed length.

Bishop John Habgood (Church of England), a Vice-Moderator, stressed the inter-relatedness of the many topics touched upon in the report. Technological society tends to fragment such topics and deal with each in isolation, but the Church must attempt to see the picture whole. It is not enough to denounce, he said: the churches must do some hard thinking if they are to influence decisions that will shape the future.

Rev. Dr Josef Smolik (Czech Brethren) underlined the need to build confidence and counter propaganda that fosters distrust and fear. Several speakers, including the General Secretary, regretted the deletion of the theological introduction, and Dr John Howard Yoder (Mennonite, USA) encouraged the WCC to pursue theological study of the ethics of war and peace. The churches should be asked to provide pastoral and practical support for Christians engaged in non-violent civil disobedience opposing militarism, argued Rev. Hamish Christie-Johnston (Uniting Church in Australia), and Bishop Karoly Toth (Reformed, Hungary) wanted an unequivocal statement that the avoidance of nuclear war is today's most urgent moral imperative. Bishop Victor Premasagar, of the Church of South India, felt the document depicted technology too much in negative terms, ignoring what the third world saw as its promise. Dr Aaron Tolen (Presbyterian, Cameroun) registered reservations about the term "appropriate technology": it is appropriate only when controlled by the country concerned, not when it increases dependency.

The Issue Group's Moderator responded positively to most of the concerns that had been raised. He explained, however, that there had been several strains of theological thinking in the Group. "We have not yet come to an ecumenical consensus on peace theology which can be stated in two paragraphs!" he said.

The substance of the report was approved and commended to the churches for study and appropriate action.

Part A: Justice, peace and militarism

1. Christ, the life of the world, is our peace (Eph. 2:14). Our hopes for a world where life is not threatened by nuclear holocaust, or slow starvation, for a world where justice and peace embrace each other, are based in Jesus Christ, the Crucified and Risen One who has triumphed over the powers of evil and death, and therefore

will not allow the ultimate triumph of injustice and war. True peace comes only from God, who can turn even the wrath of man to God's praise (Ps. 76:10). True peace is more than the absence of war: it means restored relationships of love, compassion and justice.

2. The Spirit of God works through people and nations, as they become open to God's guidance, and seek peace. Christians themselves are often guilty of hating the "enemy", of seeking vengeance, and of causing division and discord. But as we witness to our genuine desire for peace with specific actions, the Spirit of God can use our feeble efforts for bringing the kingdoms of this world closer to the kingdom of God.

3. We recognize that an unjust peace can be unbearable. Many of us have only recently been liberated from the unjust peace of colonialism. Others are in the thick of the struggle for emancipation from an injustice which precludes peace, from systems buttressed by brute force, by torture and murder and even by attempts at genocide. A peace based on racism, sexism, domination, greed and militarism cannot be what Christians seek.

Common security

4. Human beings have a right to live in security. This implies economic and social justice for all, protection and defence of life within a political framework designed to ensure this. It is legitimate for each nation to seek its own security and protection from outside attack, without endangering the security of other nations.

5. Current concepts of national security are to be challenged where they conflict with the demands of justice, exceed the needs to legitimate defence, or seek economic, political and military domination of others. Prevailing doctrines of national security lead to the preparation for war becoming an almost permanent way of life for nations and societies. Military conditioning of the population, including children, distorts priorities in political, social and cultural planning, and often seeks to legitimize the systematic violation of human rights in the name of national security.

6. This applies on the international plane also. So long as economic injustice prevails between nations, lasting international security cannot be achieved, either by collective defence systems or by negotiated weapons reduction alone. Only a common enterprise undertaken by all the nations of the world together can ensure dependable international security.

7. No nation can achieve security at the expense of others, through seeking military superiority or interfering in the life of other nations. Deterrence or peace by terror should give place to

the concept of common security for all, which includes people's security in each nation.

8. Common security implies:

a) respect for the legitimate rights of all nations and peoples;

b) promoting mutual understanding and appreciation among cultures, religions and ideologies, through open communication, rejecting propaganda of mistrust and fear, and promoting confidence-building measures;

c) broad international cooperation in science and technology, economy and culture;

d) conversion of all economies from military to civilian production;

e) using and strengthening the United Nations Organization and other international institutions with similar objectives;

f) promoting adequate international legislation and providing means for adjudication of international disputes and for implementation of decisions;

g) making the machinery for peaceful settlement of international conflicts more effective.

Militarism in relation to economic injustice

9. We believe that the present military build-up and arms race are integrally related to the practices of an unjust world economic order. The worldwide trend towards militarization is not a mere confrontation and tension between the major powers, but also an expression of the desire to repress those emerging forces which seek a more just world order. It is this latter which poses a fundamental threat to peace. Whereas people's aspirations for and expectations of a more just order have been supported as legitimate, the big powers still use military might to buttress the unjust order in order to protect their own interests. The defence of these interests can often be disguised as appeals for national security, the upholding of law and order, the defence of democracy, the protection of the "free world", the need to maintain spheres of influence and sometimes even the cause of peace.

10. Among the factors promoting militarism one can identify: technological advances enhancing the effectiveness and power of military and police forces; growing integration of military and civilian sectors; a conscious promotion of psychological insecurity to justify the further acquisition of arms; a growing worldwide military trade network; alarming increase in the number of foreign military bases; unhealthy competition between the USA and the USSR to achieve military and technological superiority; creation and maintenance of spheres of influence by major developed nations

and some of the two-thirds world nations; the egomania and prestige-seeking of certain political leaders; religious fanaticism.

11. The arms trade is a new form of intervention, maintaining and developing dominance-dependence relationships, and encouraging repression and violation of human rights. Militarism leads to massive allocation of human and material resources to research and production in the military sector in all countries, at the cost of lowering the priority of meeting the needs of human development. The process seems already out of political control.

12. As the opposition to nuclear weapons grows, new non-nuclear or so-called conventional weapons of mass destruction develop at frightening speed, evading public attention. The churches should do more research about these, and help the public to assess these developments and to oppose them where necessary.

Nuclear arms, doctrines and disarmament

13. It would be an intolerably evil contradiction of the Sixth Assembly's theme, "Jesus Christ – the Life of the World", to support the nuclear weapons and doctrines which threaten the survival of the world. We now affirm, as a declaration of this Assembly, the conviction expressed by the 1981 Amsterdam Public Hearing on Nuclear Weapons and Disarmament and commended to WCC member churches by the Central Committee in 1982:

> We believe that the time has come when the churches must unequivocally declare that the production and deployment as well as the use of nuclear weapons are a crime against humanity and that such activities must be condemned on ethical and theological grounds.

Furthermore, we appeal for the institution of a universal covenant to this effect so that nuclear weapons and warfare are delegitimized and condemned as violations of international law.

14. Nuclear deterrence, as the strategic doctrine which has justified nuclear weapons in the name of security and war prevention, must now be categorically rejected as contrary to our faith in Jesus Christ who is our life and peace. Nuclear deterrence is morally unacceptable because it relies on the credibility of the *intention to use* nuclear weapons: we believe that any intention to use weapons of mass destruction is an utterly inhuman violation of the mind and spirit of Christ which should be in us. We know that many Christians and others sincerely believe that deterrence provides an interim assurance of peace and stability on the way to disarmament. We must work together with those advocates of interim deterrence who are earnestly committed to arms reduction. But the increasing probabilities of nuclear war and the spectre of an arms race totally

out of control have exposed the cruel illusions of such faith in deterrence.

15. Nuclear deterrence can never provide the foundation of genuine peace. It is the antithesis of an ultimate faith in that love which casts out fear. It escalates the arms race in a vain pursuit of stability. It ignores the economic, social and psychological dimensions of security, and frustrates justice by maintaining the status quo in world politics. It destroys the reality of self-determination for most nations in matters of their own safety and survival, and diverts resources from basic human needs. It is the contradiction of disarmament because it exalts the threat of force, rationalizes the development of new weapons of mass destruction, and acts as a spur to nuclear proliferation by persistently breaking the "good faith" pledge of disarmament in the Non-Proliferation Treaty, thus tempting other governments to become nuclear-weapon states. It is increasingly discredited by first-strike and war-fighting strategies which betray the doubts about its reliability.

16. We urge our member communions to educate their members in the urgency of delegitimizing nuclear weapons and demythologizing deterrence.

17. In the meantime we affirm our support for the following specific measures:

a) a mutual and verifiable freeze on the development, testing, production and deployment of nuclear weapons and delivery vehicles;

b) completion of a Comprehensive Test Ban Treaty;

c) early and successful completion of the Geneva negotiations between the US and USSR for substantial reductions in strategic nuclear weapons;

d) non-deployment of Pershing II and ground-launched cruise missiles, major reductions of Soviet intermediate range missiles including SS-20s, and successful conclusion of intermediate nuclear forces (INF) negotiations in Geneva;

e) creation of nuclear-free zones wherever possible;

f) cessation of all nuclear weapons and missile tests in the Pacific and a programme of medical and environmental aid to promote the health of Pacific peoples affected by nuclear activities;

g) the negotiation of a treaty providing for the total demilitarization of space, including the banning of all nuclear, anti-satellite and anti-missile systems in space;

h) commitment by all nuclear-weapon states to a policy of no first use of nuclear weapons;

i) independent, non-negotiated initiatives such as a moratorium on the testing or development of nuclear weapons, renunciation of a specific weapon system, cessation of production of fissionable materials for weapons purposes, or reductions in existing arsenals or projected military expenditures.

Proposals to the member churches
18. We therefore propose to the churches that they:
- undertake and support educational programmes on peace with justice as an integrated part of a UN-related World Disarmament Campaign and especially address themselves to all people working in production and research for military applications;
- set up and support study centres with the special aim of defining positive alternatives to militarism and to military defence;
- strongly support continued and intensified programmes for peace and conflict research and make widely available the statistical and factual data about expenditure on militarization and development;
- establish links with movements working to resist militarism and its social, cultural and economic effects;
- develop ecumenical theological reflection on circumstances justifying civil disobedience for Christians, and explore possible non-violent ways of protest action;
- support pastorally and practically those who oppose militarism and take a conscientious stand on refusal to participate in war or in preparations for war, including the manufacture of nuclear warheads and delivery systems;
- support efforts for a just World Economic Order as a basis for global security.

Part B: Science, technology and the human future

The theological challenge
19. The churches can adequately face the threats to human survival today only if they take up the problems and promises of science and technology for the human future. The dialogue initiated by the World Council of Churches with scientists, and technologists, which found its fullest expression in the Conference on Faith, Science and the Future at MIT, needs to be continued and deepened.
20. Among the insights gained in this dialogue so far are:
a) the growing consensus in theology that we must understand God, humanity and nature in relation to one another, a relation which finds its central expression in Christ;
b) the increasing recognition by scientists that science is not a value-free or neutral activity, but takes place in a world of ethical decisions and values;
c) theology and science operate with different languages which

continue to raise problems for the dialogue, which need to be
tackled through a deeper understanding, by each discipline, of
the other's approaches and limitations;

d) humanity has to recognize the two poles around which and
between which life develops and evolves – the Creator and the
Creation. The attempt to ignore one of the poles has disastrous
consequences.

21. Therefore, conversation between the Church and the world
of science and technology should continue on all levels; it should
include those who must live with the consequences of technological
development. This dialogue is part of the Church's witness to the
world's responsibility for the future of creation. It is therefore part
of theology and of ecumenical social ethics.

22. Today science and technology are decisively involved in three
threats to survival in the contemporary world: the world arms race,
economic domination and exploitation, and the ecological crisis.
How they are involved, what structures and powers play a role
therein, needs more accurate analysis. How they can be made to
serve a just, participatory and sustainable society needs to be spelt
out continually in practical terms.

In a world of many religions and ideologies, all must be involved
in the common search for solutions.

23. Mutual exchange and consultation within the Christian
community must be continued. We need ethical guidelines for a
participatory society which will be both ecologically responsible and
economically just, and can effectively struggle with the powers
which threaten life and endanger our future.

Key issues for dialogue

24. It is suggested that the continuing dialogue with the scientific
community should focus on the following areas:

a) *Technology experienced as destructive power:* In the industrialized
countries the economic power gained through systems of mass
production and distribution has now been more widely diffused.
However, the social and environmental costs have been heavy and a
price continues to be paid by large numbers of people. The problems
arising from pollution and from hazards to health and safety
continue to threaten people's lives. In a time of economic recession
there is a danger that these problems will be overlooked or accorded
a lower priority.

In the developing countries the use of science and technology by
the industrialized nations is perceived as a continuing instrument of
domination. Technology is the springboard of modern economic
life and in seeking to achieve economic progress these countries feel

they are caught in an endless and unwinnable technological race in which they will never be able to play a leading part. The price paid by entire communities is very high. The introduction of advanced technology will almost certainly be destructive of traditional ways of life and the cycle of exploitation of resources and the associated pollution of the environment will be repeated.

b) *Appropriate technology:* Appropriate systems of technological development should take into account indigenous resources and culture in relation to patterns of sustainable development. But the power of science and technology in economic development poses major questions about systems of control that can be exercised particularly by the developing countries. The principal agents involved in technological transfer are the transnational companies, which often distort patterns of development. They can stifle initiative, exercise undue influence on national decision-making and, especially in mixed economies, undermine the public sector. The economic forces deciding the location of a particular industrial plant take little account of the social, cultural and environmental factors governing the lives of whole communities. In these circumstances careful attention to forms of appropriate technology drawing on indigenous resources both human and physical fall very quickly by the wayside. The sharing of experience between highly industrialized and less industrialized countries may help to achieve patterns of human development appropriate for varying situations. The churches have an important role in making such sharing possible and in emphasizing that the appropriate technology for a country is the technology which that country can control.

c) *Automation, micro-electronics and patterns of employment:* New technologies continue to disturb and distort the pace of economic planning. The churches need to keep abreast of these developments and the World Council of Churches has a special role in keeping the churches informed.

Three facets have been identified:
– technology has tended to lead science, and commercial interests, with practically no public accountability, tend to dominate;
– there is little systematic overall planning, with advance assessment of the social impact of these innovations;
– the idea of technology-led growth is used to justify harsh economic policies ("automate or liquidate").

Micro-electronics raises questions about technology in a particularly acute form because of its rapid development and the vast range of its applications. Technology may be used to enhance human capacities, to replace them or to transform them. The question is:

"What are the ethically appropriate criteria for the adoption of this technology in this particular social and cultural context?"

The control of science and technology

25. Science and technology are both forms of power, and can be used as forces deployed in the struggle for power. Certain forms of direct control are exercised through their social settings, e.g. academic and research institutions, industrial enterprises and departments of governments. But the possibilities of other kinds of control vary. One cannot tell in advance what direction pure science may take, and freedom may here be the paramount consideration. Technology is more controllable, and it may be useful to categorize different technologies in terms of long-term and short-term benefits and disadvantages.

26. In some countries, science and technology are centralized under government control. In all countries governments can exercise some control, but may be unwilling to do so, or may exercise it in destructive ways. Pressure groups can draw attention to the worst abuses. But both governments and pressure groups are part of larger socio-economic and cultural contexts which themselves may need fundamental changes if science and technology are to serve truly human ends. There is a task for the churches in criticizing expectations and priorities.

27. A wide variety of consultative bodies with public participation can play an important role in developing guidelines for development in science and technology and in monitoring results. Scientists and technologists can also be helped to exercise more discerning control over their own activities. In particular:

a) science education must take social responsibility seriously; scientists in training must not become a separate élite, alienated from the cultural inheritance of their people and unaware of the social and ethical implications of their work;

b) the freedom of scientific research and the free exchange of information are of the essence of science; scientists should be supported in their resistance to the growth of secrecy;

c) the increasing number of organizations concerned with the deepening of conscientious awareness is an encouraging sign, and provides an area for common work between the scientific and religious communities.

Areas of particular concern

28. *Bio-ethics:* Rapid advances in genetic engineering, *in vitro* fertilization and related techniques have raised urgent questions about the integrity of human nature, the dignity and value of the human

body, the relationship between begetting and parenting, and the social implications of direct interference with the human genetic inheritance. Far-reaching decisions on these matters are already being made, and we believe it is essential for the churches to monitor them and to bring to their discussion a deeper theological understanding of human nature.

29. The Church and Society report on *Manipulating Life* (1982) highlights some of the issues and we endorse its recommendations. We strongly support the report's recommendation that "scientists throughout the world (should) not participate in any research associated with the production of chemical and biological weapons". We urge that the work begun in that report should be continued and given a stronger theological base. We also note the beneficial effects of genetic technology, especially in agriculture, noting at the same time the possible harmful effects in view of the competition in the world food market. The benefits should become available to all the poor of the world.

30. We draw attention to equally serious issues in bio-ethics such as the use of human beings for scientific research without their full knowledge or clear consent and the indiscriminate export of harmful medicines to third world countries.

31. *Energy options*: Long-term choices about renewable and non-renewable energy supplies for all countries still have to be made and must continue to be a concern for the churches and the WCC.

32. The MIT conference represented a major landmark in Church and Society's energy programme. It followed up the Sigtuna hearing (1975) on the implications of civil nuclear power programmes, and led to a further development of the Energy for my Neighbour Programme. This resulted in a series of third world regional energy consultations. Since MIT, the lowering of demand for petroleum and a *de facto* moratorium on the construction of new nuclear plants have distorted energy planning. The underlying problem of diminishing supplies of irreplaceable traditional fuels and acute deforestation remain. Following the Harrisburg debacle, the nuclear power industry now seeks to export new varieties of small prefabricated reactors to the third world. This raises major moral, economic and political issues which merit serious evaluation against the background of wider energy issues.

33. The alleviation of the fuel crisis during the next few decades is therefore an issue of desperate urgency for the poorest of the poor, and hence a matter of high priority for the churches of the world.

★ ★ ★

34. We mention only a few of the technological, ethical and social issues raised by science and technology. In the years ahead there will be many more. It is imperative therefore for the churches to set aside resources and develop appropriate structures to tackle such problems as: the power of technology over culture, the human and social consequences of the continuing theological revolution, criteria and structures for the social control of science and technology, and the new issues in the ongoing dialogue between science and faith.

3.6   STRUGGLING FOR JUSTICE
AND HUMAN DIGNITY

Ms Theressa Hoover (Methodist, USA), Moderator of the sixth Issue Group, presented its report.
A number of particular concerns surfaced in the debate. Dr K. V. Varughese (Mar Thoma, India) highlighted the role of small action groups within the churches. Ms Heather Johnston, of the Presbyterian Church in Canada, wanted mention of the WCC's Ecumenical Development Cooperative Society as one tool the churches have for assisting the poor and powerless. Mr Arno Glitz (Lutheran, Brazil) said the document reflected his country's situation, and Ms Nancy Pereira speaking for Bishop Isac Aco (Lutheran, Brazil), asked churches in the affluent nations to pay more attention to the relationship between international capital and the growing impoverishment of countries in the southern hemisphere.
The major criticism, however, concerned the tenor of the report as a whole. Rev. Horst Becker (EKD, Federal Republic of Germany) found the militant language and apocalyptic imagery inappropriate. Rev. Ron O'Grady (Churches of Christ, New Zealand) agreed; he called for less triumphalism and a more sophisticated analysis of the structures of oppression. Dr Ulrich Duchrow (EKD, Federal Republic of Germany) defended the language of struggle and conflict: anything less would fail to reflect the experience of people in so many parts of the world today. The Assembly agreed with the critics, however, and the report was referred back to the Issue Group's officers so that a revised text could be considered by the Central Committee.

Introduction
1. Since the Fifth Assembly of the World Council of Churches (Nairobi 1975), churches and the ecumenical movement have made substantial progress in their commitment to justice. They have deepened and broadened their struggle for the human dignity of peoples all over the world.
2. Significantly, the poor, the oppressed and the discriminated peoples are awakening everywhere to resist unjust powers and to forge their own destiny. This is a sign of life.
3. At the same time, the powers of injustice and of oppression attempt to absolutize and to defend their security through ideological and religious justification.
4. A new context emerges, therefore, in which the people strive for justice and human rights in various areas of their lives.

I. Our basic biblical and theological convictions

> In (Christ) the whole fullness of deity dwells bodily, and you have
> come to fullness of life in him, who is the head of all rule and authority
> (Col. 2:9–10).

5. We confess our faith in the triune God, the giver, redeemer
and sanctifier of life. This is why, as Christians and churches, we
hope, pray and search for signs of God's kingdom in God's creation.
Since Nairobi we have struggled towards the vision of a just, participatory and sustainable society.

5.1 We confess Jesus Christ, who died on the cross and was
resurrected, in whom the whole universe was created, as Lord over
all principalities and powers (Eph. 1:9–19). We anticipate the victory
of the Lamb (Rev. 12:11) who inspires suffering and gives courage
to martyrs everywhere.

5.2 The machine of the prevailing economic order starves millions
of people, and increases the number of unemployed every year.
Science and technology are misused to oppress the people and to
destroy the earth in an insane arms race. More and more people are
detained and "disappear", are tortured, deprived of religious liberty,
forcibly displaced or exiled.

5.3 We interpret this development as idolatry, stemming from
human sin, a product of satanic forces. We are in a situation where
we must go beyond the normal prophetic and intercessory actions
of the churches.

5.4 God created human beings in God's own image. The power
God shared with human beings involved the sharing of responsibility for the world with them (Gen. 1:26–28). But human beings
failed to exercise their responsibility creatively (Gen. 3:5). In
contemporary terms, the powers of dominion over "nature" (earth,
native peoples, manual labour, women) and limitless possessions
have become idols. This culture of violence has engendered international security systems designed to assert possession at any cost.
It has become an obsession with industrialized nations and spreads
to others as well.

6. Some fundamentalist sects and church people, political parties
and governments would legitimize this development as "Christian".
These groups are against the identification of the churches with the
poor in their witness to God's kingdom.

6.1 The Church is thus challenged not only in what it does, but
in its very faith and being. Many are alert to the danger, implicit,
for example, in the heresy of apartheid. However, there are also
those who provide so-called "Christian" arguments to defend
exploitative transnational systems, the uncritical applications of

science and technology, and the production of mass nuclear weapons. In confessing Jesus Christ, churches must also confess their sins; they should recognize their complicity in or tolerance of the processes of death, and be prepared to confront the dangers inherent in exorcizing such evils.

7. The spiritual struggle of the Church must involve it in the struggles of the poor, the oppressed, the alienated, and the exiled. The Spirit is among struggling people. The Spirit kindles love and fills us with courage. The Spirit imparts creative vision. Christ's Church celebrates the eucharist as the manifestation of God's love and as the source of spiritual strength among God's people (Ez. 37:10; Rev. 11:11).

7.1 Christians are called to resist any power that demands complicity in sin. People are constantly tempted to misuse power. Therefore, justified by faith, the people struggle to affirm life as a sign of the coming kingdom. The widow argued persistently and stubbornly with the judge (Luke 18:2–5), strongly suggesting to Christians the attitude and persistence required to achieve justice and human dignity. The Lord of the Church gives a transcending vision and the patience of martyrs to resist structural support of a sinful system, when he promises "I will be with you always, to the end of the age" (Mat. 28:20).

II. Oppressive powers and the power of liberation

8. God, as the giver of life, is the source of all powers, even of those that can be used against God's own being (John 19:11). God provides to life the ability to act upon life, and with love expects that power will be exercised according to the divine will. Hence power and authority exist with God's permission (Rom. 13:1–2) so as to work for the good of God's creation.

9. In our time power is widely abused. In spite of the abundance of resources, social disparities widen. Internationally racism is condemned, yet South African apartheid continues to be justified on biblical bases, and even threatens the territorial integrity of its neighbours. Discrimination, extrajudicial executions, political regression, genocide and violations of socio-economic rights demonstrate the use of power against the people. Power elites concentrate wealth for the control of political and economic instruments and institutions. Alliances are built across institutions through continuous economic, military and political collaboration and justified by distorted doctrines of national security. Such doctrines do not guarantee the security of the people, whom the powerful thus control through the control of technology. Social relations are dehumanized and manifestations of life perverted.

9.1 A special manifestation of this injustice is the prevailing international economic order. It has institutionalized domination by Northern economies of trade, finance, manufacturing, food processing and knowledge. Handled mainly through transnational corporations, this economic order subordinates and renders dependent the Southern economies.

9.2 In sum, we witness the emergence of a new type of abuse of power. As never before, economic interests, military might, technological knowledge and international alliances form a constellation of forces arrayed against the dignity of life in the world – Jesus Christ himself! The consequences are formidable: immense human suffering, degradation and death.

10. Let us not give way to pessimism. As a gift of God, power should be used to oppose those who worship the idols of death. It represents the ability of human beings to share God's creation. This positive power is operative among those who love and appreciate the beautiful gift of the triune God in their very situation of powerlessness. The underprivileged and the poor through the ages have manifested potentialities and powers which affirm dignity and celebrate justice. This is gathering momentum in our day. People seek liberation with justice, with creativity and courage which are the signs of hope in our time. The power of the mighty is confronted with the power of people: blacks in South Africa, women in peace movements, Minjung (the people) in Korea, poor peasants in Central America. Their struggles show the spiritual force of those who have been called by our Lord "heirs of the kingdom".

11. In order to struggle for justice and human dignity we must resist oppressive powers. We are called to be in solidarity with those who build up people's power designed to shape a more participatory society through the legitimate exercise of power. Thus, international networks of support, facilitated by the churches, should be strengthened and widened. Churches are called to support people who resist oppression, combat the roots of injustice and take risks in the search for a new society. Networks help accumulate forces among the poor to resist oppressive power. The lives of the poor, considered disposable by the powerful, are in fact of infinite value, because they are God's own gift.

III. The web of oppression and injustice

12. The interlinkages among various manifestations of injustice and oppression are becoming more and more clear. Racism, sexism, class domination, the denial of peoples' rights, caste oppression, are all woven together, like a spider's web. Singly and together they are at the root of many injustices which cause much suffering and

death. The instruments of oppression which maintain and sustain this web vary from the subtle smile of denial to mammoth military machines.

13. *Racism*: The global reach of racism was highlighted in the 1980 WCC consultation on "Churches responding to racism in the 1980s". Although the legalized apartheid system in South Africa is its most blatant and hideous form, racism rears its head in all parts of the world. Violence, even genocide against indigenous groups, has become endemic in many parts of the world.

13.1 Racism is often aggravated by international systems backed by powerful economic and military factors. Land rights claims of indigenous peoples are often rejected in the name of development and national security. Immigration policies and practices discriminate on the basis of race in many parts of Europe and North America. Education policies deny equality of opportunity and employment on the ground of race. In South Africa, so-called homelands have become dumping grounds for thousands deprived of their birthright and exiled from their homes in the interests of maintaining white supremacy. Resistance often results in banning, arbitrary arrest, detention without trial, and sometimes deaths under imprisonment. The proposed constitutional changes in South Africa promise to reinforce white rule, alienate blacks from one another and prevent their participation in shaping a common, just and peaceful society.

13.2 Some churches have begun to deepen their understanding of the root causes of contemporary racism. They also take some courageous action to confront the forces of racism nationally and globally. This has given new hope to the racially oppressed as they defiantly resist entrenched forces of racism. Racism is on the increase, but so are the struggles of the racially oppressed.

14. *Sexism*: Just as any attitude, action or structure that treats people as inferior because of race is racism, so any domination or exclusion based on sex is sexism. Behind many of the diverse manifestations of sexism are economic factors leading to exploitation and manipulation. Despite the considerable change in the traditional division of labour between men and women, women still have a long way to go in their struggle for equality. The growing phenomenon of sex tourism organized by international tourist agencies – affecting primarily but not exclusively women and girls in some third world countries – is an alarming development. The abuse of children adds to the gravity of the situation.

14.1 Violence against women is another reprehensible form of sexism. Rape is an example of such violence, when individuals and groups of men take advantage of the physical vulnerability of women and express their dominance over them. Women are often subjected to physical violence; they are beaten up, and humiliated. To counteract such violence more study and information is required about its causes and consequences.

14.2 The pernicious influence of the media must be recognized, and addressed in such a way as to transform the media into a positive instrument, to eliminate stereotyped prejudices and discriminatory attitudes with regard to race and sex values.

14.3. The WCC study on the Community of Women and Men in the Church, carried out since Nairobi and culminating in the 1981 Sheffield consultation, contributed to identifying the root causes of the oppression of women, and furthered the understanding of power as empowerment. In this view, power is not a finite quantity, diminished for one group if acquired by another. Rather, empowerment can be limitless. It is not conceived of as power over someone, or over against another. It allows those who are oppressed to stand up for themselves and to be full partners in the struggle for justice and dignity, towards the creation of a true community.

15. Underlying many manifestations of sexism and of racism is *class domination* based on economic exploitation and profit-motive, cultural captivity, colonialism and neo-colonialism.

16. It is a sad reality that the *churches* often support or tolerate oppression and domination. In too many instances church life merely reflects its social environment while society's weakest members – the poor, the racially oppressed, women – have no part in leadership roles and decision-making processes.

IV. The rights of the people

17. The dominant and oppressive powers collaborate in various forms, and violate people's rights in manifold ways, including their religious rights and the rights of the disabled.

18. The rise of authoritarian and dictatorial powers, the perversion of the doctrine of national security, militarization, and the misuse of systems of science and technology are integral elements in the oppressive process that denies the civic, political and cultural rights of the people in many countries.

19. Gross and systematic violations of human rights occur in most societies. People suffer arbitrary arrests, torture, summary executions and disappearance – almost always in extrajudicial forms – and on an unprecedented scale in our time.

20. Economic domination and unjust social structures suppress the socio-economic rights of people, such as the basic needs of families, communities, and the rights of workers.

21. Racial domination denies land rights to indigenous, ethnic

and aboriginal peoples, often leading to the unlawful imprisonment of entire groups of the population.

22. Churches are called to be in solidarity with the people, especially those who struggle among and alongside them in defending their rights, including those among the churches and Christian communities whose witness – even to martyrdom – has galvanized the worldwide ecumenical fellowship.

V. Conclusions

23. Christ rules the world. His people are called to participate in his struggle against the demonic powers of the world.

24. Churches are called to be a steadfast and faithful witness. As allies of those who struggle for liberation, churches must witness to the reign of the Lamb and must become a sure sign of hope in the world.

VI. Recommendations to the churches for ecumenical action

25. *Covenanting*
a) That the churches at all levels – congregations, dioceses/synods, networks of Christian groups and base communities – together with the WCC, enter into a covenant in a conciliar process:
– to confess Christ, the life of the world, as the Lord over the idols of our times, the Good Shepherd who "brings life and life in its fullness" for his people and for all creation;
– to resist the demonic powers of death inherent in racism, sexism, class domination, caste oppression, and militarism;
– to repudiate the misuse of economic organization, science and technology, in the service of powers and principalities and against people.
b) That we ourselves make a clear covenanting commitment to work for justice and peace as it was made here in Vancouver by Central American and US delegates as a sign of clear resistance to any kind of oppression and as a step forward towards peace with justice.
c) That we reject the heretical forces which use the name of Christ or "Christian" to legitimize the powers of death.

26. *Spirituality*
a) That churches explore forms through which Christian spirituality is manifested in the struggle for justice and human dignity. For this purpose, we call churches to cultivate and strengthen the spiritual life among the people, through prayer, Bible study and worship, making justice and human dignity an integral part of the churches' life.

b) That churches and Christians affirm the values which popular cultures, other faiths and ideologies contribute to people's common action in the struggle for justice and human dignity.

27. *Solidarity*

a) That the churches be in solidarity with the poor, oppressed, and discriminated against, in order to empower their movements and organizations.

b) That in order to be in solidarity with those who are struggling to change unjust power structures, especially those who are victims of torture and other forms of violence, all churches increase their efforts of concrete action through:

   i) public exposure and denunciation of torture and all other forms of violence, especially against women and children, including domestic violence and rape;

   ii) assistance to victims and their families;

   iii) the provision of material and legal aid to prisoners of conscience;

   iv) prayer meetings of intercession and other expressions of public concern;

   v) providing sanctuary to refugees facing expulsion without due process of law;

   vi) the establishment of effective international measures to protect refugees against attacks and "refoulement" and to assure them access to due process.

c) That member churches demonstrate their international ecumenical solidarity in combating unjust economic structures through:

   i) theological reflection on the principles of work and human dignity, and on a new economic paradigm aiming at a just, participatory and sustainable society;

   ii) engaging in an intensive process of education of their members regarding the nature of oppressive economic structures and their own complicity in bolstering them;

   iii) exposing the role of transnational corporations in buttressing unjust economic structures, in undergirding racist regimes, in exploiting women as cheap labour resources; and in using technologies which result in the expulsion of labourers from their jobs and thus create unemployment;

   iv) a careful examination by churches of their investment portfolios and investment in alternative development and trading networks.

28. *Networking*
a) Churches must continue to consolidate and expand solidarity linkages and networks between North and South, especially among the "Southern" countries; and foster mutual dialogue between the Eastern and Western churches.
b) Churches are called to affirm their commitment to a process of continuous dialogue and mutual visitation, aiming at mutual support for their ministry and solidarity work.
c) Churches must contribute to efforts which promote confidence-building measures among governments in order to reduce tensions and create a favourable climate for healthy international relations.
d) Churches are urged to initiate regional commissions and/or programmes for the implementation of human rights. Such bodies prove to be very important at the international level in supporting people's struggles for their rights.
e) Churches are urged to deepen their understanding of the exercise of power for social justice, human liberation, and on matters of political ethics. For this purpose they should engage in an intensive process of education of their members regarding both the nature of the principalities and powers which exercise oppression and their own complicity in them.

29. *Financing*
a) Churches are called to support the 2% Appeal as a tool for continuous solidarity with the poor, and for the support of people's movements working for justice and human dignity.
b) In this regard, the Ecumenical Development Cooperative Society (EDCS), created by the WCC in 1974 to use the investment capital of the member churches for the development projects of the poor and powerless, should be given a high priority.
c) Churches are urged to give concrete expression of their concern for the work on human rights and social justice through increased financial commitment.
d) Churches are urged to continue and increase their support for the Special Fund of PCR.

Above: A small group at the Pre-Assembly women's meeting. Below: A televised Issue Group debate during the second week of the Assembly

3.7   LEARNING IN COMMUNITY

Ms Mercy Oduyoye (Methodist, Nigeria), Moderator, presented the report of the seventh Issue Group.
Prof. H. B. Kossen (Mennonite, Netherlands) and Ms Frieda Haddad (Orthodox, Lebanon) were uneasy about references to the congregation as an extension of the natural family, and to forms of family other than the traditional one. Experiencing unity within the congregation itself is a vital part of congregational learning, said Church of England delegate Ms Jean Mayland. Ms Ruth Elizabeth Knapp, of the United Church of Christ (USA), spoke from her wheelchair and recalled the Fifth Assembly's historic statement on the handicapped and the wholeness of the family of God. "We are still the invisible people of our churches and congregations," she said. Ms Ellen Christiansen, Church of Denmark, stressed the importance of women in theological education. Ecumenism would be furthered by joint preparation of Christian education curricula and by a greater commitment by the churches to campus ministry, suggested Dr Zablon Nthamburi (Methodist, Kenya). Dr Alexandros Papaderos (Ecumenical Partriarchate, Greece) saw dialogue with the world of science and technology as an important part of the Church's calling. More should be said about informal popular education, said Ms Nancy Pereira (Methodist, Brazil), and church schools should become examples of participation by enabling the wider community to share in their decision-making. Metropolitan Chrysostomos of Greece wanted more clarity in the way theology was understood, in particular its link with the truth objectively revealed in Christ.
Ms Oduyoye on behalf of the Issue Group undertook to incorporate a number of these concerns in the report, which was then approved in substance and commended to the churches for study and appropriate action.

I. Introduction
1. We have come from different backgrounds with a variety of experiences, hopes and frustrations in learning. We were prepared to learn from each other to find out how the Church may become a learning community. Therefore, we tried to understand ourselves as partners in a learning community and have had the following experiences of learning during our discussions.
2. We discovered various hindrances on the way to becoming a learning community, such as:
- language limitations which hindered full communication among us;
- different and even conflicting cultural, social and economic back-grounds which made it difficult to encounter each other in a trusting way;

- different theological approaches that sometimes led to misunderstandings and conflicts;
- under time pressure, we discovered painfully that learning in
  community requires much time, patience, and readiness to listen
  to one another.

3. At the same time we became convinced not only by our issue
group experience, but also in the whole Assembly process that:

- through the willingness to assist one another, we can overcome
  language barriers;
- through the readiness to share frankly our differing positions,
  concepts and experiences, we can create openness for trust, and
  thus learn from one another;
- the fellowship among churches is both a challenge and an enrichment, and is therefore an indispensable prerequisite for learning
  in community.

4. Both the painful and the positive experiences have answered
to a large extent our initial question: "Which kind of community
do we seek?" They also helped us to discover and reflect on future
goals of learning in community – like the following:

- to help each other to believe in Jesus Christ as the source of life
  and to grow in faith as Christian persons;
- to discover together that God has given us *one world*;
- to participate in the struggle for global justice and peace;
- to participate in communities of prophetic witness;
- to relate our local struggles to global perspectives.

5. This is the overarching vision we see for the future of the
ecumenical movement as a fellowship of learning. It was discussed
and expressed in our Issue Group in six major sections: family
education, liturgical education, congregational education, formal
education, theological education and development education. In each
and all of these areas the phrase "learning in community" implies
for Christians that it is both a personal and communal process, that
both method and message are important, that full participation of
all affected is crucial, that in various ways all participants are both
teachers and learners, that an important goal of learning is the
creation of a richer and more inclusive human community, and that
community of whatever size does not just happen but must be
struggled for in the power of the Holy Spirit and according to the
criteria of the Gospel image of the kingdom.

II. Six aspects of the issue

Family education

6. Family education is considered as a process through which the Church enables members of a home to take the responsibility to live according to their faith in Church and society. Family education is an essential part of congregational education. On the one hand we must clearly see that following Christ means transcending the confines of one's own family. On the other hand sisterhood and brotherhood in a local congregation or in the Church as a whole can be experienced as life in the family of God. Family, local congregations, and the whole Church inter-relate. The congregation acts as extended family to the home-based family and the community acts as the extended family to the congregation in an inter-relationship expressing the "oikoumene".

In some respects, family education may be considered as a special instrument in the Church's ministry with families. But there is also a learning through families: families can show how Christians should live and how the Church's ministry as a whole should be fulfilled. Therefore, instead of speaking of the education of the family, it is more appropriate to speak of learning in community with the family.

7. Our traditional image of family, however, no longer corresponds to the reality of family in some segments of today's society. The fundamental responsibility of the Church is clear and not controversial, namely to support the complete family consisting of parents, united in marriage and faithful to each other, learning together with their children. At the same time the Church must recognize the social reality of other forms of family life, e.g. single-parent families, one-parent families, and separated families. It also needs to examine new concepts of "mothering", "fathering", personal relationships and parenting.

8. Christian education in the parish should be family-oriented and also oriented towards learning between the generations and different groups. In view of the increasing separation from each other of seniors, adults, men, women, youth, children and disabled, inter-generational learning activities in the Church should contribute to stronger family unity. In all places, but especially where there is major adult illiteracy, church programmes of family education should incorporate drama, art, crafts, audio-visuals, etc.

Liturgical education

9. It is through liturgy that the worshipping community expresses itself. Liturgy carries in itself the dimension of learning in community. Liturgical learning includes the following elements:

- the experience of God's presence within the worshipping community;
- the revelation of Christ as a living reality transmitted through the proclamation of God's word and received in the sacraments; and
- our response to God in repentance, offering, thanksgiving, praise and remembrance.

10. All of this is fulfilled in communion with God and expressed in a specific order and language. Such language is not merely verbal but includes non-verbal expressions – signs, symbols, drama, rites and gestures.

11. The purpose of the liturgical life is:
- to rediscover and actualize the ongoing heritage of the Church as a Christian community which lives by the grace and under the judgment of God;
- to bring as an offering our present experience into the corporate life of the Church, offering it up to God on behalf of all; and
- to carry from the liturgy our common experience and vision of God into a life of service and witness in the world.

Congregational learning

12. The following elements of learning help persons to grow into community, into a congregation of God's people:
- liturgical education as the spiritual centre of congregational learning;
- family education as the foundation for Christian life and growth;
- formal education as the necessary opportunity for reflection on religious experience throughout life.

13. From a theological perspective, we understand the congregation to be:
- based on the gospel of Jesus Christ with a deepening commitment to the demands of the kingdom and open to the liberating power of the Holy Spirit;
- grounded in tradition and sustained by worship, open to be renewed and transformed through active commitment in the world;
- engaged in living the faith, interpreting the gospel in new and different contexts, mutually supportive and open to the world, as sign and instrument of new forms of human relationships;
- a coming together of persons who are constantly being built up into the body of Christ;
- rooted in solidarity with the least of God's children, ready to stand by their side, seeking to enable the participation of all: women and men, old and young, poor and rich, persons with disabilities, and those whose voice is not heard; and

– ready to deal with conflicts openly and to see them as an opportunity for learning in community.

14. Within such a community, congregational learning becomes ecumenical learning. It enables a unified Church to become an instrument for God's caring work in the world, i.e. to make the whole inhabited earth habitable for all creation.

Formal education

15. The churches, each in its own local situation, need to develop strategies for witnessing in the field of formal education, that is, in structured programmes of general education, whether of church or state.

16. In most of our schools the educational programmes and learning objectives are oriented to the progress of the individual within a framework of competition. Educational institutions sometimes divide rather than build up communities. But the task of schools is not to impose prejudices, a narrow vision or artificial divisions, but rather to develop global understanding. The churches should support communal learning and foster the attitude of sharing.

17. We need to make special provision for those who suffer from any kind of handicap or disadvantage, to ensure that they have equitable access to educational opportunities. Usually the school system of a nation has to serve national interests. But this does not always mean that the schools serve the people. In some parts of the world they are an instrument of the ruling social class. The churches should contribute to a school system that is administered and supported by all sections of the people and thus becomes a true public institution. Within such schools, teachers, students, and parents should jointly strive to grow into a community.

18. Education should combine a concern for persons, a concern for truth, and a concern for skills. A system of education which neglects any one of these is defective. Today churches have a special responsibility to see that concerns for justice, peace and ecological survival feature in the curriculum. In all educational institutions, the ethical implications of the issues of natural sciences and technological advance should be highlighted, if possible within theological perspectives, so that those who will bear responsibility in the respective fields will be able to orient their work towards the purpose of a just, peaceful and meaningful human life.

19. While recognizing that the existence of church-related schools is itself a Christian witness, we believe that the churches need to give attention to nurturing the Christian presence in secular institutions as well. This means that priority should be given to teacher training,

development of curricula, and, where possible, the training of school chaplains.

Theological education

20. Theological education is a process of learning which belongs to the whole people of God. It is more than the development of ministerial skills or the gaining of theological knowledge by individuals. Theological education involves the transformation of concepts and people for faithful leadership. In this context, theology is understood as a reflection on faith in God as human response to the given truth. This reflection includes issues of life-style and decision-making, equipping people for action in society, as well as the relationship with God and persons.

21. Theology and theological education are always to be understood in the cultural, social, spiritual, political and other contextual realities of society. Theological education therefore is called to address the particular problems and opportunities of local and regional community, against a background of wider global awareness.

22. In addition, theological education must deal with the relationships between action and reflection, experience and tradition, the personal and the corporate, the local and the global. Theological learning includes spiritual development and ecumenical understanding, towards the goal of a new human community. However, there is a need for fresh curricula and appropriate criteria for the evaluation of learners, which should be consistent with wider and fuller participation in human community (*oikoumene*).

Development education

23. Development education has to be an essential dimension in all programmes and activities of the churches and the WCC. It varies in content, shape and methods according to the cultural and economic context of the developed or developing regions of the world. In its substance, however, it must everywhere enable the churches to take the side of the poor. The growing poverty in both North and South makes this undertaking more urgent today than at the time when the Council's Development Education Programme was first started.

24. Significant activities in the field of development education point towards new models of learning through the whole of the community, through participation and especially by sharing in the struggles of those who suffer from the injustices within our societies. Such injustices often prevent many children, youth and adults from receiving any education. Churches should help provide ways of

informal education and training besides the formal educational institutions. Development education opens the door for our credible witness to Jesus Christ as the life of the world. Development education must find ways to engage the peoples of North and South, and East and West, in fruitful interchange.

 25. As an international and ecumenical group, however, we discovered that the term development education sometimes creates misunderstandings and inhibits communication and collaboration. The churches as well as the WCC, therefore, may wish to consider a change of name from "development education" to "education for justice and peace".

III. Recommendations to the churches

26. *Concerning family education*
a) Churches should encourage the production of simple literature and learning materials on how all members of the family are involved in the life and work of the Church from infancy, through baptism, confirmation and other special Christian events.
b) Church workers should have the expertise to meet the constant demand of parents, especially mothers, for Christian answers to family life issues. This calls for the restructuring of ministerial education to include various counselling and educational skills.
c) Churches should help families gain understanding and ecumenical perspectives at both the local community and global levels. Worship in other congregations, visits, and exchange of correspondence between families and children living in different countries should be encouraged.

27. *Concerning liturgical education*
In order to enable the formation of liturgical ecumenical communities, we recommend that local congregations:
a) use the Ecumenical Prayer Cycle;
b) link intercessions with offerings or gifts;
c) incorporate hymns that convey community rather than individualistic attitudes; that are peace-oriented rather than militaristic or militant; that use inclusive language and music reflecting cultural diversity; that incorporate justice and peace concerns as well as love, freedom, openness, and the respect for human rights;
d) foster the expression of community in a variety of visible and tangible ways: the exchange of peace greetings, the sharing of agape meals, holding processions, and encouraging intergenerational participation;

e) implement the vision acquired through worship in acts of service and mission in the world.

28. *Concerning congregational learning*
   We recommend that the member churches:
   a) encourage the participation of children in worship, including (where appropriate) the receiving of holy communion;
   b) encourage the full participation in worship of persons with disabilities, including the receiving and serving of the holy communion;
   c) develop opportunities for intergenerational learning in the congregation;
   d) help clergy to be sensitive to and equipped for processes of community learning in the congregation and for a sharing of their ministry;
   e) encourage congregations to be open to local groups struggling for peace and justice, to give them a place in the congregation, and to learn together with them by sharing their commitment and reflecting on it from a perspective of faith; this could include opening the doors to migrants, refugees, disabled people's civil/ human rights groups, marginal groups, and those struggling for fuller life and seeking community;
   f) help all members of congregations, young and old, to develop together new life-styles based on the demands of the gospel and a new spirituality grounded in worship, prayer and active commitment.

29. *Concerning formal education*
   We urge the member churches:
   a) to ensure that their educational programmes and institutions include among their goals the upbuilding of community, giving priority in their thinking and action to the educational needs of all disadvantaged groups including the disabled, the poor, ethnic minorities, speakers of minority languages, etc;
   b) to take seriously their responsibilities for all forms of formal education, whether church-related or state-sponsored, to ensure ecumenical sharing, planning and evaluation of educational activities among all churches, and to discover opportunities for Christian service and witness, both in terms of governing structures and teaching content and practices, and to support those who serve in such schools in their witness;
   c) to consider the inter-relatedness of changing technology/the unemployment of young people/the implications of changing patterns of education, and to take appropriate action;
   d) to take initiatives to ensure that in both church-related and state-

68346

governed schools, the concern for peace, justice and ecological survival is featured in the curriculum;

e) to take advantage of opportunities for including religious education in the school curriculum, using if possible common catechetical programmes of several denominations, and common programmes of training of religious education teachers and evaluation of processes of teaching religion in schools;

f) to take advantage of opportunities for training and placement of school and college chaplains, leading to the formation of regional and global networks for mutual support and exchange of ideas.

30. *Concerning theological education*

a) We recommend that the increased participation by lay persons in theological education programmes be recognized and furthered, the creative dimensions of this change be welcomed, their experiences shared, and their theological, pedagogical and missiological significance examined.

b) We urge the churches to promote global awareness, interaction and solidarity in theological education. This might include reciprocal ecumenical visits, staff exchange between continents and regions, development of curricula with a global focus, ecumenical sharing of resources and greater openness to the spiritual and liturgical heritage as well as the theologies emerging in different parts of the world. This could lead to the formation of national, regional/global networks for mutual support of and interaction between the wide variety of theological programmes now scattered around the world.

c) We recommend that churches and theological schools be encouraged to include in their ecumenical education the contribution of people and situations of diverse social, economic, cultural and confessional backgrounds.

d) The churches are asked to encourage theological education to develop Bible study and other resources to support the widespread study of Baptism, Eucharist and Ministry, and to enable the churches to participate fully in the reception process.

31. *Concerning development education*

a) We urge the member churches to take seriously the ecumenical dimension of learning and include it in all educational activities and programmes. In particular we urge the revision of curricula of schools and seminaries and the activities of congregations to provide for ecumenical perspectives.

b) The preparation for Vancouver has brought to light a valuable tool for ecumenical learning and development education in the form of ecumenical team visits. We believe individual churches and Christian councils should use this model, and link their local experience of development education with global concerns and vice versa.

c) Working together is one of the most valuable ways of learning. In particular, we think young people in the Church throughout the world should be exposed to the issues of justice and peace in their own communities and in the global context.

Daily press conferences drew regular attendance from the 850 media representatives who came to Vancouver

3.8   COMMUNICATING CREDIBLY

This report made ecumenical history by switching from prose to poetry before offering a number of recommendations for consideration by the churches. It was presented by Ms Dafne de Plou (Methodist, Argentina), a Vice-Moderator of the Issue Group, and Rev. Ron O'Grady (Churches of Christ, New Zealand). Dr Fridolin Ukur, of the Kalimantan Evangelical Church (Indonesia), read his poem that was included in the report.

Rev. Walter Arnold (EKD, Federal Republic of Germany) thought the document too negative in its assessment of the potentiality of the media. His proposal that it be sent back for reworking did not, however, win support.

The report was approved in substance and commended to the churches for study and appropriate action.

Who we are

1. The people who contributed to this report are not all communication experts. Like many other delegates at the Assembly, we are ordinary Christians trying to live a life of faith in a world in which mass media★ have a pervasive and often dominant role.

2. It is a world which brings us much anxiety. We fear the loss of privacy and of control over our own lives and communities. We fear the possibility that the new media could be used to bring further injustice and add to the sufferings of the weak and the dispossessed. Most of all we are concerned about our children, and we face the possibility that some of the new developments may adversely affect their future.

3. It is also a world which offers much that is good. The new media,★ put to proper use, may enhance life rather than diminish it. They too must belong within the purpose and providence of God.

4. We approach our report with this ambivalence. We want to guard against manipulation by power groups. We are also anxious to find ways to make communication serve the people rather than have people serving communication: we want to affirm that communication serve the people rather than have people serving communication.

★ The term "mass media" is used here to include newspapers, magazines, books (print media), radio and television (electronic media), records/discs, audio and video cassettes/discs. "New media" or "new electronic media" refers to the storage of information using the technology of the silicon chip (transistor, computer) and the overcoming of distance by satellite. The word "information" usually denotes the linear sender-receiver model of mass media. "Communication" on the other hand is a process which involves several persons in active sharing, interacting and participating.

Where we are

5. Our participation here in the Sixth Assembly of the World
Council of Churches at Vancouver has been a decisive event in our
lives. We appreciate the many attempts which have been made to
make the Assembly representative of the whole *oikoumene*. Voices
have been heard of the handicapped, children, youth, women and
men, persons of different languages, cultures, political ideologies
and different religious faiths. We have listened to one another not
only in words but also through sign language, art, drama, song,
and most of all through our liturgical life which brought us closer
to one another in communion and community.

6. Vancouver has indeed been for us a parable of communication.

7. More specifically, it has been a parable of human encounter.
The Assembly has provided an agora, a market place of experience
and conviction, through which we found that communication arises
from community, and in the process enhances community. As we
encountered one another in the fellowship of the WCC our individual lives have been challenged, enriched and sometimes changed
dramatically. As human persons we survive and develop only by
relating to one another and communicating with one another.
Authentic communication must bring people to experience and
affirm: I–you–we. And this we discover as we open ourselves to
God's own communication.

What we affirm

8. "In many and various ways God spoke of old" (Heb. 1:1).
God spoke through those who told stories, composed poems, and
spoke the prophetic word. "In these last days God spoke through
God's own Son" (Heb. 1:3). Jesus Christ is God's communication
at its clearest, costliest and most demanding.

9. "It was there from the beginning: we have heard it; we have
seen it with our own eyes; we looked upon it and felt it with our
hands; and it is of this we tell" (1 John 1:1). That was Christian
communication. That still is. Its theme is "the word of life". Christian communication is about Jesus Christ – the Life of the World.

10. Christian communication happens when the Holy Spirit acts,
as on the day of Pentecost. It is the Spirit that leads us from the
discord of Babel to the ecumenism of Pentecost (Acts 2:5–12).

11. At its most effective Christian communication is person-to-
person communication, like Jesus conversing with Nicodemus or
the Samaritan woman. At its most effective it is what comes out of
authentic experience. It shares one's own life with others, as Jesus
did. It meets people where they are, as Jesus did. It empowers people

to tell their stories, as happened in the case of Zacchaeus. It builds community, as it did in the early church.

The context of communication

12. The technologies of mass media are here to stay and their use is bound to increase in all parts of the world. When we met in regional groups we were deeply conscious of the uneven distribution of media growth and the control of those media by a few powerful countries and transnational corporations.

13. We find ourselves in a situation where some few attempt to speak in the name of all, and to all, at both the national and the international level. Too often, the mass media serve only to confirm that injustice. Most ordinary men and women are excluded, except as objects of the media; they have accepted the fact that only those with political and economic power, or those who possess professional skills, have the right to disseminate information, ideas, images and experiences.

14. The mass media in many affluent countries distort and diminish the life of the world, by packaging it as entertainment, or simply as propaganda. This is partly due to the limits inherent in the media themselves, partly because a communication industry or a government or a powerful group want us to perceive life and the world in their own image, for commercial or political reasons.

15. There is also much that is positive about public media. For example, the attempt to be popular enough (in terms of language, imagery and format) to be accessible to all, the need to be open and accountable to the whole community, the redemptive glimpses present in secular programmes, the fact that mass media take our human needs for recreation and celebration more seriously than many churches – such features are easily forgotten.

16. So the mass media commentators who refuse easy answers, the producers of song, dance and drama that celebrate the human spirit, the satirists who prevent a community from taking itself too seriously, the reporters who expose corruption in high places or find the images and stories that open up new space and possibility in a society – in all such instances the goodness of God's creation and the value of God's people are being recognized and served.

17. In many parts of Africa, Asia, Latin America, the Caribbean and the Pacific, the new media scarcely exist and are not likely to reach the people in the near future. Where they are in place they have often further entrenched economic and political interests. Such dangers are no less prevalent in the North, whether in existing mass media or the new electronic information systems being developed. There is urgent need to create decentralized, community-based, local

media outlets to counter this possibility. In regions where new media systems are not established, there is an active search for those media which are indigenous and which the people can own and manage (e.g. drama, oral literature, music, cassettes, film, etc.). And where participation by the people in the media is denied by oppressive political forces, the Church fulfills its vocation by affirming the basic human right of the people to communicate as a foundation on which other human rights can be built.

18. The media assume special importance in countries under oppressive rule. In these places, the Church has sometimes become the only source of credible information on human rights violations and injustice of every kind. By using its international network in a creative way, the Church can become a strong advocate for justice and peace. Credible communication serves the cause of justice and peace by setting standards that resist national, cultural, racial stereotypes and the building of enemy images, and provide space and time for the views of minority and marginalized groups.

19. The dilemmas we have tried to summarize in this short section on the context of communication have led many countries, especially in the South, to call for a new world information and communication order, so that they can assert their own values, affirm their own culture and determine their own priorities. Their demands for a new order have been largely ignored.

20. The new electronic media will enlarge and confirm the global domination of a few countries and make it almost irreversible. It will widen the gap between the information-poor and information-rich, both within and between individual nations.

21. In some countries children already spend most of their time immersed in electronic media. In others, it is hard to obtain the simplest materials, such as newsprint for a literacy campaign, a radio receiver or textbooks for schools.

22. It is an issue of decision-making and power-sharing. As some communication technologies become cheaper and more widely used they have the potential to enrich the quality of life everywhere. They allow expression of great diversity and choice. They give new possibilities for individual feedback and group participation, for education and community building, which have hardly been tried.

The question of credibility

23. Many of us have become cynical about sources of information, and there is a special urgency in our search for credibility. Credibility involves more than simply telling the truth. It must take the following into account:

a) Intention: What is the motivation of the communication? Does it affirm or exploit the people? Are cultural differences being respected?

b) Content: Does the communication make peace, build justice and promote wholeness? Does it present a complete picture, or is it based on national or sectarian prejudice?

c) Style: Does the communication have clarity, economy, precision, variety and a sense of humour?

d) Dialogue: Does the receiver have the opportunity to respond or is the communication totally one-way? Does communication listen, as well as speak? Does it call for informed choice and active response to the issues presented? Does it respect the reality of pluralism and provide for the voicing of diverse views?

e) Appropriateness: Is the form of the communication appropriate and does the choice of media suit the task?

To these, from a Christian perspective, we may add two more:

f) Mystery: Does the communication respect the "otherness" of the Gospel by refusing to explain everything and by avoiding quick judgments?

g) Value reversal: Does the communication reflect the Gospel's reversal of the normal order of importance and value: i.e. last before first, foolish before wise, weak before powerful, poor before rich?

The churches and the media

24. The Church must relate to the media in a manner which is pastoral, evangelical and prophetic. Pastorally it must try to understand the tensions of those who work in the media and assist them to perform their work in ways which affirm human values. Evangelically, the Church must resist the temptation to use the media in ways which violate people's dignity and manipulate them, but rather should proclaim with humility and conviction the truth entrusted to it.

25. The Church also has a prophetic role; it must provide a continuing critique of the performance, content, and techniques of the mass media, and the ideologies which lie behind them. It should assist churches in developing media awareness so that a critical analysis might emerge in local churches and congregations.

26. Media perceptions of events like the Vancouver Assembly provide striking illustrations of the difference between the words and actions which the Church considers important and those which speak to the mass media. A knowledge of this distinction will greatly assist local churches in their own use of the media.

The WCC and communication

27. Communication, in the widest sense of the term, is one of the primary responsibilities of the WCC. While this is the function of the whole Council, the Communication Department has a particular role. It must support the efforts of churches to communicate between themselves and to deepen their understanding of ecumenical communication. Churches need to be encouraged to make their own practice of communication more inclusive and less denominational.

28. The member churches set the policy of the WCC and they therefore have the primary responsibility for the interpretation of the Council. The WCC can play a supportive role by providing information resources and personnel.

29. In places where the WCC is under attack, the member churches and national or local ecumenical agencies need to take a leading role in making any response. (The way in which the American churches promptly and effectively responded to recent attacks on the Council illustrates the potential of member churches to play this role.) Churches may use attacks on the WCC as an educational opportunity through which congregations and churches may deepen their understanding of the work of the ecumenical movement.

30. We conclude this statement with a poem which an Indonesian delegate contributed to our discussion, as a reflection on our work as a group and on our understanding of communication.

> In the depth of silence
> no words are needed,
> no language required.
> In the depth of silence
> I am called to listen.
>
> Yes, there I sat
> there in that corner,
> listening for silence,
> longing for community.
>
> Suddenly the room is crowded,
> crowded with speeches
> voices in many languages
> announcing
> denouncing
> proclaiming
> demanding
> self-justifying
> shattering the silence.
> Christian communication must announce
> No, Christian communication must denounce,

No, Christian communication must promote sharing,
No, Christian communication must create community,
Yes, Christian communication must be hopeful
No, it must be graceful
Yes, it must have integrity
No, it must call for response.

> Please stop, please!
> Silence!
> Listen to the beating of your heart
> Listen to the blowing of the wind.
> the movement of the Spirit,
> Be silent – said the Lord,
> and know that I am God.

And listen to the cry of the voiceless
Listen to the groaning of the hungry
Listen to the pain of the landless
Listen to the sigh of the oppressed
and to the laughter of children.

For that is authentic communication:
listening to people
living with people
dying for people.

Recommendations

31. The discussion in sections made clear the central importance of language and culture in ecumenical communication. In many places our practice of communication is not rooted in our national and local cultures. We are yet to reckon with the cultural renaissance of our time. We commend to churches a programme of study and dialogue in the area of communication and culture. We are convinced that credible communication demands special efforts to listen to those whose languages are not widely used in the ecumenical community. We were made aware of the depth of alienation which many groups are made to feel when their language and culture are disregarded. Churches must recognize this deep concern and provide an environment in which full respect for culture is shown so that communication can take place.

32. Churches are encouraged to experiment with alternative forms of communication. We commend to the consideration of church communicators such forms as are described in the book *Opening Eyes and Ears.*★ Other alternatives involve the search for

---

★ This book, recently published by the WCC in cooperation with the World Association for Christian Communication and the Lutheran World Federation, presents examples of alternative media experiments. We commend it to the consideration of communicators within and outside churches.

new symbols in order to make ecumenical communication more effective. (In recent years, the WCC has made use of team visits, given grants to oppressed groups, and made use of new symbols. From Vancouver we will remember the tent, the baby at the communion table, the wisp of smoke rising from a sacred fire and the many symbolic acts of worship that have deepened our understanding of the faith.)

33. Given the growth and change in the mass media industry, it is of great importance that churches in every place seek to enter into a critical encounter and more confident dialogue with those who work in the media. As a preparation for this dialogue, churches should assist congregations to develop media awareness so that an informed analysis can be made. Agencies like the World Association for Christian Communication have resources available for such study, and we commend these to the churches.

34. Recognizing that WCC communication resources are used primarily by those churches which pay for them, the member churches of the Council which can afford such materials for themselves are urged to enable the purchase of resources by churches which lack the money to buy them.

35. In order to improve the quality and effectiveness of Christian communication, the study of communication in its broadest sense should be integrated into theological training programmes.

36. We recommend the booklet *Credible Christian Communication*, as a study resource for churches and communication agencies for further reflection on the issues raised by this report.

4. REVIEWING THE PAST: CHARTING THE FUTURE

At each assembly, the member churches through their delegates must review what they are seeking to be and do together as the World Council of Churches. They consider reports on the WCC's policies and programmes, review the relationships they have within and through it, set directions for the years ahead and choose those who are to steer the ecumenical ship for the ensuing seven or eight years.

4.1 Reports and responses

At the first session of the Assembly, the Most Rev. Edward Scott presented his report as Moderator of the Central Committee. He surveyed developments since the 1975 Assembly: the gain of twenty new member churches plus five associate members, the withdrawal or suspension of membership by five, an improved state of financial health, the growth of better communications with member churches and an advance beyond the "polite ecumenism" of the previous decade. Commenting on world developments he suggested that we may be at the end of an era, for despite their incredible achievements it was clear that the two dominant ideologies, communism and capitalism, could no longer satisfy humanity's deepest aspirations. The WCC must remain faithful to its original vision, avoid defensiveness and allow the integrity of its commitment to speak for itself (for the full text, see Appendix II).

In the report of the General Secretary, Dr Philip Potter compared the ecumenical milieu of 1983 with that prevailing when, twenty-nine years before, another World Council Assembly had convened on North American soil. Dwelling on the image of the Church as a house of living stones (1 Pet. 2:4–10), he spoke of how the WCC was helping its constituents discover afresh what it means to be the Church. He referred to the Church, under eight points, as a fellowship of confessing, learning, participation, sharing, healing, reconciliation and unity. "Can the churches go on behaving", asked Dr Potter, "as though the Council belongs to their external rather than their internal relations? Can the Council allow itself, through the decisions of representatives of the churches, to go its own way with programmes and activities reaching to groups and others, but not conceived, planned, communicated at all stages, and carried out with the active involvement of the churches? Can the churches conduct themselves as though they exist in isolation from each other and from their fellowship in the World Council, carrying on their programmes and activities with little relation with other churches around the world? Can we go on acting as though we are just stones ineffectually scattered around, or shall we allow ourselves to be living stones being gathered together and built into the house of our triune God?" (for the full text, see Appendix III).

The Moderator of the Finance Committee of the retiring Central Committee, Dr J. Oscar McCloud, drew attention to the finance section of the Central Committee's report *Nairobi to Vancouver*. "A considerable degree of stability" was how he characterized current Council finances, noting that there have been significant increases in member church contributions and reductions in some running costs. Yet present trends raise serious questions for the World Council. "Do the member churches raise, receive, contribute and spend their financial resources in relationship to the WCC in ways that the unity of which we speak is manifested? Is non-competitive funding possible between programmes in the Council and between WCC, regional and national church bodies?" On present projections, he said, the Council would not be able to sustain its existing structure much beyond 1985, and the new Central Committee would need guidance from the Assembly on how to deal with the problem.

Responses to the reports, in particular that of the General Secretary, were heard in a subsequent plenary session. Several speakers raised questions about what Dr Potter had said regarding the Church as a fellowship of participation and his critique of ecclesiastical power structures. Others referred to Faith and Order, evangelism, and the local congregation as the focal point of the Church's renewal. The General Secretary, replying, said that his challenge was directed not against authority *per se*, but against the way authority is sometimes exercised which belies our biblical faith.

Further comments surfaced relating to the life and work of the Council when the Clusters reported on discussions that had gone on in Small Groups. Proposals that bore directly on the WCC's future programme had been channelled to the appropriate committee or Issue Group.

Towards the end of the Assembly, Policy Reference Committee I commented on the reports of the Moderator and the General Secretary:

The Moderator's report

1. (The Committee resolved) to express its gratitude to the Moderator for his report which reflected his deep pastoral concern for the churches and for the work of the World Council of Churches. By reminding us of the vision which was so clearly articulated in the message of the Amsterdam Assembly, and of the costly discipleship that is called for if that vision is to come to pass, he has challenged us to be faithful to Jesus Christ, the Life of the World.

2. In his capacity as Moderator of the Central Committee he has indeed provided us with a model of faithfulness, for despite the stressful events of ecclesiastical and world history that have unfolded during his term of office, he has conducted himself with dignity and courage, all the while continuing to give significant leadership to his own church and nation. We express our profound gratitude for his service to the Council, and to its member churches.

3. We are particularly grateful for his support of the pre-Assembly team visitation programme which has proved such a stimulus to the life of the churches, and of the series of significant international gatherings, the Church and Society Conference on "Faith, Science and the Future", held in Boston in 1979, the Commission on World Mission and Evangelism conference, "Thy Kingdom Come", held in Melbourne in 1980, the Faith and Order meetings held in Bangalore in 1978 and Lima in 1982, and the Sheffield consultation on "The Community of Women and Men in the Church", held in 1981. It is our hope that his lifting up of these important gatherings will lead to a fuller analysis of their place in the life of the Council.

The General Secretary's report

The Committee unanimously expressed its desire to receive with deep gratitude the report of the General Secretary. Dr Potter's report was seen as an expression of his passionate involvement in the ecumenical movement and dynamic leadership of the WCC. Appreciation was expressed for the sketching of the vision and activities of the Council in their totality over the last 35 years by means of developing the image of "living stones". Particular mention was made of its broad biblical basis, its existential and dynamic ecclesiology, and its reference to the servanthood of ministry and our need for continuing dialogue with those of other faiths. His reaffirmation of the central calling of the ecumenical movement and therefore of the WCC as a "fellowship of unity" was welcomed.

Important issues were raised in the section describing the churches as a "fellowship of participation". Of these the most important were the exercise of magisterial authority, the understanding of episcopé and the relation between the ordained ministry and the laos of God. From Dr Potter's response to discussion in the first plenary considering this report, in which he stated that "the ordained ministry is indispensable to the life of the Church" and "our calling to the ministry. . .must be one. . .in the totality of the family of God in which I teach but also I learn", and from his unqualified support of the statement on ministry in the BEM document, it is clear that he was questioning how teaching authority and episcopé are to be rightly exercised, not their fundamental place in the life of the Church. With regard to the General Secretary's statement that "even as we reverence Christ so we must reverence those with whom we have dialogue, as an encounter of life with life", we would understand that the use of "reverence" in the second part of this statement means holding those with whom we enter into dialogue in profound respect.

The General Secretary has served us well by pointing to important further studies, along lines already initiated by Faith and Order, regarding ecclesiology, the nature of the Church's teaching authority, and the relation of the ordained ministry to the whole people of God. These studies, though they will inevitably involve discussion of the Toronto Declaration, must clearly be understood as growing out of that foundational document, rather than as challenges to it.

4.2 The WCC and its member churches

On the recommendation of the Executive Committee, the Assembly accepted two churches as members of the World Council of Churches: the Baptist Convention of Nicaragua (35,000 members) and the Evangelical Presbyterian Church of South Africa, formerly the Tsonga Presbyterian Church (30,000 members). With this action, WCC membership increased to 301 churches in more than 100 countries.

Metropolitan Chrysostomos (Ecumenical Patriarchate, Turkey), Moderator of Policy Reference Committee I, presented that part of the Committee's report which dealt with WCC/member church relationships. Noting that the Salvation Army had changed its status from one of member church to that of a Christian World Communion, the report asked for a clarification of the Army's understanding of the new relationship.

The Salvation Army had suspended its membership in the Council in 1978. In a letter dated 31 July 1981 it had expressed the wish to move from full membership to fraternal status under the provision in the Constitution (Sections VI.I and XII of the Rules). The 1981 Central Committee had accordingly passed the following motion:

> Having learned of the request of the Salvation Army to withdraw from membership of the WCC, the Central Committee regretfully accepts this withdrawal and approves the request for fraternal status.

In a statement in response to the report of Policy Reference Committee I, Commissioner Victor Keanie, a delegated observer representing the Salvation Army, said that the Army had not meant to withdraw from the WCC itself; it had simply changed its mode of continuing in the World Council's fellowship to a form more appropriate to its international structure. His suggestion for a more positive wording of this part of the report was greeted with applause and accepted by the Committee.

The relevant sections of the Committee's report read as follows:

1. Since Nairobi and as an encouragement to the development of covenant relationships and mutual accountability the WCC has greatly increased its relationships, contacts and communication with member churches.

1.1 Orthodox participation in the life of the Council has considerably increased with, as has been noted elsewhere, the contribution of the Orthodox churches having become more dynamic, valuable and creative. Besides Orthodox consultations on relevant ecumenical themes, a special consultation with official representatives of Eastern Orthodox churches was held in 1981. Several issues were discussed and have since been pursued, such as the inclusion of baptism in the Basis of the WCC, procedure and method of voting on matters of ecclesiological significance, and adequate Orthodox representation in the life of the Council. Further efforts should be made for strengthening relations with Orthodox member churches.

1.2 Great attention has been paid to united and uniting churches which, though they continue to feel the pull of their historic confessional allegiances, have made further steps towards unity. The WCC should encourage their unique ecumenical contribution.

1.3 In the period 1977–1983 significant improvement has been noted in relations with member churches in Eastern Europe and other regions. The experience in Eastern Europe proved of great value in spiritual enrichment, greater awareness of church life and activity, and in a sense of mutual support. In the light of such achievements we are able to recognize the importance of regular, regional consultations, as well as of opportunities to share the experience of member churches living in different circumstances.

2. From 1975 to 1982, our koinonia has grown with the addition of twenty full, and five associate, member churches. During this period the Salvation Army entered into dialogue with leaders of the WCC and requested agreement to its continuing its support for the World Council as a world confessional body (Constitution VI.1). To facilitate this, the Salvation Army relinquished its full membership, and at the 1981 meeting of the Central Committee was invited to assume this new relationship.

3. Staff travel, consultations and publications, team visits to some churches and regions facing various difficulties, as well as the visits of various related delegations to the Ecumenical Centre, have all contributed to this enriched relationship. The most significant achievement, however, has been in the 79 team visits to over 90 countries in preparation for the Assembly. These visits succeeded in communicating a living experience of the WCC and, while increasing local awareness of the Council, encouraged greater participation in its life. In the light

of this experience we have submitted several recommendations for consideration by the Programme Guidelines Committee.

4. *Related groups and networks*

4.1 At the same time as the WCC acts in the ways outlined above with and for member churches, its programmes are also carried out in various parts of the world through networks, study and action groups, lay centres, base communities and charismatic renewal groups, not all of which are closely related to institutional, denominational structures.

4.2 We recall that such groups for renewal played a significant part in the birth of the ecumenical movement, and their continuing creative potential is still a needed stimulus for the Council.

4.3 The inevitable tensions created by this necessary plurality of relationships calls for vigilance on the part of all partners to ensure that member churches and groups in any one place are aware of existing relationships. The WCC needs to play a supportive role as the people of God in a particular place work towards mutual understanding, dialogue and, if need be, reconciliation.

5. *Criticism of the WCC*

5.1 In the period under review various levels of criticism of the Council can be distinguished. Criticism from outside the Council falls into two categories: general misinformed comment and leafletting on ecumenical events, and highly organized, often politically motivated hostile campaigns of criticism of the Council and its work. Internal criticism also takes two forms: that which is concerned for constructive discussion of genuine theological differences, and negative challenges to the very purposes and programmes of the Council. This latter criticism is most destructive of the life of the Council and could call into question the essential meaning of membership in the WCC.

5.2 Undoubtedly some analysis of the source and information of particular criticisms would be of value, and would enable those responsible to make clear factual statements about issues and events.

5.3 The programme of team visits provides significant opportunity for personal sharing about WCC programmes and serves to counter media misinterpretation.

5.4 Such criticisms, however, are inevitable. While not in themselves a guarantee that the Council is faithfully following the way of the cross, it has to be stated that the link between costliness and discipleship is unmistakably clear, and in the end the work of the Council will be judged by other standards than those of its critics.

4.3 Relations with the Roman Catholic Church

The Fifth Report of the Joint Working Group (JWG) between the Roman Catholic Church and the World Council of Churches (see *The Ecumenical Review*, Vol 35, No. 2, April 1983) was considered by Policy Reference Committee I.

Responding to the Committee's comments, Prof. Duncan Forrester (Church of Scotland) asked for a stronger expression of concern about what he felt was a lack of progress and a hesitancy about the relationship on the Roman Catholic side. However Msgr Basil Meeking, a delegated observer of the Roman Catholic Church, spoke of the relationship in terms of "substance and maturity". It had, he said, gone beyond the stage of polite friendship. Recently Pope John Paul II asked that collaboration with the WCC be intensified in all fields where it is possible – a commitment that is seen, for example, in the fact that every episcopal conference has been asked to study the BEM document. Welcoming the Assembly's positive response to the Joint Working Group report, Msgr Meeking suggested that the JWG would need to find "suitable symbolic gestures of solidarity" to exemplify the present relationship and the commitment of both partners to it.

The relevant section of the Committee's report, as amended in the light of the discussion, reads as follows:

> This is the third time that a WCC assembly officially discusses the relationship between the Roman Catholic Church and the World Council of Churches and its member churches. The Assembly approves the Fifth Report of the Joint Working Group between the Roman Catholic Church and the World Council of Churches. The Report offers a frank, realistic description of the present ecumenical situation, an accurate summary of the activities of the JWG since the Nairobi Assembly, and clear proposals for future work. For its response, the Assembly also gratefully acknowledges the response of "general approval" from the Roman Catholic Church, in the official letter to the WCC General Secretary Dr P. Potter by Johannes Cardinal Willebrands, the President of the Secretariat for Promoting Christian Unity (4 July 1983).

> A. *General considerations*
> Two affirmations deserve to be underlined:
>   1. Overarching all considerations of continual relationships between the RCC and the member churches, whether on the world, regional or local levels, should always be the awareness of the common ground and the vision of the common goal of the ecumenical movement: "a oneness based on the real, though imperfect communion existing between all who believe in Christ and are baptized in his name" (Report, I.3); and the goal of "visible unity in one faith and in one eucharistic fellowship expressed in worship and in common life in Christ" (Constitution of the WCC, Article III). Only by a firm commitment in faith to this goal can the churches accept "their mutual responsibility and accountability before the world" as agents of reconciliation, humbly see their need already to express visibly in common witness that growing communion which already exists among the

churches (cf. Report, IV. 2), and to overcome the obstacles which impede the manifestation of full ecclesial communion (cf. I.3).

2. With this shared commitment and vision, the RCC and the WCC and its member churches have general criteria to evaluate various forms of collaboration in ecumenical solidarity. Since the 1972 answer to the membership question – "not in the immediate future" – still stands and the question is not yet ready to be taken up again (cf. I.7), the realistic question already posed in the Fourth Report 1975 remains valid and should ever be kept in mind: "How can the RCC and the WCC, without forming one structured fellowship, intensify their joint activities and thereby strengthen the unity, the common witness, and the renewal of the churches?" Or, in the words of Cardinal Willebrands, if such increased collaboration "is to mean something it must be taken seriously on both sides. There must be the will to utilize the possibilities."

B. *Ongoing and future collaboration*

The Fifth Report provides a helpful summary of the activities of the JWG since Nairobi, its achievements, encountered problems, and attempts to learn from failures. Five aspects in the Report deserve to be underlined, but they should not detract from the other main points and their details.

1. As in its Nairobi periods, the JWG has had its most visible success in initiating a number of joint studies. The study "Towards a Confession of the Common Faith" already identifies that such a common expression of the apostolic faith today is one of the requirements for visible unity, and now this long-term study project of the Faith and Order Commission will complement the convergence texts on baptism, eucharist and ministry. This coordinated effort is strengthened by the full RC membership in the Faith and Order Commission. The other joint study, "Common Witness", evaluates the "new tradition" of experiences which draw the churches closer to one another and to the ground and source of their unity in Christ. Diversity in witness which responds to different pastoral situations and contemporary challenges is no longer seen as a sign of dividedness in faith; rather, it can be considered as enriching the understanding of the common faith of the Church. The churches assign different degrees of significance to formulated doctrine and authoritative teaching as criteria for the unity within and among the churches. The experiences of common witness can help them to discover afresh the source of their faith beyond the differences of inherited doctrinal formulations.

These two studies have opened fresh perspectives which need to be pursued. How much unity of doctrinal expressions of the faith is required in order to enable the churches to witness together? How do we evaluate the claim of some that there are moral issues that are "confessional" and therefore potentially divisive? How much diversity in doctrine, moral teaching, and witness is compatible with the confession of the one faith in the one Church? Behind these questions is the unavoidable issue: the teaching authority of and in the Church.

2. While these observations and questions indicate the fruitfulness of the studies initiated by the JWG, the Fifth Report also reveals the unevenness of collaboration between the WCC Programme Units and Sub-units and the corresponding offices of the Holy See. One notices, for example, the visible relationship and active, ongoing RC involvement in the Faith and Order Commission, the Commission for World Mission and Evangelism, Dialogue with People of Living Faiths and Ideologies.

But in the area of social collaboration, new difficulties have occurred. The Report outlines the emerging ecumenical convergence on affirmations about Christian social responsibility, particularly in the areas of human development, peace and human rights (IV. 3). But the strong, visible symbol of common effort which was given by SODEPAX (Committee on Society, Development and Peace) was diminished by the 1979 decision to terminate SODEPAX. Many on both sides interpreted this decision as a weakening or even a withdrawal from a shared commitment to active collaboration.

The JWG acknowledges the influences of different structures and ways of operation (III.3.b) and emphasizes that what "ultimately matters. . .is the will to work together effectively" (*ibid*). The Assembly thus welcomes every effort of the new Joint Consultative Group for social thought and action to find realistic visible "flexible forms of collaboration on the international as well as on the national and local levels" (IV.3), for example, in common witness for peace, for the defence of human rights, including the right to religious freedom.

3. The Fifth Report focuses on relationships between the RCC and the WCC at the world level. But the JWG also acknowledges that the initiative for common witness has moved more and more to the local and national levels, and involves a wide variety of agents from both the members churches and the RCC; i.e. regional, national and local councils of churches, ecumenical groups, centres and organizations, religious orders, etc. The JWG has tried through surveys and analyses of case studies to assess the new experiences of local ecumenism and their implications for the relationship between the RCC and the WCC at world level (highly recommended for wide circulation and joint use is the JWG *Common Witness* study). It would seem that a continuing, more comprehensive analysis and understanding of the various levels is needed if future creative opportunities are to emerge. Included in such studies should also be analyses of those situations in which there is little, if any, common witness or its noticeable decrease.

4. Many of the member churches of the WCC have entered into bilateral dialogues with the RCC at national or world levels. At the same time, these dialogues complement the multilateral dialogue which takes place within the Faith and Order Commission or within other WCC theological and pastoral studies. Some of the bilateral dialogues "have reached a stage that is of considerable significance for the partners

and the ecumenical movement as a whole" (I. 6). What are the ways in which all of the churches can be mutually edified and enriched by the results of both the bilateral and multilateral dialogues? How can the RCC help the WCC to benefit from the insights which are gathered from its varied experiences in these bilateral conversations? Are there some emerging common concerns which now can be discussed within the fellowship of the WCC?

5. The Assembly strongly supports the Report's insistence on "the present urgency of the task of ecumenical formation" (IV. 4) and the recommendation that this be the first priority for the coming period. As Cardinal Willebrands remarks, "we have tended to take too much for granted that there is a sound knowledge of the ecumenical movement, of its history, and of the principles which are at stake". Indeed, "the ecumenical dimension is an indispensable part of all processes of Christian formation and nurture, be it the formation of laity, youth work, programmes of catechesis and religious training, or theological training" (IV.4).

C. *The Joint Working Group*

The Assembly accepts the JWG's self-description of its ongoing role and future tasks (V). The JWG in itself is important for the visibility which it gives to the RCC/WCC relationship – a symbol of a shared commitment to the one ecumenical movement. The new emphasis on ecumenical formation has implications for the organization, composition and style of the JWG. For example, besides being a necessary liaison body between two administrative and programme structures on the world level, the JWG should also be the direct listener and responder of local insights and should provide a framework for the sharing of experiences between different contexts, · whether local, national or regional.

In approving the Fifth Report of the JWG, the Assembly recommends that:

a) The Central Committee nominate to the JWG persons with experiences in local and regional ecumenical collaboration with the RCC. Such persons should be greater in number than representatives of the administrative structures of the parent bodies, in order to explore more adequately both problems and opportunities for significant ecumenical dialogue.

b) The JWG be enabled to hold at least some of its meetings outside its previous site, i.e. Western Europe. On the occasion of its meeting, the JWG would participate in local ecumenical activities.

c) The JWG should consider for implementation not only the specific recommendations above (part B) but also all of those recommendations which are offered in the Fifth Report under "Proposals for Future Work" (cf. V).

d) The parent bodies be even more concerned with the higher visibility of the JWG and with the communication of its findings to interested member churches and to the wider RC constituency.

4.4 Christian World Communions

Policy Reference Committee I reported to the Assembly in the following terms:

1. Since the time of the Nairobi Assembly (1975) where a special report on "Relationships between the World Council of Churches and World Confessional Families"* was adopted, a deeper partnership has developed between the WCC and the Christian World Communions (CWCs) within the one ecumenical movement as they have faced the common calling to Christ. Several significant joint programmes and consultations have taken place which mark important progress within the relationships between the WCC and the CWCs in response to moving towards the goal of Christian unity and common witness, including concerted action and cooperation in the fields of theological dialogue, interchurch aid, international affairs, human rights and religious liberty.

2. In this period of growing partnership and mutual trust, four joint ventures of special significance are noted:

a) building upon the ongoing dialogues from Nairobi regarding the relationship between the WCC and CWCs, a joint meeting was held in October 1978, to explore the possibilities for developing more fruitful relationships in responding to the present and future challenges of the common calling to visible unity;

b) a series of three meetings of a "Forum on Bilateral Conversations" took place in April 1978, June 1979 and October 1980, to facilitate the exchange of information and to review recent developments in the bilateral dialogues; to promote the interaction between bilateral and multilateral discussions; to study the implications of bilateral findings for the ecumenical movement as a whole; and to examine issues of method relevant to all bilateral conversations;

c) two important discussions have taken place regarding the relationship of united and uniting churches to the CWCs, including the recent meeting in October 1982 at the Conference of Secretaries of CWCs growing out of the Colombo Consultation of United Churches in November 1981; fruitful dialogues have also been held between representatives of united churches and the Vatican Secretariat for Promoting Christian Unity (February 1983) and with members of Orthodox churches (February 1983);

d) a special consultation on relations between the WCC and the Lutheran World Federation (May 1981) produced an "Aide Memoire" outlining several guiding principles on relationships between the WCC and the LWF and several areas for future reflection, study and cooperation.

---

* In 1979 the identification of "Christian World Communions" (CWCs) was chosen to replace "World Confessional Families" as a more accurate description of those organizations.

3. From its discussion of the reports of these joint ventures, Policy Reference Committee I recommends:

a) that the Assembly *recognize* the ecumenical importance of the CWCs and the Conference of Secretaries of CWCs as partners in the quest for the full visible unity of the Church and *encourage* the development of closer collaboration between the WCC and the CWCs. This collaboration should include mutual challenge to greater advance in the search for the nature and unity of the Church and the renewal of human community, and cooperation in common witness to the Gospel's proclamation in today's world;

b) that the WCC, in partnership with the CWCs, should *pursue* the task of seeking clarity as to the goal of the unity we seek within the one ecumenical movement, and in identifying steps and possibilities in achieving that goal;

c) that the Assembly *express* its hope that a new series of ad hoc meetings of the "Forum on Bilateral Conversations" be held, with the specific request that attention be given to the reception of the *Baptism, Eucharist and Ministry* text and to its relations to the bilateral dialogues among CWCs (refer to "The Three Reports of the Forum on Bilateral Conversations", Faith and Order Paper 107);

d) that, in light of the ongoing work of the Faith and Order Secretariat over several years in giving assistance to the united and uniting churches to witness to their particular experiences of Church unity across confessional traditions in the national context, the Assembly *support* the fostering of discussions between united Churches and the CWCs regarding possible areas of common exploration and common witness (refer to "Unity in each place. . .in all places. . .", Faith and Order Paper 118);

e) that the Assembly *express* gratitude for the fact that within the General Secretariat in the recent past a liaison function between the WCC and the CWCs has been faithfully carried out by Prof. Todor Sabev, and its hope that this important function be continued.

The Report of Policy Reference Committee I was received and its recommendations adopted.

4.5 Nominations, elections

The Nominations Committee began its complicated task by securing the Assembly's assent to the following principles:

1) the Nominations Committee should "make full use of the provisions of Article V,2(b) of the Constitution of the WCC, according to which the Central Committee can include up to 145 members coming from full member churches" (Central Committee *Minutes*, Geneva, July 1982, p.54);

2) the new Central Committee should reflect the composition of the Assembly – not only in the representation of confessions and regions, but also in the representation of women, youth and

lay persons, remembering that the Dresden Central Committee affirmed that "the principles of equal participation between men and women be a goal towards which we move, starting with the composition of the WCC decision-making and consultative bodies during and after the Sixth Assembly" (Central Committee *Minutes*, Dresden, August 1981, p. 29);

3a) care should be taken to have adequate representation for the Orthodox churches. "The final decision of the Central Committee regarding the allocation of seats provided for approximately 23% to be filled by Orthodox churches (Eastern and Oriental)" (Central Committee *Minutes*, Geneva, July 1982, p. 51);

3b) "It is considered desirable that as far as possible within the present rules each Orthodox member church be represented on the Central Committee by at least one person, and that the total Orthodox membership of the Central Committee be in accordance with both the size and the specific nature of the Orthodox churches" (Central Committee *Minutes*, Geneva, July 1982, p. 51).

Mr Harry Ashmall (Church of Scotland), Moderator of the Nominations Committee, explained the statistical base the Committee was proposing to use for the allocation of Central Committee places and the time-table the Committee would follow in presenting its lists for the Assembly's consideration. These were approved.

Having given the required notice, Mr Ashmall moved an amendment to Rule II.1 to read

> The Assembly shall elect one or more Presidents but the number of Presidents shall not exceed seven.

The addition of a seventh President would, he said, enable the representation of an additional region in response to changes that have taken place in the WCC since 1948. The amendment was approved.

A first list of names for the new Presidium and Central Committee was presented at the beginning of the second week, and written comments were invited by the Nominations Committee. A revised list was presented on Friday, 5 August, provoking some strong reactions to what, from an assortment of viewpoints, were seen as serious imbalances in the categories of names proposed. Why were there not more youth, many asked, noting that only 9.66% of the names put forward for the Central Committee were aged thirty or less (as against 13.44% of delegates in the Assembly itself). Women made up 26.21% of the list (29.49% in the Assembly). Other protests were with regard to the representation of southern Europe, francophone Africa, Brazil, the Netherlands, the Middle East, and the disabled.

The following day the Moderator ruled, in response to an appeal, that the Nominations Committee had acted properly in terms of Rule III.4 and had, to the best of its ability, tried to be faithful to the three principles earlier affirmed by the Assembly. Proposals for changes were then considered; each had to be directed to the replacement of one name on the list by another, and each required the backing of six delegates. A counter-nomination for the Presidium won insufficient support, and the Presidium as proposed was elected. Dr W. A. Visser 't Hooft was re-elected Honorary President by acclamation.

The Central Committee list proved more difficult. First, by mutual agreement between the delegations concerned, the names of Rev. Dr Ako Haarbeck (EKD, Federal Republic of Germany) and Rt Rev. Ulises Hernandez B. (Methodist, Mexico) were withdrawn in favour respectively of Rev. Dr R. J. Mooi (Netherlands Reformed Church, Netherlands) and Rev. Meinard Piske (Lutheran, Brazil). Then, by counter-nomination, Ms Margot Kaessman replaced Dr Helga Gilbert (both EKD, Federal Republic of Germany), and Ms Rose Jarjour (Evangelical Synod of Syria and Lebanon) replaced Ms Frieda Haddad (Greek Orthodox Patriarchate of Antioch and All the East).

A remaining counter-nomination that would have resulted in a further erosion of Orthodox representation evoked strong expressions of concern, and debate was adjourned so that advice could be sought from the Officers. At a later session the Moderator indicated that the person nominated to replace the Ecumenical Patriarchate's Mr George Lemopulo had withdrawn her name. Further, the General Secretary explained that notwithstanding the replacement of Ms Haddad all Orthodox churches would still be represented in the Central Committee: the Patriarch of her church was one of the Presidents, and Rule IV.1(c) meant that in his absence a substitute could be appointed with the right to speak and vote. By the time the above changes were completed, the proportion of those aged 30 or under had been raised to 11.72%.

The list as amended (see Appendix IX) was then adopted, although a not insignificant number abstained from voting to register their frustration at the Assembly's inability to achieve the goal for representation that it had set itself.

Reduced to statistics, the Assembly's agonizing had produced a Central Committee with an interesting profile.

	Male Number %	Female Number %	Youth Number %	Ordained Number %
Outgoing CC	103 77.44	30 22.56	13 9.77	87 65.41
Sixth Assembly delegates	591 70.27	248 29.49	113 13.44	445 52.91
New CC	107 73.79	38 26.21	17 11.72	86 59.31

Confessional participation by women and youth on new Central Committee

	Total Seats	Women	Youth
Anglican	15	6	1
Baptist	7	1	–
Brethren	1	–	–
Disciples	2	–	1
Friends	1	1	–
Independent	2	–	–
Kimbanguist	1	–	–
Lutheran	22	5	4
Mar Thoma	1	–	–
Mennonite	–	–	–
Methodist	14	7	–
Moravian	1	–	1
Old Catholic	1	–	–
Orthodox	32	3	2
Pentecostal	2	1	1
Reformed	29	10	6
United	14	4	1
Others	–	–	–
	145	38	17

Thirty-nine of the 145 (26.89%) had served on the Central Committee in the period from Nairobi to Vancouver.

Finally, the Nominations Committee identified several problems that it felt require further attention before this exercise is repeated. Time precluded any discussion of its final report, which was bounced forward for consideration by the incoming Central Committee. It highlighted the following issues.

1. *Orthodox representation*
The Committee feels this matter needs continuing discussion and for the following reason: although the number of the faithful in the Orthodox churches will continue to grow, the number of the Orthodox member churches in the WCC is not likely to increase and the

Committee is sympathetic to the case made by the members of the Orthodox family that even 23% does not meet adequately their needs in terms of representation in view of the fact that the Protestant membership will continue to increase.

2. *Regional representation*
Arguments have been advanced in the Assembly for a review of regional representation and the Committee feels such a review would be helpful.

3. *Smaller church representation*
A number of the original member churches are small and would not now qualify by numbers for full membership or even for associate status. It is difficult for them to be represented on Central Committee so that consideration should be given to their pleas for periodic representation.

4. *United churches*
Concern was expressed that uniting churches can sometimes be penalized for uniting by losing seats on committees, etc. The matter should be studied.

5. *Youth representation*
A number of different suggestions have been made in the effort to improve youth representation. The Committee has not had time to recommend any one approach but it agrees that the Central Committee should urgently study the options.

In asking the Assembly to pass this document to the Central Committee for action the Nominations Committee wishes to inform delegates that suggestions for review made in discussion will be extracted from the Minutes and included in a dossier, along with all the written suggestions submitted by individuals, groups or church delegations seated in the Assembly.

4.6 Programme Guidelines and Finance
Prof. José Miguez Bonino (Methodist, Argentina) and Dr Janice Love (Methodist, USA) presented the report of the Programme Guidelines Committee.

The Committee had received comments bearing on WCC programmes and priorities throughout the Assembly, particularly from Issue Groups and Hearings. Its report evoked a rather confused discussion, as some delegates spoke to the report itself while others used the opportunity to raise a variety of specific concerns to which they felt the World Council should address itself. Some interventions led to minor amendments in the report. Other speakers were invited to channel their concerns via the new Central Committee. Inevitably a number of recommendations from Issue Groups and Hearings were not included in the Committee's report, but the General Secretary assured the Assembly that all such would be accessible in another form to the Central Committee or the core groups of particular Units, as appropriate.

Subject to amendment by the Committee's officers in the light of the debate, the report of the Programme Guidelines Committee was adopted (see Appendix VIII).

Rev. Patricia McClurg (Presbyterian, USA), Moderator of the Assembly's Finance Committee, presented the Committee's report. The pressure of time prevented any extended debate, but Dr H. J. Held (EKD, Federal Republic of Germany) drew attention to the fact that all member churches, not only the more affluent among them, were being challenged to make substantial increases in their undesignated giving to the World Council in the period up to the next Assembly.

The Finance Committee's report was adopted and the recommendations contained therein approved (see Appendix VII).

5. WORLD AFFAIRS
IN ECUMENICAL PERSPECTIVE

The making and breaking of human life anywhere and for whatever reason is the legitimate and necessary concern of Christ's Church: on that score the churches as they work together through their World Council have never had any doubts. Moreover, an Assembly that had meditated at length on the Vancouver theme was bound to try to bring the insights of the Gospel to bear, quite specifically, on the life-denying forces rampant in the Year of our Lord 1983.

But where to start? Where to stop? And how to select? The Sixth Assembly, like its predecessors, was in that quandary. Like them it will be charged by some with having said too much on too many issues and by others with having uttered too little on too few.

The *Assembly Work Book* contained some helpful advice on the problem. A public statement, it pointed out, is not the only way of responding to a situation. Other forms of action include pastoral visits to churches in difficult or critical situations, discussions with governments or intergovernmental bodies, delegations which study and report on specific issues or situations, confidential representations to governments, and support for action groups. Statements too, can be of different kinds – some appealing to member churches, others making representations to governments or the UN, yet others in the form of pastoral letters.

In 1976 the Central Committee tried to make explicit the criteria that help the Council select the issues on which it makes statements. It listed:

1) areas and issues on which the WCC has had direct involvement and long-standing commitment;
2) emerging issues of international concern to which the attention of the churches should be called for action;
3) critical and developing political situations which demand the WCC to make known its judgment and lend its spiritual and moral voice;
4) expectations from the member churches that the WCC should speak;
5) to set a policy mandate for the WCC secretariat.

This is not a set of hard and fast rules – sensitivity to the special nature of each situation takes priority – but it was hoped that listing the criteria might help delegates sort out the issues on which the Assembly, advised by its Business Committee and Policy Reference Committee II, should attempt to formulate its thinking.

Even so, the Assembly ran into difficulties. World Council officers were showered with something like fifty requests for Vancouver to utter on issues ranging from caste in India to religion in Albania, from imprisoned clergy in the Soviet Union, Ethiopia and South Korea to a resurgent Ku Klux Klan in the United States. Eventually the Assembly attempted to deal with six general statements, four more focused resolutions and four brief minutes, leaving the remaining concerns to be picked up after the Assembly by the WCC's regular programmes and procedures.

5.1   STATEMENT ON PEACE AND JUSTICE

Mr William P. Thompson (Presbyterian, USA), Moderator of Policy Reference Committee II, presented the draft statement entitled "Peace and Justice". Supporting presentations were made by Bishop Henry Okullu (Anglican, Kenya), Archbishop Kirill (Orthodox, USSR) and Ms Aruna Gnanadason (Church of South India).

In an extended debate there were calls to strengthen the justice component of the statement. Dr Avery Post (United Church of Christ, USA) wanted a sharper note of prophetic urgency in the document, while Bishop John Habgood (Church of England) and others argued for a more pragmatic, less "utopian" emphasis. Greater specificity was needed, said some, about conditions of injustice and what the churches could do about them.

A revised document was submitted to a subsequent session of the Assembly. Debating it, Dr Gerhard Grohs (EKD, Federal Republic of Germany) asked for a stronger statement advocating church support for the right of conscientious objection to military service. Mr Thorsten Manson (Church of Sweden) and Bishop Victor Premsagar (Church of South India) urged that the WCC seek to send a delegation to the presidents of the USA and the USSR; they were advised to make the proposal as a notice of motion, not by trying to amend the statement. Dr Alan Geyer (Methodist, USA) proposed an amendment referring to the danger of nuclear proliferation in the southern hemisphere. However, Mr Bena-Silu (Kimbanguist, Zaire) was uneasy about the implication that nuclear weapons may be tolerable in the hands of some nations but not in the hands of others. He and Dr Geyer were invited to formulate an acceptable wording.

The statement, with several amendments accepted on behalf of the committee, was adopted.

1. Humanity is now living in the dark shadow of an arms race more intense, and of systems of injustice more widespread, more dangerous and more costly than the world has ever known. Never before has the human race been as close as it is now to total self-destruction. Never before have so many lived in the grip of deprivation and oppression.

2. Under that shadow we have gathered here at the Sixth Assembly of the World Council of Churches (Vancouver, 1983) to proclaim our common faith in Jesus Christ, the Life of the World, and to say to the world:
– fear not, for Christ has overcome the forces of evil; in him are all things made new;
– fear not; for the love of God, rise up for justice and for peace;
– trust in the power of Christ who reigns over all; give witness to him in word and in deed, regardless of the cost.

Growing threats to justice and peace

3. Still we are moved to repentance as we consider with alarm the rapidity with which the threats to justice and survival have grown since we last met. The frantic race towards nuclear conflagration has accelerated sharply. In an incredibly short period of history, we have moved from the horrors of Hiroshima and Nagasaki, and the threat that they might be repeated elsewhere, to the likelihood, unless we act now, that life on the whole planet could be devastated. A moment of madness, a miscalculated strategic adventure, a chance combination of computer errors, a misperception of the other's intention, an honest mistake – any one could now set off a nuclear holocaust.

4. As we have been reminded dramatically during this Assembly, nuclear weapons claim victims even in the absence of war, through the lasting effects of nuclear bombings, weapons testing and the dumping of nuclear wastes.

5. For many millions, however, the most immediate threat to survival is not posed by nuclear weapons. Local, national and international conflicts rage around the world. The intersection of East-West and North-South conflicts results in massive injustice, systematic violation of human rights, oppression, homelessness, starvation and death for masses of people. Millions have been rendered stateless, expelled from their homes as refugees or exiles.

6. The World Council of Churches has consistently drawn the attention of the churches to the economic threats to peace. Even without war, thousands perish daily in nations both rich and poor because of hunger and starvation. Human misery and suffering as a result of various forms of injustice have reached levels unprecedented

in modern times. There is a resurgence of racism, often in itself a
cause of war. Peoples continue to be driven, as a last resort, to take
up arms to defend themselves against systematic violence, or to
claim their rights to self-determination or independence.

7. While the equivalent of nearly two billion dollars (US) is being
expended globally each day for armaments, the world economy is
engulfed in a prolonged and deepening crisis which threatens every
country and international security. The spectre of trade warfare,
competitive devaluation and financial collapse is omnipresent. This
crisis has contributed to even greater injustice for the developing
countries, denying millions the basic necessities of life. The failure of
UNCTAD VI has dashed hopes for meaningful North-South dialogue.
While many factors are involved, the link between the arms race
and economic development, the effects of rising defence budgets
and accelerated reliance on arms production in the industrialized
nations, and the ensuing strain on the international system as a
whole pose special threats to peace and justice.

No peace without justice

8. The peoples of the world stand in need of peace and justice.
Peace is not just the absence of war. Peace cannot be built on
foundations of injustice. Peace requires a new international order
based on justice for and within all the nations, and respect for the
God-given humanity and dignity of every person. Peace is, as the
Prophet Isaiah has taught us, the effect of righteousness.

9. *The churches today are called to confess anew their faith, and to
repent for the times when Christians have remained silent in the face of
injustice or threats to peace. The biblical vision of peace with justice for
all, of wholeness, of unity for all God's people is not one of several options
for the followers of Christ. It is an imperative in our time.*

10. The ecumenical approach to peace and justice is based on the
belief that without justice for all everywhere we shall never have
peace anywhere. From its inception, peace with justice has been a
central concern of the ecumenical movement. The World Council
of Churches was conceived amid the rumblings of looming world
wars. Ever since it was formed it has condemned war, and engaged
almost constantly in efforts to prevent war, to aid the victims of
war and to keep war from breaking out anew. It has exposed the
injustices that lead to conflict, affirmed its solidarity with groups
and movements struggling for justice and peace, and sought to
establish channels of communication leading to the peaceful resolution of conflicts. It has repeatedly called the attention of the churches
and through them the governments and the general public to the
threats to peace, the threats to survival, and the deepening crisis.

But we face an even more critical situation now. More than ever before it is imperative that Christians and churches join their struggles for peace and justice.

Rampant militarism

11. Through the Council's work on militarism since the Fifth Assembly (Nairobi, 1975), we have come to understand more fully the dire consequences for justice of the increasing reliance of the nations on armed force as the cornerstone of their foreign – and often domestic – policies. Priorities have been dangerously distorted. Attention has been drawn away from the fundamental rights and needs of poor nations and of the poor within the rich nations. The number of military regimes has grown, contributing further to a largely male-dominated process of global militarization. Justice is often sacrificed on the altar of narrowly perceived national security interests. Racial, ethnic, cultural, religious and ideological conflicts are exacerbated, corruption is rife, a spirit of fear and suspicion is fostered through the increasing portrayal of others as the enemy: all this further contributes to disunity, human suffering and increased threats to peace.

12. We strongly reiterate the Central Committee's appeals to the churches to:

a) challenge military and militaristic policies that lead to disastrous distortions of foreign policy, sapping the capacity of the nations of the world to deal with pressing economic and social problems which have become a paramount political issue of our times;

b) counter the trend to characterize those of other nations and ideologies as the "enemy" through the promotion of hatred and prejudice;

c) assist in demythologizing current doctrines of national security and elaborate new concepts of security based on justice and the rights of the peoples;

d) grapple with the important theological issues posed by new developments related to war and peace and examine the challenges posed to traditional positions;

e) pay serious attention to the rights of conscientious objectors;

f) continue . . . to call attention to the root causes of war, mainly to economic injustice, oppression and exploitation and to the consequences of increasing tension including further restrictions on human rights.

Justice and security

13. The blatant misuse of the concept of national security to justify repression, foreign intervention and spiralling arms budgets

is of profound concern. No nation can pretend to be secure so long as others' legitimate rights to sovereignty and security are neglected or denied. Security can therefore be achieved only as a common enterprise of nations but security is also inseparable from justice. A concept of "common security" of nations must be reinforced by a concept of "people's security". True security for the people demands respect for human rights, including the right to self-determination, as well as social and economic justice for all within every nation, and a political framework that would ensure it.

Peaceful resolution of conflicts

14. In this connection the growing refusal of many governments to use the opportunities afforded by the United Nations to preserve international peace and security and for the peaceful resolution of conflicts, or to heed its resolutions, is deeply troubling. We call upon the governments to reaffirm their commitment to the United Nations Charter, to submit interstate conflicts to the Security Council at an early stage when resolution may still be possible short of the use of massive armed force, and to cooperate with it in the pursuit of peaceful solutions. *We draw special attention to the United Nations International Year of Peace (1986) and the World Disarmament Campaign, urging the churches to use them as important opportunities for the strengthening of international security and the promotion of disarmament, peace and justice.*

Nuclear weapons and disarmament

15. It is now a full decade since there has been any substantial, subsequently ratified measure of arms control. Since our last Assembly, global military expenditures have tripled. This past year has marked a new peak of confrontation between NATO and the Warsaw Treaty Organization. There is the real prospect, if the current negotiations in Geneva between the USA and the USSR fail to prevent it, that the world stockpile of nuclear weapons may increase dramatically in the next decade. The growing sophistication, accuracy and mobility of new generations of weapons now ready for deployment or currently being designed make them more dangerous and destabilizing than ever before. The failure of arms control among nuclear-weapon states has made the non-proliferation treaty, in practice, an instrument of invidious discrimination, incited the spread of nuclear weapons, and compounded the prospects for nuclear war in several areas of regional tension in the Southern hemisphere. Until the super-powers move decisively towards nuclear disarmament, efforts to contain nuclear proliferation are bound to fail.

16. *We call upon the churches, especially those in Europe, both East and West, and in North America, to redouble their efforts to convince their governments to reach a negotiated settlement and to turn away now, before it is too late, from plans to deploy additional or new nuclear weapons in Europe, and to begin immediately to reduce and then eliminate altogether present nuclear forces.*

17. *We urge the churches as well to intensify their efforts to stop the rapidly growing deployment of nuclear weapons and support systems in the Indian and Pacific Oceans, and to press their governments to withdraw from or refuse to base or service ships or airplanes bearing nuclear weapons in those regions.*

18. The risk of nuclear war is compounded by the rapidly escalating reliance on conventional weapons. Stockpiles of non-nuclear weapons of mass destruction and indiscriminate effect are growing almost uncontrolled. The volume of highly profitable trade in conventional weapons has nearly doubled in the past five years, a very large part of it in the direction of the developing nations and regions where armed conflict already defies containment. The destructive power of these weapons steadily increases, blurring the distinction between conventional and nuclear warfare; and many nuclear disarmament strategies call for major increases in conventional arms production and deployment.

19. Since the Nairobi Assembly, a number of consultations and conferences have been held by the WCC, providing churches with opportunities to deepen their understanding of these issues. From them have come valuable reports and recommendations to the churches for concrete action. The most recent was the Public Hearing on Nuclear Weapons and Disarmament (Amsterdam, 1981). The published report contains careful, thoroughgoing analyses and spells out urgent tasks for the churches. We urge the churches once again to study attentively these reports and to pursue their recommendations.

20. The Central Committee urged the churches to pay special attention to and take clear positions on a number of points developed in the report of the Amsterdam Hearing. We reiterate that appeal with respect to the following:

a) a nuclear war can under no circumstances, in no region and by no social system, be just or justifiable, given the fact that the magnitude of devastation caused by it will be far out of proportion to any conceivable benefit or advantage to be derived from it;

b) nuclear war is unlikely to remain limited, and therefore any contemplation of "limited" use of nuclear weapons should be discouraged as dangerous from the outset;

c) all nations now possessing nuclear weapons or capable of doing so in the foreseeable future should unequivocally renounce policies of "first use", as an immediate step towards building confidence;

d) the concept of deterrence, the credibility of which depends on the possible use of nuclear weapons, is to be rejected as morally unacceptable and as incapable of safeguarding peace and security in the long-term;

e) the production and deployment of nuclear weapons as well as their use constitute a crime against humanity, and therefore there should be a complete halt in the production of nuclear weapons and in weapons research and development in all nations, to be expeditiously enforced through a treaty; such a position supports the struggle to cause one's own nation to commit itself never to own or use nuclear weapons, despite the period of nuclear vulnerability, and to encourage and stand in solidarity with Christians and others who refuse to cooperate with or accept employment in any projects related to nuclear weapons and nuclear warfare;

f) all nations should agree to and ratify a comprehensive test ban treaty as a necessary step to stopping the further development of nuclear weapons technology;

g) all means leading to disarmament, both nuclear and conventional, should be welcomed as complementary and mutually reinforcing: multilateral conferences leading to effective decisions, bilateral negotiations pursued with daring and determination and unilateral initiatives leading to the relaxation of tensions and building of mutual confidence among nations and peoples.

21. In addition, we urge the churches to press their governments to abstain from any further research, production or deployment of weapons in space; and to prohibit the development and production of all weapons of mass destruction or indiscriminate effect, including chemical and biological means.

Challenge to the churches

22. In our efforts since the last Assembly to accomplish the purpose of the World Council of Churches "to express the common concern of the churches in the service of human need, the breaking down of barriers between people, and the promotion of one human family in justice and peace", we have been encouraged and strengthened by the movement of the Holy Spirit among us, leading the churches to undertake new initiatives. In this process of conversion the insights and the leadership of women and youth have often been

decisive. But our common faith and the times now demand much more of us as stewards of God's creation.

23. Christians cannot view the dangers of this moment as inherent in the nature of things. Nor can we give ourselves over to despair. As believers in the one Lord and Saviour, Jesus Christ, the Prince of Peace, we are stewards of God's hope for the future of creation. We know God's love and confess a Lord of history in whom we have the promise of the fullness of life. God's mercy is everlasting, and the Holy Spirit is moving among us, kindling the love which drives out fear, renewing our vision of peace, stirring our imaginations, leading us through the wilderness, freeing us and uniting us. The peoples of the world are coming to their feet in growing numbers, demanding justice, crying out for peace. These are present signs of hope.

24. We have recognized that our approaches to justice and peace often differ, as do the starting points for discussion among the churches, due to the wide diversity of our histories, traditions and the contexts in which we live and witness. *We call upon the churches now to:*

a) *intensify their efforts to develop a common witness in a divided world, confronting with renewed vigour the threats to peace and survival and engaging in struggles for justice and human dignity;*

b) *become a living witness to peace and justice through prayer, worship and concrete involvement;*

c) *take steps towards unity through providing more frequent opportunities for sharing in and among the churches in order to learn more about and understand better each other's perspectives, defying every attempt to divide or separate us; and*

d) *develop more innovative approaches to programmes of education for peace and justice.*

25. According to the 1980 Geneva Convention, the use of certain weapons of indiscriminate effect is forbidden under international law. We believe nuclear weapons must be considered within that category. We join in the conviction expressed by the Panel of the WCC Public Hearing on Nuclear Weapons and Disarmament after it had examined the testimony of a broad range of expert witnesses:

"We believe that the time has come when the churches must unequivocally declare that the production and deployment as well as the use of nuclear weapons are a crime against humanity and that such activities must be condemned on ethical and theological grounds. The nuclear weapons issue is, in its import and threat to humanity, a question of Christian discipline and faithfulness to the Gospel. We recognize that nuclear weapons will not disappear because of such an affirmation by the churches. But it will involve the churches and their members in a

fundamental examination of their own implicit or explicit support of policies which, implicitly or explicitly, are based on the possession and use of these weapons."

We urge the churches to press their governments, especially in those countries which have nuclear weapons capabilities, to elaborate and ratify an international legal instrument which would outlaw as a crime against humanity the possession as well as the use of nuclear arms. We ask the churches as well to urge their governments to acknowledge the right of conscientious objection to military service and to provide opportunities for non-violent alternative service.

26. On the same basis, and in the spirit of the Fifth Assembly's appeal to the churches "to emphasize their readiness to live without the protection of armaments", *we believe that Christians should give witness to their unwillingness to participate in any conflict involving weapons of mass destruction or indiscriminate effect.*

27. It is with a deep sense of pastoral responsibility that we make these affirmations. To live up to them will be no simple matter for any Christian or church, but we recognize that the consequences of taking such positions will be far more serious for some than for others. We state these convictions not as a condemnation or in judgment of others, but confessing our own weakness, *calling on the churches and Christians to support one another in love as in these ways we seek together to be faithful to our common calling to proclaim and serve our one Lord, Jesus Christ, the Prince of Peace, the Life of the World.*

5.2   STATEMENT ON HUMAN RIGHTS

A draft statement on human rights was presented by Mr Thompson, with the request that suggestions for changes be made in writing to Policy Reference Committee II.

In the ensuing discussion, Bishop Marjorie Matthews (Methodist, USA) said that the question of the ordination of women should be seen in this context. Dr David Russell (Baptist, UK) and Rev. Jean Pierre Jornod (Reformed, Switzerland) asked for more emphasis on violations of religious freedom, and two Canadian delegates wanted specific mention of the land claims of Aboriginal Canadians. Archbishop Ajamian (Armenian, Israel) pleaded for a word of hope in the face of a thoroughly depressing human rights situation worldwide.

When a revised text reached the plenary there were several requests that particular areas be mentioned: specifically Ethiopia, India and the Middle East. Rev. Michael Oleksa of the Orthodox Church in America said churches should not only press governments to come to terms with the land claims of Aboriginal peoples but should also monitor the implementation of such settlements. Rev. Dr Theodore Stylianopoulos (Ecumenical Patriarchate, USA) asked that the WCC extend its concern to embrace the human rights of the unborn. The reference to migrant workers should make special mention of people who are made migrants even in the lands of their birth, said Ms Virginia Gcabashe (Methodist, South Africa). Bishop Aram Keshishian (Armenian, Lebanon) urged a stronger denunciation of genocide.

Mr Thompson, in the name of the Committee, resisted suggestions that the document should start singling out particular countries by name, but incorporated several of the amendments proposed.

The statement, as amended, was adopted.

1. The World Council of Churches' Sixth Assembly rejoices and gives thanks to God for the increasing commitment to work for the realization of human rights which has been demonstrated in the life and work of the churches throughout the world since the Nairobi Assembly. Many persons, including Christians and their leaders, have been imprisoned, tortured or have lost their lives in service to God and humanity. The ecumenical community has increasingly participated in concrete expressions of international solidarity in the struggle for human dignity, often through the World Council of Churches and regional, national and local ecumenical bodies.

2. Cooperation in the field of human rights is emerging between the Christian community and peoples of other living faiths and ideologies, based on their common commitment to human values and social goals.

3. And yet, the tasks have become more difficult, the violations of human rights in many parts of the world have become more widespread and severe, and churches must confess in humility that they have not done enough to counter the forces of evil and death, at times even being in complicity with them.

4. As the theme of this Assembly affirms, Jesus Christ is the life of the world. All human beings, regardless of race, sex or belief, have been created by God as individuals and in human community. Yet the world has been corrupted by sin, which results in the destruction of human relationships. In reconciling humankind and creation with God, Jesus Christ has also reconciled human beings with each other. Love of our neighbours is the essence of obedience to God.

Lessons from the past

5. Drawing on the International Bill of Human Rights (the Universal Declaration of Human Rights, the United Nations International Covenant on Economic, Social and Cultural Rights, and

the United Nations International Covenant on Civil and Political Rights together with its Optional Protocol) and after extensive consultations among the churches, the Nairobi Assembly affirmed its commitment to the promotion of human rights under the following categories: the right to basic guarantees of life; the rights to self-determination, to cultural identity and the rights of minorities; the right to participate in decision-making within the community; the right to dissent; the right to personal dignity; and the right to religious freedom. Following Nairobi, the churches have seen the need to broaden their understanding of human rights to include the right to peace, the right to protection of the environment, the right to development and the right to know one's rights and to struggle for them. We have also come to appreciate more clearly the complexity and inter-relatedness of human rights. In this regard we recognize the need to set individual rights and their violation in the context of society and its social structures.

6. We are increasingly aware of the fact that human rights cannot be dealt with in isolation from the larger issues of peace, justice, militarism, disarmament and development. The fuller the rights that every person enjoys in society, the more stable that society is likely to be; the fuller the implementation of human rights globally, the more stable international relations are likely to be. Injustice in a society, including the corruption of public officials, may contribute to domestic, economic and political disorder, which in turn may lead to the deterioration in relations among nations.

7. We have moved beyond mere reflection to concrete engagement in human rights struggles. In doing so, however, we have discovered how difficult and painful it is to cope with human rights and their violations. We have found that in promoting the rights of women, youth, children, and disabled persons, for example, the churches need to examine and often alter their own structures and methods of operation. In struggling for justice many Christians are experiencing the way of the cross.

Future agenda
8. While recognizing the positive work undertaken by churches, we cannot ignore the general deterioration in the quality of life and the emergence of new forms of human degradation. The prolonged economic disorder has further aggravated an already grave situation, driving some countries to the brink of bankruptcy, leaving millions unemployed and, especially in the developing nations, denying additional millions the basic necessities of life. Of the many pressing problems and emerging trends facing the Christian community, the

following call for our special concern and commitment at the time of our Sixth Assembly.

8.1 Many Christians have discovered that freedom of expression and freedom of association are indispensable as means to promote a life of dignity in their societies. We must reaffirm our commitment to those freedoms and our support for those who in exercising them are suffering.

8.2 Increasingly sophisticated forms of physical and psychological torture, the practice of "disappearances" and extrajudicial executions have not only been used more widely throughout the world, but have in many countries become standard procedures of military and police forces. The Sixth Assembly endorses the Central Committee statements that condemn the practice of torture (1977) and extrajudicial executions (1982), calls upon the churches to engage in extensive human rights education programmes with a view to improving public understanding of these atrocities, and urges member churches and their governments to cooperate with the UN and other governmental and non-governmental bodies in this regard.

8.3 We have been vividly reminded during this Assembly of the plight of indigenous people. Deprived of any real political power, they are often unable to resist the expropriation of their lands, their physical relocation and the denial of their right to maintain their cultural identity. In supporting the Central Committee statement on the "Land Rights of Indigenous People" (1982), we call upon the churches to identify with the struggle of the indigenous people, including the provision of financial and human resources; to cooperate with indigenous people's organizations, to urge their governments to ratify and implement all relevant UN instruments; to make determined efforts to settle outstanding land rights claims of indigenous people, including those involving churches; and to monitor implementation of such settlements to assure that governments respect the spirit as well as the letter of these laws.

8.4 The employment of a doctrine of national security to justify the denial of basic human rights has in recent years acquired a wider geographical application. While national security is a legitimate concern of all states, the churches must resist its perversion such as the ever-increasing militarization of society to preserve an unjust status quo or ensure the perpetuation of those in power thereby sanctioning a persistent and widening violation of human rights, including in some cases genocide.

8.5 In some areas, the growing climate of religious fanaticism and the rise of political fundamentalism have seriously threatened the rights of churches and other religious communities to manifest their faith in worship, observance, practice and teaching. While we welcome the long-awaited adoption of the UN Declaration on the Elimination of All Forms of Intolerance and Discrimination based on Religion or Belief, we fear that the Declaration does not offer sufficient protection against specific problems facing religious communities today. It is therefore imperative that member churches and the WCC continue to identify and denounce gross violations of religious freedom and extend moral and material assistance to those who suffer oppression and even persecution because of their religious beliefs and practices. Churches and church communities which suffer repression or even persecution because of their spiritual, cultural and ethnic identity or minority position should enjoy the solidarity of other churches particularly within their own nation, as an expression of their fellowship in the one body of Christ.

8.6 In many countries churches are called to take new and firm steps to support the right of workers to establish and join trade unions which genuinely represent their interests, and their freedom to cooperate actively with each other both within their nation and internationally.

8.7 Of growing concern to the ecumenical community is the present predicament of refugees throughout the world. A new dimension added to the existing suffering of refugees involves the difficulty they have had in availing themselves of effective protection. This new factor is due to the refusal by many governments to admit asylum-seekers across their boundaries and the imposition of visa requirements to curtail the flow of refugees; to arbitrary detentions and expulsions without due process of law; and to attacks on defenceless refugees by military and paramilitary forces. We appeal to the WCC and member churches to intensify their efforts at the national and international levels to ensure compliance of all refugee-receiving countries with international conventions and to identify and respond to situations that lead to the creation of refugees.

8.8 We express great concern for migrant workers who, in ever increasing numbers, face the prevailing problems of unemployment and deprivation of civil liberties in their own countries or in the countries of their adoption. We urge the World Council of Churches to encourage the churches in those countries to take positive action on their behalf.

Implementation

9. In the name of Jesus Christ, the life of the world, we reaffirm in fellowship our common commitment to work even more fervently for the elimination of all forms of inhumanity, brutality, discrimination, persecution and oppression, both within our own countries and situations and in ecumenical solidarity on a regional

and world level. As discrepancies inevitably exist between what we profess and what we practise, we must move beyond making declarations about human rights and duties to making more effective use of existing mechanisms and to devising, where necessary, new means for meeting this challenge.

9.1 In working for the implementation of human rights, we urge the World Council of Churches and its member churches to continue their practice of a pastoral approach, which combines prayer, preaching and practical efforts in action.

9.2 We appeal to the churches to dedicate themselves with renewed vigour to raising the consciousness of the people concerning their profound responsibility for the implementation of human rights and for the demonstration of their biblical foundation.

9.3 The churches and the ecumenical movement should strengthen their work of monitoring, advocacy and study in which they are already engaged.

9.4 Additional financial resources must be made available by the churches to carry out their own programmes in human rights and to cooperate ecumenically.

9.5 Considerable thought needs to be given to the development of new initiatives in order to improve the churches' record of implementation. Among the possible initiatives that might be undertaken are the announcement of an international day of prayer for human rights, the creation of a world action week for the education of church members and the promotion of human rights, and the establishment of a series of regional and global review conferences to evaluate the work done by the churches in the field of human rights.

9.6 We urge the continuation of the World Council of Churches' Human Rights Programme and recommend that the Human Rights Advisory Group, meeting regularly and with a more clearly focused mandate, should be maintained to assist the churches and the World Council of Churches in their promotion of human rights.

9.7 While recognizing that East-West tensions are only part of the tragic divisions of humanity, we welcome the work of the Churches' Human Rights Programme for the Implementation of the Helsinki Final Act, as a model of regional and inter-regional consultation and cooperation, complementing and strengthening initiatives at the world level.

10. We urgently appeal directly to all governments of the world to adopt and ratify intergovernmental instruments of human rights, to respect the rights included in these agreements and to promote by all means both in law and in practice their fuller realization in every country.

11. In the midst of a world of suffering and death, we are called

to witness to Jesus Christ, the life of the world. We affirm God's gift of life which is entrusted to our care and nurture, to be lived fully in unity with all those who share this precious gift and therefore in respect of the rule of law in defence of justice. It is life lived in Christ which unites us in prayer and active solidarity with all those whose lives are threatened by the forces of death in our world.

5.3   STATEMENT ON THE INTERNATIONAL FOOD DISORDER

On the recommendation of Policy Reference Committee II, the following statement was adopted by the Assembly.

1. The scandal of hunger calls for the immediate attention of the churches. Estimates are that at a minimum there are 400 million people in the world who do not receive adequate sustenance of food. Many die for lack of food; many more suffer from diseases and disabilities caused by insufficient or unbalanced diet. It is often children who are the victims of malnutrition and who are deprived of the possibility of fullness of life.

2. The World Council of Churches has for years responded to calls for emergency help in situations of drought and famine. At its Fifth Assembly in Nairobi, 1975, the WCC lifted up for the churches' attention the crises of famine and mass malnutrition and the questions related to policies of food production and distribution. The Assembly called for response to both "present-day hunger problems and to the difficult long-term solutions". The WCC Central Committee, meeting in 1980, again placed before the attention of the churches and the public the scandal of hunger, noting its belief that access to adequate nutrition is a fundamental human right.

3. There has been in recent years a significant increase in world food production but starvation and malnutrition are at a crisis level in many countries due to the inability of the rural and urban poor to produce or purchase food. The present international food disorder is rooted thus in mismanagement of food resources. The current misuse of natural resources also calls for attention to the problems which may arise in providing adequate food for future generations.

4. The present patterns of production and distribution of food have led to a serious disorder in the international food markets. Many countries of the South produce food which is often insufficient for a balanced diet for their people. They are therefore forced to buy from the world market and to depend on external food aid.

Much of their agricultural production is aimed at and therefore dependent on markets of the wealthier nations. The agricultural infrastructure, research and finance are often aimed at improving the production of crops for export, rather than producing food which can be consumed by the people of the producing countries. At the same time, industrialized countries are seeking to reduce production levels on their land so that prices for their crops will continue to rise.

5. Food has also been used in international affairs as a political weapon for bargaining among nations and within nations. Where persons or nations have been perceived to be unfriendly or strategically unimportant, food has often been denied. We emphasize that food must not be used as a political weapon. Every person has a fundamental and unconditional human right to adequate food. Furthermore, every nation has the right to self-determination and self-reliance, and under no circumstances should food supplies be used to control or limit that right.

6. The development of technologies of food production, which require the use of chemical inputs, has in certain instances hampered food production in the developing countries which have received chemicals banned as unfit for use in the industrially developed world. It is critical that the distribution of unsafe chemicals be halted and that education about the use of chemical substances be provided for farming communities.

7. The causes of the food disorder are also located within nations. In many countries, in both industrialized and developing nations, much of the productive land is controlled by large land-owners and transnational corporations who exploit the land and do not allow the farmers, peasants, and landless rural workers to participate in making decisions which would benefit them. As a result, small farmers are often forced off their land and reduced to poverty. In addition, efficient transportation and marketing of food for domestic consumption are often lacking. Within many countries both land reform and a reorientation of agricultural research, extension, infrastructure and marketing to serve the interests of peasant farmers are urgently needed if the growth of rural and urban malnutrition is to be halted and reversed.

8. Related to these concerns about the policies of food production and distribution is the effect of these policies on the natural resources of the earth. Natural calamities have been exacerbated by the mismanagement of resources. The problems which hamper food production today and which cause grave concern for the future include not only soil erosion, deforestation, drought, ineffective water conservation and irrigation systems, but also the under-utiliz-

ation of land and human resources, sometimes due to war and refugee crises. In addition, unequal land allocation and resettlement of refugees sometimes result in over-utilization of land, reducing its long-term potential.

9. The Sixth Assembly of the WCC, meeting in Vancouver, Canada, in 1983, has as its theme "Jesus Christ – the Life of the World". We believe that this theme calls us to respond urgently to the international food disorder.

10. The reality of hunger reminds us of the many biblical accounts which link one's response to Christ with a response to the hungry of the world. To feed or not to feed them is indeed to do likewise to Christ (Matt. 25:35, 42). Through the miracle of the feeding of the five thousand, Jesus showed his disciples that by his will there could be ample food to feed the hungry (John 6:1–14) and in this context he said "I am the bread of life" (John 6:35). During this Assembly we have celebrated the gift of life in its fullness, the eucharistic life to which Jesus calls his Church. The ecumenical text on "Baptism, Eucharist and Ministry" reminds us that "the eucharistic celebration demands reconciliation and sharing among all those regarded as brothers and sisters in the one family of God, and is a constant challenge in the search for appropriate relationships in social, economic and political life" (Eucharist, p. 14).

11. We believe that food is a gift from God which through human labour serves for the sustenance of life in its fullness. The ordinance of the jubilee year in Leviticus 25 reminds us that the life-sustaining resources of the world as gifts from God are to be distributed justly among all people and redistributed regularly to allow for self-reliance of all.

12. We are called to confess our failure. The fact that so many are hungry shows that we have failed to be faithful and responsible stewards of God's creation.

13. We call upon member churches to take action to redress the international food disorder by:

a) strengthening ecumenical structures for meeting emergency and short-term food needs;

b) building ecumenical support for long-term solutions to the problem of hunger through appropriate policies, including increased access to land and to work for rural and urban poor, husbanding and renewing of natural resources, greater self-reliance in basic food production and more equitable structures of international trade in agricultural products;

c) continuing educational programmes on the causes of hunger and the international food disorder;

d) monitoring policies of governments, international agencies and transnational corporations regarding food production, distribution and land reform;

e) developing programmes of advocacy and support for the participation of the poor in the production of food and in the distribution of food resources;

f) recognizing and encouraging specific programmes of international aid for agricultural research in support of the production of food for consumption by the people of the producing country;

g) engaging in more generous and effective sharing within congregations and communities, as well as nationally and internationally, of resources relevant to the provision of food and to the ability to produce it;

h) supporting efforts for peace and justice and human rights which will counteract the forces which divert resources from production and just distribution of food;

i) taking leadership in preparing for the future, working with the scientific community to ensure that the causes of the international food disorder will be addressed in any technological developments;

j) being advocates for communities and movements of farmers and landless rural workers;

k) denouncing current policies that the International Monetary Fund imposes on nations in debt, which result in the reduction of food available to the poor, thereby increasing malnutrition, hunger-related diseases and infant mortality;

l) investigating and taking action on the investments of church funds and use of church land so that they support agricultural and rural development in which people participate fully;

m) supporting churches and movements which are working to alleviate the effects and causes of hunger in various nations and communities throughout the world.

5.4 STATEMENT ON THE MIDDLE EAST

Mr Thompson, on behalf of Policy Reference Committee II, presented the text of a proposed statement on the situation in the Middle East. After a brief debate the statement was adopted.

1. The increasingly dangerous situation in the Middle East threatens the peace of the whole world and places heavy demands on all those striving for justice and freedom.

The Middle East is a region of special interest as the birthplace of three monotheistic religions. The churches in the area have their roots from apostolic times. Their continued presence and active participation in the life of the whole area, despite suffering at various periods, is a remarkable witness to the faith. They are facing new challenges and attempting to respond through new forms of witness. While only the churches of the Middle East can determine the nature and forms of their witness, it behoves all churches to strengthen their presence and support their ministry, especially the ministry of reconciliation and witness for peace. Historical factors and certain theological interpretations have often confused Christians outside in evaluating the religious and political developments in the Middle East.

2. Recent developments in the region have further pushed back prospects for peace. The agony of the Lebanese war is not yet over. The integrity and independence of Lebanon are in greater danger than ever. The Israeli settlement policy on the West Bank has resulted in a *de facto* annexation, giving final touches to a discriminatory policy of development of peoples that flagrantly violates the basic rights of the Palestinian people. There are fears of relocation of the inhabitants on the West Bank and their expulsion. A large number of Palestinians are under detention in the prisons on the West Bank and in camps in Lebanon. There is escalation of tension in the occupied territories. The consensus among the Arab nations appears to have been lost. External and internal pressures have caused serious rift within the Palestinian movement. In many situations there are increasing violations of human rights, especially of minorities, and religious fanaticism is a bane of many communities. The Iran-Iraqi war continues to claim an increasing toll of lives and complicates inter-Arab relations. Tension is increasing in relation to Cyprus.

3. The Israeli-Palestinian conflict

(i) We reaffirm the principles previously enunciated by the WCC as the basis on which a peaceful settlement can be reached. The UN Security Council Resolution 242 and all other relevant UN resolutions need to be revised and implemented, taking into account changes that have occurred since 1967, and such revisions should express the following principles in a manner that would ensure:

.a) the withdrawal of Israeli troops from all territories occupied in 1967;

b) the right of all states, including Israel and Arab states, to live in peace with secure and recognized boundaries;

c) the implementation of the rights of the Palestinians to self-determination, including the right of establishing a sovereign Palestinian state.

(ii) We reaffirm that the Middle East conflict cannot be resolved through the use of force but only through peaceful means. Negotiations for a comprehensive settlement in the Middle East should include all those parties most intimately involved: the state of Israel, the Palestine Liberation Organization and neighbouring Arab states. The interests of the world at large are best represented through the United Nations, and the USA and the USSR have a special responsibility in this matter.

(iii) Churches should undertake the following with a view to facilitating processes towards negotiations:

a) to build greater awareness among the churches about the urgency and justice of the Palestinian cause. In this connection active support should be extended to the UN International Conference on the Question of Palestine to be held at the end of August 1983 in Geneva. The churches should bring to bear their influence on states to participate in it;

b) to encourage the dialogue between Palestinians and Israelis with a view to furthering mutual understanding and enabling recognition;

c) to remind Christians in the Western world to recognize that their guilt over the fate of Jews in their countries may have influenced their views of the conflict in the Middle East and has often led to uncritical support of the policies of the state of Israel, thereby ignoring the plight of the Palestinian people and their rights. In this context we welcome the more open and critical stance adopted by Christian churches in the traditional Jewish-Christian dialogue, but we also urge the broadening of the dialogue to include larger segments of both Christian and Jewish communities;

d) to support movements within Israel, which are working for peace and reconciliation.

4. Lebanon

The ecumenical community shares the agony of the peoples in Lebanon who have been tragically suffering over the last nine years and who have been carrying too large a burden of the problems of the region.

(i) We reiterate that the recovery of Lebanese territorial integrity and sovereignty is a key to peace and justice in the region and that for this to be realized all foreign forces must be withdrawn from Lebanese territory.

(ii) We appeal to the ecumenical community:

a) to support the efforts of the Lebanese government to reassert the effective exercise of its sovereignty over all Lebanese territory and to support full independence and unity of the Lebanese people;
b) to assist the churches within Lebanon in their attempts with leaders of the religious communities for reconciliation, with a view to achieving harmony and unity among all communities in the country;
c) to continue to support generously the Middle East Council of Churches and the churches in Lebanon in their humanitarian and social programmes of relief for all in Lebanon;
d) to collaborate with the churches in the area in their contribution to the promotion of justice, dignity, freedom and human rights for all in Lebanon.

5. Jerusalem

(i) We reaffirm that "Jerusalem is a Holy City for three mono-theistic religions: Judaism, Christianity and Islam. The tendency to minimize Jerusalem's importance for any of these three religions should be avoided" (WCC Fifth Assembly, Nairobi 1975). The WCC should implement the proposal of the WCC Central Committee (August 1980) that dialogue be initiated with Jews and Muslims so that members of the three religions can understand each other's deep religious attachment to Jersualem and so that together they can contribute towards political processes that would lead to a mutually acceptable agreement for sharing the city. The churches should give priority to this while continuing efforts to secure a general settlement of the Middle East conflicts. The special legislation known as the *Status Quo* of the Holy Places must be safeguarded and confirmed in any agreement concerning Jerusalem.

(ii)
a) We call the attention of the churches to the need for:
– actions which will ensure a continuing indigenous Christian presence and witness in Jerusalem;
– wider ecumenical awareness of the plight of the indigenous Muslim and Christian communities suffering from the repressive actions of the occupying power in East Jerusalem and other occupied territories.
b) We call upon all churches to express their common concern that although Israeli law guarantees free access for members of all religious traditions rooted in Jerusalem to their holy places, the state of war between Israel and Arab states, the political reality created by the Israeli annexation of East Jerusalem and continuing occupation of the West Bank means that Arab Muslims and

Christians continue to experience serious difficulties and are often prevented from visiting the Holy City.

6. We uphold the churches in the Middle East in our intercessions as they respond to the new challenges in the difficult circumstances through their witness in the service of Christ. We assure them of the solidarity of the community of faith around the world as we have gathered together here in the name of Jesus Christ, the Life of the World. We pray for the healing of the wounds in the nations of that region.

We stand together with other religious communities in a spirit of servanthood seeking to be faithful in our common calling to be peace-makers and reconcilers and to bring hope for all.

5.5 STATEMENT ON SOUTHERN AFRICA

A proposed statement on Southern Africa was presented by Mr William P. Thompson, in his capacity as Moderator of Policy Reference Committee II.

The General Secretary of the South African Council of Churches, Bishop Desmond Tutu, asked for a clear statement that the loving care of the Church embraces whites in his country as well as blacks. "The WCC is not anti-South African," he said, "it is anti-injustice." Mr Bena-Silu, Kimbanguist from Zaire, thought the churches should challenge more energetically the arguments from history that are used to bolster apartheid, and Ms Birgit Weinbrenner (EKD, Federal Republic of Germany) wanted a stronger call to the churches for action. Mr Stig Utnem (Church of Norway) proposed that a recommendation regarding sanctions should include specific reference to the major oil-exporting nations.

The Assembly acted on the document in two stages. First, the statement with the exception of recommendation (1) regarding economic disengagement and sanctions was put to the vote and adopted. Recommendation (1) was then voted on separately and adopted.

I. Preamble

1. Institutionalized racism in South Africa continues to be the central problem of justice and peace in the region, although there are several other situations in which human rights are infringed. We recall that in Nairobi (1975) the Assembly of the World Council of Churches declared that "racism is a sin against God and against fellow human beings. It is contrary to the justice and the love of God revealed in Jesus Christ. It destroys the human dignity of both the racist and the victim." We would wish to add that it is a denial

of the fullness of life which is Christ's gift to the world, for in him there is neither Greek nor Jew, there is neither slave nor free, there is neither male nor female, but all are one. Christ on his cross tore down the barriers of hostility which keep people apart (Eph. 2:14–16), thus establishing peace.

2. Apartheid raises barriers and denies the fullness of life in Christ. Christians and the churches are called in obedience to Jesus Christ the life of the world, and to maintain the integrity of the Church, to oppose apartheid in all its forms, to support those who struggle against this sinful system of injustice, and to denounce any theological justification of apartheid as a heretical perversion of the Gospel.

II. South Africa

3. The apartheid system perpetuates white minority rule at the cost of enormous suffering. Widespread and flagrant violations continue to be an everyday part of South African life. Restriction of movement, arbitrary arrests, detention without trial, torture and death have become an institutionalized way of intimidating black people and their supporters. Although a number of banning orders have recently been lifted, several people, including some leading Christians, continue to suffer from arbitrary banning orders.

4. Furthermore, large numbers of people are experiencing ongoing forced removals and relocation in resettlement camps, often in conditions of destitution, and violent government efforts to eliminate so-called "black spots" such as Driefontein as well as urban squatter areas such as Crossroads. The cost of these policies in terms of human suffering, the break-up of family life and the creation of bitterness and despair is immense, and creates an extremely explosive climate.

5. In such a context a church which seeks to be the Church and to proclaim the liberating Gospel and the divine demand for justice cannot avoid a confrontation with the government. The Church did not seek a confrontation; it prayed that it would not happen. It continues to strive to be faithful to its own calling as it summons the state to fulfill the mandate which has been given to it by God.

6. In confessing the faith it is impossible in South Africa not to call for a fundamental change in the political, social and economic order of the country, not to speak for the oppressed and defend the rights and human dignity of the powerless. As the South African Council of Churches (SACC) has said, such a confession is "a cry from the heart, something we are obliged to do for the sake of the Gospel". As a consequence of the life and witness of the Christians and the churches, there is unrelenting pressure on them and the

SACC, most recently shown in the activities of the Eloff Commission which appears to be an effort to muzzle and destroy the SACC.
7. Bantustan rule is in many instances as oppressive and arbitrary as that of white rule in the area, and has resulted in the proscription of churches and the systematic persecution of people. The willingness of some black leaders to accept this form of "independence" furthermore threatens to become the single most divisive and potent force militating against black solidarity and liberation in South Africa.
8. This Bantustan policy whereby blacks are being deprived of any kind of citizenship rights in other parts of South Africa and allocated to a variety of nominally independent "tribal home-lands", has been followed by further constitutional proposals affecting Asians and "coloureds". According to these, Asians and "coloureds" would have specifically limited representation in a multicameral South African legislature with Asians and "coloured" ministers of state being appointed. It is necessary to indicate, however, that these proposals do not involve any sharing of political power. This will remain securely in white hands as constitutionally entrenched. These proposals are inherently racist and emphasize separation between the races rather than integration, and underscore the fact that blacks continue to be excluded entirely from the political process. In effect, these proposals, like the Bantustan policy, reaffirm the racist principles of apartheid.

III. Namibia
9. The remarkable courage of the Council of Churches in Namibia (CCN) in witnessing to Jesus Christ the life of the world, by standing with the oppressed, defending human rights and dignity and pressing for freedom and independence deserves wide recognition. The illegal South African occupation of the country is oppressive and generates many acts of terror against civilians. We endorse the open letter to the South African Prime Minister in January 1983 in which the Executive Committee of the CCN wrote:

> With no regard to the rights or the will of the people of Namibia, your Administrators-General continue a regime of draconian laws, proclamations and amendments which have destructive effects upon the people. We condemn the existence of all those laws that allow for the detention of people without recourse to a court of law, and call upon your government to charge or release all those who are detained under the so-called "security laws", including the survivors of Carsinga who are kept in a detention camp near Mariental. Further suffering and death are caused by curfews, conscription for military service and by brutal and unprovoked attacks on innocent people. Deportations,

the refusal of passports and visas and the stifling of the true situation through bannings, also arouse our strong condemnation.

10. Negotiations for independence are stalled owing to obstruction by the South African government and its relentless refusal to recognize SWAPO as the legitimate representative of the Namibian people. This, together with the lethargy and apparently ineffectual influence of the Western Contact Group, motivated by short-term political and economic interests, only contributes to the prevailing conflict. Such a situation emphasizes the need for the Western Contact Group either to bring the South African government to the negotiation table or to disband. The insistence on linking the withdrawal of Cuban troops from Angola to Namibian independence is "an irrelevance" as was pointed out by the CCN. "The Cuban presence in the Sovereign State of Angola", CCN stated, "is not a threat to the Namibian people." Absolute priority must be given to both the termination of the illegal South African occupation of Namibia and to Namibian independence in accordance with United Nations Resolution 435.

IV. Destabilization

11. During the last decade South Africa, with the active collaboration of major Western powers and Israel, has been engaged in a massive military build-up which now includes nuclear weapons capability. This dangerous development poses a major threat to the peace and stability of the region. President Reagan's policy of "constructive engagement" and the recent loan of US$1.25 billion to South Africa on very favourable terms by the International Monetary Fund are widely interpreted as signs of increased outside support for the South African regime which is pursuing a concerted policy of an "undeclared war against its neighbours" through destabilization and aggression.

12. A large area of Angola has been under South African occupation since 1981 and there have been numerous incursions deep into Angolan territory resulting in considerable loss of life. Subversive and military attacks have taken place in Mozambique and Lesotho and there is clear evidence of attempts at destabilization in Zimbabwe. This process of destabilization is clearly intended to perpetuate white dominance in the region.

V. Recommendations

13. The WCC Assembly, meeting in Vancouver, Canada, 24 July–10 August 1983:
a) *reiterates* its conviction that apartheid stands condemned by the

Gospel of Jesus Christ the life of the world, and that any theology which supports or condones it is heretical;

b) *expresses* its admiration and support for the prophetic and courageous stand for human dignity, justice and liberation taken by the South African Council of Churches and the Council of Churches in Namibia;

c) *calls* on the member churches to intensify their witness against apartheid and the continuing oppression in South Africa and Namibia, and to deepen their solidarity with those forces – including the liberation movements recognized by the UN – which oppose apartheid and racism, and struggle for liberation;

d) *assures* the white people of South Africa that its opposition is to apartheid as a system and that it loves them as brothers and sisters made in the image of God and prays that they may seek an end to apartheid and work for the establishment of a just and caring society;

e) *condemns* Bantustan "independence" as a divisive and destructive force militating against black solidarity and liberation in South Africa;

f) *condemns* the new constitutional proposals in South Africa as fraudulent and racist because they do not provide for the real sharing of power and exclude blacks entirely from the political process;

g) *commends* the South African Council of Churches for rejecting the new constitutional proposals and *draws* the attention of the member churches to the full implications of the racist and divisive character of this proposed legislation;

h) recognizing the necessity for a society of justice in this subcontinent and reaffirming its abhorrence of all forms of violence, *urges* the member churches to do all in their power to promote freedom of association, equality, democratic rights and the dismantling of apartheid as the essential ingredients of a political climate in which a national convention can be held;

i) *calls for* the independence of Namibia by the immediate implementation of UN Resolution 435 and *requests* the churches in the countries of the western contact group to intensify pressure on their governments to give urgent and effective support;

j) *further deplores and condemns* attacks on neighbouring countries and efforts at destabilization by the South African government;

k) in view of the increasing number of refugees from this region, *calls upon* the member churches to use all appropriate means to render assistance to the people and also to work through existing refugee programmes;

l) *renews* its call to member churches to a disengagement from those institutions economically engaged in South Africa; *affirms* the need for mandatory and comprehensive sanctions and further *urges* governments which, through their fleets, are involved in transporting oil to South Africa, to take immediate steps, unilaterally or in cooperation with others, to bring an effective halt to the fuelling of apartheid;

m) *calls on* churches and Christian people throughout the world to express their support for and fellowship with the oppressed people of South Africa in prayer and every other appropriate way;

n) *calls on* member churches to discourage their people from emigrating to South Africa; and

o) *supports* the ongoing process of consultation and solidarity among the churches in Africa, in cooperation with the All Africa Conference of Churches, in their witness and struggle for liberation against apartheid and its consequences.

5.6 STATEMENT ON CENTRAL AMERICA

The Vancouver Assembly convened at a time of tensions in Central America. Press reports indicated that units of the United States navy had begun manoeuvres in the area. A vessel had been stopped on the high seas and its captain questioned about his cargo and destination. Official statements by the US administration sounded increasingly militant. Concern ran high about current and possible future developments in the region.

Early in the Assembly, the WCC's Moderator and General Secretary cabled the UN Secretary General as follows:

> *Participants in the Sixth Assembly of the World Council of Churches meeting in Vancouver, BC, Canada, have in various ways expressed deep concern about the recent escalation of threats to use massive armed force against Nicaragua. As Officers of the WCC we wish to acknowledge your efforts to resolve peacefully the Central American conflict. We urge you to renew those efforts, using your good offices to further the process of negotiation, to bring about the withdrawal of foreign military forces from the region, and to ensure the sovereignty of Nicaragua and the inviolability of its national borders. Be assured of our prayers and our readiness to support your efforts in every way available to us.*

There were intensive discussions involving the representatives of churches in the USA and Central America. These culminated, on 5 August, in the endorsement of a "Covenant of Life" by more than 300 participants from the US, Nicaragua, Guatemala, El Salvador, Costa Rica, Puerto Rico and Mexico. Congregating on the university's soccer field, they signed the two-page covenant as part of a brief service of commitment to solidarity and unity. The document committed its signers to unite in prayer and fellowship for study and "educational and political actions to reverse the US policy in Central America", to serve as "agents of justice and reconciliation" and to promote a "process of peaceful negotiation" respecting the rights of all peoples.

Hence a good deal had been done to hammer out a common mind by the time a draft statement reached the Assembly from Policy Reference Committee II. Debate was brief. An amendment that would have deleted explicit reference to military intervention by the United States was defeated. The need to rephrase a sentence about Guatemala, in the light of a coup d'etat there the day before, was accepted.

The statement was adopted.

1. Promising signs of life are appearing within Central America. They are like a young plant striving to rise from the earth, yearning to grow and to be a blessing for the world. Thus, Jesus Christ, the life of the world, teaches us, his disciples, that life must be nourished and defended against the powers of death and of oppression which oppose it.

> God remembers those who suffer;
> He does not forget their cry,
> And he punishes those who wrong them.

> The needy will not always be neglected;
> The hope of the poor will not be crushed for ever.
> (Ps. 9:12,18)

2. Central America is caught up in an agonizing struggle to recast the foundations of its peoples' life. The struggle of life confronting death is a daily one. The depth of this struggle – political, economic, ideological, social, cultural, spiritual – is of historic proportions. Grounded in a common history of harsh colonialism, of exploitation of the poor and of the concentration of power and wealth, countries in the region are, in different ways, under siege.

3. The current United States administration, acting on its perception of the nation's security, has adopted a policy of military, economic, financial and political initiatives designed to destabilize the Nicaraguan government, renew international support for Guatemala's violent military regimes, resist the forces of historic change in El Salvador, and militarize Honduras in order to insure a base from which to contain the aspirations of the Central American peoples. This policy is publicly articulated as a framework within which objectives of peace, reform, economic development and democracy

can be achieved and communism and "export of revolution" prevented.

4. Indeed the opposite prevails: fear and tensions are heightened; scarce resources needed to meet basic human needs are diverted; the chances of war, potentially devastating to Central America and the Caribbean, escalate; and, in the long term, the legitimate interests and security of the nations and peoples of the American hemisphere are threatened. There can be no security in the region without fidelity to the persistent, yearning struggle of the Central American peoples for peace with justice.

5. International price declines in the region's key export crops have severely strained the region's economies, further exacerbating political, economic and social tensions. Adding to these economic problems, the United States administration has successfully harnessed international financial institutions to its Central American strategy.

6. In this context, the churches, endeavouring to respond to the needs of the region's suffering population, are also having to face the divisive effects of an aggressive new wave of mainly US-based and financed religious groups. They are a source of great concern to the churches, particularly as these groups appear, in the churches' analysis, to be used for political purposes in legitimizing policies of repression.

7. Guatemala in the past year has witnessed massacres of civilian non-combatant populations, a large number of extrajudicial executions and the extermination of thousands of people among the Indian population in ways which defy belief. Despite the magnitude of economic, political and military resources provided to the regime by the United States, the El Salvadoran government has demonstrated an inability to curb human rights violations and implement needed reform. The Legal Aid Christian Service, of the Roman Catholic Archdiocese of San Salvador, reports a number of over 2,000 civilians and non-combatants who have been executed outside the law during the period running from January to April of this year, by members of the armed forces, by paramilitary organizations and by death squads, for political reasons. The policies of the Honduran government threaten the territorial sovereignty of Nicaragua and cause considerable harassment to refugees from El Salvador. Churches report severe human rights violations committed by intelligence and security forces. Other countries – such as Belize, Costa Rica and Panama – have been the object of pressures brought to bear upon them so as to affect events within Guatemala, El Salvador, Honduras and Nicaragua.

8. Refugees, displaced persons and divided families are a powerful

testimony to the bloodshed and terror perpetrated on the poorest of the region's people. Approximately 500,000 human beings have been forced to flee their country and one million more have been displaced from their homes in Guatemala alone. El Salvadoran refugees in Honduras and Guatemalan refugees in southern Mexico continue to be vulnerable to incursions by military forces into camps.

9. In the context of the theme of the Sixth Assembly, "Jesus Christ – the Life of the World", and given the escalation of aggressive acts against Nicaragua, we lift up our concern for the people of the entire region by drawing attention to the life-affirming achievements of the Nicaraguan people and its leadership since 1979. Noteworthy was the decision of the government to abolish the death penalty and to release several thousand members of Somoza's National Guard. In addition, an internationally-acclaimed literacy programme, the eradication of poliomyelitis and reduction of malaria, an effective land reform scheme and significant progress in constitutional development, preparatory to holding elections in 1985, have helped to give concrete expression to the region's aspirations. The government has demonstrated its openness in acknowledging the inappropriateness of some policies related to the Miskito Indian and other ethnic groups of the Atlantic Coast, and is moving towards reconciliation. It is also important to note that the Nicaraguan process has involved the full participation of Christians, both Roman Catholic and Protestant, at every level of reconstruction and nation-building.

10. This life-affirming process is having to confront death on a daily basis. The United States-financed former National Guard, now based in Honduras, have thus far claimed 700 lives, mainly Nicaraguan young people who are members of the volunteer militia. Tensions with Honduras have escalated dangerously. Nicaragua's call for bilateral talks with Honduras has failed. In the interests of peace, Nicaragua has now indicated its willingness to enter multilateral talks. However, United States support for the former National Guardsmen continues and the Reagan administration, pleading peace and dialogue, takes steps to assemble weaponry and support troops in Honduras and to deploy naval vessels off both Nicaraguan coasts.

11. Nicaragua's destabilization is an affront to life and is fully capable of plunging not only the countries of Central America but also those of the Caribbean into deeper suffering and widespread loss of life. It undercuts the legitimate call and struggle of the poor throughout the region for an end to exploitation and for an opportunity to determine their own path on the difficult pilgrimage of those who seek to enjoy life in all its fullness.

12. The Sixth Assembly affirms the right of the Central American peoples to seek and to nourish life in all its dimensions. It therefore:

i)   *expresses* to the Central American churches the profound concern and solidarity of the worldwide ecumenical community, as Christian sisters and brothers experience and respond to the critical threats to life, reiterating its strong commitment to the churches' witness, ministries and presence. It commends the Nicaraguan Christian community for its active participation in the building up of national institutions and reconciliatory processes leading to peace with justice;

ii) vigorously *opposes* any type of military intervention by the United States, covert or overt, or by any other government, in the Central American region. The Assembly commends the churches in the United States for their prophetic expressions of the condemnation of such intervention, and calls upon them to intensify their efforts to press for a radical change of US policy in the region. It urges member churches in other countries to make strong representations to their governments so as to press the United States administration to reverse its military policies, as a positive step towards the building of peace in the region;

iii) *calls upon* the new government of Guatemala to reverse the policies of repression by which large numbers of its population have been exterminated and to take immediate steps to restore respect for human rights;

iv) *urges* the government of El Salvador to enter into a fruitful process of dialogue with representatives of its political and military opposition, so as to bring long-lasting peace to the country;

v)   *calls upon* the churches and the ecumenical community to throw their full weight into supporting peace initiatives, such as that of the "Contadora" group of Latin American states;

vi) *encourages* the churches in Central America to redouble their efforts to gather and communicate, to the worldwide ecumenical community and other international constituencies, information on the developing critical situation affecting the region, as long as it is necessary;

vii) *affirms* and *encourages* the process of reconciliation among Nicaraguan minorities and the Spanish-speaking majority and *urges* the Nicaraguan government to maintain its openness and commitment to increasing the sensitivity of its policy and practice in this area.

5.7 RESOLUTION ON AFGHANISTAN

A resolution on Afghanistan was presented by the Moderator of Policy Reference Committee II. Mr Thompson explained that the proposed wording was intended to support efforts by the UN Secretary General to find a formula for ending the conflict.

Bishop Gunnar Lislerod (Church of Norway), Rev. Giorgio Bouchard (Waldensian, Italy) and Rev. Guy Deschamps (United Church of Canada) found the document insufficiently critical of the USSR. Bishop Alexander Malik (Church of Pakistan), calling for a condemnation of Soviet aggression and the unconditional withdrawal of Soviet troops, moved that the document be sent back to the committee for reworking. After the Assembly declined to send it back, Bishop David Preus (Lutheran, USA) proposed amendments that would have emphasized the withdrawal of Soviet troops as the first condition to be met and deleted reference to ending the supply of arms to opposition groups. Archbishop Kirill, of the Russian Orthodox Church, urged the Assembly against making changes that would only be used for propaganda purposes. What mattered, he said, was resolving the conflict for the sake of the people of Afghanistan, and the committee's text pointed to the most promising way of doing that. The amendment was defeated. Dr Jean Woolfolk (Disciples, USA) suggested, and the committee agreed, that the wording should be reordered in order to make it clearer that the formulation of conditions in the document was in support of a United Nations initiative.

The resolution was adopted.

The Sixth Assembly recalls the concern regarding the Afghan situation expressed in earlier statements by the World Council of Churches.

We note that the continuing fighting there has led to tremendous suffering for vast sections of the population, many of whom have become refugees. The UN estimates that there are more than three million Afghan refugees in Pakistan and Iran.

We note initiatives, including that of the non-aligned movement, for peaceful resolution of the conflict. We welcome specially the initiatives taken by the Secretary General of the United Nations for resolving the conflict, summarized as follows:

- an end to the supply of arms to the opposition groups from outside;
- creation of a favourable climate for the return of the refugees;
- guarantee of the settlement by the USSR, the USA, People's Republic of China, and Pakistan;
- withdrawal of Soviet troops from Afghanistan in the context

of an overall political settlement, including agreement between Afghanistan and the USSR.

We support the Secretary General's current efforts and hope that the negotiations among the parties concerned will lead to a comprehensive settlement.

We believe that this would enable the Afghan people to follow freely their own path of development and to progress towards a more just society. We also believe that such an agreement would reduce tension in the region and also contribute to improvement of relations between the USA and USSR and of international relations in general.

Meanwhile, the WCC should continue to provide humanitarian assistance to the Afghan refugees.

5.8 RESOLUTION ON CYPRUS

After rejecting an amendment that would have included reference to Turkish violation of the independence, sovereignty and territorial integrity of Cyprus, the Assembly adopted the following resolution proposed by Policy Reference Committee II.

The Sixth Assembly recalls the statements and actions of the World Council of Churches since 1974 related to the situation in Cyprus created by the military intervention by Turkish forces. The Assembly is deeply concerned about the lack of progress towards a peaceful and just solution of the question of Cyprus.

The Assembly reaffirms the calls already made by the World Council of Churches:

– for immediate implementation of all relevant United Nations resolutions on Cyprus;
– for immediate resumption in a meaningful and constructive manner of the negotiations between the representatives of the Greek Cypriot and Turkish Cypriot communities under the auspices of the Secretary General of the United Nations, to be conducted freely and on the basis of equality, with a view to reaching a mutually acceptable agreement ensuring their fundamental and legitimate rights;
– for due respect for religious and sacred places.

The Assembly asks the General Secretary of the World Council of Churches and its Commission of the Churches on International Affairs to pursue further the question of missing Cypriots, in cooperation with member churches especially in Western Europe and North America, and with appropriate intergovernmental and international bodies.

5.9 RESOLUTION ON THE PACIFIC

From its venue on the edge of the Pacific basin, the Sixth Assembly had good reason to pay special heed to the voice of the region's island churches. A plenary presentation on the Pacific, organized by them, articulated the main concerns.

Later, the Assembly learned that delegates of the French churches had made a public statement asking the Pacific peoples "for forgiveness for France's continued use of your ocean as a testing area for nuclear weapons", and pledging their solidarity with the campaign to make the Pacific a nuclear-free zone.

With minor amendments, the Assembly adopted a resolution proposed by Policy Reference Committee II.

The WCC Sixth Assembly has heard the personal and collective testimonies emanating from the inspiring life and witness of Christians and churches in the South Pacific. We give thanks to God for this witness, and express our solidarity with the pastoral and prophetic roles which the churches of the Pacific and the Pacific Conference of Churches have been playing with regard to a number of urgent problems affecting the present and future Pacific societies:

- the continued nuclear weapons testing in French Polynesia, the effects of radiation on the health and environment of present and future generations in the Marshall Islands;
- dumping of nuclear wastes by outside powers;
- military, notably naval, manoeuvres undertaken by the great powers, which include nuclear-weapons carrying submarines, and which reinforce the militarization of the region;
- threats to the indigenous Pacific cultural identities through colonial and neo-colonial structures involving transnational corporations, foreign media and tourism;
- persistence of foreign domination in French Polynesia and Micronesia;
- the as yet unresolved problem of the self-determination and independence of the Melanesian people of New Caledonia.

The Assembly urges the member churches to strengthen their support for and solidarity with the Christians and churches of the Pacific in their struggles for political and economic independence and for a nuclear-free Pacific, by concrete educational and advocacy activities, combined with a pastoral approach involving prayers and intercession. It is recommended that the WCC programmes involving the Pacific be intensified.

5.10 RESOLUTION ON THE RIGHTS OF THE ABORIGINAL PEOPLES OF CANADA

Delegates had many opportunities to hear the voices of Canada's Aboriginal peoples and to learn of the support given to them by the Canadian churches. As a result of that listening and learning, the Assembly adopted without amendment the following resolution.

The World Council of Churches' Central Committee (August 1982) has called upon the member churches "to listen to and learn from indigenous people in order to deepen Christian understanding of (and solidarity with) their legal rights, their political situation, their cultural achievements and aspirations, and their spiritual convictions." At this Sixth Assembly in Vancouver, BC, Canada, we have been privileged to hear personal testimonies from and to share experiences with Aboriginal peoples of Canada. We give thanks to God for this witness and for the consistent support of the Canadian churches for these peoples' struggles to:
- gain recognition within Canada as distinct peoples uniquely attached to their traditional lands; and
- assert and gain respect for their human rights, including especially their fundamental rights to their land.

The Assembly expresses its solidarity with those struggles and, in the light of the First Ministers Conference on the Canadian Constitution on Aboriginal rights, title and treaty rights, urges the Federal and Provincial Governments of Canada to recognize and enact Aboriginal title, Aboriginal rights and treaty rights in the Canadian Constitution in a manner and form acceptable to the Aboriginal peoples themselves. We further urge these governments to make no amendment or alteration to Aboriginal and treaty rights without the consent of the affected peoples.

The Assembly appeals to the member churches to support the Aboriginal peoples of Canada and the Canadian churches as they seek to achieve these ends; and requests the General Secretary to communicate this resolution to the appropriate governments and the Working Group on Indigenous Populations of the United Nations Commission on Human Rights.

5.11 MINUTES ON PUBLIC ISSUES
OF CONTINUING CONCERN TO THE WCC

Policy Reference Committee II reported that it had received from the Business Committee requests from several member churches regarding concerns arising in their own situations. Most of these would be dealt with in the normal way by the General Secretariat, one or another of the Programme Sub-units, the Central Committee or the Executive Committee.

Speaking to a point of order, the General Secretary explained how the World Council responds to appeals received from bodies other than the member churches. On receiving such appeals, the member churches are contacted, and when there are well-founded documents, appropriate approaches are made to state authorities.

The Policy Reference Committee recommended that the Assembly adopt minutes on the following due to recent changes in circumstances or the particularly pressing issues they present. The proposed minutes would recognize the continuing work being done in these areas by the WCC and provide guidance for future actions.

With minor changes, the minutes as proposed were adopted.

Minute on the Armenian genocide

1. During this Assembly's discussion of violations of human rights our attention has been drawn to the historical reality and present threat of genocide to some peoples. Far too often these occurrences are passed over in silence. In certain current instances this is being used by groups to justify wholly unacceptable acts of violence.

2. In this context we have been reminded once again of the tragic massacre of one-and-a-half million Armenians in Turkey and the deportation of another half million from this historic homeland at the beginning of this century. The silence of the world community and the deliberate efforts to deny even historical facts have been consistent sources of anguish and growing despair to the Armenian people, the Armenian churches and many others.

3. The Commission of the Churches on International Affairs of the World Council of Churches has raised this concern in the United Nations Commission on Human Rights with reference to the latter's study of the Question of Prevention and Punishment of the Crime of Genocide.

4. The Assembly requests the General Secretary to provide information to the churches on this, and to continue to pursue the matter in appropriate contexts. Public recognition of those events is essential in order that they do not continue to engender violent acts

of retribution, and that through remembering the history of the Armenian people other peoples might be spared a similar fate.

Minute on the United States military bases in the Philippines

1. In its discussion on peace and justice, the Assembly has drawn attention to the misuse of the concept of national security to justify repression and foreign intervention in denial of the sovereignty and legitimate security interests of other peoples. It has called for a halt to the rapidly growing deployment of nuclear weapons and support systems in the Indian and Pacific Oceans.

2. Our attention has been drawn to the negative effects of the continuation of US military bases in the Philippines. The presence of these foreign conventional and nuclear forces poses threats to the sovereignty, security and human rights of the Filipino people. These threats have been frequently discussed in WCC consultations since the last Assembly and detailed information about them has been provided to the churches.

3. The Assembly requests the General Secretary, particularly through the CCIA, to keep this concern under constant review, and to recommend to the churches appropriate actions in support of the churches in the Philippines and the efforts of the Filipino people for the withdrawal of the bases, and in their continuing struggles for human rights and against the militarization of their society. The WCC should also support the US churches in their efforts for changes in the policies of the USA as they affect the Philippines.

Minute on the situation in Sri Lanka

1. During the first week of the Assembly, we received the news about the violence in Sri Lanka which resulted in the death of many and which made thousands homeless. The Officers of the Council sent cables to the President of Sri Lanka and the churches there expressing profound concern. They assured the churches and all the people of Sri Lanka of the prayers of the Assembly.

2. There have been earlier actions by the WCC protesting against the Prevention of Terrorism Act and other legislative enactments and criticizing the violation of human rights in Sri Lanka.

3. The WCC has now received first-hand information on the situation there. The Assembly commends the churches in Sri Lanka for their praise-worthy efforts in relief and rehabilitation and for their ministry of reconciliation under difficult circumstances.

4. It asks the General Secretary:

a) to intensify the efforts through CICARWS to assist the churches in their programmes of relief and rehabilitation;

b) to give priority through the programmes of PCR and CCIA to

the underlying racial conflicts and the violation of human rights especially as they affect the Tamil community, and to assist processes that will lead to a cessation of the violence and to a political settlement;
c) to provide information and analysis of the situation in Sri Lanka to member churches.

Minute on the situation in Lesotho

1. In the recent period there has been a disturbing increase in the violation of human rights in Lesotho, with arbitrary arrests, detentions, torture and even political killings.

2. Responding to the demands of the Gospel, the Lesotho Evangelical Church has witnessed boldly in defence of justice and human rights for all people in the country. This has created considerable difficulties for the church, and many of its members had to pay a heavy price for their service to God and people.

3. The Assembly requests the General Secretary to extend all possible support to the Lesotho Evangelical Church in its ministry especially in the area of human rights and to disseminate information among member churches on the situation there.

APPENDICES

NEW WCC CENTRAL COMMITTEE OFFICERS: *Rev. Dr Heinz J. Held, FRG, Moderator; Dr Sylvia Talbot, USA, Vice-Moderator; and Metropolitan Chrysostomos of Myra, Ecumenical Patriarchate, Vice-Moderator*

NEW WCC PRESIDENTS

Dr Marga Bührig
Switzerland

Most Rev. W. P. K.
Makhulu, Botswana

Dame R. Nita
Barrow, Barbados

Very Rev. Dr Lois M.
Wilson, Canada

Metropolitan Paulos
Mar Gregorios, India

Patriarch Ignatios IV
Syria

Bishop Johannes
Hempel, FRG

Rev. Dr W. A. Visser 't Hooft
Honorary President

I. ASSEMBLY PROGRAMME

Sunday, 24 July
9.30	Opening worship
14.45	Public celebration, Pacific Coliseum

Monday, 25 July
8.15– 8.45	Worship
9.00–10.30	Plenary session: opening actions, report of the Moderator
11.00–12.30	Plenary session on Assembly theme: "Jesus Christ – the Life of the World" Prof. Theodore Stylianopoulos, USA Dr Allan Boesak, South Africa
14.30–16.00	Small Groups
16.30–18.00	Plenary session: finance report, appointment of Committees and other business
21.30	Evening prayers

Tuesday, 26 July
8.15– 8.45	Worship
9.00–10.30	Plenary session: report of the General Secretary
11.00–12.30	Small Groups
16.30–18.00	Plenary session on Sub-theme I: "Life – a Gift of God"
20.00–21.30	Regional meetings

Wednesday, 27 July
8.15– 8.45	Worship
9.00–10.30	Plenary session on Sub-theme II: "Life Confronting and Overcoming Death"
11.00–12.30	Small Groups
14.30–16.00	Plenary session on Sub-theme III: "Life in all its Fullness"
16.30–18.00	Plenary session: discussion of reports of Moderator, General Secretary and finance; first reports of Nominations and Credentials Committees
21.30	Evening prayers

Thursday, 28 July

8.15– 8.45	Worship
9.00–10.30	Plenary session on Sub-theme IV: "Life in Unity"
11.00–12.30	Small Groups
14.30–18.00	Committee meetings
20.00–21.30	Programme Hearings

Friday, 29 July

8.15– 8.45	Worship
9.00–10.30	Plenary session: presentation by the Canadian churches
11.00–12.30	Small Groups and Committee meetings
14.30–18.00	Clusters
18.00	Canadian Native night, including raising of totem pole
21.30	Evening prayers

Saturday, 30 July

8.15– 8.45	Worship
9.00–10.30	Plenary session: Pacific
11.00–12.30	Small Groups and Committee meetings
14.30–18.00	Clusters
20.00	Worship: service of preparation for the eucharistic celebrations

Sunday, 31 July

9.30	Worship: celebration of the eucharist (ecumenical liturgy)
Evening	Festival of Cultures

Monday, 1 August

8.15– 8.45	Worship
9.00–10.30	Plenary session: presentation of the eight Issues; new member churches and second report of Nominations Committee
11.00–12.30	Small Groups
14.30–18.00	Issue Groups
21.30	Evening prayers

Tuesday, 2 August

8.15– 8.45	Worship
9.00–10.30	Plenary session: discussion of the theme, with reporting from Clusters
11.00–12.30	Small Groups

| 14.30–1800 | Issue Groups |
| 21.30 | Evening prayers |

Wednesday, 3 August

8.15– 8.45	Worship
9.00–10.30	Plenary session: discussion on the theme, with reporting from Clusters; second report of Credentials Committee
11.00–12.30	Small Groups
14.30–18.00	Commitee meetings
20.00–21.30	Issue Groups

Thursday, 4 August

8.15– 8.45	Worship
9.00–10.30	Plenary session: first presentation of Peace and Justice statement
11.00–12.30	Small Groups and Committee meetings
14.30–18.00	Issue Groups
21.30	Evening prayers

Friday, 5 August

8.15– 8.45	Worship
9.00–12.30	Plenary session: Nominations
14.30–16.00	Plenary session: report of Policy Reference Committee I; new member churches
16.30–18.00	Issue Groups
19.30–22.00	Public witness for peace and justice
22.00–	Worship and all-night vigil

Saturday, 6 August

– 6.30	All-night vigil
7.30	Celebration of the eucharist (liturgy of St John Chrysostom)
10.30–12.30	Programme Hearings
14.30–16.00	Small Groups and Committee meetings
16.30–18.00	Plenary session: first report of Message Committee; Nominations
21.30	Evening prayers

Sunday, 7 August

Visits to local congregations

A meeting of the newly elected Central Committee was scheduled for the afternoon, but had to be postponed.

Monday, 8 August
8.15– 8.45	Worship
9.00–12.30	Plenary session: reports of Message Committee, Issue Group 2, Nominations and Policy Reference Committee II
16.30–18.00	Regional meetings
20.00–21.30	Regional meetings, and meeting of newly elected Central Committee

Tuesday, 9 August
8.15– 8.45	Worship
9.00–12.30	Plenary session: reports
14.15–15.30	Small Groups
16.00–18.15	Plenary session: reports
21.30	Evening prayers

Wednesday, 10 August
8.15– 8.45	Worship
9.00–12.30	Plenary session: reports
14.00–18.00	Plenary session: reports
18.15–19.00	Closing worship
20.00–22.00	Reports and closing actions

II. REPORT OF THE MODERATOR OF THE CENTRAL COMMITTEE
Edward Scott

It is my privilege and joy to welcome you to the Sixth Assembly of the World Council of Churches. It is also my responsibility to report on the work of the Central Committee and the staff since the last Assembly.

Preliminary remarks

Previous Moderators' reports have made mention of a number of persons who have been active in the formation of the Council. As the history of the Council has become longer and the number of such persons has increased, I have decided only to mention presidents, officers and key staff persons who have gone on ahead on a road we all must travel:

Bishop Hanns Lilje
Metropolitan Juhanon Mar Thoma
Metropolitan Nikodim
Mr Charles Parlin
Dr Ernest Payne
Bishop Henry Knox Sherrill

Mr Frank Northam
Mr John Taylor
Mr Luiz Carlos Weil

We are surrounded by a great cloud of witnesses into whose labours we have entered. I want to mention only two other persons; both served as General Secretaries:

- Dr W. A. Visser 't Hooft, our Honorary President, who will in a few weeks celebrate his 83rd birthday (and who recently wrote a new book – *The Genesis and Formation of the World Council of Churches*). He is not able to travel but is very much present with us in thought and prayer.
- Dr Eugene Carson Blake, the second General Secretary who, we are sorry to hear, will not be with us as we had hoped, due to failing health.

★   ★   ★

This report has been difficult to prepare, for several reasons.

1. The activities and relationships of the Council have increased enormously; it is not easy to discern the issues of greatest importance.

2. The conditions of the world in which we live have become ever more turbulent; it is not easy to read the signs of the times.

3. You are an extremely diverse company. A few, I believe, have been present at every Assembly; others at several, still others at only one, but the majority (80%, I am told) are attending their first Assembly. I very vividly recall Nairobi, how I did not find it easy to follow the two superb addresses presented by the Moderator (Dr M. M. Thomas) and our General Secretary (Dr Philip Potter) in the light of my limited knowledge of the life and work of the World Council of Churches. I have decided, therefore, to prepare this address keeping in mind primarily those attending their first Assembly.

Whenever I preach a sermon or give an address there are always many more than one. There are the various draft addresses prepared; there is the one actually given; and there are the many different addresses heard by those who listen, because each person listens out of the context from which he or she has come. There are few gatherings drawn from as many different cultural, geographic and religious contexts as are represented here. Each of you will be listening to my words influenced by the realities of the context where you live and move and have your being. I want you quite consciously to evaluate all I say from the light of your own experience.

Yet in the face of these complexities of communication I continue to preach and give addresses, because in the process of speaking and listening God is very often active. He is present in us and with us. Let us then begin with a moment of silence.

> O God, forasmuch as without you we are not able to please you, mercifully grant that in this time of speaking and listening, and in all the activities of this Assembly, your Holy Spirit may direct and rule our hearts and minds; through Jesus Christ our Lord. Amen.

The call to faithfulness

The biblical call to persons and groups is to be "faithful". The ultimate focus of our "faithfulness" is the living God in whose image we are created and who, Christians believe, has made and is making God's nature known to human beings through the life, teaching, death and resurrection of Jesus Christ and through the continuing activity of the Holy Spirit in both the Church and the world. Our faithfulness is expressed in seeking to know and to do God's will:

by acknowledging God's sovereignty and by recognizing our accountability to God in every aspect of life and work. Faithfulness to God cannot be expressed simply by talking about it. It embraces responsibility for relationships with our neighbours – other human beings, those we like and those we find hard to like – as well as our stewardship of the created order over which we exercise dominion and which we are called to replenish. We love God, in part, by loving those whom God loves and by loving the world which God created and loves so deeply.

This Assembly has both the right and the responsibility to ask if the Central Committee and the staff of the WCC have been "faithful" to the responsibilities given to them by the Council. In seeking to give an account of the stewardship of these two groups, I draw your attention to three questions that must be considered:

1. Have we been faithful to the vision set forth in the Message of the Amsterdam Assembly?

> Our coming together to form a World Council will be vain unless Christians and Christian congregations everywhere commit themselves to the Lord of the Church in a new effort to seek together, where they live, to be His witnesses and servants among their neighbours. We have to remind ourselves and all men that God has put down the mighty from their seats and exalted the humble and meek. We have to learn afresh together to speak boldly in Christ's name both to those in power and to the people, to oppose terror, cruelty and race discrimination, to stand by the outcast, the prisoner and refugee. We have to make of the Church in every place a voice for those who have no voice, and a home where every man will be at home. We have to learn afresh together what is the duty of the Christian man or woman in industry, in agriculture, in politics, in the professions and in the home. We have to ask God to teach us together to say "No" and to say "Yes" in truth. "No" to all that flouts the love of Christ, to every system, every programme and every person that treats any man as though he were an irresponsible thing or means of profit, to the defenders of injustice in the name of order, to those who sow the seeds of war or urge war as inevitable; "Yes" to all that conforms to the love of Christ, to all who seek for justice, to the peace-makers, to all who hope, fight and suffer for the cause of man, to all who – even without knowing it – look for new heavens and a new earth wherein dwelleth righteousness.

2. Have we been faithful to the programme guidelines, to the general instructions and to the many specific requests directed to the Central Committee and to the staff by the Nairobi Assembly?

3. Have we been faithful to the growing number of member churches who together make up the World Council of Churches and who together accept a common accountability to God? The

churches, like the Council, are not static. In the past seven and a half years they have all changed, responding in their separate contexts to our rapidly changing world. New leaders have replaced those who have died or retired. Often structures or patterns of work have altered. The World Council of Churches is called to be a servant to the churches in the midst of all this change.

Faithfulness and accountability always involve relationships. Even as this Assembly has a right and responsibility to ask questions about the faithfulness of the Central Committee and staff, so they for their part have the right and responsibility to ask if the member churches and their representatives have been faithful to the vision of the Council which they helped to form or chose to join. The relationship between the Council and the member churches is a covenant relationship and so involves mutual accountability. The Assembly is an occasion to reflect together about this mutual accountability. Many of us may be called by this Assembly to take messages back to our churches about their responsibilities as members of the World Council of Churches. I trust that each person here will be stimulated by the Assembly to be a leader in ecumenical undertakings at home as well as an interpreter of the work of the World Council. The WCC has always recognized the vital importance of local ecumenism, which depends upon local leadership. It also recognizes the need to keep the local and global concerns in living relationship with each other. This is only possible when people like you and me, who have some experience of global relationships, are prepared to give continuing leadership.

A report of our work

At the Nairobi Assembly, the Programme Guidelines Committee presented its report in the form of guidelines rather than priority directives, to enable the Central Committee to assess the total programme and take account of the Assembly's guidelines in a responsible manner.

Three guidelines called for an overall programme to be conceived and implemented in a way:
- "which enables the member churches to grow towards a truly ecumenical conciliar fellowship";
- "that engages the churches in the effort to reach a common understanding of the Gospel and the tradition and, under the guidance of the Holy Spirit, to make possible a fuller common witness . . . and search for an authentic incarnation of the Christian faith in the historic circumstances of a given place";
- "that expresses the basic Christian imperative to participate in the struggle for human dignity and social justice and, at the same

time, maintains the integrity of action and engagement by the churches as rooted in the biblical faith . . . . (and) enable(s) the churches to become communities generating hope, reconciliation, liberation, and justice".

The Assembly called for a Council which:

a) clearly sees itself as the servant of the living God who in Christ calls us into liberation and unity and which is dependent on him;

b) has a stable basis of financial support;

c) has a sound, comprehensive, coordinated, balanced programme; and

d) has developed a new flexibility so that it may:

  – utilize its human and financial resources more effectively;

  – have its programmes and priorities under constant review;

  – operate with a deep sense of accountability to the priorities set by this Assembly; and

  – carry on its work with increased mutual consultation with the churches which constitute it.

The Assembly did not stop there. It also called for many special undertakings in addition to the regular continuing programme, and recognized the need for procedures which would help bring about:

– greater coordination of all aspects of the Council's work;

– more adequate support of Programme Units and Sub-Units within the total programme; and

– a greater sense of confidence on the part of the member churches and agencies in the work of the Council.

The Nairobi Assembly took these actions in the face of a very critical and confused financial picture internally in the Council and of a very uncertain world economic situation where inflation and extremely erratic exchange rates (over which the Council had no control) were having a very detrimental impact.

The Officers, Central Committee members and staff were aware of the difficult tasks confronting them but, as the title of Leon Howell's popular report suggests, they did not become immobilized; they "acted in faith" – faith thay they were called by God and would be empowered by God on whose faithfulness they could depend as they undertook their work.

What has been accomplished? A careful reading of *Nairobi to Vancouver* is required, but it will give only a bare outline of the work of seven and a half years. I want to highlight a number of points which may help this Assembly to evaluate the work accomplished.

a) The Central Committee developed four major areas of concentration to give expression to the programme guidelines which had been adopted at Nairobi:

1) the expression and communication of our faith in the triune God;
2) the search for a just, participatory and sustainable society;
3) the unity of the Church, and its relations to the unity of humankind;
4) education and renewal in search of true community (*Nairobi to Vancouver*, p. xvi).

b) In addition to continuing many studies already under way, and others arising out of the regular work of Units and Sub-units, the Central Committee commissioned a number of special studies in response to requests made by the Assembly. Many of these are reported in *The Ecumenical Review* and the *International Review of Mission*, but many are published separately. It would be impossible to mention them all and dangerous to pick out what I think are the most important. Rather, I call your careful attention to the catalogue of WCC publications you have all received. These studies are not published as authoritative policy statements. They are offered to assist the member churches and others to be involved internally and ecumenically in a continuing process of exploration, and to help churches make decisions concerning appropriate action in relation to new insights.

c) The Central Committee authorized a number of international gatherings; some of them – like the Church and Society conference on "Faith, Science and the Future" held in Boston in 1979, and the Commission on World Mission and Evangelism conference "Thy Kingdom Come" held in Melbourne in 1980 – involved large numbers of people. Others, just as important, involved smaller numbers and dealt with more specific issues. These included the Sheffield conference on "The Community of Women and Men in the Church"; "The International Hearing on Nuclear Weapons and Disarmament"; the meeting on "Dialogue in Community", held at Chiang Mai, Thailand, which produced "Guidelines for Dialogue"; consultations on racism in the 80s. Many regional consultations were also held, such as the series conducted by the Christian Medical Commission which led to the study on Health, Healing and Wholeness. All these gatherings produced reports that are rich resources for the member churches.

d) The Committee increased the consultative process. More consultations have been held to bring together members of the ecumenical family from different parts of the world in the years since Nairobi than in the entire previous history of the Council from 1948 to 1975.

Direct contact with the member churches was intensified in five ways.

1. The Committee encouraged official delegations and key officers from member churches to visit the headquarters in Geneva and meet with staff to share information and discuss areas of concern.
2. It encouraged the visits of Officers, staff, Central Committee members, and members of Unit and Sub-unit committees to member churches.
3. It increased regional consultations with member churches and with families of churches. Of particular importance here is a series of consultations with representatives of the Orthodox churches which has enabled these churches to make a much greater contribution to the life of the Council and to interpret their self-understanding to other churches within the Council and beyond.
4. It convened consultations of persons from member churches and agencies who have similar functional responsibilities, e.g. finance officers, staff with responsibility for development concerns and development education.
5. It inaugurated the pre-Assembly visitation programme in which many of the delegates here present had an important role. Seventy-nine teams visited member churches in some ninety-one countries. In addition, more visits of individual officers and staff to member churches were made in the pre-Assembly period than ever before.

e) The Central Committee made changes in its internal structures which have resulted in much greater integration in programme planning and much greater cooperation of staff and resources. This emphasis on integration, cooperation and coordination is continuing.

f) The Committee implemented and refined staff policies adopted prior to Nairobi (e.g. the nine-year rule – which has become a ten-year rule) and made provision for more responsible patterns of support and supervision of staff.

g) More books have been published since 1975 than in the period 1948–1975. The publications, in addition to books, include a wide range of periodicals, newsletters, films, photos, posters, cassettes and records. One of the most important books in your bag is "WCC Publications 1983". But we face a major problem in communication: it is the limited circulation of this excellent material. We need the help of every Assembly delegate to enlarge this circulation and widen the range of languages in which publications are available. I hope each of you will spend some time in the publications display room during the course of this Assembly.

h) In the financial realm the Central Committee has taken action enabling the Council to move from crisis to stability, from "seven budgets to one budget". All the financial problems have not been solved (they never will be!), but we come to this Assembly in a responsible financial position. The major problems have been identified, and clear and adequate information can be provided to enable us to seek solutions together. This was not the case at Nairobi.

I could add many other points but these are sufficient to indicate that the Central Committee and staff have worked hard to be accountable to the decisions of Nairobi.

One of the calls of Nairobi, mentioned above, was "to take steps which could lead to a greater sense of confidence on the part of the member churches and agencies in the work of the Council". What can be said about achievements in this area?

First, the membership of the Council has increased since Nairobi. Twenty churches – all but two from the "two-thirds world" – have become full members of the Council, and five other churches have become associate members. Six national councils have been recognized as associate councils of the WCC (total associate councils: 34). In addition, 31 other councils are associated with CWME and there are working relations with 34 other councils where official affiliation does not exist.

Relations with non-member churches, particularly the Roman Catholic Church, have been maintained and in many instances deepened. *Nairobi to Vancouver* and the General Secretary's report provide additional information about relations with the Roman Catholic Church, and the study document "Common Witness" (1981) is of particular importance. The relationship with the Christian World Communions is being further clarified.

In this same period two churches, the Congregational Union of New Zealand and the Seventh Day Baptist Conference USA, resigned membership without giving specific reasons. Three other churches suspended membership following the 1978 grant to the Patriotic Front from the Special Fund of the Programme to Combat Racism. Consultations have been held with all three: the Presbyterian Church of Ireland which withdrew from membership; the Salvation Army which withdrew from full membership but remains in a fraternal relationship with the Council as a Christian World Communion (it has been actively involved in the preparation for the Assembly); and the Evangelical Lutheran Church of Schaumberg-Lippe which has taken no further formal action since suspending membership.

During the period there have been and there remain points of tension both within member churches and affiliated councils, and also between member churches and affiliated councils and the WCC. This is to be expected. Without tension there is little possibility of growth. I believe the situation is now much more positive than it was in 1978. Member churches are taking greater initiative in contracting, entering into dialogue with, and challenging the Central Committee and staff – and this is good. Relationships are more open, more frank, and therefore much deeper, more realistic and forward-looking than they were during the previous decade of "polite ecumenism". I believe, however, that the Council is more willing to be challenged by the member churches than the churches are to be challenged by the Council. Relations between churches and councils (all of which are facing constant changes of personnel and also having to respond to new challenges locally, regionally and internationally) must always be worked at. We must re-covenant continually, to build and maintain relationships of trust. That means learning to relate to each other openly and frankly, knowing that our actions influence one another, and avoiding feelings of moral superiority in the relationship. It is a difficult and demanding art, but one that is essential for maintaining and deepening Christian community.

It is not easy to measure levels of trust and confidence. One fact which suggests increased confidence is that many of the member churches, in spite of internal financial problems resulting in part from the unsettled world economic situation, have increased their financial support of the Council – some very substantially. This increase in support has been received in different ways. Some has come through increased financial contributions. Some, particularly in the case of such churches as those in Eastern Europe which cannot export hard currency, has come by indirect contributions in various forms. Often it has been by hosting and bearing the major costs of delegates from a number of churches. Another way is by paying the travel costs and/or including on charter flights delegates from other churches or countries to World Council gatherings such as the Assembly. The Russian Orthodox Church has contributed in this way on various occasions.

These points, taken together, seem to indicate greater confidence in the work of the Council. But there is need for still more action on the part of both the Council and the member churches in the area of relationships, so that the level of trust may be deepened.

One area of particular concern to me (perhaps partly because I was the Moderator of the Finance Committee in Nairobi) is that 113 churches (38%) make no financial commitment to the Council. There are a variety of reasons for this. It is partly the result of history and of Council policy, a carry-over from the not-yet-extinct paternalistic attitudes and practices which characterized some of the earlier relationships in the period of the Western missionary movement. I am convinced that one of the most unkind and destructive things which a person or group can do to another is to allow dependency relationships to continue. The Council has never made financial support a condition of membership and this is as it should be. I do believe, however, that the Council should encourage a growing sense of interdependence with all member churches which will lead to a desire to share in the financial support of the Council's work.

The Central Committee and staff have taken very seriously the mandate given to them at Nairobi, and I believe that an examination of their work indicates they have been "faithful". But what about faithfulness to the vision developed when the Council was formed?

The achievements listed above have *not* been made by sacrificing this vision. There has been no attempt to avoid dealing with difficult controversial issues which needed to be faced. The Committee and the staff have sought to speak boldly by word and in action, as faithful witnesses of the Lord. They have sought both to challenge member churches and, at the same time, to surround them with strength, to stand in solidarity with them where they are. They have invited member churches in a series of world conferences and consultations to be involved in an analysis of the world situation from a Christian perspective and to share in decision-making concerning appropriate responses to the analysis. They have sought to increase the sense of unity within and among the member churches – not by avoiding issues but by encouraging a common response to them by member churches and the Council acting together. In doing this they have attempted to be true to the vision which inspired the foundation of the Council. They have also worked far harder to keep in continuous contact with member churches than was previously the case, particularly by developing a policy of informing churches about actions that may be controversial before they are announced publicly. No doubt the most graphic illustration relates to the Programme to Combat Racism, which has been both controversial and creative. It has led to tensions which continue, but has also led to study within member churches, regional consultations, and an international consultation on racism. It is evident that the international consultation helped churches to begin to make concern about racism much more a part of their own agendas so that it is not seen only as a concern of the World Council.

It will be up to you, in the light of the report *Nairobi to Vancouver* and the presentations here at the Assembly, to make your judgment about our faithfulness. I hope you will feel free both to ask questions and to offer constructive criticism following your assessment.

I have set forth this positive affirmation of the accountability of the Central Committee and staff because I am convinced it is true. I am aware, as many of you are, of the very vocal criticism of the World Council which exists both within and outside member churches. In many cases this comes from lack of knowledge or from very inaccurate or partial information, gained primarily from the secular media. When this is the case, the criticism very often provides an educational opportunity for persons knowledgeable about the Council and its work. I do not suggest that the Council has not made mistakes – it involves very fallible human beings like you and me. Nevertheless, I am convinced of the basic soundness of our work and believe it can stand up under careful scrutiny. There is, however, growing documentation indicating that persons and groups who do not want certain kinds of issues raised or discussed are deliberately seeking to misinterpret or misrepresent the Council. This should not surprise us – Jesus warned his followers that such would happen. We must avoid becoming overly defensive, be true to our calling and commit our work to God.

The contribution of the Central Committee and the staff

The accomplishments that have been made were only possible because of the deep commitment and high level of competence exhibited by the Central Committee members and by the staff. I want to express, on my own behalf and on behalf of the member churches, deep appreciation to both groups. It has been a demanding and joyful privilege to work with them and my life has been enriched by this experience. The presidents also have all played a very active and important role.

My closest contacts have in the very nature of things been with the two Vice-moderators, Miss Jean Skuse and His Holiness Karekin II, and with the two persons who have served as Moderators of the Finance Committee, Dr Robert Marshall and Dr Oscar McCloud. All four carry heavy responsibilities in their own churches but have been very generous in making time for WCC responsibilities, and have served the Council with deep and steady devotion.

My closest contact on the staff has been with the General Secretary whose wisdom, vast knowledge of the ecumenical movement, deep biblical insights, broad grasp of world affairs, strong faith and great courage have been an inspiration to me and many others. He has served as General Secretary at a very difficult period in the life of the world, of the Council, and also in his own personal life, and has done so with deep devotion. We share with him in the loss of Doreen, his wife. The Council and its member churches owe more to him than most of us realize.

The Council also owes a particular debt to the four Deputy

General Secretaries, Dr Alan Brash (now retired), Dr Konrad Raiser, Professor Todor Sabev, and Mrs Marie Assaad, as well as to two persons who have served as Assistant General Secretaries – Mr Wesley Kenworthy and Mr Patrick Coïdan. These persons brought to the work of the Council outstanding competence and great loyalty.

I do want to make some comments about the relation of staff to the Central Committee and the Council, as well as about the responsibility of the Assembly, the Central Committee and member churches to the staff.

The Church is not the same as a business organization, and the staff relationships should be different – although both should strive to be efficient in accomplishing their purposes. The churches and their councils do not simply employ staff. The staff, in the vast majority of cases, are a part of the Church – members of the body that employs them. As members, they have a right to share in the decision-making, in the policy-formation, because they, like Central Committee members, are part of the one body. We have worked hard at giving living expression to this reality in the life and work of the Council. I am aware we have not completely succeeded, but we have been involved in a participatory pattern of decision-making – sometimes very frustratingly so! But we have no right to call for a participatory society unless we seek to give expression to that principle in our own life. I am deeply grateful to the Central Committee members and to the staff for the part they have played in making this possible.

Now a more particular word about relations with and support of staff. Most of us here are members of a particular church and work in and for it. Most of us are firmly rooted in a particular cultural context and many of us (but certainly not all) are accustomed to working in a single language. Because this is so, it is very easy for us to be unaware of, or to forget, the very many additional pressures which are connected with work in a world organization concerned about the whole inhabited earth, where there is constant need to relate to people living in a variety of cultural contexts, under political structures representing different ideologies, and who speak and think in a wide range of languages. During the days of the Assembly, we shall all be involved to some degree in such a context. Those for whom it is a new experience will find it exciting but often frustrating; they will find it demanding and most tiring. This is the context in which the staff members work almost constantly.

Every staff member is important, and I want to say "thank you" to each one: General Secretary; shipper; librarian; field worker; those in high profile positions and those whose names and faces are unknown to most of us; those who speak and think in many languages and those who, like me, are largely limited to one; those who develop ideas and write, and those who translate and interpret; those who are continually facing new challenges and those who do the dull routine things that enable an organization to be strong. The gratitude the Council owes to this staff cannot be adequately expressed by financial remuneration alone. It must also be expressed by honouring and encouraging our mutual accountability with them as fellow members of the Body of Christ.

Church leader and Moderator

It has been suggested that it might be useful to reflect with you about the experience of being Moderator and a titular head of a member church – in my case, Primate of the Anglican Church of Canada. To do this, I must say a few words about the Anglican Church of Canada and my responsibilities in it. Our national church is composed of thirty dioceses, each with considerable autonomy. It is spread over a vast area – 4½ time zones – in a country where there are many regional differences. I am called to have pastoral concern for the whole church and also carry executive responsibility in the development and implementation of the national policy of our church. This position involves me in considerable travel nationally and internationally.

Serving as Moderator has brought me into direct personal contact with outstanding church leaders from churches in all parts of the world, with many of the great ecumenical thinkers of our day, and with persons living under a wide variety of different cultural, economic, political and social conditions. I have become conscious of the truth of a statement made by our General Secretary, Dr Philip Potter, in his address to the Nairobi Assembly:

> The most striking fact of our time is that all the major issues, whether political, economic, social, racial, or of sex, are global and inter-related in character. What happens in one place affects all places. What appears to be a political issue tends, on closer examination, to have many other dimensions. As St Paul reminds us about the body, "If one member suffers, all suffer together" (1 Cor. 12:26). This is as true of the body politic as it is of the Body of Christ.

I have become sharply aware of the seriousness of the global issues and of the very great need to take action – often radical action – in the light of this new knowledge. New knowledge always brings new responsibilities. The context of my thinking, my theological reflection, my decision-making, has been incredibly widened.

The contact with people from other communions forced me to examine theological assumptions which as a member of one commu-

nion I had tended to take for granted. Contacts with people seeking
to express their belief in Jesus Christ as Lord and Saviour in other
contexts made me much more aware of the extent to which my
Christian thinking had been culturally conditioned.

These experiences complicated my life as Primate here in Canada.
I came to see all the realities of the life of both Church and state in
a much wider context which raised many new issues. This increased
sense of complication was most clearly expressed in the thirty or
more weekends I spend each year in local parishes across the
country. In these parishes I constantly meet persons of integrity,
persons of faith, whose context of experience and thought is much
more limited. Many do not yet acknowledge the reality and truth
of the General Secretary's comment – their personal experiences
have not led them to these insights. In these settings I find I have
to challenge and disturb, but at the same time I have to try to
support and to provide strength. Above all, I have to point to
sources of strength far greater than my own. The challenging and
the disturbing are to help people gain a new vision of what it means
to be a part of the people of God – a worldwide community called
into existence by God's activity in history in Jesus Christ. As Verna
Dozier puts it:

> God came into history to create a people who would change the world,
> who would make the world a place where every person knew that he
> or she was loved, was valued, had a contribution to make, and had
> just as much right to the riches of the world as every other person
> (*The Authority of the Laity*, p. 5).

In this process I have to help people develop increased understanding of the biblical message and become much more consciously
aware of God's concern for the whole world. I have found, for
example, that most Anglicans know John 3:16 – "God so loved the
world that he gave his only Son, that whoever believes in him
should not perish but have eternal life", but only a small group are
aware of John 3:17 – "For God sent the Son into the world, not to
condemn the world, but that the world might be saved through
him." My experience as Moderator has led me to realize that need
for a much deeper sense of God's concern for the whole of creation,
and to see the need of members of the church I belong to, and of
other churches in Canada, to deepen their understanding of the
breadth of God's concern. Many in Canada seem to feel that God
loves only individuals and is not concerned about the totality of life,
every aspect of life.

On the other hand, I have found that I have to keep reminding
myself (and sometimes members of the Canadian church and the

WCC staff) that many things which seem self-evident to us as a result of *our* experience, contacts, and learning opportunities, are not that clear to people who live in more limited and localized contexts in Canada (or elsewhere). I find I live in a constant tension, trying to interpret the thinking, attitudes and actions of people in one context to those of people who live in different contexts. This is stimulating but not easy to accomplish.

The most disturbing part of this process is the all-too-human tendency of some persons in each context to blame or condemn those in other situations who think, feel, and act differently; rather than to struggle, to analyze, find common ground, understand and seek to act as part of the one worldwide community. When people do not understand our position, it is easy to say they are perverse or stubborn − or that they refuse to listen. In some cases, however, although people share general faith affirmations, the different contexts in which they live may make it extremely difficult for them to understand and respond to the insights which people from another range of experience are trying to share with them.

I could say much more about some of the experiences resulting from holding these two positions, but I have focused particularly on this one aspect of holding two offices because I know that all who are privileged to attend this Assembly, particularly if it is their first international gathering, will find themselves facing something of this same tension when they get home. Being able to communicate effectively when the contexts of our experience are very different is a difficult and a demanding art. This is one reason why the Issue Group on communicating credibly is so important. We always communicate something, but often it is not what we want or intend to communicate. We often convey blame or condemnation, rather than a desire to share, to deepen understanding, and to learn to work in community. We need constantly to remind ourselves that the Church is called to be a loving, accepting, challenging and supportive community. This relates directly to the unity of the Church.

The world context in which we meet

The General Secretary has set forth in *Nairobi to Vancouver* some of the realities of the world in which we meet. I want to share some personal perspectives about existing conditions and my interpretation of them.

The situation today is in very sharp contrast with that of the 1960s. The sixties saw the zenith of the post-war prosperity boom as the reconstruction of Europe and Japan progressed. It was a decade marked by optimism − one which heralded a hope for the

unity of humankind and a world of plenty. The eighties have quite
a different feel. Langdom Gilkey expresses it this way:

> It feels as if we were reaching the end of an historical era, and reflection
> on the elements making up that feeling tends to substantiate it. (*The
> New Watershed in Theology*)

I agree. We are, I believe, at the end of an era. It was an era
dominated by what, for brevity, I would call urban industrial
culture. This culture grew out of the discovery of the scientific
method and the technological development which followed. Science
and technology were seen by many to be offering ultimate answers
to human aspirations. This culture came to be expressed in two
major competing ideologies – capitalism and communism. There
are many differences between them but there are also some very
great similarities. Both, in practice if not in theory, are materialistic,
and both tend to limit their focus of achievement to what happens
in space and time. Both are very much concerned about the production and delivery of goods and services, and both tend to place
emphasis upon persons as units of production and consumption and
tend to measure progress, in a country or in the world, in terms of
the Gross National Product. The material achievements of this
culture in both the ideological expressions have been and continue
to be almost incredible.

It is my conviction, however, that neither of these present ideological expressions of this culture is adequately responding to the
challenges of our day. These ideologies are no longer satisfying the
deepest human aspirations, and neither is displaying the power to
galvanize adherents and so provide unity, direction, standards and
courage to their respective communities. Both are on the defensive
and, in the present struggle between them, involving power of a
magnitude previously unknown in human history, there lies the
possibility of the destruction not only of civilization as we know it
but also of life on this planet. I believe that both of these ideologies,
although they remain powerful, are no longer adequately responding
to the challenges which confront us. An era is ending.

Where have the churches been in this cultural process? We have
to be honest and admit that to a very large degree they have been
in cultural captivity. They have too often retreated from criticizing
culture from their own faith affirmations, their own theological
insights, and have instead accommodated themselves to the cultural
values of the world. If they had remained truly faithful, they would
have affirmed much more positively that human beings are not mere
units of production or consumption, but relationship beings: being
made in the image of the Creator and called to seek the meaning of

life not in the abundance of things possessed, but in the quality of relationships with God, with one another and with nature. I believe we are witnessing today a concerted effort on the part of the churches to break out of their cultural captivity, and I am convinced that the World Council of Churches has given great leadership in this effort.

If churches are to break out of their cultural captivity and avoid the ever-present danger of substituting a limited emphasis on individual piety for the proclamation of the sovereignty of God, they must again discover a transcendent loyalty which is strong enough to enable them "to be in the world but not of it". In this endeavour they will be much helped by the statement on "Baptism, Eucharist and Ministry", the report of the conference on "Faith, Science and the Future", and the document entitled "Mission and Evangelism: an Ecumenical Affirmation". All these reports can play a vital role in this search.

It is in this turbulent period, when there is and will continue to be much suffering, much pain, much despair and no easy answers, that you and I from many different churches and countries meet under the theme "Jesus Christ – the Life of the World".

The theme affirms life, it affirms the source of life, it implies "good news"; it points to evangelism, but it will be a demanding evangelism. It makes a heavy demand upon us as we meet together at this Assembly, and upon the churches we represent here. We must ask ourselves this question: Will a new vision, which enables us, under God, to break out of our cultural captivity, be found?

If this happens here and continues to happen after we all return home, we shall find the power to galvanize adherents and so provide the unity, direction, standards and courage so desperately needed in the world today.

How shall we start? According to the Synoptic Gospels, Jesus began his ministry with the call: "Repent ye, for the kingdom of God is at hand." Let us relate this call to our theme: "Turn about, focus attention on Jesus Christ who is the life of the world."

What do we learn as we focus attention on Jesus Christ? We learn that we are important, we are loved, we are called to say "no" to "all that flouts the love of Christ, to every system, every programme, every person who treats any human being as though he or she were an irresponsible thing or a means of profit" – and we must say "yes" to "all that conforms to the love of Christ, to all who seek for justice, to the peace-makers, to all who hope, fight and suffer for the cause of man (humanity), to all who – even without knowing it – look for new heavens and a new earth wherein dwelleth righteousness". These are some of the ways in which we seek first the kingdom of God and God's righteousness.

What a magnificent and demanding calling!

Given to us by a God who in his gracious faithfulness enables human beings like you and me to accomplish things which seem impossible!

Thanks be to God, who gives us the victory through Jesus Christ our Lord. Amen.

III. REPORT OF THE GENERAL SECRETARY
Philip Potter

May I once again greet you warmly at this Sixth Assembly of the World Council of Churches in Vancouver. This is the second time in the thirty-five years of its existence that the Council's Assembly has met in North America. The last time was the Second Assembly at Evanston, Illinois, in the USA, in 1954, with the theme, "Jesus Christ the Hope of the World". We gathered together then, at a time of fear and despair, in the midst of the confrontation between the East and West and the struggles of peoples for political, economic and racial injustice around the world. The witch-hunt of McCarthyism was raging in the USA, and its effects were felt in the Assembly. And yet, we were able to say together in the Message:

> Here where we stand (under the judgement of God and in the shadow of death), Jesus stood with us. He came to us, truly divine and truly human, to seek and to save. Though we were the enemies of God, Christ died for us. We crucified him, but God raised him from the dead. He is risen. He has overcome the powers of sin and death. A new life has begun. And in his risen and ascended power, he has sent forth into the world a new community, bound together by his spirit, sharing his divine life, and commissioned to make him known throughout the world.

These words are still appropriate as we meet nearly thirty years later under the theme: "Jesus Christ – the Life of the World". We come to Vancouver as those who share the divine life in Christ and desire to offer it in all its fullness to the peoples of the world. In contrast to the Evanston Assembly, we meet now as a much more representative gathering of people from all over the world. We meet, too, under an even darker cloud of fear and despair. The confrontation between East and West and between North and South, and the conflicts within countries between sexes, races, classes and religions, have become much fiercer and more complex. The very survival of the human race is daily threatened.

At the Fifth Assembly in Nairobi in 1975, we had a feeling of being in the wilderness, as the children of Israel were after the Exodus, full of doubts and fears. Nevertheless, despite the pain and conflicts we experienced during that meeting, there was no retreat from the positions we had taken and the programmes we had launched after the Fourth Assembly at Uppsala in 1968. Indeed, we committed ourselves to go forward and undertake more specific, even controversial programmes in obedience to our calling. When we examine the official report, *Nairobi to Vancouver*, we can see that in the wilderness of our time we have been able to receive and proclaim God's word of life. We have had contact with a wider variety of people, and more churches have been visited than ever before. We have laboured for the unity of the Church and for the renewal of humankind. We have tried to meet human need in every part of the globe, and to be in solidarity with the oppressed and the deprived. We have spoken and acted in situations of conflict.

There is a profound sense in which the Church is by its very nature always in the wilderness on its pilgrim way to the City of God or, as the Letter to the Hebrews puts it, to the world (*oikoumene*) to come (2:5). The Church is the people of God called and consecrated through the Exodus in the death and resurrection of Christ. It is called to participate in the sufferings of Christ for the salvation of our broken, divided world. At the beginning of the Church's history it was seen as a community of people scattered all over the Roman Empire, having no legal or social status, and subject to harassment, persecution and death.

It was to such diaspora churches that the First Letter of Peter was addressed. We have been drawing from that Letter one of the "Images of Life" in our Bible studies in preparation for this Assembly – the image of "The House made of Living Stones" which is intended to be an image of the Church. I invite you to meditate on what it means to be "the house of living stones" in a hostile world which nevertheless yearns to be such a house, a living community of sharing in justice and peace. This biblical meditation should help us to reflect on what we have learned during these thirty-five years of the existence of the World Council of Churches about the nature and calling of the churches and about the Council as a fellowship of churches.

Peter exhorts the diaspora churches:

> Come to him, to that living stone, rejected by people, but in God's sight chosen and precious: and like living stones be yourselves constantly built into a spiritual house, to be a holy priesthood, to offer spiritual sacrifices acceptable to God through Jesus Christ (1 Pet. 2:4–5).

Christ is God's delegated and precious living stone. The Psalmist declared, "the stone which the builders rejected has become the chief cornerstone" (118:22); so Christ, rejected and crucified, is now the risen, life-giving Lord. That is the foundation of our faith and the basis of the World Council of Churches.

Actually, according to the Gospels, it was Jesus himself who drew attention to this Psalm, which is the last of a group of Psalms called *Hallel* (Praise) and sung during and after the great feasts at Jerusalem (Pss. 111–118). Ps. 118 was sung after the Passover – the meal which served as the binding force of the people of Israel on the eve of the Exodus. Jesus quoted this verse of Ps. 118 in his controversy with the religious authorities who plotted his death (Mark 12:1–12), on the eve of what Luke called his exodus (Luke 9:31). He spoke to his disciples of being rejected and killed and of rising again after three days (Mark 8:31). In recalling his experience with Jesus and what he learned from it, Peter is saying to the diaspora churches in Asia Minor, as he says to us today, that confessing Christ means entering into his sufferings and sharing his risen life. He invites them and us to keep on coming day after day to Christ the living stone, so that we may ourselves become living stones, share his life and continue his ministry of suffering for humankind in joyful hope.

But becoming living stones means that believers and communities of believers do not remain isolated, alone, petrified, dead. They are made alive and are being built into a house, an *oikos* which is enlivened by the Spirit. Christ is the cornerstone, and the Spirit enables those who come to Christ to be built into his house.

A living house

The word "house" was rich in meaning for the peoples of the ancient Middle East. It signified community, nation, culture, way of life, structure as well as environment. Abraham was called by God out of his father's *bayith*, or *oikos* – that is, out of his nation and culture – to form a new *oikos*, a house based on faith in and obedience to God (Gen. 12:2; 15:6; 17:12–13). This new house, this new people of God found themselves swallowed up into "the house of bondage" in Egypt. They were delivered from Pharaoh (a word which comes from the Egyptian *per-aa*, the Great House) through the Exodus, and were made "the house of Israel". That is to say, they were given a way of life based on their deliverance from Egypt and directed by the liberating word of the Covenant (Ex. 19–23). As a means of keeping the house of Israel fully and continuously conscious of the nature of their existence and task there was established the house of God, the place of worship, the temple, where people offered their life and their labour to God and received God's renewing grace.

The drama of Israel was that again and again they lost their loyalty to the founder of the house and accommodated themselves to the ethical and spiritual attitudes of the surrounding cultures or *oikoi*. They also failed to live as a household according to the covenant, to share a common life in truth, justice and peace. Hence the prophets again and again challenged them, as for example, Jeremiah when he told them:

> Do not trust in these deceiving words: "This is the temple of the Lord, the temple of the Lord, the temple of the Lord." For if you truly amend your ways and your doings, if you truly execute justice one with another, if you do not oppress the widow, or shed innocent blood in this place, and if you do not go after other gods to your own hurt, then I will let you dwell in this place, in the land that I gave of old to your fathers for ever . . . Has this house, which is called by my name, become a den of robbers in your eyes? Behold, I myself have seen it, says the Lord (Jer. 7:4–7, 11).

For Jeremiah, the people of God, the house of Israel, are founded on certain qualities and obligations: justice and mercy, and utter loyalty to God, the Lord of the house. These are based on the Torah, the Law, the words of the Covenant. A house is truly built on those qualities which enable its inhabitants to live together in community and in common wellbeing, *shalom*. Where these qualities are lacking the house cannot stand. Institutions and structures acquire a demonic character when people lose that strength of being, that clear integrity and sense of purpose which enable them to discern, correct and change their situation. There comes a time, therefore, when existing structures have to be destroyed in order that new structures, a new *oikos*, can be built up based on a new covenant and enabling people to be responsible for themselves and for one another before God (Jer. 31:27–34). This is what Jesus meant when he said that the old temple would be destroyed in his crucifixion and that he would rebuild it in three days through his resurrection (John 2:19–21).

Peter affirms that in the crucified and risen Christ this new house has been built and that all who come to him are living stones forming an integral part of the house, sharing a common life and offering their whole life and that of all to God in the Spirit and through Jesus Christ. He goes on to adopt in a new way some of the other ancient images for Israel when he calls believers "a chosen race, a royal priesthood, a holy nation, God's own people" (1 Pet. 2:9a). Believers, as living stones, overcome the separations of racism and become the true human race made in the image of God. Both women and men become the priests of the king and ruler of their lives, offering themselves and the world to God through their worship and their witness. Nationalism with all its exclusivist attitudes gives place to a community consecrated to God and his purpose to unite all nations in their diversity into one house. All are the people of God as a sign of God's plan to unite all peoples into one human family in justice and peace. It is this house which is called to proclaim the wonderful deeds of God who called it out of darkness into his marvellous light (1 Pet. 2:9). This is Peter's way of confessing the "one, holy, catholic and apostolic church".

It is this image and understanding of the living house which has motivated the ecumenical movement. As is well known, the word ecumenical is derived from the Greek word *oikoumene*, meaning the whole inhabited earth. It is a word which came into common use when Alexander the Great was conquering the world of the Middle East and beyond. The intention was that peoples should give up their cultural isolation and participate in a cosmopolitan life through which they would discover their true humanity. That was the *oikoumene*. When the Romans conquered the Hellenists, their rulers were hailed as lords and saviours of the *oikoumene*.

Against the background we can understand how this word was appropriated by the Greek translators of the Old Testament and the writers of the New Testament. In Psalm 24:1 we read: "The earth is the Lord's and its fullness; the world and those who dwell on it." Not Caesar, but Yahweh, the one who has been and is present in the world, is the Lord and Saviour of the *oikoumene*, ruling it in truth, justice and peace, and manifesting his purpose through the covenant people, the house of Israel. God's purpose is that the whole *oikoumene* will recognize him as the true Lord and Saviour. It is through God that true humanity becomes a promise and a reality. In the New Testament we are told, for example, of Paul and his companions preaching at Thessalonica and of their forming a house church. They are accused before the city authorities as "people who have turned the world, the *oikoumene*, upside down . . . and are acting against the decrees of Caesar, saying that there is another king, Jesus" (Acts 17:6–7).

The ecumenical movement is, therefore, the means by which the churches which form the house, the *oikos* of God, are seeking so to live and witness before all peoples that the whole *oikoumene* may become the *oikos* of God through the crucified and risen Christ in the power of the life-giving Spirit. The World Council of Churches was formed in 1948 precisely to be a means of enabling this process to take place in the totality of the life and witness of the churches in response to the totality of God's claim on the life of the *oikoumene*. What then have we learned during this ecumenical journey of thirty-five years about the nature and calling of the churches which have committed themselves to the fellowship of the World Council of Churches?

The reflections which follow are based on my experience and active involvement in the life of the Council from 1948. They should also be read alongside my introduction to the official report, *Nairobi to Vancouver*.

A fellowship of confessing

First, we have been learning to be a fellowship of confessing. In fact, according to its basis, the World Council is "a fellowship of churches which confess the Lord Jesus Christ as God and Saviour according to the scriptures and therefore seek to fulfill together their common calling to the glory of the one God, Father, Son and Holy Spirit".

After centuries of separation the churches have been drawn together in a fellowship of confessing communities which live "according to the scriptures". It is through the biblical renewal of the past fifty years that the churches themselves have been heeding the words of Peter: "The time has come for judgment to begin with the house of God" (1 Pet. 4:17). That was the revolutionary discovery of Martin Luther, the 500th anniversary of whose birth we celebrate this year. He brought back to the centre of the life of the Church the sovereignty of God's judging and redeeming word, that it may constantly be reformed in order to become a true house of living stones.

Through the World Council the churches have been constrained to share with one another the ways in which they confess their faith and have, through mutual correction, from time to time become conscious of their own failure to live up to the claims of the gospel. The ecumenical movement is first of all a call to the churches to penitence, a change of heart and mind in the direction of the offer and demand of Christ, the living stone, and a greater openness to confess together their faith boldly and joyfully in the storm of the world's life.

I want to give one illustration of the ways we have advanced as a fellowship of confessing. When the Orthodox churches and the churches of the Reformation got together to form the World Council, there was great diffidence between them. Apart from the fact that they did not accept each other as churches in the full sense, there was also a history of proselytism – churches confessing their faith in a competing way and seeking to win converts from other churches. At the Third Assembly at New Delhi, 1961, when the International Missionary Council was integrated into the World Council, there was an agreed statement on "Christian Witness, Proselytism and Religious Liberty". The churches were called upon to disavow all forms of proselytism so as to render their common witness to Christ more faithful and more convincing. In the same spirit the Second Vatican Council produced a Declaration on Religious Liberty in 1965. Then in 1970 the Joint Working Group of the Roman Catholic Church and the World Council of Churches issued a study document on "Christian Witness and Proselytism" where the emphasis was already more on common witness. By 1980, the same Joint Working Group agreed to publish a statement on "Common Witness", giving many stories of ways in which Christian communities have been confessing their faith together in word and act. The churches have thus been enabled, through the World Council, to clear away many obstacles to their common witness, whether as churches, base communities, or action groups. This amazing fact has too often been taken for granted.

Moreover, we have been learning the meaning of the words of Peter's letter: "In your hearts reverence Christ as Lord. Always be prepared to make a defence to any one who calls you to account for the hope that is in you, yet do it with modesty and reverence" (3:15). I do not here refer to the notable theological reflections carried out on "Giving an Account of the Hope that is in Us", but rather to the way in which the churches have been encouraged to carry out a dialogue with people of living faiths and ideologies and with those without faith. The nature of dialogue is as Peter presents it. Even as we reverence Christ, so must we reverence those with whom we have dialogue as an encounter of life with life. In a profound sense Christ is present besides the other putting his or her claim upon us. Therefore, we must be ready to listen to the other to receive a word of judgment and promise, with the scriptures as our criterion, and be open to be renewed in faith as we pray that God's Spirit will do God's own work with the other. In this spirit, the churches and Christians are being renewed to be confessing communities, and so facilitate the building of "the house of living stones".

A fellowship of learning

Secondly, we have gained a fresh understanding of the churches as a fellowship of learning. Of course, this has been a characteristic of the Church from the very beginning. Peter uses a very moving image to describe what happens to those who are baptized – who, as in the early Church on the eve of Easter, put off their old clothes and descend into the waters of baptism and are crucified with Christ and rise from the waters in the risen Christ and put on new clothes. Before he evokes the images of the house of living stones, he writes:

> Put off all malice and deceit, and insincerity and jealousy and recrimina-
> tion of every kind. Like newborn babies, long for the pure spiritual
> milk, that by it you may grow up to salvation: for you have tasted
> that the Lord is good (2:1–3).

The Christian is like a newborn baby who eagerly sucks at its mother's warm breast to receive the food which will enable it to grow and be a person in its own right. Learning is that intimate process of tasting the goodness of God, what God has done and wills to be done that the world may become truly a home (*oikos*). Peter quotes Psalm 34 which describes how we learn the goodness of God in the travail of our existence with others in the world.

Learning in the Bible is a process by which people relate to God and God's way of truth, righteousness and peace, that they may in obedience practise that way in relation to each other and extending to the nations. Moses declares:

> The Lord said to me: "Gather the people to me, that I may let them hear my words, so that they may learn to reverence me all the days that they live upon the earth and that they may teach their children." . . . And the Lord commanded me at that time to teach you statutes and ordinances, that you might do them in the land which you are going over to possess (Deut. 4:10, 14).

And the prophet Isaiah prays to God:

> My soul yearns in the night,
> my spirit within me earnestly seeks thee.
> For when thy judgments are in the earth,
> the inhabitants learn righteousness (Isa. 26:9).

In these and many other passages in the Old and New Testaments we discern that learning does not simply mean acquiring knowledge or skills, or being intellectually equipped, or just memorizing some catechism of faith. Rather it means so entering with our whole being and with all the people into a relationship with God through God's self-revelation, that our horizons are widened and our wills are strengthened to be right with God and with one another in word and deed. Isaiah indicates clearly the global motivation of learning; he says that when believers yearn for God, like the baby at its mother's breast, this is no individual or parochial matter. They do so as those who dwell in the *oikoumene* and whose life should be governed by righteousness – right relations with God and others. Learning involves a global consciousness of God's will and way. This is a concept which is incredibly difficult to communicate through present mass media and educational structures and programmes.

It is not surprising therefore that the World Council has put a lot of emphasis on ecumenical learning during these last years. All its programmes and meetings are means by which people allow themselves to be opened to the realities of God's word in the context of the harsh realities of our world. They do so by being opened to each other and being opened to go beyond their local ways of thinking and acting. This Assembly is a living example of what we mean by ecumenical learning. So, too, are the many team visits between our churches which have helped to prepare us for this event. Such learning is a precondition for any effective action in the cause of truth, peace and justice, and the building of true community. However, it has to be admitted that this perception of learning has not been sufficiently built into the programmes of the World Council and that the churches themselves have not sufficiently appropriated the insights and perspectives received through this process of ecumenical learning. And insofar as we fail to take such learning seriously, we fail to become a house of living stones.

A fellowship of participation

Thirdly, we have become acutely aware that the churches should be a fellowship of participation. In fact, in New Testament Greek, *koinonia* was the word for "fellowship" and "participation"; it meant a community which is bound together in mutual support, service and sharing. Peter's image of the house of living stones also points to this *koinonia*. He speaks of "a holy priesthood offering spiritual sacrifices acceptable to God through Jesus Christ" (2:5), and later of "a royal priesthood" (2:9).

One of the great merits of the Reformation was the discovery, based on the very word of Peter, that everyone – woman and man alike – is a priest before God, offering the life of the world to God and receiving his or her life through the eucharistic sacrifice of Christ for the life of the world. But it is one of the curiosities of our history as churches that this conviction that we are a holy, consecrated priesthood, a priesthood which owes its allegiance to the king and ruler of our lives, has degenerated into a kind of individualistic, pietistic religion. This has, on the one hand, destroyed a sense of our mutual accountability and our common bond as the house of living stones. On the other hand, it has exposed the churches to various forms of hierarchical and institutional exclusiveness, with a concentration of power in bureaucratic ways which are alien to all that God has ordained and promised to the ancient people of Israel – that all the earth was God's and that they should be a kingdom of priests (Ex. 19:6). God willed that people should act as priests of the king and ruler of the earth sustaining and caring for the earth as God cares for them. Instead we have followed the ways of the rulers of the earth and created stratified and petrified structures of power in the churches, thus depriving us of our true priesthood to the world and of being living, dynamic stones fitted into a growing habitable house for all.

This has been a persistent concern of the ecumenical movement. We have reminded each other that the Church is, as Peter affirmed, the people, *laos*, of God, and not principally the ordained ministry which, though indispensable, constitutes less than 1% of the house of living stones. We have endeavoured to encourage the churches to recognize that young people are not the church of tomorrow but of today. More insistently in recent years we have painfully tried to come to terms with the fact that the house of living stones is a community of women and men fulfilling a common ministry of witness and service to the world. We recall that the first account we have of the Lord's Supper, what we call holy communion, is given by Paul when he rebukes the rich, upper-class members of the church in Corinth for excluding the poorer and socially despised members (1 Cor. 11:17–34). We are also learning to recognize the right and privilege of the disabled to participate as living members of the body of Christ.

Our communion in the body and blood of Christ, our spiritual sacrifices, the offering of the gift of the spirit we have received, demands that we exorcise the heresies of magisterial authority and power in the Church and become a true priesthood of all believers among whom the gifts and functions are not imposed but mutually accepted, whether ordained or lay. At the heart of our divisions as churches is this disparity and concentration of power in the life of the churches, which weakens our credibility in a world which is full of power-grabbing and individualism. The challenge to the churches and to the Council is, therefore, how far we are willing to be obedient to the convictions of our faith that we really become a priesthood of the whole house of living stones, dedicated to God and God's kingly rule, sharing God's gifts as we offer them to the world. That is what is involved in being a fellowship of participation exercising, in love, our priestly task by being with and among the people.

A fellowship of sharing

Fourthly, we have experienced the blessing of the churches being a fellowship of sharing. Since the end of World War II, while the World Council of Churches was still in process of formation, churches have shown a clear will to share their resources as a demonstration of being a house of living stones, crossing the barriers of division caused by war and political conflicts, and meeting human need wherever it arose and with no other motive than caring love. We are now in a difficult process of developing, within the Council itself, a means by which we can show the inter-related character of our sharing of material, technical and above all spiritual resources.

Peter develops his image of the house of living stones by urging the diaspora churches:

> Above all hold unfailing your love for one another, since love covers a multitude of sins. Practise hospitality ungrudgingly to one another. As each has received a gift, employ it for one another, as good stewards of God's varied grace (1 Pet. 4:8–10).

God's grace, his self-giving love, has been manifest in Christ, he who gave his body and blood for us and for the world. We share his grace through his gifts, *charismata*, which are for the good functioning of the house. That is why we are called stewards, *oikonomoi*, "economists" whose basic understanding of policy is love. Peter also reminds us that Christ's bearing of our sins in his body means that we might die to our selfish rebellion from God and become "alive to righteousness, justice" (2:24), a term which for Peter who was brought up in the Hebrew tongue, meant right relations with God and therefore with one another – the relationship of sharing the life which God has given us.

It has become fashionable to accuse the World Council and some churches of being too involved in social and economic concerns. This very accusation raises the question of how the churches themselves relate to one another. There is far too little real sharing within and between the churches, not only of material and technical resources which so much dominates our thinking, but of all the gifts of grace which we have received. We have learned in the ecumenical movement that our disunity as churches is in large measure due to our incapacity to practise this genuine sharing of gifts. We tend too much to hang on to the inherited forms of power and prestige and to the petrifying habit of self-sufficiency or of obsequious begging.

There is another element in this fellowship of sharing. Within and around the churches are Christian groups or communities which are seeking to use the gifts of the Spirit in ways which are renewing and enriching for all, often to the point of suffering and even death. But the gifts of these groups are not well shared among themselves and with the churches in each country. The churches are sometimes very aloof from these groups, and the groups are equally aloof from the churches' institutional authorities. This is a particularly acute issue for the World Council, because many of its programmes are carried out with the active groups which dare to use their gifts for the life of the world in personal, costly ways. This has often exacerbated the relations between the churches and the Council. How do we get out of this impasse? How can we together develop a fellowship of sharing, remembering that fellowship and sharing are in fact one reality, *koinonia*, the communion in the body of Christ for the life of the world? This is one of the critical issues to which I hope this Assembly will address itself.

A fellowship of healing

Fifthly, we have been learning that the churches are called to be a fellowship of healing. The Council and the churches have been greatly helped to understand this through a series of consultations around the world on "Health, Healing and Wholeness". The operative understanding of health now emerging is that it is " . . . a dynamic state of wellbeing of the individual and of society; of physical, mental, spiritual, economic, political and social wellbeing; of being in harmony with each other, with the material environment and with God". It is this holistic approach to health which has caught our attention, and which is demonstrated in the healing ministry of Jesus.

Scientists have discovered that matter, and especially the body, is not a mechanistic phenomenon. Therefore, when any part of the mechanism is not functioning properly it cannot be treated in isolation. The body is indeed an organism in which both body and mind, our social and natural environment play a decisive role. We have to be enabled to participate in the process of understanding the interconnectedness of the house of our bodies in terms of the house of our environment. We must be permitted to share in the process of healing, through mobilizing the stronger elements to support the weaker. Above all, our total state of being in living fellowship with God is essential for health, even if the body dies. There is a healthy and an unhealthy way of dying.

This view of health challenges the separations we have created by our present ways of looking at the world and of operating, whether in church or society. We divide the soul from the body, the mind from matter, rational thought from feeling. These dualisms have played havoc with our world, but even more in the churches which have developed these dualisms in systems of dogmas, ethical norms, and attitudes towards persons and society which are quite alien to our biblical and especially Christian heritage. Pursuing his image of the house of living stones, Peter refers to Isaiah 53, saying that it was by the wounds of Christ's whole self-offering that we are healed (2:24). In this way he calls us to live for righteousness, justice, being in right relations with God and with one another and, we must add, with our environment.

The image of the house of living stones is relevant here, because it calls for an understanding of our life as churches in which the house is made up of the living stones being fitted together and functioning as a whole beyond the separateness which marks our existence. The only separateness which our faith entertains is that separateness or holiness which means our total devotion and orientation to the triune God, whose inner being and manifestation as Father, Son and Holy Spirit is that of mutual exchange, co-inherence within the divine life. It is this co-inherence in our life together which makes for wholeness and peace, that integrated wellbeing, when even death is swallowed up into victory.

There is a great need in this area for the churches and the Council to rethink their theological and ethical systems and their style of life, and to overcome their indifference to the natural environment. The image of the house of living stones includes the whole *oikoumene*, the whole cosmos in which people and all living things have their being.

A fellowship of reconciliation

Sixthly, we have become deeply mindful of our calling as churches and as a Council to be a fellowship of reconciliation. We have, indeed, been entrusted with the ministry of reconciliation (2 Cor. 5:18). This is particularly urgent at a time of fierce confrontation, the hurling of anathemas between nations and peoples, especially the powerful ones, and the helpless drift to the apocalyptic annihilation of the *oikoumene*. As Peter reminds us, the churches are diaspora communities, barely tolerated minorities, ignored, reviled or persecuted if they take a stand for the way of reconciliation. When, therefore, Peter calls these scattered communities to become a house of living stones, and to assume the sufferings of Christ for the world, he is calling for a courageous confrontation with the forces of evil and destruction in the world.

Peter does not shirk the fact that reconciliation is not possible without bringing out, rather than pushing under the table, the things which are contrary to God's purpose for his creation. In his image of the stone, he also quotes from Isaiah 8:14–15. It is instructive to quote the full passage:

> The Lord said: "Do not call conspiracy all that this people call conspiracy, and do not fear what they fear, nor be in dread. But the Lord of hosts, him you shall regard as holy; let him be your fear, and let him be your dread. And he will become a sanctuary, and a stone of offence, and a rock of stumbling to both houses of Israel, a trap and a snare to the inhabitants of Jerusalem. And many shall stumble thereon; they shall fall and be broken; they shall be snared and taken."

Isaiah warns the house of Israel that they should not be seduced by the power games that were going on in the surrounding nations, nor should they make alliances, or for fear be submissive to one side of the conflicts or another. They should expose the conflicts between the powers as denials of the covenant purpose of God, because the outcome of such conflicts is that all will be broken on the rock of offence to God's will and purpose. It has been a continuing task of the World Council to analyze and expose the underlying causes of injustice and war and to work for the peaceful resolution of conflicts.

It was that great early ecumenical pioneer, John R. Mott, who used to say: "We must turn our stumbling blocks into stepping stones." The Chinese characters for "crisis" mean "danger" – "opportunity". At this dangerous time in which we meet as an Assembly, I hope that we who represent the house of living stones, coming from the diaspora, will take a clear and unequivocal stand for God's will for peace and justice, which are inextricably bound together, and will not be tempted to echo the doomed policies of the nations from which we come. The credibility of the gospel of reconciliation is at stake here. It is significant, in this regard, to remember that the Sermon on the Mount, which calls us to such a ministry of reconciliation, ends with the image of two houses – one built on sand which is bound to fall, and the other built on the rock of God's way of peace. The world will be watching us to know whether we will meet the test of being truly a house of living stones, built on the rock of faith in God who wills peace for all, and the rights of all to be fully themselves whatever their creed or sex or race or class or nation.

A fellowship of unity

Seventhly, we have tried to be attentive to the prayer of our Lord that we should be a fellowship of unity. I have mentioned this central calling and task of the ecumenical movement and of the churches at this point, because many are all too prone to say that the World Council is indifferent to our primary task of becoming what we are in the work of God in Christ, one house of living stones offering the eucharistic sacrifice as one people who are destined to offer the sacrifice of their lives for the unity of the *oikoumene*. On the contrary, I have mentioned this essential calling of the churches here precisely because all that has been said before is about the confession of the one, holy, catholic and apostolic Church.

We can claim notable advances in the way towards unity, especially during these thirty-five years. We started timidly and with much mutual suspicion by covenanting to stay together. We tried to describe as openly and honestly as possible to each other the major doctrinal blocks to unity. We moved from there to consider our given unity in the undivided Christ whose crucified and risen life we share, and pledged to let this Christ do his work among us as we seek to be obedient to him. We have since expressed the goal of unity in each place and in all places and all ages in one eucharistic fellowship expressed in worship and in common life in Christ that the world may believe. We have gone further and engaged in bilateral and multilateral discussions between the different communions, and the Council has assisted in bringing these together into a forum of assessing where we are and where we are going. We see the way forward in working for conciliar fellowship, expressed in various ways, however feebly, not least in the World Council. And we have now asked the churches to facilitate a process by which the congregations can be involved in receiving convergent statements on baptism, eucharist and ministry.

The reactions so far received on this long march towards unity are mixed. But they certainly are marked by the fact that the churches have not yet sufficiently advanced in being a fellowship of confessing, of learning, of sharing, of healing, of participation and of reconciliation to overcome the stumbling blocks which have deeply divided them. Unity consists in the living stones being constantly built into the house of the living God and not in rearrangements within static structures. It is an inter-related process in which the diaspora churches are engaged.

I hope therefore that all that we say and decide during this Assembly will be judged by whether it promotes the unity of God's people as the house of living stones and as a sign and sacrament of God's design to unite all peoples as the *oikoumene* under the loving rule of the one God, Father, Son and Holy Spirit.

A fellowship of expectancy

Finally, we have learned afresh during these years that the churches are a fellowship of expectancy. Their existence is not an end in itself. They point to and are called to be a sign of the kingdom of God. Their constant prayer is: "Your kingdom come, your will be done on earth as it is in heaven." The image of the house of living stones is based on an act of celebration:

> Blessed be the God and Father of our Lord Jesus Christ! By his great mercy we have been born anew to a living hope through the resurrection of Jesus Christ from the dead, and to an inheritance which is imperishable, undefiled, and unfading, kept in heaven for you, who by God's power are guarded through faith for a salvation ready to be revealed in the last time (1 Pet. 1:3–5).

At this Assembly we shall be overwhelmed with the dangers facing our world. Some may be tempted to adopt an attitude of resignation as though all that is necessary is that we keep the faith and let the world go up in flames, an attitude which often goes along with accommodation with the deathly military policies of the powers. Many will be impatient that we are not doing enough and urgently enough to proclaim the gospel to the world, or to work for peace and justice for all, or to achieve the unity of the churches. We are called to be steadfast in faith, and we will not shrink from speaking and acting boldly in hope and love.

Nevertheless, we can only do this as we celebrate our faith in Christ the living stone and as living stones being fitted together into the house of God. Our worship, our prayers, our sharing of our faith with one another will be central to all we say and do. But, as Peter tells the diaspora churches, our living hope as those born anew through the living and abiding word of God (1:23) and as those who taste that the Lord is good, must make us enter into the sufferings of the world as we share the sufferings of Christ. The way ahead is one of pain and suffering, of persecution and death for many. It is the way of faithful living by the deeds of God, but it is also the way of joy. As Peter says:

> Rejoice in so far as you share Christ's suffering, that you may also rejoice and be glad when his glory is revealed (1 Pet. 4:13).

* * *

What does all this say to us about the nature and calling of the churches and of the Council? Soon after the Council was formed, there was a big debate about "the ecclesiological significance of the World Council of Churches" at the Central Committee meeting in Toronto in 1950. It was recognized that the Council "represents a new and unprecedented approach to the problem of interchurch relationships" and that it "exists to break the deadlock between the churches". Over thirty years after, we are able to say that the calling of the churches to be a fellowship of confessing, of learning, of participation, of sharing, of healing, of reconciliation, of unity and of expectancy, has precisely been the preoccupation and task of the World Council. What consequences does this reality pose for the churches and for the Council?

Can the churches go on behaving as though the Council belongs to their external rather than their internal relations? Can the Council allow itself, through the decision of representatives of the churches, to go its own way with programmes and activities reaching to groups and others, but not conceived, planned, communicated at all stages, and carried out with the active involvement of the churches? Can the churches conduct themselves as though they exist in isolation from each other and from their fellowship in the World Council, carrying on their programmes and activities with little relation with other churches around the world? Can we go on acting as though we are just stones ineffectually scattered around, or shall we allow ourselves to be living stones being gathered together and built into the house of our triune God? Certainly, Peter's image of the house of living stones reminds us of the inescapable fact that it is only as the churches relate to each other as living stones that they will discover new realities about their essential calling to be the Church, the house of the triune God. And this common calling demands a fellowship of confessing, learning, participating, sharing, healing, reconciliation, unity and expectancy, to the glory of God, Father, Son and Holy Spirit. The task of the World Council of Churches, as well as of regional and local councils, is to promote this common calling.

At Nairobi in 1975 I reminded the Fifth Assembly that it would "have failed in its purpose if we did not advance to a new covenant relationship between the member churches at all levels of their life and the World Council at all levels of its activities". This reminder is even more urgent here at Vancouver, especially because during this period the relations between several member churches and the Council have been strained, and the Council has come under heavy attack from the media for the actions it has taken in response to the mandate of the Assembly and of the Central Committee. However, our fellowship has become deeper and more lively as we have faced the conflicts openly and frankly under the victorious cross of Christ.

There is no life without sharing. Our theme, "Jesus Christ – the Life of the World" is a clear call to let his life permeate our life together as we go forward in hope and with joyous courage to be living stones built into the house which will point to God's *oikoumene*, being filled with his life.

IV. MESSAGES

Messages were received from a number of heads of member churches, partner ecumenical bodies, international non-governmental organizations, and host organizations within Canada.

Reproduced below are the full texts of the messages from Pope John Paul II and the first General Secretary and current Honorary President of the World Council of Churches, Dr W. A. Visser 't Hooft.

1. Message from the Pope

The message from Pope John Paul II was conveyed by the Most Rev. James Carney, Archbishop of Vancouver. It read:

"The grace of the Lord Jesus be with you" (1 Cor. 16:23). As the delegates and other participants of the Sixth Assembly of the World Council of Churches gather in Vancouver, I wish to assure you of my deep pastoral interest and closeness in prayer.

"I am pleased that, for this important meeting in the service of the ecumenical movement, you have decided that the central theme would be: 'Jesus Christ – the Life of the World'. In doing this, you have reached out to Christians everywhere, to all who confess faith in Jesus Christ, believing that there is salvation in no one else, for there is no other name under heaven given among men by which we must be saved (Acts 4:12). You have affirmed our common belief that Jesus is the crucified Saviour, the Redeemer of all, the Lord of life who was designated Son of God in power according to the Spirit of holiness by his Resurrection from the dead (Rom. 1:4), the Risen Christ whose oneness with us in all things but sin has firmly established the dignity and worth of every human being.

"Ecumenical endeavours such as this bear witness to the ever increasing longing of Christians today that the prayer of Christ must be fulfilled: that they may be one (John 17:22). This urgent task, which still encounters many difficulties, is indeed challenging and multi-faceted. It requires obedience to the will of God and cooperation with his grace. It demands persevering faith and steadfast hope. Above all, it impels us to constant prayer and continual conversion.

"As I have made pastoral visits to the Catholic Church in various parts of the world, it has been a special pleasure for me to have met with representatives of a number of the member churches of the World Council. Many also have come to Rome to further our common efforts of dialogue and mutual understanding. Such contacts have advanced the cause of Christian unity, and I trust that the present gathering in Vancouver will bring about even further progress towards this goal for which we all long.

"Upon all taking part in the Sixth Assembly of the World Council of Churches, I invoke the wisdom, light and peace of the Holy Spirit. With the words of Saint Paul I say: My love be with you all in Christ Jesus (1 Cor. 16:24)."

2. Message from Dr W. A. Visser 't Hooft

"Since I am not able to make the journey to Vancouver, I can only express through this message that I try to accompany you by my thoughts and prayers. Not to attend a World Council Assembly makes me feel that the translator from a Latin country was right when he identified me recently in a church publication as 'the *ancient* General Secretary of the World Council of Churches'. It is good to know that the memory of the first five Assemblies is represented among you by the present General Secretary himself, who was the effective spokesman of the youth delegation at the first Assembly in 1948.

"You meet at a difficult moment in the history of the ecumenical movement. In the first phase of that history the discovery of the rich heritage of the churches and the declaration of our intention to grow together gave the movement its dynamic. Now we have reached the moment when we must draw the consequences and take concrete steps on the road to unity. In the meantime the climate in our environment has changed. The weather conditions are not favourable for ecumenical action.

"At such a moment we must remember the *raison d'être* of our Council. It is not the product of a nice-weather ecumenism. The basic motive in the creation of the World Council was not to respond to the contemporary mood of facile internationalism or to build up a more powerful ecclesiastical structure. It was simply to respond to the urgent prayer of our Lord, that his disciples should be one. The Amsterdam Assembly message put it very simply: 'Christ has made us his own and he is not divided. Here at Amsterdam we have committed ourselves to him and have covenanted with one another in constituting this World Council. We intend to stay together.' A movement with such a foundation need not fear a change of climate. Conscious of the fact that Christ gathers us at the foot of his cross, it knows that the criterion by which its life is judged is not outward worldly success but true obedience.

"As we hold on to the conviction that the commandment and promise of our Lord give us our marching orders, we can be witnesses that Jesus Christ who is the life of the Church is also the life of the world, and come to grips with the powerful forces which make the life of humankind in our time such a tragic story.

"May the life-giving Spirit guide and inspire you during this Assembly."

V. PRESENTATIONS
ON THE ASSEMBLY THEME

1. By Theodore Stylianopoulos

Glory to God who lives and reigns for ever!
Glory to the Father and the Son and the Holy Spirit, one kingdom,
one power, one life!
Glory to the sovereign Lord "who is and who was and who is to
come, the Almighty!" (Rev. 1:8, RSV) "For from him and through
him and to him are all things. To him be glory for ever" (Rom. 11:36)

Dear brothers and sisters in Christ, one of the joys of faith which
has sustained Orthodox Christians through many centuries of persecution is the celebration of Easter. Holy Pascha, as we call it, is a
new passover, a passing from death to life, a festival of life, light
and joy. With lighted candles in our hands, we spend much of
Pascha morning singing hymns to Christ, victor over death and
giver of life:

The day of resurrection! Let us be radiant in splendour!
Pascha of the Lord! Christ, our God, has led us from death to life,
from earth to heaven!
Christ is risen from the dead, trampling death by death, and to those
in the tombs granting life!

St John's prologue

For the paschal liturgy the appointed Gospel reading is the
prologue of St John, the magnificent hymnic expression of the faith
of the Church in all ages that Christ is life, truth, and grace. Let us
join in spirit the saints of all times and places in confessing "Jesus
Christ – the Life of the World" by reciting with one heart St John's
prologue as a hymn to Christ.

In the beginning was the word,
and the word was with God,
and the word was God.
He was in the beginning with God.

All things were made through him,
and without him was not anything made that was made.
In him was life,
and the life was the light of humankind.

The light shines in the darkness,
and the darkness has not overcome it.
          . . .
The true light that enlightens every person was coming to the world.
He was in the world,
and the world was made through him,
yet the world knew him not.
He came to his own home,
and his own people received him not.

But to all who received him,
who believed in his name,
he gave power to become children of God,
who were born, not of blood
nor of the will of the flesh
nor of the will of man,
but of God.

And the word became flesh
and dwelt among us,
full of grace and truth;
we have beheld his glory,
glory as of the only Son from the Father.
          . . .
And from his fullness have we all received grace upon grace.
For the law was given through Moses;
grace and truth came through Jesus Christ.
No one has ever seen God;
the only Son,
who is in the bosom of the Father,
he has made him known.

            (John 1:1–5, 9–14, 16–18)

My brothers and sisters, by faith we have gathered in this hospitable city of Vancouver from all around the globe, from Russia to South Africa, from England to Argentina, from Japan to India, that we may both confess and also witness to Christ as the true life, the giver of life, and the life of the world. What an enormous challenge! We have come together relying not "on ourselves but on God who raises the dead" (2 Cor. 1:9), that we may lift up Jesus Christ who was lifted up on the cross that the world may live.

The early Christian hymn that we read a moment ago extols Jesus Christ, the pre-existent and incarnate word of God, as the cosmic mystery of God's revelation in all things, especially in human beings. The pre-existent word, the life and light of all, according to this song of faith, reveals divine life through *creation*, through *incarnation*, and through *sanctification*. Life in him is a life of grace and truth, adoption as children of God, and a beholding of God's glory. The eternal word himself is the instrument of the revelation of God's glory throughout the material and spiritual cosmos, to the end that all creation may be disclosed in its true nature as a burning bush ablaze with the glory of the triune God, Creator, Redeemer, and Sanctifier.

But the doxological affirmations of faith and the hymnic language of St John's Gospel should not lead us to overlook the reality of evil, the tragedy of sin, the realm of darkness, which resist God's work. True life is not recognized. The light is rejected. Although the light overcomes the darkness, God's victory is achieved only through the cost of the cross. Just as the hands and feet of the crucified Christ were pierced by spikes, so also God's creative, redemptive, and sanctifying activities in the world are attacked by demonic forces ever ready to destroy life. Grace and sin, truth and falsehood, love and hatred, so we are told by the evangelist of the Fourth Gospel, everywhere engage one another. The battleground is the human heart and will. Our choice is God's gift of abundant life or the terrible emptiness of death.

All things were made through him

What does it mean to confess God as Creator? By confessing that "all things were made through him" (John 1:3) we affirm that life is a gift of God and achieves its true purpose in closest link with God – whereas alienation from God is death. Life in its amazing multiplicity of forms, species, and levels is cohesive, sacred, and inviolate. Like the bread and wine of the eucharist, all of it can be consecrated to God and mirror the glory of God. By confessing God as the source of life and the Lord of life we recognize that all creation is a eucharist in his presence. It is to be received thankfully and responsibly as a common table of God's love, not as an unclaimed or unprotected treasure for hoarding and abuse.

St Kosmas Aitolos, an itinerant monk, priest, evangelist, and martyr, working among peasants in northwestern Greece during the late eighteenth century, expressed this truth about life as a gift of God with powerful simplicity:

> God has many names, my brothers. The principal name of God is love. He is a Holy Trinity: Father, Son, and Holy Spirit, one nature, one glory, one kingdom, one God. We should first love God, my brothers, because he gave us such a large earth to live in, so many thousands of people. And he gave us plants, fountains, rivers, oceans, fish, birds, night and day, sky, sun and moon. . . For whom did he create all of these if not for us? What did he owe us? Nothing. They

are all his gifts. . . . Now I ask you, my brothers, tell me whom do you want, God or the devil?[1]

In the perspective of St John's Gospel creation has simultaneously a Christological and anthropological focus. The pre-existent word is the creative power that upholds all things but the primary goal of his loving action is humanity: "In him was life, and the life was the light of humankind" (John 1:4).[2] For the Fourth Gospel the term *cosmos* signifies not so much nature but chiefly the world of human affairs, personal and corporate. In deep, often inarticulate ways we human beings most clearly sense that we do not possess life of ourselves. Rather we partake of the gift of life and seek fullness of life. The message of St John's Gospel is that God offers not mere life, that is, natural existence which is assumed, but true life, eternal life, a quality of life penetrated by God's presence and will. The tragic problem of humanity is that we often seek to secure life in selfish ways which breed evil and corruption. Caught in our self-blindness, we refuse to trust in the Creator and obey God's truth. Hence our hatred and violence, our injustice and oppression, our love of possessions and hedonism, all expressions of the will to live gone wild. Behind all this is refusal to believe, wilful evil, insecurity, slavery to the survival instinct, and fear of death. The result is a cosmos ruled by demonic powers, darkness, and deadness. It is in this sense that, according to the Fourth Gospel, the term cosmos takes on the negative connotation signifying a world deliberately choosing to remain in darkness, a world set against its Creator, a world wholly "in the power of the evil one" (1 John 5:19). But the darkness does not overcome the light!

And the word became flesh

"And the word became flesh and dwelt among us" (John 1:14). What is meant by incarnation? The Gospel of St John, unlike those of St Matthew and St Luke, tells us nothing about the birth of Jesus. Although the fourth evangelist clearly affirms the *fact* of the word's incarnation, his emphasis falls on the incarnate word's *activity* in the

---

1. N. M. Vaporis, *Father Kosmas, the Apostle of the Poor*, Brookline, Holy Cross Orthodox Press, 1977, pp. 19 and 91. I have combined two of Kosmas' statements in the above citation. See also the excellent study by P. S. Vallianos, "St Kosmas Aitolos: Faith as Practical Commitment", *Greek Orthodox Theological Review*, 25, 2, 1980, pp. 172–186.
2. The RSV reads "men" instead of "humankind". I am also aware of the alternate punctuation of vss. 3b–4a translated: "That which has been made was life in him". But this seems improper to me because the prologue's reference here is not to created but uncreated life, the word himself, who is the life and light of humankind.

world. For St John's Gospel incarnation is above all the reality of the unique presence of God in the person, words, and works of Jesus of Nazareth. Through his historical ministry Christ discloses God's creative, redeeming, and sanctifying power: "My Father is working still, and I am working" (John 5:17).

Jesus healed the official's son. He restored the health of the paralytic. He fed the multitude. Jesus healed the blind beggar by a special act: "He spat on the ground and made clay of the spittle and anointed the man's eyes with the clay, saying to him, 'Go, wash in the pool of Siloam' ". In this act of making clay the Church fathers saw a symbol of the creation of humanity now being "recreated" by the incarnate word. St John Chrysostom comments that Christ, the self-same Creator, and not the pool of Siloam, healed the blindman.[3] Through such signs, as well as through his person and words, the Johannine Christ reveals his intimate relationship to the Father and also his divine prerogative of granting life as an act of grace (John 5:21,26). He is "the bread of God", "the only Son from the Father", indeed God the word in the flesh, giving life to the world.

The incarnation may be interpreted in several ways. First, it is an expression of God's unconditional love for humanity. The entire mission of the Son is prompted by divine love (John 3:16). "In this the love of God was made manifest among us, that God sent his only Son into the world, so that we might live through him" (1 John 4:9). The incarnate word *became* flesh that the love with which the Father loved him may *abide* in us (John 17:26).

The incarnation is also a sharing, an embrace of life by Life, a total identification of God with the object of God's love. The word "pitched his tent" (eskenōsen, John 1:14) among us that he might be "touched with our hands" (John 1:1). In his treatise *On the Incarnation* St Athanasius writes that the incarnate word moved among people, becoming an object of their senses, healing and teaching by word and deed.[4] "To all who received him. . . he gave power to become children of God" and to be his "friends" (John 15:14–15) and "brothers and sisters" (John 20:17). John, Irenaeus, Origen, Athanasius, Chrysostom and others all interpret the incarnation in the light of a theology of sharing – the Son of God became man in order that human beings might become children of God by grace. In this light the unity of Christ's full divinity and full humanity is the fundamental soteriological truth behind the trinitarian and Christological teaching of the Church.

---

3. Homily 57.1 on St John. See: *The Nicene and Post-Nicene Fathers*, First Series, Vol. 14, Grand Rapids, Eerdmans, 1969, p. 204.
4. *De Incar.*, iii, 14–15.

Finally the incarnation is redemption, the liberation of life, "life confronting and overcoming death", according to the formulation of the second sub-theme of the Sixth Assembly. The presence of the incarnate word in the world is an invasion of life into the realm of darkness. Especially Christ's passion, death, and resurrection, viewed as one movement of return to the Father,[5] represent his "hour of glory", the hour when the powers of sin, satan, and death are decisively defeated and new life takes hold in the world. Christ is Redeemer. "Behold the Lamb of God, who takes away the sin of the world!" (John 1:29). An Orthodox icon of the resurrection depicts the risen Christ shattering the gates of Hades, breaking to pieces the bonds of death, and raising up Adam and Eve to new life. This same theme resounds frequently in Orthodox hymns:

> When you descended into the realm of death, O immortal life, you put Hades to death by the dazzling light of your divinity. When you raised up the dead from the dark abyss, all the powers of heaven cried out: Christ, our God, giver of life, glory to you!

And from his fullness have we all received

The sufferings of Christ should not cause us to overlook his moments of joy with people. One of them was the marriage in Cana where Jesus turned water into wine. The fourth evangelist alone reports this miracle and places it at the beginning of Jesus' ministry. Already much wine had been drunk. But Jesus made between one hundred twenty and one hundred eighty more gallons of new wine (John 2:6–9), a hyperbole. The joy of the marriage, the festivity of the wedding banquet, and the abundance of wine – all symbolize the fullness of life brought to the world by Christ upon whom the Spirit descended and remained (John 1:32). The incarnate word was rich in "grace and truth" (John 1:14). The Law, *given* through Moses, was a gift of God. The only Son bearing the glory of the Father now brings "grace upon grace" (John 1:16). The pairing of "grace" and "truth" is well attested in the Jewish tradition (*hesed* and *'emet*). God was revealed to Moses on Sinai as a merciful and gracious God "*abounding in steadfast love and faithfulness*" (or rich in *hesed* and *'emet*, Ex. 34:6). "Truth" is faithfulness, constancy, or fidelity. "Grace" is steadfast love, covenant love, merciful love, or loving kindness.[6]

Abundant life in Christ is life in community. "We have beheld his glory" (John 1:14). "And from his fullness have *we all* received"

---

5. See R. Brown, *The Gospel According to John I–XII, The Anchor Bible*, Vol. 29, New York, Doubleday, 1966, p. 507.
6. *Ibid.*, p. 14.

(John 1:16). The community consciousness is especially high in the farewell discourses of St John's Gospel (chapters 13–17). Against the background of the washing of the disciples' feet and the Last Supper, Jesus shares with the disciples the bread of divine love in the world, their mutual relationship, and his abiding presence among them through the Spirit. He reveals to them his relationship to the Father and the Spirit; he prays to the Father that they may be sanctified in the truth and may share his glory; and he prepares them for mission. He is departing to the Father but he gives to them the Spirit to teach them all things. He also leaves with them his peace, assurance of victory, and commandments of love, mutual service, and unity. This is the risen Christ speaking to his Church in all ages about who he is, who the disciples are, what they are to do in the world and how to do it. The Lord and his Church are like the vine and the branches bearing fruit for the life of the world.

An example of a disciple who heard his Master's voice is Ivan Ilyich Sergiev, better known to the Orthodox as St John of Kronstadt, an amazing witness to the abundant life of Christ lived in community. A pastor of a large cathedral, a man of the eucharist, a man of the scriptures, a man of prayer – truly a beloved disciple of the Lord – he washed with the waters of divine love the feet of thousands upon thousands of beggars and tramps, who were concentrated in the port city of Kronstadt on the Baltic by government policy.[7] The slums of Kronstadt were described as follows: "Those places were terrible – one found in them darkness, dirt and sin: there, even a seven-year-old child might be a profligate and a thief."[8] Father John shared with these poor people the richness of his life in Christ not only through the encouraging joy of the good news but also through an immense community project of which Father John, yes Christ in him, was the life-power. He advertized in the *Kronstadt Herald*,[9] pleaded with the public,[10] mobilized

---

7. Bishop Alexander Semenoff-Tian-Chanksy, *The Life of Father John of Kronstadt*, Crestwood, St Vladimir's Seminary Press, 1979, p. 13.
8. *Ibid.*, quoting the words of the writer A. V. Knuglov.
9. *Ibid.*, p. 17. Father John perceived not only the private but also the social causes of poverty as, e.g. in this advertisement: "Who does not know of the swarms of beggars in Kronstadt?. . . The reasons for their extreme poverty are many; for instance: poverty from birth; poverty due to orphanhood; poverty deriving from accidents such as fire and theft; poverty due to loss of work or incapacity to work owing to old age or illness; laziness; weakness for alcoholic drinks; and, mainly, lack of the equipment necessary to start work, such as decent clothing, tools or instruments."
10. *Ibid.*, p. 18, quoting Father John: "Do not be afraid of the immensity of such an enterprise; God will help us in a good work and with God's help everything which is needful will be forthcoming."

people of education and means,[11] and finally in 1882 the Home for Constructive Labour was opened, a phenomenal success. According to statistics, by 1902, 7,281 men worked in its bag-and-hat shops, 259 children were enrolled in its free elementary school, and up to 800 meals per day were served in its public eating house. The home also featured job training in carpentry, shoe-making, and sewing, a library, a Sunday school, and even a summer camp boasting its own vegetable garden. Father John's biographer comments: "Such organized welfare, initiated by a parish priest, was at that time an unusual, a novel event. . . and it is the more exceptional, because his practical activity did not prevent him from remaining in a state of constant, profound prayer and spiritual contemplation."[12] This "praying priest" as he was called, a splendid example of orthodox evangelical Christianity, who knew nothing about the neat distinction between the "vertical" and "horizontal" dimensions of Christian life, most surely knew who was his life-source and the life-power of his work:

> The Lord is everything to me: he is the strength of my heart and the light of my intellect. He inclines my heart to everything good; he strengthens it; he also gives me good thoughts; he is my rest and my joy; he is my faith, hope, and love; he is my food and drink, my raiment, my dwelling place.[13]

The only Son from the Father

While the prologue as well as the entire content of St John's Gospel extols the incarnate word's significance for the world as the creative, redeeming and sanctifying presence of the triune God, the limelight is cast on the grandeur of the person of Christ himself whose glory is "glory as of the only Son from the Father" (John 1:14). Christ does not merely *teach* about or *transmit* life, light and truth; he *is* also all these. He is "the Son of God and the King of Israel", the "Holy One of God" with life-giving words, and the

---

11. *Ibid.*, quoting Father John: " 'The strong ought to bear the infirmities of the weak' (Rom. 15:1). Therefore in the presence of such diverse potentialities in our Kronstadt society, with all its talents, its great numbers of educated, active and often wealthy people, it would be a sin before God and men to leave so many of our members alienated, isolated and deprived of their share of prosperity."

12. *Ibid.*, p. 21. For the statistics see pp. 19–21.

13. *My Life in Christ: Extracts from the Diary of Saint John of Kronstadt*, Part I, transl. E. E. Goulaeff and reprinted by Archmandrite Panteleimon, Jordanville, Holy Trinity Monastery, 1977, p. 225. A thematic selection of St John's diary extracts has been compiled by W. Jardine Grisbrooke, *Spiritual Counsels of Father John of Kronstadt*, Westminster, Clarke, 1966, and reprinted by St Vladimir's Seminary Press, 1982.

Lord and God (John 20:28). He who comes to give abundant life to all declares: "you will die in your sins unless you believe that I am he" (the divine name, *egō eimi*, John 8:24; cf. Ex. 3:13). By virtue of his unique relationship to God the Father (1:1,18) the incarnate word reveals: "I am the way, and the truth, and the life; no one comes to the Father, but by me" (John 14:6). The whole Gospel of St John was written to the end "that all may believe that Jesus is the Christ and that believing they may have life in his name" (John 20:21).

How can this absolute claim that Christ is not *a* but *the* life of the world be properly interpreted in the contemporary world of religious and ideological pluralism, a world shrunk to the extent that a satellite can travel around it in a few hours? Ours is a problem of affirming a Christology neither "from above" nor "from below" but from both – that is the theological witness of St John. To be sure, this is not a scientific or philosophical but confessional claim – the central spiritual claim of the Christian faith. We must freely admit that this claim, as other transcendent claims by other religions, has from the early days of Christianity led Christians to sinful patterns of triumphalism, intolerance, and persecution unworthy of Christ who preached love of enemies and forgave his crucifiers from the cross. We need to repent of our sins before the world and seek in the mystery of the cross to find ways of lifting up Christ as an invitation of faith, love, and freedom, an invitation which must not be abused either for selfish ends or to force anyone's conscience.

St Maximus the Confessor,[14] St Isaac the Syrian,[15] and other Church fathers taught that divine love knows no distinctions between sinner or righteous, friend or enemy, believer or unbeliever, but rather is ready to be sacrificed equally for all. Woe to those who would lay claim to Christ, the incarnate love of God, that they may breed self-righteousness and intolerance, prejudice and polemics, injustice and oppression, hiding all manner of sin and ignorance. It is only through the pursuit of the perfect love of Christ that we can discover the freedom of confessing the glorious name of Christ, while in love respecting the spiritual claims of others. Only through such love can we perceive differing transcendent claims among Christians themselves and also among others as the

---

14. "For him who is perfect in love and has reached the summit of dispassion there is no difference between his own or another's, or between Christians and unbelievers, or between slave and free, or even between male and female," in *The Philokalia, The Complete Text*, Vol. 2, trans. and ed. G. E. H. Palmer, P. Sherrard, and K. Ware, London & Boston, Faber & Faber, 1981, p. 70.

15. See *Mystic Treatises by Isaac of Nineveh*, trans. A. J. Wensinck, Amsterdam, 1923, reprinted Wiesbaden, 1969, pp. 38–39.

cherished values of their historical experience without feelings of disloyalty to Christ.

That Christ is the life of the world, therefore, is above all a call to Christians themselves for radical repentance, spiritual renewal, urgency on the walk towards unity, common witness, prophetic action, being ready to die for others in Christ's name. Are we willing to die for others in his name? That is a key question. We ourselves then become, and only then, convincing in our confession of Christ as the life of the world. Christ came not to judge the world but to save it. By his grace, that is also our task. In the words of St Dimitrii of Rostov, let us confess Christ as our Life, Light, and Lord, and pray to him to cleanse us from sin and to energize us for this task:

> Come, our Light, and illumine our darkness.
> Come, our Life, and revive us from death.
> Come, our Physician, and heal our wounds.
> Come, Flame of divine love, and burn up the thorns of our sins, kindling our hearts with the flame of your love.
> Come, our King, sit upon the throne of our hearts and reign there.
> For you alone are our King and our Lord.[16]

2. By Allan Boesak

Jesus Christ the life of the world! These are words that speak of joy, of meaning, of hope. For some, they may even speak of triumph and victory. These are words that have a ring of certainty in them. Yet, in the uncertain world of suffering, oppression and death, what do they mean? The realities of the world in which we live suggest the cold grip of death rather than the freedom of life.

Violence, greed and the demonic distortion of human values continue to destroy God's world and his people. Economic exploitation is escalating rather than abating and economic injustice is still the dominant reality in the relationships between rich and poor countries. Racism is as rampant as ever, not only in South Africa, but also in other parts of the world. In its alliances with national security ideologies it has acquired a new cloak of respectability and has become even more pervasive. In South Africa apartheid and injustice still reign supreme. Inequality is still sanctified by law and racial superiority is still justified by theology. Today, with the

---

16. K. Ware, *The Orthodox Way*, St Vladimir's Orthodox Theological Seminary, 1979, p. 21–22. I have rendered the prayer in the plural.

blatant support of so many Western governments, apartheid seems stronger than ever and the dream of justice and human dignity for South Africa's black people more remote than ever.

In our world, it is not the joyful, hopeful sound of the word of life that is being heard. No, that word is drowned by the ugly sound of gunfire, by the screams of our children and the endless cry of the powerless: "How long, Lord?"

In too many places too many children die of hunger and too many people just disappear because they dare to stand up for justice and human rights. Too many are swept away by the tides of war and too many are tortured in dungeons of death. In too many eyes the years of endless struggle have extinguished the fires of hope and joy and too many bodies are bowed down by the weight of that peculiarly repugnant death called despair. Too many young people believe that their youth and their future are already powdered to dust by the threat of nuclear destruction. And even in the face of all of this, too many in the Christian Church remain silent. We have not yet understood that every act of inhumanity, every unjust law, every untimely death, every utterance of faith in weapons of mass destruction, every justification of violence and oppression is a sacrifice on the altar of the false gods of death; it is a denial of the Lord of life.

No, for millions of people it is true: we are not uplifted by the word of life, we are crushed by the litany of death.

Yet the gospel affirms: Jesus Christ is the life of the world. That means he is the source of life, he is the giver of the sacred gift of life. He intends for us a life filled with abundance, joy and meaning. He is the Messiah in whose eyes our lives are precious.

But this is precisely the problem. Dare we believe this? Can we believe this without making of our faith a narrow, spiritual escapism? Can we avoid the cynicism of "reality"? Can we find a way to live with that painful dilemma: "Lord, I believe, please help my unbelief!" And even more painful: can we accept the reality of hope and the call to battle that lie in this affirmation? In other words, is the joyous affirmation, this confession that Jesus Christ is the life of the world, really meant for the millions who suffer and die, who are oppressed and who live without hope in the world today? While discussing this theme with a group in my congregation, a woman said quietly, almost despairingly: "It seems you have to be white and rich to believe this."

Good news for the weak

But there are two things we must remember when talking about this. First, in the Gospels this affirmation is never a triumphalistic war-cry. It is never a slogan built on might and power. It is a confession in the midst of weakness, suffering and death. It is the quiet, subversive piety which the Christian Church cannot do without. Second, we must be reminded that in the Bible this affirmation is given to people who in their situation *were* the poor, the oppressed and the weak. They were the people who lived on the underside of history. And it is they who are called upon to confirm this truth: Jesus Christ is the Life of the World.

In the Gospel of John, chapter 4, the story of Jesus and the Samaritan woman is a good illustration of this truth. She is the paradigm *par excellence* of the despised, the weak and the oppressed. She becomes the very example of the dejected people of this world. First of all, she is a woman, with all that that means in the society of her day. Notice how John makes a point of stating the disciples' astonishment that Jesus was in discussion with a woman. She is also a Samaritan, and therefore despised and rejected by the Jews. Her religion is considered inferior and in her own community she is an outcast because of her way of life. This is probably the reason why she goes to that well alone, at a most unusual hour of the day. But it is precisely to her that Jesus speaks of these unfathomable things: the life-giving waters, and the waters of life.

Likewise, the Revelation of John is written to a weak, scattered underground church, suffering severely under the persecution of a ruthless tyrant. They were people who had no recourse, no protection under the law, no "connections" in high and powerful places, no political or economic power. Their lives were cheap. They were completely and utterly surrendered to the mercy of a man who did not know the meaning of the word, whom John could only describe with the telling title: "beast". From a purely human point of view, they had not a chance in the world, there was precious little upon which they could build their hopes for the future. But like the Samaritan woman, *they* are the ones who hear the message and to whom this is proclaimed: "I am the first and the last and the living One. . ." They knew with a certainty not born of earthly power: Jesus Christ, not the Caesar (in spite of all *his* power!), is the life of the world. The claims of divinity, of immortality, of omniscience and power are the lies, the half-truths, the propaganda without which no tyrant can survive. But the truth stands: Jesus Christ is the life of the world, and he is indeed Lord of life.

The Church understood this confession not only as a comfort in times of trial and darkness, but as essential part of that basic, subversive confession: Jesus Christ is Lord. In this way it became not only comfort to the persecuted, oppressed Church, but also a ringing protest against the arrogance of earthly potentates who wanted so desperately to create the impression that *they* decided over the life and death of the people of God. And the Church knew this to be the truth, not only for the life hereafter, but the truth for the very life and the very world in which they struggled to believe, to be faithful, to be obedient. To understand that is to understand the power, nay more, to experience the power of the life-giving Word. It is to drink of the life-giving and living waters even while facing suffering, destruction and death. It is to understand and experience what it means to worship the living One in spirit and in truth. This worship is not confined to certain moments only. This is a worship which encompasses all of our life, so that every prayer for liberation, every act for the sake of human dignity, every commitment in the struggle for true human freedom, every protest against the sinful realities of this world, becomes an offering to the living One for the sake of his kingdom.

Jesus says: "The hour comes, and it is now. . ." Here the present and the future coalesce. The moment of the hesitant, yet faithful human response and the moment of the favour of the Lord come together.

This is the source of the acts of sublime courage sometimes displayed in the witness and the life of the Christian Church. This is what led to the witness of the Christian Church at the martyrdom of St Polycarp:

> The blessed Polycarp died a martyr's death on 23 February, on the Great Sabbath, the eighth hour. Herod imprisoned him when Phillip of Tralles was the High Priest, and Statius Quartus was the Pre Consul, whilst for ever is King our Lord Jesus Christ. His be the glory, honour, majesty and an everlasting throne from generation to generation. Amen.

And indeed, it may seem as if for the moment the dictators of this world, the powerful and the mighty have full control over this world. Their arrogance seems to have no bounds. Their power seems unchecked. But the Church knows: Jesus Christ is Lord of history, he is Lord of life, and his truth shall have the final word.

In the same way Christians in South Africa begin to understand that for us God's moment is brought together with our present reality, as we discern that the Church is called to an extraordinary courageous witness for the sake of the gospel. So we hear Bishop Desmond Tutu, the General Secretary of the South African Council of Churches, saying to the Minister of Law and Order: "Mr Minister, we must remind you that you are not God. You are just a man. And one day your name shall merely be a faint scribble on the pages of history, while the name of Jesus Christ, the Lord of the Church, shall live forever. . ."

The Christian Church can take this stand, not because it possesses earthly power, nor because it has "control" over the situation. Over against the structures of political, economic and military powers who seek to rule this world, the Church remains weak and in a sense defenceless. But it takes this stand because it refuses to believe that the powers of oppression, death and destruction have the last word. Even while facing these powers the Church continues to believe that Jesus Christ is Lord and therefore the life of the world. And it is this faith in the living One, this refusal to bow down to the false gods of death, that is the strength of the Church.

But this affirmation has another ramification. Jesus Christ is the life of the *world*. His concern is not only for the Church but for the world. In his life, death and resurrection lies not only the future of the Church, but the future of the world. In the letter to the Ephesians, Paul is persistent in proclaiming Jesus Christ as Lord of the Church and of the cosmos. Therefore, his being our peace has consequences not only for the Church but also for the world. Therefore, the Church must proclaim, clearly and unequivocally, that Jesus Christ came to give meaningful life to the world, so that all of human history, all human activity can be renewed and liberated from death and destruction.

The life of the world, the destruction of this world, the future of this world, is therefore the concern of the Church. We have a responsibility for this world, for it is God's world. And if this world is threatened by the evils of militarism, materialism, greed, racism, it is very much the concern of the Church. It is the Church which has heard the words: "Today I am giving you a choice between good and evil, between life and death. . . choose life!" It is the Church which has heard the words: "I have come so that they may have life, and that abundantly. . ." And because we have heard this, and because we confess Jesus Christ as the life of the world, we dare not be silent.

Speaking out on peace and justice

This Assembly must speak out. We must confess, humbly but without any hesitation, our faith in Jesus Christ, the life of the world. We must, humbly, but without any hesitation, renew our commitment to Jesus Christ, the life of the world. And this faith, this commitment, must be the basis of our action on the issues of peace, justice and human liberation. We must not hesitate to address ourselves to the question of peace and to the possibility of total nuclear destruction. We must be clear: the nuclear arms race, the employment of God-given human talents and possibilities for the creation of ever more refined weapons of mass destruction, and the call to put our faith in these weapons so as to secure our peace, is not simply a temporary madness, it is essentially sinful and contrary to the purposes of God for this world and for the people of his heart.

I am not persuaded that the issue of peace is simply one of fashion, a fad that will go away tomorrow. I do not agree with those who believe that this issue is simply one of political and military calculations, so that the Church should withdraw from the debate and let the problems be solved by the politicians and the military strategists. I remain convinced that the issue of peace as it faces us today, lies at the very heart of the gospel.

But there is something else I must say about this. When the World Alliance of Reformed Churches met in Ottawa last August, we spent considerable time discussing a statement on peace. During the debate, a delegate from Africa made a remark that very poignantly raised some of the tensions surrounding this issue in the ecumenical movement today. He said: "In this document, the word 'nuclear' is used a number of times, but I don't ever see the word 'hunger'. In my village, the people will not understand the word 'nuclear', but they know everything about hunger and poverty."

What he was really talking about was the concern of many Christians in the "third world" that the issue of peace will be separated from the issue of justice, making of peace primarily a North Atlantic concern. This should not happen. First of all because ideologies of militarism and national security are international in character and cause deprivation and the continuation of injustice everywhere, but especially in the so-called "third world" countries. But secondly, and more importantly, in the Bible peace and justice are never separated. Peace is never simply the absence of war, it is the active presence of justice. It has to do with human fulfilment, with liberation, with wholeness, with a meaningful life and wellbeing, not only for the individual, but for the community as a whole. And the prophet Isaiah speaks of peace as the offspring of justice.

So it may be true that the issues of justice, racism, hunger and poverty are largely unresolved issues for the ecumenical movement. It may be true that these issues present the churches with painful dilemmas, but it cannot be true that we will be willing to use the issue of peace to avoid those dilemmas. One cannot use the gospel to escape from the demands of the gospel. And one cannot use the issue of peace to escape from the unresolved issues of injustice, poverty, hunger and racism. If we do this we will make of our concern for peace an ideology of oppression which in the end will be used to justify injustice.

Separating truth from falsehood

But there is one last point we have to make. Jesus Christ is the life of the world because he reveals the truth about himself, the Church, humankind and the world. He is the Messiah, the chosen One of God who proclaims the acceptable year of the Lord. In him is the fulfilment of the promises of Yahweh. He is the Servant of the Lord who shall not cease his struggle until justice shall triumph on the earth (Is. 42:1–3; Matt. 12:17–21). In him shall the nations place their hope.

Jesus, in his life, death and resurrection, is himself the guarantee of life, peace and human dignity. He is the Messiah who struggles and suffers with his people. And yet, he is the victor. He is King in his suffering, not in spite of it. There is therefore an inseparable link between Pontius Pilate's "Ecce homo!" and his "There is your King!" (John 19:4,19). So it is that the Book of Revelations speaks of Jesus both as the lamb that was slaughtered and as the rider on the white horse. The One who died is the One who lives forever. The suffering servant of the Lord is the ruler of the kings of the earth. The One who was willing to give up his life is Jesus the Messiah, the life of the world.

This is the truth that is revealed to the Church even as we speak the words: Jesus Christ is the life of the world. The Revelation of John reminds us of the victory of the saints. But again, it is not a victory brought about by earthly powers. "They won the victory over (satan) by the blood of the lamb, and by the truth they proclaimed, and because they did not love their life unto death" (Rev. 12:11). This truth is the basis upon which the Church stands. It is the essence of the witness of the Church in the world. It is the essence of the confession: Jesus Christ is the life of the world. The Church can say this only if we are willing to give our life for the sake of the world. We can say this only if we are willing to accept that the survival of the Church is secondary to the survival of the world. We can say this only if we truly believe that there are some things so dear, some things so precious, some things so eternally true that they are worth dying for. And the truth that Jesus Christ is the life of the world is worth giving our life for.

The truth that the Messiah reveals is contrary to the lies, the propaganda, the idolatrous, the untrustworthy in the world. His truth is the truth that holds the freedom and the life of the world. And this we are called to proclaim. And so, as we begin these two weeks together as the assembled churches of the world, let us affirm this truth, and let us believe:

– It is not true that this world and its people are doomed to die and be lost –

This is true: For God so loved the world that he gave his only begotten Son, that whosoever believes in him, shall not perish, but have everlasting life.

- It is not true that we must accept inhumanity and discrimination, hunger and poverty, death and destruction –
  This is true: I have come that they may have life, and that abundantly.
- It is not true that violence and hatred should have the last word, and that war and destruction have come to stay forever –
  This is true: For unto us a child is born, and unto us a Son is given, and the government shall be upon his shoulder, and his name shall be called wonderful counsellor, mighty God, the everlasting Father, the Prince of peace.
- It is not true that we are simply victims of the powers of evil who seek to rule the world –
  This is true: To me is given all authority in heaven and on earth, and lo I am with you, even unto the end of the world.
- It is not true that we have to wait for those who are specially gifted, who are the prophets of the Church, before we can do anything –
  This is true: I will pour out my Spirit on all flesh, and your sons and your daughters shall prophesy, your young men shall see visions, and your old men shall have dreams. . .
- It is not true that our dreams for liberation of humankind, of justice, of human dignity, of peace are not meant for this earth and for this history –
  This is true: The hour comes, and it is now, that the true worshippers shall worship the Father in spirit and in truth. . .

So let us use these two weeks to dream, let us use these two weeks to prophesy; let us use these two weeks to see visions of love, and peace and justice. Let us use these two weeks to affirm with humility, with joy, with faith, with courage: *Jesus Christ – the Life of the World.*

VI. ASSEMBLY COMMITTEES AND ISSUE GROUPS

BUSINESS COMMITTEE

Scott, Most Rev. E.W., mo, Anglican, Canada, *Moderator*
Karekin II, His Holiness, mo, Oriental Orthodox, Lebanon, *Vice-Moderator*
Skuse, Ms Jean, fl, United, Australia, *Vice-Moderator*

Abayasekera, Ms Annathaie, fl, Anglican, Sri Lanka
Antonie of Ardeal, Metropolitan, mo, Eastern Orthodox, Romania
Ashmall, Mr Harry A., ml, Reformed, UK
Baechtold, Ms Janete, yfl, Lutheran, Brazil
Chrysostomos, Metropolitan, mo, Eastern Orthodox, Turkey
Fischer, Ms Nicole, fl, Reformed, Switzerland
Getaneh Bogale, Ato, ml, Oriental Orthodox, Ethiopia
Gregorios, Metropolitan Paulos Mar, mo, Oriental Orthodox, India
Hempel, Bishop Johannes, mo, Lutheran, GDR
Hoover, Ms Theressa, fl, Methodist, USA
Ilia II, His Holiness, mo, Eastern Orthodox, USSR
Ingelstam, Ms Margareta, fl, Congregational, Sweden
Ionita, Father Viorel, mo, Eastern Orthodox, Romania
Jiagge, The Hon. Ms Justice A.R., fl, Reformed, Ghana
John of Helsinki, Metropolitan, mo, Eastern Orthodox, Finland
Lohse, Bishop E., mo, Lutheran, FRG
Mayland, Ms Jean, fl, Anglican, UK
McClurg, Rev. Patricia, fo, Reformed, USA
Miguez-Bonino, Prof. Jose, mo, Methodist, Argentina
Nababan, Rev. Dr S.A.E., mo, Lutheran, Indonesia
Nabulivou, Rev. Inoke, mo, Methodist, Fiji
Nyomi, Rev. Setri, ymo, Reformed, Ghana
Oduyoye, Ms Mercy, fl, Methodist, Nigeria
Philaret of Kiev, Metropolitan, mo, Eastern Orthodox, USSR
Simatupang, Dr T.B., ml, Reformed, Indonesia
Sundby, Most Rev. Olof, mo, Lutheran, Sweden
Thompson, Mr William P., ml, Reformed, USA
Vassilios of Caesaria, Metropolitan, mo, Eastern Orthodox, Jerusalem
Wedel, Dr Cynthia, fl, Anglican, USA
Williams, Ms J., yfl, Anglican, South Africa
Wilson, Dr Lois M., fo, United, Canada

Key to abbreviations: m = male; f = female; o = ordained; l = lay; y = youth

Consultants to the Business Committee

Bena-Silu, Mr, ml, Kimbanguist, Zaire
Gatu, Rev. John G., mo, Reformed, Kenya
Kang, Dr Won Yong, mo, Reformed, Korea
Kirill, Archbishop, mo, Eastern Orthodox, USSR
Leite, Rev. Jose, mo, Reformed, Portugal
MacDonald, Rev. David, ml, United, Canada (Adviser)
McCloud, Rev. J. Oscar, mo, Reformed, USA
Preus, Bishop David M., mo, Lutheran, USA
Sampath, Ms Dorinda, fl, Reformed, Trinidad
Than, Prof. Kyaw, ml, Baptist, Burma
Trautwein, Dr Dieter, mo, Lutheran, FRG (Adviser)
Webb, Ms Pauline, fl, Methodist, UK

CREDENTIALS COMMITTEE

Mayland, Ms Jean, fl, Anglican, UK, *Moderator*
Habib, Rev. Dr Samuel, mo, Reformed, Egypt, *Secretary*

Abbey-Mensah, Ms Dinah, fl, Reformed, Ghana
Fiehland, Ms Astrid, yfl, Lutheran, FRG
Hernandez B., Rt Rev. Ulises, mo, Methodist, Mexico
Huston, Rev. Dr Robert, mo, Methodist, USA
Ieriko, Rt Rev. Siaosi, mo, Congregational, New Zealand
Jacobson, Rev. S.T., mo, Lutheran, Canada
Kivambe, Dr David, ml, Lutheran, Tanzania
Ursache, Most Rev. Victorin, mo, Eastern Orthodox, USA

FINANCE COMMITTEE

McClurg, Rev. Patricia, fo, Reformed, USA, *Moderator*
Jornod, Rev. Jean Pierre, mo, Reformed, Switzerland, *Vice-Moderator*
Samuel, Rt Rev. John, mo, United, Pakistan, *Vice-Moderator*
Laham, Mr Albert, ml, Eastern Orthodox, Switzerland, *Secretary*

Abel, Ms Carol, yfl, Anglican, UK
Abloh, Ms Ophelia, fl, Reformed, Ghana
Aitken, Mr I.C., ml, Reformed, South Africa
Akande, Rev. Dr Ola, mo, Baptist, Nigeria
Asay de Benech, Ms Kathy, yfl, Reformed / Argentina
Baker, Ms Christina, fl, United, Canada
Binhammer, Rev. Dr Robert J., mo, Lutheran, Canada
Bradley, Mr Edgar G. ml, Anglican, New Zealand

Clarke, Mr Raymond, ml, Reformed, UK
Engelen, Dr O.E., ml, Reformed, Indonesia
Gathuka Ngumi, Mr George, ml, African Christian, Kenya
Held, Rev. Dr Heinz J., mo, United, FRG
Kerry, Mr Jonathan, yml, Methodist, UK
Kim, Rev. Dr Hyung Tae, mo, Reformed, Korea
Kok, Dr Govaert, ml, Old Catholic, Netherlands
Koob, Ms Kathryn, fl, Lutheran, USA
Kruse, Mr Max, ml, Lutheran, Denmark
Kumar, Mr Uttam, ml, Lutheran, India
Lemopulo, Mr George, yml, Eastern Orthodox, Switzerland
Lethunya, Ms E.S., fl, Reformed, Lesotho
Lislerud, Rt Rev. Gunnar, mo, Lutheran, Norway
Ludwig, Mr Marvin, ml, United, USA
Makary of Uman, Most Rev., mo, Eastern Orthodox, USSR
Manoogian, Archbishop Torgom, mo, Oriental Orthodox, USA
Manson, Mr Thorsten, ml, Lutheran, Sweden
McCloud, Rev. J. Oscar, mo, Reformed, USA
McGregor-Lowndes, Mr Myles, yml, United, Australia
Natho, Rt Rev. Eberhard, mo, United, GDR
Nugent, Dr Randolph, mo, Methodist, USA
Pesonen, Dr Pertti, ml, Lutheran, Finland
Poitier, Ms Annette, fl, Methodist, Bahamas
Quiambao, Ms Ligaya N., fl, United, Philippines
Radjagukguk, Mr M.H., ml, Lutheran, Indonesia
Randell, Mr Clarence, ml, Anglican, Canada
Rangelov, Mr Rangel, ml, Eastern Orthodox, Bulgaria
Rocha Souza, Mr Enilson, ml, Pentecostal, Brazil
Romanides, Rev. Prof. John S., mo, Eastern Orthodox, Greece
Sepulveda Barra, Rev. Narciso, mo, Pentecostal, Chile
Valcu, Mr Vergil, ml, Eastern Orthodox, Romania
Vassilios, Metropolitan, mo, Eastern Orthodox, Israel
Vuakatagane, Mr Emosi, ml, Methodist, Fiji
Yongui, Ms Marie Thérèse, fl, Reformed, Cameroon

MESSAGE COMMITTEE

Wilson, Dr Lois, fo, United, Canada, *Moderator*
Gqubule, Rev. Dr Simon, mo, Methodist, South Africa, *Vice-Moderator*
Zizioulas, Prof. Dr John, ml, Eastern Orthodox, UK, *Vice-Moderator*
Thorogood, Rev. Bernard, mo, Reformed, UK, *Secretary*

Aco, Bishop Isaac, mo, Methodist, Brazil
Britten, Ms Elizabeth, fl, Anglican, Australia
Carter, Dr Lawrence, mo, Baptist, USA
Dalla, Rev., yfo, Lutheran, Iceland

Flax, Ms Patricia, yfl, Anglican, Antigua
Fuchs, Ms Erika, fl, Reformed, Austria
Havea, Rev. Dr Sione 'Amanki, mo, Methodist, Tonga
Ibrahim, Archbishop Gregorios Y., mo, Oriental Orthodox, Syria
Jesudasan, Most Rev. I., mo, United, India
Kauma, Rt Rev. Misaeri, mo, Anglican, Uganda
Lah, Ms Oknah Kim, fl, Methodist, Korea
Philaret of Kiev, Metropolitan, mo, Eastern Orthodox, USSR
Radjawane, Rev. Dr Nico, mo, Reformed, Indonesia
Sandner, Rev. Peter, mo, United, FRG
Smolik, Rev. Dr Josef, mo, Reformed, Czechoslovakia
Vasile, Bishop, mo, Eastern Orthodox, Romania
Zoe-Obianga, Ms Rose, fl, Reformed, France

NOMINATIONS COMMITTEE

Ashmall, Mr Harry, ml, Reformed, UK, *Moderator*
Than, Prof. Kyaw, ml, Baptist, Burma, *Vice-Moderator*
Yuvenaly, Metropolitan, mo, Eastern Orthodox, USSR, *Vice-Moderator*
Sonnenday, Dr Margaret, fl, Methodist, USA, *Secretary*

Arnold, Rev. Walter, mo, Lutheran, FRG
Athanasios, Rt Rev., mo, Oriental Orthodox, Egypt
Baumer, Rev. Martha A., fo, United, USA
Bhandare, Most Rev. Dr R.S., mo, United, India
Bozabalian, Bishop Nerses, mo, Oriental Orthodox, USSR
Buku, Mr Joel, ml, Anglican, Kenya
Currens, Rev. Dr Gerald E., mo, Lutheran, USA
Cuthbert, Rev. Raymond A., ymo, Disciples, Canada
Denton, Mr J.G., ml, Anglican, Australia
Doom, Mr John, ml, Reformed, Tahiti
Fabiny, Rev. Tamas, ymo, Lutheran, Hungary
Gcabashe, Ms Virginia, fl, Methodist, South Africa
Haddad, Ms Frieda, fl, Eastern Orthodox, Lebanon
Hoyt, Jr, Dr Thomas, mo, Methodist, USA
Kim, Rev. Choon Young, mo, Methodist, Korea
Kotto, Rev. Jean, mo, Reformed, Cameroon
Larsson, Ms Birgitta, fl, Lutheran, Sweden
Linn, Rev. Gerhard, mo, United, GDR
Maximos, Bishop, mo, Eastern Orthodox, USA
Misang, Mr Jobson, yml, United, Papua New Guinea
Muchena, Ms Olivia, fl, Methodist, Zimbabwe
de Oliveira, Rev. Orlando S., mo, Anglican, Brazil
Pankraty, Metropolitan, mo, Eastern Orthodox, Bulgaria
Payne, Rt Rev. Roland, mo, Lutheran, Liberia
Plou, Ms Dafne De, fl, Methodist, Argentina

Sihombing, Rev. P.M., mo, Lutheran, Indonesia
De Souza, Rt Rev. Neville, mo, Anglican, Jamaica
Van der Veen-Schenkenveld, Rev. M.J., fo, Reformed, Netherlands
Wade, Ms Jinny, fl, Anglican, Uk

POLICY REFERENCE COMMITTEE I

Chrysostomos, Metroplitan, mo, Eastern Orthodox, Turkey, *Moderator*
Haggart, Most Rev. Alastair, mo, Anglican, UK, *Vice-Moderator*
Henry, Rev. Harry Y., mo, Methodist, Benin, *Vice-Moderator*
Johnston, Ms Heather, fl, Reformed, Canada, *Secretary*

Alexander Mar Thoma, Most Rev. Dr., mo, Mar Thoma, India
Andrino, Bishop Rodriguez, mo, Methodist, Brazil
Antonie of Ardeal, Metropolitan, mo, Eastern Orthodox, Romania
Bouchard, Rev. Giorgio, mo, Reformed, Italy
Brown, Rev. Neville C., mo, Moravian, Antigua
Browne, Archbishop George D., mo, Anglican, Liberia
Cabreza, Ms Ella, fl, Independent, Philippines
David, Ms Susy, fl, Mar Thoma, India
Faatauola, Ms Sauiluma, fl, Congregational, Western Samoa
Farah, Archdeacon Rafic, mo, Anglican, Lebanon
Galbraith, Ms Jane, yfl, Anglican, Ireland
Garima, Bishop Dr, mo, Oriental Orthodox, Ethiopia
Jaeger, Superintendent Joachim, mo, United, GDR
Kaessmann, Ms Margot, yfl, United, FRG
Kishkovsky, Very Rev. Leonid, mo, Eastern Orthodox, USA
Matthews, Bishop Marjorie, fo, Methodist, USA
Nagy, Bishop Gyula, mo, Lutheran, Hungary
Ngcobo, Rev. Samuel, mo, Reformed, South Africa
Patelos, Dr Constantin, ml, Eastern Orthodox, Greece
Pattiasina-Toreh, Rev. C.E., fo, Reformed, Indonesia
Philaret of Minsk, Metropolitan, mo, Eastern Orthodox, USSR
Piske, Rev. Meinard, mo, Lutheran, Brazil
Popescu, Rev. Prof. Dumitru, mo, Eastern Orthodox, Switzerland
Ruokanen, Ms Katariina, yfl, Lutheran, Finland
Rusch, Dr William, mo, Lutheran, USA
San Lone, Rev. Victor, mo, Baptist, Burma
Seddoh, Ms Akuyo, fl, Reformed, Togo
Smith, Rev. Robert F., mo, United, Canada
Webley, Rt Rev. Stanford, mo, United, Jamaica

POLICY REFERENCE COMMITTEE II

Thompson, Mr William, ml, Reformed, USA, *Moderator*
Kim, Rev. Kwan Suk, mo, Reformed, Korea, *Vice-Moderator*
Konie, Ms G., fl, United, Zambia, *Vice-Moderator*
Toth, Bishop Karoly, mo, Reformed, Hungary, *Secretary*

Abebaw Yegzaw, Mr L.M., mo, Oriental Orthodox, Ethiopia
Akoma Mozogo, Ms Albertine, fl, Reformed, Gabon
Bos, Dr Jone, ml, Reformed, Netherlands
Branch, Mr Keith, yml, Anglican, Guyana
Buevski, Mr A.S., ml, Eastern Orthodox, USSR
Bullimore, Chancellor John, ml, Anglican, UK
Carter, Ms Aiko Y., fl, United, Japan
Carvalho, Bishop Emilio de, mo, Methodist, Angola
Chrysostomos, Metropolitan, mo, Eastern Orthodox, Greece
Doll, Ms Ulrike, yfo, United, GDR
Englezakis, Dr Benedictos, ml, Eastern Orthodox, Cyprus
Farah El-Khoury, Ms Mahat, fl, Eastern Orthodox, Syria
Forrester, Rev. Prof. Duncan, mo, Reformed, UK
Hamalian, Prof. Arpi, fl, Oriental Orthodox, Canada
Khumalo, Rev. Samson, mo, Reformed, South Africa
Komla Dzobo, Rt Rev., mo, Reformed, Ghana
Kruse, Dr Martin, mo, United, FRG
Lewis, Mr Michael, ml, United, Canada
Mehany, Dr Makram, ml, Oriental Orthodox, Egypt
Narzynski, Rt Rev. Janusz, mo, Lutheran, Poland
Neff, Rev. Dr Robert, mo, Brethren, USA
Pajula, Konsistorialrat Kuno, mo, Lutheran, USSR
Pannell, Ms Tammy, yfl, Anglican, Canada
Pereira, Ms Nancy C., yfl, Methodist, Brazil
Perera, Rev. Somasiri K., mo, Methodist, Sri Lanka
Petrova, Ms G. Stefka, fl, Eastern Orthodox, Bulgaria
Reinich, Rev. R.R., mo, Reformed, Argentina
Salonga, Dr Jovito, ml, United, USA
Shehadeh, Mr Raja, ml, Anglican, Israel
Sitahal, Rt Rev. Harold, mo, Reformed, Trinidad
Stalsett, Rev. Gunnar, mo, Lutheran, Norway
Supardan, Ms E. Wilandari, fl, Reformed, Indonesia
Tehindrazanarivelo, Mr Emmanuel, yml, United, Madagascar
Tellez, Mr Thomas, ml, Baptist, Nicaragua
Varughese, Dr K.V., ml, Mar Thoma, India
Wood, Rev. Bertrice, fo, United, USA

PRESS COMMITTEE

Macdonald, Rev. David, mo, United, Canada, *Moderator* (Adviser)

Gatwa, Mr T., yml, Reformed, Rwanda
Holloway, Mr John, yml, Anglican, USA
Ingelstam, Ms Margareta, fl, Congregational, Sweden
Kerepia, Ms Anne, fl, United, Papua New Guinea
O'Grady, Rev. Ronald M., mo, Disciples, Australia
Okullu, Bishop Henry, mo, Anglican, Kenya
Pitirim, Most Rev., mo, Eastern Orthodox, USSR
Ukur, Dr Fridolin, mo, Reformed, Indonesia

PROGRAMME GUIDELINES COMMITTEE

Miguez-Bonino, Prof. Jose, ml, Methodist, Argentina, *Moderator*
Okullu, Bishop Henry, mo, Anglican, Kenya, *Vice-Moderator*
Parthenios, H.E. Metropolitan, mo, Eastern Orthodox, Greece, *Vice-Moderator*
Love, Dr Janice, fl, Methodist, USA, *Secretary*

Bena-Silu, M., ml, Kimbanguist, Zaire
Bettenhausen, Dr Elizabeth, fl, Lutheran, USA
Campbell, Rev. Dr Robert, mo, Baptist, USA
Capo, Rev. Enrique, mo, Reformed, Spain
Christie-Johnston, Rev. Hamish, mo, United, Australia
Cuthbert, Rev. Robert W.M., mo, Moravian, Jamaica
David, Archbishop, mo, Eastern Orthodox, USSR
Dean, Ms Katherine, fl, Reformed, USA
Douglas, Ms Barbara, yfl, United, Canada
Duchrow, Rev. Dr Ulrich, mo, United, FRG
Faa'alo, Rev. Puafitu, ymo, Congregational, Tuvalu
Garkusha, Ms Valentina, fl, Baptist, USSR
Halim, Ms Inge, yfl, Reformed, Indonesia
Havea, Ms Maata, fl, Methodist, Tonga
Hempfling, Ms Helen, yfo, Disciples, USA
Herbst, Ms Ursula, fl, Lutheran, GDR
Jarjour, Ms Rose, yfl, Reformed, USA
Jivi, Mr Aurel, ml, Eastern Orthodox, Romania
Julkiree, Ms Boonmee, fl, Reformed, Thailand
Kawabata, Mr Junshiro, ml, United, Japan
Kirill, Archbishop, mo, Eastern Orthodox, USSR
Kitagawa, Rev. John E., mo, Anglican, USA
Knoblauch, Rev. Bruno, mo, United, Argentina
Koev, Prof. Totiu, ml, Eastern Orthodox, Bulgaria
Lidell, Rev. Elisabeth, fo, Lutheran, Denmark

Musoko, Ms C.L., fl, Reformed, Cameroon
Niemczyk, Prof. Jan, mo, Lutheran, Poland
Nxasana, Ms Vuyiswa, fl, Anglican, South Africa
Orr, Ms Lesley, yfl, Reformed, UK
Pall, Rev. Laszlo, mo, Reformed, Hungary
Palma, Ms Marta, fl, Pentecostal, Chile
Peers, Most Rev. Michael G., mo, Anglican, Canada
Persson, Rt Rev. William, mo, Anglican, UK
Pu, Ms Katherine, fl, Baptist, Burma
Razivelo, Ms Mariette, fl, Lutheran, Madagascar
Santram, Rev. Pritam, mo, Reformed, India
Saraneva, Rev. Dr Tapio, mo, Lutheran, Finland
Seah, Dr I.S., mo, Reformed, Taiwan
Silva, Mr Paulo Lutero, yml, Pentecostal, Brazil
Sumo, Mr K., yml, Lutheran, Liberia
Supit, Dr B.A., ml, Reformed, Indonesia
Talbot, Bishop Frederick, H., mo, Methodist, USA
Terpstra, Mr Gerrit, ml, Reformed, Netherlands
Uwadi, Rt Rev. Rogers, mo, Methodist, Nigeria
Youssef Abdou, Dr, mo, Eastern Orthodox, Egypt
Zumach, Ms Hildegard, fl, United, FRG

WORSHIP COMMITTEE

Trautwein, Dr Dieter, mo, Lutheran, FRG, *Moderator* (Adviser)

Bayiga, Rev. Dr Alfred, mo, Reformed, Cameroon (Adviser)
Cuffie, Ms Daphne, fl, Anglican, Trinidad
Gnanadason, Ms Aruna, fl, United, India (Adviser)
Hoiore, Ms Celine, yfl, Reformed, Tahiti
Micks, Prof. Marianne, fl, Anglican, USA (Adviser)
Samuel, Archbishop Athanasius, mo, Oriental Orthodox, USA
Sosa, Rev. Pablo, mo, Methodist, Argentina (Adviser)
Sotirios, Rt Rev. Bishop, mo, Eastern Orthodox, Canada
Suleeman, Rev. C., mo, Reformed, Indonesia
Vladimir, Most Rev., mo, Eastern Orthodox, USSR
Williams, Ms J., yfl, Anglican, South Africa

ISSUE GROUPS

1. WITNESSING IN A DIVIDED WORLD
Moderator: Rev. Inoke *Nabulivou*, mo (Fiji, Methodist)
Vice-Moderators: Bishop Eli *Korban*, mo (Syria, Eastern Orthodox)
   Ms Valerie *Russell*, fl (USA United)

Rapporteurs: Rev. Dr Zablon *Nthamburi*, mo (Kenya, Methodist)
　　Rev. Dr James *Veitch*, mo (New Zealand, Presbyterian)
Staff: Rev. Emilio *Castro*, mo (Uruguay, Methodist)

2. TAKING STEPS TOWARDS UNITY
Moderator: Metropolitan *John*, mo (Finland, Eastern Orthodox)
Vice-Moderators: Rev. Albert *Burua*, mo (Papua New Guinea, United)
　　Ms Marthe *Westphal*, fl (France, Reformed)
Rapporteurs: Rev. Dr Paul *Crow*, mo (USA, Disciples)
　　Dr J.N.O. *Fernando*, ml (Sri Lanka, Anglican)
Staff: Dr Michael *Kinnamon*, mo (USA, Disciples)

3. MOVING TOWARDS PARTICIPATION
Moderator: Ms Nicole *Fischer*, fl (Switzerland, Reformed)
Vice-Moderators: Ms Maud *Nahas*, fl (Lebanon, Eastern Orthodox)
　　Rt Rev. Victor P. *Premasagar*, mo (India United)
Rapporteurs: Dr Gerhard *Grohs*, ml (FRG, EKD/United)
　　Ms Selena *Tapper*, fl (Jamaica, Anglican)
Staff: Rev. Bärbel *von Wartenberg*, fo (FRG, EKD/Lutheran)

4. HEALING AND SHARING LIFE IN COMMUNITY
Moderator: Rt Rev. Johannes *Hempel*, mo (GDR, BEK/Lutheran)
Vice-Moderators: Dr Erlinda *Senturias*, fl (Philippines, United)
　　Dr Harold L. *Wilke*, ml (USA, United)
Rapporteurs: Ms Mabel de *Filippini*, fl (Argentina, Methodist)
　　Rt Rev. Aram *Keshishian*, mo (Lebanon, Oriental Orthodox)
Staff: Dr Stuart *Kingma*, ml (USA, Reformed)

5. CONFRONTING THREATS TO PEACE AND SURVIVAL
Moderator: Metropolitan Paulos Mar *Gregorios*, mo (India, Oriental
　　Orthodox)
Vice-Moderators: Rt Rev. John *Habgood*, mo (UK, Anglican)
　　Ms Christina *Rogestam*, fl (Sweden, Lutheran)
Rapporteurs: Mr *Bena-Silu*, ml (Zaire, Kimbanguist)
　　Rev. James M. *Lawson*, mo (USA, Methodist)
Staff: Dr Paul *Abrecht*, mo (USA, Baptist)

6. STRUGGLING FOR JUSTICE AND HUMAN DIGNITY
Moderator: Ms Theressa *Hoover*, fl (USA, Methodist)
Vice-Moderators: Rev. Alexei *Bichkov*, mo (USSR, Baptist)
　　Rev. Rita *Panke*, fo (Brazil, Lutheran)
Rapporteurs: Rev. Nelson *Charles*, mo (Sierra Leone, Methodist)
　　Dr Yong-Bock *Kim*, ml (Korea, Presbyterian)
Staff: Prof. Dr Anwar *Barkat*, ml (Pakistan, United)

7. LEARNING IN COMMUNITY
Moderator: Ms Mercy *Oduyoye*, fl (Nigeria, Methodist)
Vice-Moderators: Dr Maurice *Assad*, ml (Egypt, Oriental Orthodox)
    Ms Johanna *Linz*, fl (FRG, EKD/Lutheran)
Rapporteurs: Dr Oscar Corvalan *Vasquez*, ml (Chile, Pentecostal)
    Ms Constance *Tarasar*, fl (USA, Orthodox)
Staff: Dr Ulrich *Becker*, mo (FRG, EKD/Lutheran)

8. COMMUNICATING CREDIBLY
Moderator: Mrs Margareta *Ingelstam*, fl (Sweden, Congregational)
Vice-Moderators: Most Rev. *Pitirim*, mo (USSR, Orthodox)
    Ms Dafne *de Plou*, fl (Argentina, Methodist)
Rapporteurs: Rev. Ronald *O'Grady*, mo (New Zealand, Disciples)
    Dr Fridolin *Ukur*, mo (Indonesia, Lutheran)
Staff: Mr T.K. *Thomas*, ml (India, Mar Thoma)

VII. REPORT OF THE ASSEMBLY'S FINANCE COMMITTEE

Introduction

The Finance Committee of this Assembly has been given the task of considering the general financial situation of the World Council of Churches and of making recommendations concerning any actions which this Assembly might need to take with regard to financial matters. The Committee has done its work in the full awareness that financial resources are one among many gifts which are shared in the ecumenical family, that giving and receiving belong to the very essence of our fellowship as churches committed to each other in the search for unity and justice as reflected in the theological foundation and programmatic relationships and goals of the World Council and this Assembly.

The Finance Committee of this Assembly has studied the information made available to it in the official report of activities since the Fifth Assembly in Nairobi, particularly the financial situation of the World Council. The Nairobi Assembly in 1975, meeting at a time of international monetary disorder, recognized that the World Council of Churches faced serious financial problems; many of them continued into the 1980s. Over this past period the Central Committee implemented many and varied measures to bring financial matters under control, and for the year 1982, the financial report reflects this greater stability: income for the Council exceeded expenditure, and the Council's budget as a whole was balanced, although many Sub-units still found it necessary to draw on reserves to cover their expenses, reserves which will be exhausted by 1984.

A. Accordingly, the Finance Committee of this Assembly *recommends* that the Assembly commend the 1975–1983 Central Committee, its Executive Committee, Finance Committee and staff, for:
1) responsibly implementing the financial directions issued by the Fifth Assembly;
2) developing policies and practices that have enabled the World Council of Churches to balance its budget;
3) securing funding for this meeting of the Sixth Assembly;

4) alerting this Assembly to the financial problems that face the Council in the years to come.

B. The Finance Committee further *recommends* that the Assembly commend the member churches and church-related agencies which through their financial contributions have made possible:
1) the programmes of the World Council of Churches as determined by the member churches and as reflected in the report of these since Nairobi;
2) the greatly improved financial situation of the Council, as reported to this Assembly, through the increase in giving by member churches and their related agencies;
3) this meeting of the Sixth Assembly. We express our special appreciation to the host churches in Canada for their contribution of inestimable human, spiritual, and material resources well beyond those actually reflected in the World Council financial accounts of this event.

Actions to be taken by the Central Committee, Executive Committee, and General Secretary of the World Council
The following recommendations of the Finance Committee are intended to enable the Central Committee to implement the programme priorities of the World Council as envisioned by this Assembly. These recommendations focus on the need to increase the Council's income as well as to increase the Council's flexibility in allocating available funds for programmes and its ability to undertake new programmes of a short-term or experimental nature within the availability of undesignated funds.

C. Accordingly, the Finance Committee *recommends* that the Assembly affirm the need for increased contributions to the Council as a whole as an important sign of the commitment of member churches to the ecumenical vision and a necessary financial base for the continuity and creativity of the World Council.

D. The Finance Committee *recommends* that the Assembly instruct the newly elected Central Committee to continue the initiatives which have been taken in developing:
1) clearer and simpler administrative and organizational structures and budgeting procedures that lead to greater coordination of the total programme of the World Council, and
2) integrated long-range programme and financial planning which reflects the wholeness of WCC programme and assures its financial stability.

This requires close and constant cooperation of all Programme Units, Sub-units, commissions, working groups, committees, and staff, and the Central Committee should fully instruct them regarding these procedures.

E. The Finance Committee *recommends* that the Assembly affirm the policy regarding the necessity of Council reserves established in 1981 by the Central Committee, and instruct the newly elected Central Committee to pursue these measures.

F. It is the further *recommendation* of the Finance Committee that this Assembly instruct the newly elected Central Committee to:
1) plan for and maintain balanced budgets for the World Council of Churches in each of the coming years;
2) include financial provision for the Seventh Assembly in each budget year throughout the period;
3) explore and implement more flexible funding patterns, including reallocation, following consultation with the donor, of part or all excess designated funds on a given programme when that programme has been over-subscribed in any budget year;
4) pursue the policy direction established in recent years regarding the sharing of central costs and direct the Central Committee to determine if more overall Council costs could be so distributed.

G. Recognizing the financial constraints still facing the WCC in the next period, the Finance Committee *recommends* that this Assembly direct the newly elected Central Committee to:
1) undertake new programmes of a short-term or experimental basis within the framework of its priorities and the availability of undesignated funds;
2) ascertain that any new World Council programmes of long-range nature can be funded within the financial structures and programmatic relationships of the Council, its member churches and their related agencies, and that such programmes would not be dependent on undesignated funds of the WCC;
3) strengthen efforts of coordinated income development to provide financial support for those programmes which the Central Committee agrees to continue, consequently reducing the dependency of such programmes on undesignated funds.

The Finance Committee notes that although the Fifth Assembly in Nairobi asserted that every member should contribute towards undesignated income based on their membership and their ability to pay, there has been no significant movement on the part of many member churches to contribute to the Council.

H. The Committee therefore *recommends* that the Assembly direct the new Central Committee to draw up a statement of the financial responsibilities of membership with a view to its ultimate inclusion in the Rules of the World Council of Churches. These responsibilities, while not a condition of membership, should be recognized as a minimum tangible sign of every member church's commitment. The new Central Committee should make it an early priority to identify specific guidelines by which the above principle could be made workable, and such guidelines should be communicated to the member churches.

I. The Finance Committee also *recommends* that the Assembly instruct the General Secretary of the World Council to:
1) continue and further a regular pattern of communication with the member churches, and their financial, ecumenical and stewardship officers, no less than once each year, whereby a financial report of the WCC's activities during the year is provided, together with pertinent information and specific guidance about current giving of each member church; these topics should be regularly included for discussion during visitations;
2) correspond with the delegates of this Sixth Assembly regarding the financial situation of the Council in order to enable them to work within their churches to better interpret the financial situation of the World Council and their contribution to it;
3) prepare a report for circulation among member churches on the type of alternative support of the World Council that could be envisaged, such as;
   a) equalization of travel costs to meetings
   b) hosting of meetings
   c) support of other churches' programmes in the same country or region
   d) contribution of time and talent in local work for the WCC
   e) local responsibility for the development of ecumenism;
4) further develop reporting methods for the receipt and use of alternative support towards the programme budget, such as material aid and in-kind contributions of the member churches.

J. The Finance Committee *recommends* that the Assembly note with appreciation the considerable improvement of the financial report compared to the one considered in Nairobi, and request that the General Secretary take steps towards making the financial report an annual report of the WCC, giving a broad outline of activities of the year under review including materials which can be readily used in interpreting the Council's programmes and finances.

Requests to the member churches and to church-related agencies

K. The Finance Committee *recommends* that the Assembly:

1) encourage all member churches to organize an annual "WCC Sunday" to interpret the WCC to local congregations; offerings made on that day could represent a new source of undesignated funding;

2) commend the vast number of projects between the churches themselves outside of the WCC programme budget and urge the churches to increase their support of the staffing and financial services which the World Council budget provides in making this sharing of resources possible;

3) note the growing trend towards bilateral funding of development projects of churches, national councils of churches and regional councils of churches, and call upon project holders, donor agencies, and all churches:

   a) to study carefully and to respond faithfully to the principles of ecumenical sharing of resources within and between regions, and

   b) to work for more transparency in the sharing of resources, sharing information about bilateral project requests and funding within the ecumenical family;

4) recognize the need to strengthen the administrative capacity of the World Council of Churches to deal more effectively with the listing, screening, funding, financing, reporting, and following up of projects of third parties (trust funds), and that such capacities must also be strengthened at regional, national and local levels.

L. The Finance Committee further *recommends* that the Assembly request those member churches and church-related agencies which have been making financial contributions to the World Council to:

1) interpret more fully and intensely the life and work of the World Council to their own constituencies as a part of and an extension of the life and work of the member church. Churches should call upon the human resources of their leadership, including ecumenical officers, financial officers, stewardship officers, and delegates and other participants here present at this Assembly to transmit information about the World Council to local church levels. Churches are called upon to assist the Council in exploring how local resources within the churches may be applied towards the implementation of WCC programmes so that participation in the international ecumenical fellowship can be more directly manifested in congregational life;

2) increase the amount of financial support to programmes of the World Council. This effort by the churches may include the identification of new sources of funds within each church, new relationships to programmes of the Council, undertaking special funding efforts in the churches, nationally or regionally, to allow the continuation of on-going WCC programmes. Churches should be encouraged to designate such funds broadly by the nature of the work they wish to support (function) rather than by pre-determining the WCC administrative unit which might implement the programme (structure);

3) find ways to contribute financially to the costs incurred by the Council in administering trust funds.

M. The Finance Committee *recommends* that this Assembly specifically challenge:

1a) the member churches in the thirteen countries identified in the official report to this Assembly as the source of 98% of Council funds, to increase their annual undesignated giving substantially in the period until the next Assembly. This request urges them to follow the leadership of member churches in other countries whose undesignated giving has doubled, after exchange loss and inflation, since the Nairobi Assembly. The challenge to the churches in these thirteen countries, depending upon their circumstances and recent history of undesignated giving, is to set a goal for themselves to increase such giving 30 to 50% over the 1982 level in 1984 and further, to make yearly adjustments to annually increase the level of undesignated funds in real terms;

1b) the member churches in all other countries to make a sizeable increase in undesignated giving in 1984 of at least 25% over 1982, and further, to make yearly adjustments to annually increase the level of undesignated funds in real terms;

2a) those member churches whose names do not appear on the list of financial contributors to the World Council of Churches in 1982 (pp. 19–32 of 1982 financial report) to make a specific financial contribution in 1984 and regularly thereafter;

2b) those churches whose support of the WCC can only be of a non-financial (alternative, or in-kind) nature, to increase their levels of giving and to work closely with the WCC to assure the most appropriate and effective means of making such contributions.

Conclusion

The World Council of Churches as a whole and in its various parts has, and does, spend its energies in working towards the unity of the Church, in promoting solidarity between the churches, in sharing good news, in combating the root causes of injustice, in comforting and defending those who suffer, and in working on behalf of peace. In this world of God's children some of the fundamental injustices with which the Council must contend are manifested in the grossly inequitable distribution of information and of the world's material resources and in the sometimes systematically demonic misuse of financial resources. The irony is that the work of the World Council itself suffers because it is not given the kind of financial resources it needs to do what the member churches ask of it and what it is being called to do by God. The measuring stick of the world is cruel, and by those standards the World Council would seem to be a small and fragile vessel indeed. *One day* of the world's expenditure on armaments (the equivalent of more than four billion Swiss francs) would fund the current level of work done by the World Council of Churches for *more than 130 years*.

And yet, because of the promises of our Lord and our faith in those promises, those of us gathered here in Vancouver have great hopes for the work of the World Council of Churches and its member churches. In obedience to our Creator we have encouraged careful stewardship of the financial resources of the World Council, and we have been insistently hopeful about the financial underpinnings for that work which will be provided by the member churches and church-related agencies.

We affirm again here the call "to support one another in love as in these ways we seek together to be faithful to our common calling to proclaim and serve our one Lord, Jesus Christ, the Prince of Peace, the Life of the World".

VIII. REPORT OF THE ASSEMBLY'S PROGRAMME GUIDELINES COMMITTEE

I. MANDATE OF THE PROGRAMME GUIDELINES COMMITTEE (PGC)

The Programme Guidelines Committee has had two tasks:
a) to receive and evaluate the official report of the Central Committee, *Nairobi to Vancouver*, and to propose formal action on this report;
b) to formulate guidelines for future WCC programmes, taking careful note of proposals that emerge at various points in the Assembly.

II. "NAIROBI TO VANCOUVER"

The PGC recommends that the Assembly receive the report with appreciation for the work it reflects, and with the following comments:

A. The report is presented in a well-organized style, and in language that is clear and accessible to persons who do not have a high degree of familiarity with the work of the WCC. We are grateful that this work can be described in such a lucid and readable form. The chapter on the Finance Committee is especially commended for the clarity of its presentation. In addition, the foreword and introduction are helpful in setting the context within which to see WCC programmes since Nairobi. The Committee also appreciates that the Report was published in all WCC official languages. The report would have been improved, however, with summary sections at the end of each chapter and an index. The section on the Youth Sub-unit discusses international youth work but does not adequately reflect the regional and national relationships of the Sub-unit. Spanish-speaking Assembly participants would have been helped if they could have received the Spanish edition of *Nairobi to Vancouver* prior to arrival in Vancouver.

The Committee notes that the popular book *Acting in Faith* (by Leon Howell), which preceded the publication of the official Report of the Central Committee, has served both as a very good introduction to the WCC and a useful preparatory piece for *Nairobi to Vancouver* and the Assembly itself.

The PGC recommends that the Central Committee issue reports to the churches in the period between assemblies, similar in style to *Nairobi to Vancouver*, so that the churches can have access to more frequent comprehensive overviews of WCC work. These interim reports could be based on Unit and Sub-unit programme reports presented in each Central Committee meeting and thus should require few additional resources.

B. We have the following observations regarding the implementation of the programme guidelines established in Nairobi:

1. Within the concern for "The Quality of a Truly Ecumenical Fellowship", the question of communication in its wider context between Geneva and the member churches of the World Council of Churches is still a major issue. Part of the problem revolves around a view that communication only comes from Geneva to the churches. Some churches, therefore, take little responsibility in initiating contact and communication with Geneva, responding to communication from Geneva, or affecting horizontal communication between the churches themselves. Conversely, however, responsibilities for relationships and communication with member churches are often too dispersed across Council programmes. There needs to be more coordination and monitoring of these relations within the Council.

The pre-Assembly visitation programme has received widespread and enthusiastic endorsement and is one good realization of the guideline concerning a truly ecumenical fellowship. The visits were living evidence that ecumenism is to be embodied fully in many relationships: among congregations, churches, related organizations, regional councils of churches, and the WCC. Ecumenical fellowship was also evidenced in the realization that the issues of peace and struggles for justice are inter-related concerns in every area visited. The programme is affirmed as an important means for wider engagement of Christians at the local level in the ecumenical movement and for education about its wider levels. Some of the criticisms received about the visits, however, are that they were often too short, that the purpose of the visit was not always clear to the visitors or the hosts, that more people in local congregations, including those not already ecumenical enthusiasts, should be involved in receiving the teams, and that commissions and working groups were unable to meet in the period immediately prior to the Assembly due to the cost of the visitation programme.

2. The second guideline adopted by the Fifth Assembly, "The

Incarnation of Our Faith", stressed the essential interdependence of unity in faith and unity in Christian life. That this interdependence has guided the work of the WCC is evident in many ways. The convergence statement on "Baptism, Eucharist and Ministry" emphasizes the organic interconnection between the sacramental life of Christians and the engagement of Christians in the human struggles of our time. The study on the Community of Women and Men in the Church holds together ecclesiology and the life experiences of women and men in Church and society. The work of the Unit on Justice and Service was conducted with constant reference to the biblical and theological visions of the kingdom of God. The renewal of congregational life was interpreted as a matter of spirituality, evangelism and social engagement. Other examples could easily be cited.

While attention to the interdependence of faith and life is evident throughout the report, it is also obvious that the appropriate tension between the two has not always been present, nor agreement reached on the nature of each element. The theological diversity among the Units and Sub-units of the Council is perceived by some as a sign of vitality, by others as a sign of too little integration and too much division. For some, there is still too great a distance between the daily struggles and anguish of human life and the technical theological discussion of traditional doctrinal questions. Others fear the disruption of careful theological deliberation precisely because of the introduction of these struggles into the deliberation process. The unconnectedness of unity of faith and unity of Christian life is also sharpened by the tension between growing confessionalism and conciliar unity. These strains in the interconnectedness envisioned in the guidelines hinder the embodiment of Christ's message of liberation and the dialogue with people of living faiths and ideologies.

3. The third guideline on "The Struggle for True Humanity" stressed "the basic Christian imperative to participate in the struggle for human dignity and social justice". Since Nairobi, the WCC has succeeded in large part in establishing a wholistic approach to understanding and participating in such struggles. For example, programmes like those on Political Ethics; Faith, Science and the Future; the Ecumenical Sharing of Resources; Health, Healing and Wholeness; and the Melbourne World Mission Conference "Your Kingdom Come" clearly established the inter-relatedness of particular issues across the world, as well as the linkages between our faith and witness in struggles for justice. Recognizing that each church must involve itself authentically in its own place and in the worldwide search for a just, participatory and sustainable society,

the task of the WCC is to facilitate this process while encouraging "the self-reliance and self-identity of the member churches" (cf. *Breaking Barriers*, p. 299).

We note that some progress has been made in increasing the opportunities for disabled persons', youth, and women's participation in the total life and work of the Council. Some programmes, however, do not yet reflect an understanding of the importance of such participation. The struggle for true humanity cannot be achieved without partnership between all people in the Church.

We also note regarding this guideline that the WCC, through Unit II, has increased its efforts to safeguard human rights, despite diminishing financial resources. Although the extent of activity may not have been as great as was envisioned in Nairobi, the Council has enabled some churches to strengthen their struggles for human rights in their own situations; and it has helped to establish a basis of mutual trust among churches so that they can more actively pursue these issues together.

III. FUTURE WORK OF THE WCC

Each Assembly of the World Council of Churches is a gathering of both continuity and new vision. The continuity lies in the functions and purposes written into the Constitution of the WCC: the goal of visible unity, common witness, evangelism, justice and peace, renewal, and ecumenical education and inter-relations. The new vision emerges as participants in the Assembly voice their hopes for the future out of their living faith and the variety of experiences in the world which they bring. Thus the continuing purposes are renewed and given a distinctive shape for the next seven years.

The Fifth Assembly at Nairobi adopted three guidelines for future programmes: the quality of a truly ecumenical fellowship; the incarnation of our faith; and the struggle for a true humanity. The Programme Guidelines Committee of the Sixth Assembly reaffirms these guidelines. The emphasis on unity, on common witness, and on the struggle for true humanity is at the heart of the continuity from Nairobi to Vancouver and into the future. Out of this Assembly a new vision has also emerged. It is a vision of growth. The theme of the Assembly – "Jesus Christ – the Life of the World" – expresses this vision. Life is the gift we receive. But unless we continue to grow, the vision of one faith and one humanity will not achieve maturity. With the vision of growing more and more into Jesus Christ, the Life of the World, we propose the following interdependent programme guidelines for the WCC for the next seven years.

A. Guidelines that should inspire all WCC activities in the coming years

1. Growing towards unity

Jesus Christ is the life of the world. This life is to be expressed through maturing ecumenical relationships among the churches. Growth towards unity in conciliar fellowship should be one of the purposes of all programmes of the WCC. New ecumenical relationships should be nurtured locally and regionally, especially among congregations, local churches, and the variety of communities, ministries and networks which express the mission of the Church. Existing relationships should be renewed and sustained to express more fully the growth towards unity of faith, eucharistic fellowship, and service.

2. Growing towards justice and peace

Jesus Christ is the life of the world. This life is to be expressed through justice and peace for the whole world and respect for the integrity of all creation. Growth towards full ecclesial, spiritual, and political commitment to this expression by all member churches, in all their dimensions, should be one of the purposes of all programmes of the WCC. Justice, peace and the wellbeing of the whole creation are inseparable. Today confessing Jesus Christ the life of the world and living this confession in the world are embodied especially in worship, action, and reflection for peace and justice. The urgency of this situation calls for cooperation with all others who share the hope for a just and peaceful social order and the wellbeing of all creation and especially with those who confess and act in direct opposition to the powers of death.

3. Growing towards vital and coherent theology

Jesus Christ is the life of the world. This life is to be expressed through biblical and theological thought and active vision. Growth towards vital and coherent theology should be one of the purposes of all programmes of the WCC. A vital theology will incorporate the rich diversity of theological approaches emerging out of the varied experiences of churches throughout the world. A coherent theological approach will incorporate tradition and methods of reflection which represent the concrete needs and call of each and all members of the ecumenical movement towards unity of life and faith.

4. Growing towards new dimensions of the churches' self-understanding
Jesus Christ is the life of the world. This life is to be expressed through discovering new dimensions in the self-understanding of the churches in response to their deepening participation in the ecumenical movement. Growth towards this enriched self-understanding should be one of the purposes of all programmes of the WCC. It is nurtured in living ecumenical engagement with the questions of the nature and calling of the Church; its ministry; the nature and exercise of authority; the diverse forms of Christian community; the challenges posed by the threats to true humanity: the full expression of the Church's ministry of healing and sharing; and the ways to live and celebrate the Church's faith. Growing self-understanding is also nurtured by dialogue with and service to all our neighbours in the world.

5. Growing towards a community of confessing and learning
Jesus Christ is the life of the world. This life is to be expressed through its compelling proclamation, ecumenical education, and spiritual formation. Growth towards maturity of these interdependent dimensions of ecumenical life should be one of the purposes of all programmes of the WCC. The Gospel must be proclaimed in order to be believed. Unity must be experienced in common life and thus also be learned. Spirituality must be formed in order to be lived. All three must be at the centre of the life of all churches for the sake of the world; all three must be embodied in worship and work. The full engagement of the laity is crucial to this embodiment. Children and youth can elicit and contribute new vitality to this engagement, invigorating the vision and deepening the commitment of adults.

B. Priority areas for WCC programme

The priority areas recommended here have arisen from the discussion at this Assembly. They are intended to provide focus and orientation for new initiatives to be undertaken by the WCC in the coming years. They presuppose the continuation of work in areas defined by the functions of the WCC, i.e. unity of the Church, mission, service, education and renewal.

1. Unity: The search for concrete steps towards the goal of *visible unity* must remain a priority in the years ahead. A new dynamic has developed in this area which should be sustained and promoted. On the one hand decades of theological work have led to significant agreements and convergences; on the other hand the search for unity has become very much a matter of "practical ecumenism" which calls for more exchange of experiences and for a more inclusive approach.

The Nairobi Assembly described the goal of unity as "a conciliar fellowship of local churches which are themselves truly united", This description has been widely affirmed and has served to open new ways for the churches to deepen their commitment to each other (e.g. covenant agreements).

In this coming period the WCC will have to give particular attention to the reception process of the statements on "Baptism, Eucharist and Ministry" in the member churches, including at the level of local congregations. The liturgical and spiritual implications of these statements are particularly important. Further work is needed on the common understanding of the apostolic faith as a presupposition of effective steps towards unity. Yet, it will be decisive in all of these efforts, whether – and to what extent – the question for unity is being perceived as the crucial point of reference for all the activities of the WCC (Issue 2, Cluster 3).

2. *Fostering ecumenical relationships* with and between churches, communities, groups and ecumenical organizations on all levels should become a priority for the WCC in the coming years. The growth and vitality of the ecumenical movement depend on the encounter and trust between people more than on institutional links. Three features of this task should receive particular attention:

a) The implementation of the new resource sharing system on the basis of the comprehensive understanding of ecumenical sharing of resources and as part of a continuing dialogue on the mission and service of the Church. The purpose should clearly be to facilitate models of ecumenical sharing and not to create a heavy, centralized structure (Issue 4).

b) The strengthening and further coordination of the instruments of communication within the WCC and its member churches with a view to enhancing mutual understanding and solidarity based on authentic and undistorted information (Issue 8).

c) The initiation of a regular process of ecumenical visits between member churches and ecumenical partners on local, national and international levels. Member churches should be encouraged to engage in such visits sharing each others' living experiences. Visits initiated by the WCC, unless of a fact-finding or pastoral nature, should be linked with the programmatic concerns of the Council. The responsibility for coordinating and monitoring this process, ensuring careful preparation and specificity of focus, should be assigned to a staff person in the General Secretariat (Issue 4; Clusters 2, 3, 7).

3. Creative *theological work* is taking place throughout the WCC.

The development of vital and coherent inter-relationships in this work should be a priority for all Units and Sub-units (Cluster 3). There should be interaction between the diversity of theological approaches. This will involve cooperation among Units and Sub-units in theological programmes such as the evaluation of the reception process of "Baptism, Eucharist and Ministry"; the study of "The Unity of the Church and the Renewal of Human Community"; emerging studies of the relationships between culture, proclamation and unity and of the biblical and theological bases of social ethics; and encountering other faiths and modern ideologies (Issues 1, 2, 5).

This cooperative work should be furthered by the formation of a Theological Advisory Group, representative of all Units, Sub-units, and theological perspectives in the WCC and drawn from the membership of working groups and commissions. It should be located for administrative purposes in Unit I: Faith and Witness. This Theological Advisory Group would consider the place, diversity and interaction of theological work in all dimensions of the WCC through critical and constructive evaluation. The General Secretary is requested to clarify the mandate of the group through appropriate consultations and to submit proposals to the Central Committee in 1984.

4. *Evangelism* should undergird the work in all WCC programmes, based on the "Ecumenical Affirmation on Mission and Evangelism" adopted by the Central Committee in 1982. The Council should assist member churches in their mission to proclaim Christ, the life of the world, and in their calling of men and women to faith and discipleship. The implementation of this priority should have three dimensions. The WCC should:

a) help member churches in developing an understanding of the relationship between evangelism and culture in respect of both the contextual proclamation of the Gospel in all cultures and the transforming power of the Gospel in any culture;

b) seek to develop dialogue with evangelicals not related to the WCC on the meaning and methods of evangelism, particularly with concern for the relation between evangelism and the wholeness of salvation and the criteria for authentic church growth;

c) help to clarify the distinction between evangelism, carried out in the spiritual freedom and power of the Gospel, and proselytism in all its forms, particularly in view of activities, some of which evidence an arrogant disregard for people's cultural integrity and which are sometimes – consciously or unconsciously – at the service of foreign political interests (Clusters 2, 7, Small Groups).

5. To engage member churches in a conciliar process of mutual *commitment (covenant) to justice, peace and the integrity of all creation* should be a priority for World Council programmes. The foundation of this emphasis should be confessing Christ as the life of the world and Christian resistance to the demonic powers of death in racism, sexism, caste oppression, economic exploitation, militarism, violations of human rights, and the misuse of science and technology. Ecumenical study and action on the ecclesiological, spiritual, and socio-ethical implications of this commitment process should be organized. New initiatives are needed to promote education for peace, justice and a caring attitude to nature. For this purpose, use should be made of earlier studies in Political Ethics; Violence and Non-violence; the programmes for Disarmament and against Militarism and the Arms Race; the Church and the Poor; Faith, Science and the Future; the Community of Women and Men in the Church; the Programme to Combat Racism, the human rights programme and others pertinent to the concern. The links as well as the tensions between the goals of justice, peace and the wellbeing of creation should be explored from biblical, socio-economic and political perspectives. Emphasis should be placed on the use and misuse of power. Contributions to understanding the fullness of life developed from the perspectives of children, young people and women should also be an integral part of this priority (Issues 5,6).

6. The development of a community of healing and sharing within the WCC and the member churches where women, men, young people and children, able and disabled, clergy and laity, *participate fully* and minister to one another should be another priority. Participation implies encounter and sharing with others, working and making decisions together in styles that enhance inclusiveness, and living together as people of God. The Council should continue to examine the roles of both laity and clergy in the churches' mission and witness in the world. It should also assist the churches in creating awareness about the needs and gifts of disabled while helping to fight fear, superstition and negative attitudes about them. Attention should be given to supporting and participating in the United Nations International Youth Year (1985) which has the theme, "Participation, Peace and Development". Laity and disabled persons should be given more opportunities for participation in decision-making bodies of the WCC; and future working groups, commissions, and committees appointed by the WCC Central Committee should, as far as possible, have a composition of at least the proportion of women and young people present at the Assembly. Steps should also be taken to ensure an increase in the

number of women appointed to WCC executive staff positions (Grades 6–10) (Issues 3, 4).

7. The *concerns and perspectives of women* should become integral to the work of all WCC Units and Sub-units. Programmes and policies of the Council should appropriate and translate the insights gained from the study on the Community of Women and Men in the Church. Monitoring the churches' participation in and reaction to this study should be emphasized; and the WCC should continue open discussions on the issues of women's involvement in the total life of the churches. Using methodology similar to that developed by the CWMC study and drawing on expertise and resources from across the Council, a systematic and contextual study of the social, religious, cultural, economic, and political causes and consequences of sexism should be undertaken. The study should include an examination of women and work, women in poverty, violence against women, sex tourism, and women as initiators and participants in social change (Issues 3, 4).

8. The strength and vitality of the ecumenical movement depends on increasing an ecumenical perspective among laity and clergy throughout the member churches. Urgent attention should be given to the methods and content of *ecumenical learning*. Three aspects of this priority are highlighted here. The first is the development of common witness, liturgical activities, and spiritual formation as ecumenical concerns. The second involves understanding the tradition and current situation of more churches than just one's own; theological and biblical literacy; and preparation for leadership in ecumenical activities. The third involves commitment to understanding the basic issues of the social order, to acting cooperatively to address its problems, and to participating in the renewal of moral and ethical perspectives among Christians and others in relation to the world.

This priority should apply to all programmes of the WCC, but examples are mentioned here to underscore the importance of inter-Unit cooperation in furthering education for ecumenism. They are: the various programmes for theological education of the laity, including those preparing for ordination; the development and promotion of ecumenical liturgical materials (e.g. the Lima liturgy); and the concern for more Bible study materials, voiced at this Assembly.

Education for ecumenism in all its forms should take seriously the methodology of the study "The Community of Women and Men in the Church", in order that the needs, perspectives, and contributions of Christians at the local level be kept at the forefront of the educational processes (Issues 5, 7; Clusters 2, 3, 7).

C. Styles of work

The implementation of the guidelines and priorities recommended above will affect the methods and style of work of the WCC. The following indications are based on the preliminary evaluation of the pre-Assembly visits and a review of structure, policies and working methods carried out by the outgoing Central and Executive Committees.

1. Strengthening local ecumenism

The pre-Assembly visits have helped to highlight the critical importance of ecumenical relations in given local situations for the future of the ecumenical movement. All activities of the WCC should be carried out in ways which respond to the expectations of local Christian communities for ecumenical support and encouragement, for effective links of solidarity and the sharing of experiences.

2. Dynamic interaction with member churches

The pre-Assembly visits and the discussions at the Assembly itself have revealed a widespread lack of information and understanding in the churches about the programmes and activities of the WCC. In the future the Council will have to find more imaginative ways and devote more time and resources to being with the member churches and developing more programmes with them. More attention to follow-up initiatives, interpretation and distribution of WCC materials, especially in third world language areas, is important. In formulating programmes more clarity is needed from the beginning about addressees and the intended consequences in the life of the churches. Assembly delegates as well as members of the Central Committee and commissions should be encouraged and enabled to participate actively in the task of intepretation. Particular attention needs to be given to increasing the transparency of the flow and use of financial resources entrusted to the Council.

3. Increased cooperation and integration

The priority areas defined above cut across the structural distinctions of Units and Sub-units. They call for determined efforts to increase cooperation and integration within and between the operational parts of the WCC structure. This affects all activities of the Council, i.e. studies, action-programmes, and efforts in fostering relationships. The outgoing Central and Executive Committees have adopted basic guidelines and policy recommendations regarding a more effectively coordinated approach to regional relationships and resource sharing. These have been affirmed by this Assembly (Policy Reference Committee I, Finance Committee) and should be implemented speedily following the Assembly. Increased efforts for coordination are needed in the area of fund-raising and allocation of resources for the activities of the WCC itself.

4. Decision-making structures of the WCC

As a result of a two-year process of review of the structures, policies and working methods of the WCC, the Executive Committee concluded that the basic operating structure of the WCC was still sound and that it reflected the main tasks given to the Council. The Executive Committee at the meeting in March 1983 adopted, however, a number of guidelines, intended to clarify the relationship between the different levels of decision-making within the WCC. These guidelines are affirmed explicitly by the Programme Guidelines Committee, as quoted below (cf *Minutes*, Executive Committee, February/March 1983, p. 21):

> i) Central Committee, which has clear responsibility and authority for determining and overseeing the implementation of policy and programme, including finance and staffing, needs to be enabled to fulfill this task more effectively.

> ii) Central Committee should be guided in its task by the Unit Committees, which function as Policy Reference Committees.

> iii) To facilitate the work of these Reference Committees, the Programme Units and a Unit for the General Secretariat should each have an executive or coordinating group to ensure continuous cooperation and coordination within the Unit, and to monitor common concerns, particularly with regard to finance and staffing. Each group would be made up of the officers and staff moderator of the Unit, the officers and directors of the Sub-units or Departments, and possibly other designated persons.

> iv) The units should function in such a way as to promote as close working relations as possible among the Sub-units and, through the General Secretariat, between the Units. To strengthen the relations with the Central Committee, the Moderators of the Units should preferably be members of the Executive Committee or be invited to attend its meetings as consultants. One of the officers of each commission or working group should be a member of the Central Committee.

In order to increase the transparency of decision-making processes, members of Central Committee and Commissions should be held responsible to report to their churches and to foster two-way communication.

D. A brief for core groups of Programme Units

The guidelines and priority areas recommended by the Programme Guidelines Committee will have to be translated into specific programme policies. This is the task of the new Central Committee. It will make its decisions in 1984 on the basis of proposals formulated by "core groups". A core group for each Programme Unit, composed of core groups of each Sub-unit, will be appointed by the Central Committee at the meeting immediately following this Assembly, based on nominations prepared by the outgoing Executive Committee. The core groups are appointed for the specific purpose of translating the guidelines, priorities and other programme-related proposals coming from various parts of the Assembly into a realistic and coherent mandate for the work of the Units and Sub-units in the years ahead; they should not be regarded as executive groups of the future commissions that are to be appointed by the Central Committee in 1984.

The core groups will do their work within the framework and on the basis of the actions by the Assembly regarding programme guidelines. The following points are offered by the Programme Guidelines Committee as additional orientation for the core groups.

1. The discussions during this Assembly in Small Groups, Clusters and Issue Groups have revealed widespread support for the basic, ongoing agenda of the WCC. The Programme Guidelines Committee notes with appreciation that the Council's work in its diversity does in fact respond to actual needs and expectations within its constituency. The frequent allegations about the "lack of balance" or "one-sidedness" in WCC programmes have been openly discussed and largely refuted by the debates during this Assembly. Diversity, complementarity or sometimes even tension are widely accepted as a necessary part of the life of the Council. This should be preserved in the future.

2. The Programme Guidelines Committee has received a vast number of specific proposals for particular programme areas from individual delegates, Small Groups, Clusters, Hearings or Issue Groups. Recognizing that the Assembly cannot act responsibly on all of these proposals, the Programme Guidelines Committee has limited itself to identifying a number of broader priority areas. All remaining proposals, including the full recommendations from Issue Groups, have been transmitted to the General Secretary who is requested to group and integrate them and to submit a memorandum to each Unit core group. The core groups should review these proposals in the light of relevant Assembly actions and should propose a consistent and realistic prospectus for future work.

3. The core groups are being formed according to Programme Units. The first task of core groups is to review the overall mandate of the Unit and its working methods in the light of the actions by this Assembly. Even though the core groups are composed accord-

ing to each Sub-unit they have to give full attention to the future orientation of the Unit as a whole and its cooperation with the other Units.

4. Each Unit core group has to make provisions for initiatives responding to the priorities identified by the Programme Guidelines Committee. This task must not be subordinated to specific Sub-unit concerns. In formulating programme policies for submission to the Central Committee, each Unit core group should consider carefully organizing cooperation, allocating staff responsibilities, timing and funding, including the possibility of intra- and inter-unit sharing of resources. Where necessary the core groups will have to consider postponing or terminating certain activities in order to make room for new tasks.

5. In assessing the validity of different proposals each Unit core group should be guided by the following questions:
- Does the proposed programme express the wholeness of the ecumenical task?
- Who will be the addressees of insights gained or action to be taken? What priority should be given by the WCC to serving this constituency within the totality of its membership?
- How are the needs for ecumenical learning and communication, as well as for continuous theological reflection to be acknowledged in the implementation of the proposed programme emphasis?
- Will the resouces available to the WCC permit the implementation of the proposal, and what adjustments would be required in terms of working patterns and allocation of resources? Could the proposal be equally or better pursued by other ecumenical agencies or in partnership with them?

6. In the light of the recommendations that ecumenical visits be regarded as a permanent feature of the work of the Council in close relationship with its programmatic activities, each unit core group should make the necessary provisions in terms of the allocation of human and material resources on the basis of proposals to be submitted by the General Secretary.

IV. CONCLUSION

The Programme Guidelines Committee presents this report hoping that it will enable the World Council of Churches to keep central in its work the confession which has inspired this Assembly: Jesus Christ – the Life of the World.

IX. THE PRESIDENTS AND MEMBERS OF THE CENTRAL COMMITTEE

HONORARY PRESIDENT
Rev. Dr W. A. *Visser 't Hooft*

PRESIDIUM

Dame R. Nita *Barrow*, Methodist Church in the Caribbean and the Americas, Barbados
Dr Marga *Bührig*, Swiss Reformed Church
Metropolitan Paulos Mar *Gregorios*, Orthodox Syrian Church of the East, India
Bishop Johannes *Hempel*, Federal of the Evangelical Churches in the GDR
Patriarch *Ignatios IV*, Greek Orthodox Patriarchate of Antioch and All the East, Syria
Most Rev. W. P. K. *Makhulu*, Church of the Province of Central Africa, Botswana
Very Rev. Dr Lois M. *Wilson*, United Church of Canada

OFFICERS

Rev. Dr Heinz J. *Held*, Evangelical Church in Germany (FRG), *Moderator*
Metropolitan *Chrysostomos of Myra*, Ecumenical Patriarchate, *Vice-Moderator*
Dr Sylvia *Talbot*, African Methodist Episcopal Church, USA, *Vice-Moderator*
Dr Philip A. *Potter*, Methodist Church in the Caribbean and the Americas, *General Secretary*

MEMBERS OF THE CENTRAL COMMITTEE

Abayasekera, Ms Annathaie, Church of Ceylon
Abebaw Yegsaw, L. M. Yegzaw, Ethiopian Orthodox Church
Abel, Ms Carol, Church in Wales
Adejobi, Primate Emmanuell A., Church of the Lord Aladura, Nigeria
Ahren, Rt Rev. Dr Per-Olov, Church of Sweden
Ajamian, Archbishop Shahe, Armenian Apostolic Church (Etchmiadzin)/Israel
Allin, Rt Rev. John M., Episcopal Church, USA
Antonie, Metropolitan of Ardeal, Romanian Orthodox Church
Arnold, Rev. Walter, Evangelical Church in Germany (FRG)
Ashmall, Mr Harry A., Church of Scotland

---

*Executive Commitee Member

*Athanasios, Rt Rev., Coptic Orthodox Church, Egypt
Ault, Bishop James M., United Methodist Church, USA
*Bena-Silu, M., Church of Jesus Christ on Earth by the Prophet Simon Kimbangu, Zaire
Bichkov, Rev. Alexei, Union of Evangelical Christian Baptists of USSR
Bobrova, Ms Nina S., Russian Orthodox Church
Borovoy, Prof. Prot. Vitaly, Russian Orthodox Church
Bozabalian, Bishop Nerses, Armenian Apostolic Church (Etchmiadzin), USSR
Briggs, Mr John, Baptist Union of Great Britain and Ireland
Buevski, Mr Alexey S., Russian Orthodox Church
Burua, Rev. Albert, United Church in Papua New Guinea and the Solomon Islands
**Calvo, Rev. Samuel, Methodist Church, Costa Rica
Campbell, Rev. Dr Robert, American Baptist Churches in the USA
Charles, Rev. Nelson, Methodist Church of Sierra Leone
Christiansen, Rt Rev. Henrik, Church of Denmark
Chrysostomos, Metropolitan, Church of Greece
Cole, Ms Kara L. N., Friends United Meeting, USA
Crow, Rev. Dr Paul, Christian Church (Disciples of Christ), USA
Crumley, Bishop James R., Lutheran Church in America
Cuthbert, Rev. Raymond A., Christian Church (Disciples of Christ), Canada
Das, Prof. Dr Vincent A., Church of Pakistan
David, Archbishop, Georgian Orthodox Church, USSR
Doll, Ms Ulrike, Federation of the Evangelical Churches in the GDR
Duku, Dr Oliver, Province of the Episcopal Church of the Sudan
Elmquist, Ms Marie, Mission Covenant Church of Sweden
Eneme, Ms Grace, Presbyterian Church in Cameroon
*Faa'alo, Rev. Puafitu, Church of Tuvalu
**Fuligno, Rev. Gioile, Baptist Union of Italy
**Funzamo, Rev. Isaias, Presbyterian Church of Mozambique
Gatwa, Mr T., Presbyterian Church of Rwanda
Gcabashe, Ms Virginia, Methodist Church of Southern Africa
Graewe, Dr W. D., Federation of the Evangelical Churches in the GDR
Grindrod, Most Rev. John, Anglican Church of Australia
Habgood, Bishop John, Church of England
Halim, Ms Inge, Indonesian Christian Church
Hannon, Rev. Canon Brian, Church of Ireland
Harmon, Ms Janice, American Lutheran Church
Hoiore, Ms Celine, Evangelical Church of French Polynesia
Hoover, Ms Theressa, United Methodist Church, USA
Huston, Rev. Dr Robert, United Methodist Church, USA
Ibrahim, His Grace Mar Gregorios Yohanna, Syrian Orthodox Patriarchate of Antioch and All the East
Imasogie, Rev. Dr Osadolor, Nigerian Baptist Convention

Jarjour, Ms Rosa, National Evangelical Synod of Syria and Lebanon
Jefferson, Rev. Canon Ruth, Anglican Church of Canada
Jeremia, Rt Rev. (Anchimiuk), Autocephalic Orthodox Church in Poland
Jesudasan, Most Rev. I., Church of South India
John, Metropolitan of Helsinki, Orthodox Church of Finland
Jornod, Rev. Jean Pierre, Swiss Protestant Church Federation
Julkiree, Ms Boonmee, Church of Christ in Thailand
*Kaddu, Ms Joyce, Church of Uganda
Kaessmann, Ms Margot, Evangelical Church in Germany (FRG)
Karefa-Smart, Rev. Dr Rena, African Methodist Episcopal Zion Church, USA
Karpenco, Mr Alexander, Russian Orthodox Church
Kawabata, Mr Junshiro, United Church of Christ in Japan
Keshishian, Bishop Aram, Armenian Apostolic Church, Lebanon
Khumalo, Rev. Samson, Presbyterian Church of Africa, South Africa
Kim, Rev. Choon Young, Korean Methodist Church
Kim, Rev. Dr Hyung-Tae, Presbyterian Church of Korea
*Kirill, Archbishop, Russian Orthodox Church
Kishkovsky, Very Rev. Leonid, Orthodox Church in America
Knall, Bishop Dieter, Evangelical Church of the Augsburg and Helvetic Confession, Austria
Knoblauch, Rev. Bruno, Evangelical Church of the River Plate, Argentina
Kok, Dr Justice Govaert, Old Catholic Church of the Netherlands
Komla Dzobo, Rt Rev. Noah, Evangelical Presbyterian Church, Ghana
Konidaris, Prof. Gerasimos, Church of Greece
Kruse, Dr Martin, Evangelical Church in Germany (FRG)
Larsson, Ms Birgitta, Church of Sweden
Lemopulo, Mr George, Ecumenical Patriarchate of Constantinople
Lethunya, Ms E. S., Lesotho Evangelical Church
Lodberg, Mr Peter, Church of Denmark
*Love, Dr Janice, United Methodist Church, USA
Luvanda, Ms Jeneth, Evangelical Lutheran Church in Tanzania
**Malakar, Dr Upendra Nath, Church of Bangladesh
Mayland, Ms Jean, Church of England
Mban, Rev. Joseph, Evangelical Church of the Congo
*McCloud, Rev. J. Oscar, Presbyterian Church (USA)
Mekarios, Archbishop of Gojam, Ethiopian Orthodox Church
Michalko, Generalbischof Prof. Jan, Slovak Evangelical Church of the Augsburg Confession in the CSSR, Czechoslovakia
Mitsides, Dr Andreas, Church of Cyprus
Mooi, Rev. Dr Remko J., Netherlands Reformed Church
Muchena, Ms Olivia, United Methodist Church/Zimbabwe
*Nababan, Rev. Dr S. A. E., Batak Protestant Christian Church, Indonesia
Nabulivou, Rev. Inoke, Methodist Church in Fiji
Nagy, Bishop Gyula, Lutheran Church in Hungary
Neff, Rev. Dr Robert, Church of the Brethren, USA
Okullu, Bishop Henry, Church of the Province of Kenya
Pajula, Konsistorialrat Kuno, Estonian Evangelical Lutheran Church, USSR

Palma, Ms Marta, Pentecostal Mission Church, Chile
Pankraty, Metropolitan, Bulgarian Orthodox Church
Parthenios, H. E. Metropolitan, Greek Orthodox Patriarchate of Alexandria and All Africa, Egypt
Pattiasina-Toreh, Rev. Ms C. E., Protestant Church in the Moluccas, Indonesia
Petrova, Ms Stefanka, Bulgarian Orthodox Church
Philaret, Metropolitan of Minsk, Russian Orthodox Church
*Piske, Rev. Meinard, Evangelical Church of Lutheran Confession in Brazil
Poitier, Ms Annette, Methodist Church in the Caribbean and the Americas
Post, Rev. Dr Avery, United Church of Christ, USA
Preus, Bishop David M., American Lutheran Church
Ravalomanana, Ms Voasoa F., Church of Jesus Christ in Madagascar
Richardson, Rev. John, Methodist Church, UK
Richardson, Dr W. Franklyn, National Baptist Convention, USA, Inc.
Ross, Dr Mary O., National Baptist Convention, USA, Inc.
Russell, Most Rev. P. W. R., Church of the Province of Southern Africa, South Africa
Sabug, Mr Fructuoso T., Philippine Independent Church
Santram, Rev. Pritam, Church of North India
Seah, Dr I. S., Presbyterian Church in Taiwan
Sekaran, Mr Premkumar, United Evangelical Lutheran Church in India
Silva, Mr Paulo Lutero, Evangelical Pentecostal Church "Brazil for Christ"
Simich, Prof., Serbian Orthodox Church, Yugoslavia
*Skuse, Ms Jean, Uniting Church in Australia
Smolik, Rev. Dr Josef, Evangelical Church of Czech Brethren
Soro, Rev. Ashur A., Apostolic Catholic Assyrian Church of the East/Canada
Souza, Rt Rev. Neville de, Church in the Province of the West Indies, Jamaica
Sowunmi, Dr Ms Adebisi, Church of the Province of Nigeria
*Stalsett, Rev. Gunnar, Church of Norway
Stylianopoulos, Rev. Dr Theodore, Ecumenical Patriarchate of Constantinople
Sumo, Mr Kpadeson, Lutheran Church in Liberia
Supit, Dr B. A., Christian Evangelical Church in Minahasa, Indonesia
Suvarsky, Archpriest Dr Jaroslav, Orthodox Church of Czechoslovakia
Than, Prof. Kyaw, Burma Baptist Convention
Thompson, Rev. Livingston, Moravian Church in Jamaica
Thompson, Mr William P., Presbyterian Church (USA)
Thorogood, Rev. Bernard, United Reformed Church in the United Kingdom
Tisdale, Rev. Leonora Tubbs, Presbyterian Church (USA)
*Tolen, Dr Aaron, Presbyterian Church of Cameroon
*Toth, Bishop Karoly, Reformed Church in Hungary
Tshihamba, Dr Mukome Leundu, Church of Christ in Zaire – Presbyterian Community
Tudu, Ms Elbina, United Evangelical Lutheran Church in India
Ukur, Dr Fridolin, Kalimantan Evangelical Church, Indonesia
**Vaccaro, Rev. Dr Gabriel, Church of God, Argentina

Varughese, Dr K. V., Mar Thoma Syrian Church of Malabar, India
Vasile, Bishop, Romanian Orthodox Church
Vassilios, Metropolitan, Greek Orthodox Patriarchate of Jerusalem
Veen-Schenkeveld, Rev. Marja J. van der, Reformed Churches in the
   Netherlands
Vercoe, Rt Rev. Whakahuihui, Church of the Province of New Zealand
Vikstrom, Archbishop Dr John, Church of Finland
Westphal, Ms Marthe, Reformed Church of France
Yao, Datuk Ping-Hua, Methodist Church in Malaysia
Zumach, Ms Hildegard, Evangelical Church in Germany (FRG)

X. MEMBER CHURCHES OF THE WCC

ALGERIA

Eglise protestante d'Algérie*
(Protestant Church of Algeria)

ARGENTINA

Iglesia de Dios*

Iglesia de los Discipulos do Cristo*
(Church of the Disciples of Christ)

Iglesia Evangélica Luterana
Unida*
(United Evangelical Lutheran
Church)

Iglesia Evangélica Metodista
Argentina
(Evangelical Methodist Church of
Argentina)

Iglesia Evangélica del Río de la
Plata
(Evangelical Church of the River
Plate)

AUSTRALIA

The Anglican Church of Australia

Australian Council of Churches**

Churches of Christ in Australia

The Uniting Church in Australia

AUSTRIA

Alt-katholische Kirche Österreichs
(Old Catholic Church of Austria)

Ökumenischer Rat der Kirchen in
Österreich
(Ecumenical Council of Austrian
Churches)**

Evangelische Kirche
Augsburgischen u.
Helvetischen Bekenntnisses
(A.u.H.B.)
(Evangelical Church of the
Augsburg and Helvetic
Confession)

BANGLADESH

Bangladesh Baptist Sangha

The Church of Bangladesh*

BELGIUM

Eglise protestante unie de Belgique
(United Protestant Church of
Belgium)

BENIN

Eglise protestante méthodiste en
République populaire du Bénin
(Protestant Methodist Church in
the People's Republic of Benin)

BOLIVIA

Iglesia Evangélica Metodista en
Bolivia*
(Evangelical Methodist Church in
Bolivia)

---

*Associate member church
**Associate council

BOTSWANA

Botswana Christian Council★★

BRAZIL

Igreja Episcopal do Brasil
(Episcopal Church of Brazil)

Igreja Evangélica de Confissão
Luterana no Brasil
(Evangelical Church of Lutheran
Confession in Brazil)

Igreja Evangélica Pentecostal "O
Brasil para Cristo"
(The Evangelical Pentecostal
Church "Brazil for Christ")

Igreja Metodista do Brasil
(Methodist Church in Brazil)

Igreja Reformada Latino
Americana
(The Latin American Reformed
Church)

BULGARIA

Bulgarian Orthodox Church

BURMA

Burma Baptist Convention

Burma Council of Churches★★

Church of the Province of Burma

BURUNDI

Church of the Province of
Burundi, Rwanda and Zaire

CAMEROON

Eglise évangélique du Cameroun
(Evangelical Church of
Cameroon)

Eglise presbytérienne
camérounaise
(Presbyterian Church of
Cameroon)

Eglise protestante africaine★
(African Protestant Church)

Presbyterian Church in Cameroon

Union des Eglises baptistes du
Cameroun
(Union of Baptist Churches of
Cameroon)

CANADA

The Anglican Church of Canada

Canadian Council of Churches★★

Canadian Yearly Meeting of the
Society of Friends

Christian Church (Disciples of
Christ)

The Evangelical Lutheran Church
of Canada

The Presbyterian Church in
Canada

The United Church of Canada

CENTRAL AFRICA

Church of the Province of Central
Africa

CHILE

Iglesia Evangélica Luterana en
Chile
(Evangelical-Lutheran Church in
Chile)

Iglesia Metodista de Chile★
(The Methodist Church of Chile)

Iglesia Pentecostal de Chile
(Pentecostal Church of Chile)

Misión Iglesia Pentecostal
(Pentecostal Mission Church)

**CONGO (People's Republic of
the)**

Eglise évangélique du Congo
(Evangelical Church of the Congo)

COOK ISLANDS

Cook Islands Christian Church

COSTA RICA

Iglesia Evangélica Metodista de
Costa Rica*
(Evangelical Methodist Church of
Costa Rica)

CUBA

Iglesia Metodista en Cuba*
(Methodist Church in Cuba)

Iglesia Presbiteriana-Reformada en
Cuba*
(Presbyterian-Reformed Church in
Cuba)

CYPRUS

Church of Cyprus

CZECHOSLOVAKIA

Ceskobratrská církev evangelická
(Evangelical Church of Czech
Brethren)

Ceskoslovenská církev husitská
(Czechoslovak Hussite Church)

Czech Ecumenical Council**

Pravoslavná církev v CSSR
(Orthodox Church of
Czechoslovakia)

Ref. krest. církev na Slovensku
(Reformed Christian Church in
Slovakia)

Slezská církev evangelická a.v.
(Silesian Evangelical Church of the
Augsburg Confession)

Slovenská evanjelická církev a.v. v
CSSR
(Slovak Evangelical Church of the
Augsburg Confession in the
CSSR)

DENMARK

Det danske Baptistsamfund
(The Baptist Union of Denmark)

Ecumenical Council of
Denmark**

Den evangelisk-lutherske
Folkekirke i Danmark
(The Church of Denmark)

EAST AFRICA

Presbyterian Church of East Africa

EGYPT

The Coptic Orthodox Church

Coptic Evangelical Church – The
Synod of the Nile

Greek Orthodox Patriarchate of
Alexandria and All Africa

EQUATORIAL GUINEA

Iglesia Reformada de Guinea
Ecuatorial*
(Reformed Church of Equatorial
Guinea)

ETHIOPIA

Ethiopian Orthodox Church

The Ethiopian Evangelical Church
Mekane Yesus

EUROPE

Europäisch-Festländische Brüder-
Unität, Distrikt Bad Boll
(European Continental Province of
the Moravian Church` –
Western District)

FIJI

Methodist Church in Fiji

FINLAND

Ecumenical Council of Finland★★

Suomen evankelis-luterilainen
kirkko
(Evangelical-Lutheran Church of
Finland)

Orthodox Church of Finland

FRANCE

Eglise de la Confession
d'Augsbourg d'Alsace et de
Lorraine
(Evangelical Church of the
Augsburg Confession of Alsace
and Lorraine)

Eglise évangélique luthérienne de
France
(Evangelical Lutheran Church of
France)

Eglise réformée d'Alsace et de
Lorraine
(Reformed Church of Alsace and
Lorraine)

Eglise réformée de France
(Reformed Church of France)

FRENCH POLYNESIA

Eglise évangélique de Polynésie
française
(Evangelical Church of French
Polynesia)

GABONESE REPUBLIC

Eglise évangélique du Gabon
(Evangelical Church of Gabon)

FEDERAL REPUBLIC OF GERMANY

Arbeitsgemeinschaft Christlicher
Kirchen in der Bundesrepublik
Deutschland und Berlin (West)
e.v.
(Council of Christian Churches in
Germany (FRG)★★

Evangelische Kirche in
Deutschland
(Evangelical Church in Germany)

Evangelische Landerskirche in
Baden

Evangelisch-Lutherische Kirche
in Bayern†

Evangelische Kirche in Berlin-
Brandenburg (Berlin West)

---

†This church is directly a member of the World Council of Churches in accordance
with the resolution of the General Synod of the United Evangelical Lutheran
Church of Germany, dated 27 January 1949, which recommended that the member
churches of the United Evangelical Lutheran Church should make the following
declaration to the Council of the Evangelical Church in Germany concerning their
relation to the World Council of Churches:
"The Evangelical Church in Germany has made it clear through its constitution
that it is a federation (Bund) of confessionally determined churches. Moreover, the
conditions of membership of the World Council of Churches have been determined
at the Assembly at Amsterdam. Therefore, this Evangelical Lutheran Church
declares concerning its membership in the World Council of Churches:
  i) It is represented in the World Council as a church of the Evangelical Lutheran
     confession.
 ii) Representatives which it sends to the World Council are to be identified as
     Evangelical Lutherans.
iii) Within the limits of the competence of the Evangelical Church in Germany it
     is represented in the World Council through the intermediary of the Council
     of the Evangelical Church in Germany."

Evangelisch-Lutherische
Landeskirche in
Braunschweig†

Bremische Evangelische Kirche

Evangelisch-Lutherische
Landeskirche Hannovers†

Evangelische Kirche in Hessen
und Nassau

Evangelische Kirche von
Kurhessen-Waldeck

Lippische Landeskirche

Nordelbische Evangelisch-
Lutherische Kirche†

Evangelisch-reformierte Kirche
in Nordwestdeutschland

Evangelisch-Lutherische Kirche
in Oldenburg

Evangelische Christliche Kirche
der Pfalz
(Protestantische Landeskirche)

Evangelische Kirche in
Rheinland

Evangelisch-Lutherische
Landeskirche Schaumburg-
Lippe†

Evangelische Kirche von
Westfalen

Evangelische Landeskirche in
Württemberg

Katholisches Bistum der Alt-
Katholiken in Deutschland
(Catholic Diocese of the Old
Catholics in Germany)

Vereinigung der Deutschen
Mennonitengemeinden
(Mennonite Church)

GERMAN DEMOCRATIC REPUBLIC

Arbeitsgemeinschaft Christlicher
Kirchen in der DDR
(Council of Christian Churches
(GDR)★★

Bund der Evangelischen Kirchen
in der Deutschen
Demokratischen Republik
(Federation of the Evangelical
Churches in the GDR)

Evangelische Landeskirche
Anhalts‡

Evangelische Kirche in Berlin-
Brandenburg‡

Evangelische Kirche des
Görlitzer Kirchengebietes‡

Evangelische Landeskirche
Greifswald‡

Evangelische-Lutherische
Landeskirche Mecklenburgs‡

Evangelische Kirche der
Kirchenprovinz Sachsen‡

Evangelisch-Lutherische
Landeskirche Sachsens‡

Evangelische-Lutherische
Kirche in Thüringen‡

Evangelische Brüder-Unität
(Distrikt Herrnhut)
(Moravian Church)

Gemeindeverband der Alt-
Katholischen Kirche in Der
Deutschen Demokratischen
Republik
(Federation of the Old Catholic
Church in the GDR)

---

‡United in a fellowship of Christian witness and service in the Federation of
Evangelical Churches in the GDR, these churches are represented in the WCC
through agencies of the Federation of Evangelical Churches in the GDR.

GHANA

The Christian Council of Ghana★★

Evangelical Presbyterian Church

The Methodist Church, Ghana

Presbyterian Church of Ghana

GREECE

Ekklesia tes Ellados
(Church of Greece)

Helleniki Evangeliki Ekklesia
(Greek Evangelical Church)

HONG KONG

The Church of Christ in China,
The Hong Kong Council

Hong Kong Christian Council★★

HUNGARY

Ecumenical Council in Hungary★★

Magyarországi Baptista Egyház
(Baptist Union of Hungary)

Magyarországi Evangélikus
Egyház
(Lutheran Church in Hungary)

Magyarországi Reformatus
Egyház
(Reformed Church in Hungary)

ICELAND

Evangelical Lutheran Church of
Iceland

INDIA

Bengal-Orissa-Bihar Baptist
Convention★

Church of North India

Church of South India

Mar Thoma Syrian Church of
Malabar

Malankara Orthodox Syrian
Church

Methodist Church in India

National Council of Churches in
India★★

The Samavesam of Telugu Baptist
Churches

United Evangelical Lutheran
Church in India

INDONESIA

Banua Niha Keriso Protestan
(Nias Protestant Christian Church)

Council of Churches in
Indonesia★★

The Evangelical Christian Church
in Halmahera

Gereja Batak Karo Protestan
(Karo Batak Protestant Church)

Gereja-Gereja Kristen Java
(Javanese Christian Churches)

Gereja Kalimantan Evangelis
(Kalimantan Evangelical Church)

Gereja Kristen Indonesia
(Indonesian Christian Church)

Gereja Kristen Injili di Irian Jaya
(Evangelical Christian Church in
West Irian)

Gereja Kristen Jawi Wetan
(East Java Christian Church)

Gereja Kristen Pasundan
(Pasundan Christian Church)

Gereja Kristen Protestan di Bali★
(Protestant Christian Church in
Bali)

Gereja Kristen Protestan Indonesia
(G.K.P.I.)
(Christian Protestant Church in
Indonesia)

Gereja Kristen Protestan
Simalungun
(Simalungun Protestant Christian
Church)

Gereja Kristen Sulawesi Tengah
(Christian Church in Central
Sulawesi)

Gereja Masehi Injili Minahasa
(Christian Evangelical Church in
Minahasa)

Gereja Masehi Injili Sangihe
Talaud (G.M.I.S.T.)
(Evangelical Church of Sangir
Talaud)

Gereja Masehi Injili di Timor
(Protestant Evangelical Church in
Timor)

Gereja Protestan di Indonesia
(Protestant Church in Indonesia)

Gereja Protestan Maluku
(Protestant Church in the
Moluccas)

Gereja Punguan Kristen Batak
(G.P.K.B.)*
(Batak Christian Community
Church)

Gereja Toraja
(Toraja Church)

Huria Kristen Batak Protestan
(Batak Protestant Christian
Church)

Huria Kristen Indonesia (H.K.I.)
(The Indonesian Christian Church)

IRAN

Synod of the Evangelical Church
of Iran

ITALY

Baptist Union of Italy*

Chiesa Evangelica Metodista
d'Italia
(Evangelical Methodist Church of
Italy)

Chiesa Evangelica Valdese
(Waldensian Church)

JAMAICA

The Moravian Church in Jamaica

The United Church of Jamaica and
Grand Cayman

JAPAN

Japanese Orthodox Church

The Korean Christian Church in
Japan*

National Christian Council of
Japan**

Nippon Kirisuto Kyodan
(The United Church of Christ in
Japan)

Nippon Si Ko Kai
(Anglican-Episcopal Church in
Japan)

JERUSALEM

Episcopal Church in Jerusalem and
the Middle East

Greek Orthodox Patriarchate of
Jerusalem

KENYA

African Christian Church and
Schools

African Church of the Holy Spirit*

African Israel Church, Ninevah

Church of the Province of Kenya

The Methodist Church in Kenya

KOREA

The Korean Methodist Church

The Presbyterian Church in the Republic of Korea

The Presbyterian Church of Korea

LEBANON

Armenian Apostolic Church

Union of the Armenian Evangelical Churches in the Near East

LESOTHO

Lesotho Evangelical Church

LIBERIA

Lutheran Church in Liberia

Presbytery of Liberia*

MADAGASCAR

Eglise de Jésus-Christ à Madagascar
(Church of Jesus Christ in Madagascar)

Eglise luthérienne malgache
(Malagasy Lutheran Church)

MALAYSIA

Council of Churches of Malaysia**

The Methodist Church in Malaysia

Protestant Church in Sabah*

MAURITIUS

Church of the Province of the Indian Ocean

MELANESIA

(see under Solomon Islands)

MEXICO

Iglesia Metodista de México
(Methodist Church of Mexico)

MOZAMBIQUE

Igreja Presbiteriana de Moçambique*
(Presbyterian Church of Mozambique)

NAMIBIA

Council of Churches in Namibia**

NETHERLANDS

Algemene Doopsgezinde Sociëteit
(General Mennonite Society)

Council of Churches in the Netherlands**

Evangelisch Lutherse Kerk
(Evangelical Lutheran Church)

De Gereformeerde Kerken in Nederland
(The Reformed Churches in the Netherlands)

Nederlandse Hervormde Kerk
(Netherlands Reformed Church)

Oud-Katholieke Kerk van Nederland
(Old Catholic Church of the Netherlands)

Remonstrantse Broederschap
(Remonstrant Brotherhood)

NETHERLANDS ANTILLES

Iglesia Protestant Uni*
(United Protestant Church)

NEW CALEDONIA

Eglise évangélique en Nouvelle Calédonie et aux Iles Loyauté
(Evangelical Church in New Caledonia and the Loyalty Isles)

NEW ZEALAND

Associated Churches of Christ in New Zealand

The Baptist Union of New Zealand

Church of the Province of New Zealand

The Methodist Church of New Zealand

National Council of Churches in New Zealand★★

The Presbyterian Church of New Zealand

NICARAGUA

Convención bautista de Nicaragua
(Baptist Convention of Nicaragua)

NIGERIA

The Church of the Lord Aladura

Church of the Province of Nigeria

Methodist Church, Nigeria

Nigerian Baptist Convention

The Presbyterian Church of Nigeria

NORWAY

Den Norske Kirke
(Church of Norway)

PAKISTAN

The Church of Pakistan

United Presbyterian Church of Pakistan

PAPUA NEW GUINEA

The United Church in Papua New Guinea and the Solomon Islands

PERU

Iglesia Metodista del Peru★
(The Methodist Church of Peru)

PHILIPPINES

Iglesia Evangélica Metodista en las Islas Filipinas
(The Evangelical Methodist Church in the Philippines)

Iglesia Filipina Independiente
(Philippine Independent Church)

National Council of Churches in the Philippines★★

United Church of Christ in the Philippines

POLAND

Autocephalic Orthodox Church in Poland

Kosciola Evangelicko-Augsburskiego w PRL
(Evangelical Church of the Augsburg Confession in Poland)

Kosciola Polskokatolickiego w PRL
(Polish Catholic Church in Poland)

Polish Ecumenical Council★★

Staro-Katolickiego Kosciola Mariatowitow w PRL
(Old Catholic Mariavite Church in Poland)

PORTUGAL

Igreja Evangélica Presbiteriana de Portugal★
(Evangelical Presbyterian Church of Portugal)

Igreja Lusitana Catolica Apostolica Evangélica★
(Lusitanian Catholic-Apostolic Evangelical Church)

ROMANIA

Biserica Orthodoxa Romana
(Romanian Orthodox Church)

Evangelische Kirche A.B. in der
Sozialistischen Republik
Rumänien
(Evangelical Church of the
Augsburg Confession in the
Socialist Republic of Romania)

Evangelical Synodal Presbyterial
Church of the Augsburg
Confession in the Socialist
Republic of Romania

Reformed Church of Romania

RWANDA

Eglise presbytérienne au Rwanda
(Presbyterian Church of Rwanda)

SAMOA

The Congregational Christian
Church in Samoa

Methodist Church in Samoa

SIERRA LEONE

The Methodist Church of Sierra
Leone

Sierra Leone United Christian
Council★★

SINGAPORE

The Methodist Church in
Singapore★

National Council of Churches of
Singapore★★

SOLOMON ISLANDS

Church of Melanesia

SOUTH AFRICA

Church of the Province of
Southern Africa

Evangelical Lutheran Church in
Southern Africa

Evangelical Presbyterian Church
in South Africa

The Methodist Church of
Southern Africa

Moravian Church in South Africa

Presbyterian Church of Africa

The Presbyterian Church of
Southern Africa

The Reformed Presbyterian
Church of Southern Africa

The South African Council of
Churches★★

The United Congregational
Church of Southern Africa

SPAIN

Iglesia Española Reformada
Episcopal★
(Spanish Reformed Episcopal
Church)

Iglesia Evangélica Española
(Spanish Evangelical Church)

SRI LANKA

The Church of Ceylon

Methodist Church

National Christian Council of Sri
Lanka★★

PROVINCE OF THE SUDAN

Episcopal Church of the Sudan

The Presbyterian Church in the
Sudan★

SURINAM

Moravian Church in Surinam

SWAZILAND

Council of Swaziland Churches★★

SWEDEN

Svenska Kyrkan
(Church of Sweden)

Svenska Missionsförbundet
(The Mission Covenant Church of
Sweden)

Swedish Ecumenical Council★★

SWITZERLAND

Christkatholische Kirche der
Schweiz
(Old Catholic Church of
Switzerland)

Schweizerischer Evangelischer
Kirchenbund
Fédération des Eglises protestantes
de la Suisse
(Swiss Protestant Church
Federation)

SYRIA

The National Evangelical Synod of
Syria and Lebanon

Patriarcat grec-orthodoxe
d'Antioche et de tout l'Orient
(Greek Orthodox Patriarchate of
Antioch and All the East)

Syrian Orthodox Patriarchate of
Antioch and All the East

TAIWAN

The Presbyterian Church of
Taiwan

TANZANIA

Church of the Province of
Tanzania

Evangelical Lutheran Church in
Tanzania

Joint Board of the Moravian
Church in Tanzania

THAILAND

The Church of Christ in Thailand

TOGO

Eglise évangélique du Togo
(Evangelical Church of Togo)

TONGA

Free Wesleyan Church of Tonga

Tonga National Council of
Churches★★

TRINIDAD

The Presbyterian Church in
Trinidad and Grenada

TURKEY

Ecumenical Patriarchate of
Constantinople

TUVALU

Tuvalu Church

UGANDA

The Church of Uganda

**UNION OF SOVIET
SOCIALIST REPUBLICS**

Russian Orthodox Church

The Union of Evangelical
Christian Baptists of USSR

Armenian SSR

Eglise apostolique arménienne
(Armenian Apostolic Church)

Estonian SSR

Eesti Evangeeliumi Luteri Usu
Kirik
(Estonian Evangelical Lutheran
Church)

Georgian SSR

Georgian Orthodox Church

Latvian SSR

Latvijas Evangeliski Luteriska
Baznica
(Evangelical Lutheran Church of
Latvia)

**UNITED KINGDOM and
REPUBLIC OF IRELAND**

British Council of Churches★★

The Baptist Union of Great Britain
and Ireland

The Church of England

The Methodist Church

The Moravian Church in Great
Britain and Ireland

The United Reformed Church in
the United Kingdom

The Church of Ireland

The Methodist Church in Ireland

The Church of Scotland

The Congregational Union of
Scotland

The Scottish Episcopal Church

United Free Church of Scotland

The Church in Wales

The Presbyterian Church of Wales

Union of Welsh Independents

Council of Churches for Wales★★

**UNITED STATES OF
AMERICA**

African Methodist Episcopal
Church

African Methodist Episcopal Zion
Church

American Baptist Churches in the
USA

American Lutheran Church

Apostolic Catholic Assyrian
Church of the East

Christian Church (Disciples of
Christ)

Christian Methodist Episcopal
Church

Church of the Brethren

The Episcopal Church

Hungarian Reformed Church in
America

International Evangelical Church

Lutheran Church in America

Moravian Church in America
(Northern Province)

Moravian Church in America
(Southern Province)

National Baptist Convention of
America

National Baptist Convention,
USA, Inc.

National Council of the Churches
of Christ in the USA★★

National Council of Community
Churches

The Orthodox Church in America

Polish National Catholic Church

Presbyterian Church (USA)

Progressive National Baptist
Convention

Reformed Church in America

Religious Society of Friends
Friends General Conference
Friends United Meeting

United Church of Christ

The United Methodist Church

URUGUAY

Iglesia Evangélica Metodista en el
Uruguay*
(The Evangelical Methodist
Church in Uruguay)

VANUATU

Presbyterian Church of Vanuatu

WEST AFRICA

The Church of the Province of
West Africa

WEST INDIES

The Church in the Province of the
West Indies

The Methodist Church in the
Caribbean and the Americas

Moravian Church, Eastern West
Indies Province

YUGOSLAVIA

Ecumenical Council of Churches
in Yugoslavia**

Reformatska Crke u SFRJ
(The Reformed Church in
Yugoslavia)

Serbian Orthodox Church

Slovenska ek.-kr. a.v. cirkev v.
Juhuslavi
(Slovak Evangelical Church of the
Augsburg Confession in
Yugoslavia)

ZAIRE (Republic of)

Eglise du Christ au Zaïre
(Church of Christ in Zaire)

Eglise du Christ au Zaïre
(Communauté des Disciples)
(Church of Christ in Zaire –
Community of Disciples)

Eglise du Christ au
Zaïre(Communauté
evangélique)
(Church of Christ in Zaire –
Evangelical Community)

Eglise du Christ au Zaïre
(Communauté Lumière)
(Church of Christ in Zaire –
Community of Light)

Eglise du Christ au Zaïre
(Communauté Mennonite)
(Church of Christ in Zaire –
Mennonite Community)

Eglise du Christ au Zaïre
(Communauté
Presbytérienne)
(Church of Christ in Zaire –
Presbyterian Community)

Eglise du Christ au Zaïre
(Communauté épiscopale
baptiste en Afrique
(C.E.B.A.)*
(Church of Christ in Zaire –
Episcopal Baptist
Community)

Eglise de Jésus-Christ sur la Terre
par le Prophète Simon
Kimbangu
(Church of Jesus Christ on Earth
by the Prophet Simon
Kimbangu)

ZAMBIA

United Church of Zambia

ZIMBABWE

Zimbabwe Christian Council**

OTHER CHURCHES

Eesti Evangeeliumi Luteri Usu
Kirik
(Estonian Evangelical Lutheran
Church)

Latvijas Evangeliski Luteriska
Baznica Eksila
(Evangelical Lutheran Church of
Latvia in Exile)

XI. ASSEMBLY PARTICIPANTS

WCC PRESIDENTS

Ilia II, His Holiness, mo, Georgian Orthodox Church, USSR
Jiagge, The Hon. Mrs Justice A.R., fl, Evangelical Presbyterian Church, Ghana
Miguez-Bonino, Prof. José, mo, Evangelical Methodist Church of Argentina
Simatupang, Dr T.B., ml, Indonesian Christian Church
Sundby, Most Rev. Olof, mo, Church of Sweden
Wedel, Dr Cynthia, fl, Episcopal Church, USA

WCC OFFICERS

Karekin II, His Holiness, mo, Armenian Apostolic Church (Cilicia), Lebanon
Potter, Rev. Dr Philip A., mo, Methodist Church in the Caribbean and the Americas
Scott, Most Rev. E.W., mo, Anglican Church of Canada
Skuse, Ms Jean, fl, Uniting Church in Australia

DELEGATES FROM MEMBER CHURCHES

Abayasekera, Ms Annathaie, fl, Church of Ceylon
Abbey-Mensah, Ms Dinah, fl, Evangelical Presbyterian Church, Ghana
Abebaw Yegzaw, L. M., mo, Ethiopian Orthodox Church
Abel, Ms Carol, yfl, Church in Wales
Abesamis, Rev. Gil S., mo, Evangelical Methodist Church in the Philippines
Ablorh, Ms Ophelia, fl, Presbyterian Church of Ghana
Abraham, Rt Rev. D., mo, Hungarian Reformed Church
Aco, Bishop Isac, mo, Methodist Church of Brazil
Adams, Dr Charles, mo, Progressive National Baptist Convention, USA
Adejobi, Primate Emmanuell A., mo, Church of the Lord Aladura, Nigeria

---

Key to abbreviations: m = male; f = female; o = ordained; l = lay; y = youth

Adhiambo, Ms C., yfl, Church of the Province of Kenya
Adhikari, Mr Michael S., ml, Bangladesh Baptist Sangha
Affeld, Mr Dietrich, ml, Federation of the Evangelical Churches in the GDR
Ahren, Rt Rev. Dr Per-Olov, mo, Church of Sweden
Aitken, Mr I.C., ml, Presbyterian Church of Southern Africa
Ajamian, Archbishop Shahe, mo, Armenian Apostolic Church (Etchmiadzin)/Israel
Akande, Rev. Dr Ola, mo, Nigerian Baptist Convention
Akoma Mozogo, Ms Albertine, fl, Evangelical Church of Gabon
Alexander Mar Thoma, Most Rev. Dr, mo, Mar Thoma Syrian Church of Malabar, India
Allin, Rt Rev. John M., mo, Episcopal Church, USA
Allsop, Rev. Ian, mo, Churches of Christ in Australia
Ambadiang, Rev. Dr Grégoire, mo, Presbyterian Church of Cameroon
Amoah, Dr Elizabeth, fl, Methodist Church, Ghana
Amosa, Mr Vaetoe, yml, Congregational Christian Church in Samoa
Andrews, Rev. James, mo, Presbyterian Church (USA)
Andriamanamihaga, Rev. Roger, mo, Church of Jesus Christ in Madagascar
Andriamiharisoa, Rev. Lala, mo, Church of the Province of the Indian Ocean/Madagascar
Andrino, Bishop Messias, mo, Methodist Church in Brazil
Angelov, Protohierey Dimitre, mo, Bulgarian Orthodox Church
Annu, Rev. Hans, mo, Evangelical Christian Church in Halmahera, Indonesia
Antonie of Ardeal, Metropolitan, mo, Romanian Orthodox Church
Arends, Mr A., yml, United Congregational Church of Southern Africa
Armstrong, Bishop James, mo, United Methodist Church, USA
Arnold, Rev. Walter, mo, Evangelical Church in Germany, FRG
Arreak, Rev. Benjamin, mo, Anglican Church of Canada
Asay de Benech, Ms Kathy, yfl, Waldensian Church/Argentina
Ashjian, Bishop Mesrob, mo, Armenian Apostolic Church (Cilicia)/USA
Ashmall, Mr Harry A., ml, Church of Scotland
Assad, Dr Maurice M., ml, Coptic Orthodox Church, Egypt
Assefa, Emahoy Askala, fl, Ethiopian Orthodox Church
Athanasios, Archbishop, mo, Syrian Orthodox Patriarchate of Antioch
Athanasios, Rt Rev., mo, Coptic Orthodox Church, Egypt
Augusto Silva, Ms Valeria Mantovani, fo, Evangelical Pentecostal Church "Brazil for Christ"
Ault, Bishop James M., mo, United Methodist Church, USA
Austin, Canon George, mo, Church of England
Azariah, Rev. M., mo, Church of South India

Baechtold, Ms Janette, yfl, Evangelical Church of Lutheran Confession in Brazil
Bailey, Ms Joyce, fl, Methodist Church in the Caribbean and the Americas/Jamaica
Baker, Ms Christina, fl, United Church of Canada

Baker, Ms Peta-Anne, fl, Church in the Province of the West Indies/
Jamaica
Balke, Rev. Dr W., mo, Netherlands Reformed Church
Banks, Ms Helen, fl, Churches of Christ in Australia
Banoet, Rev. Chr. P., mo, Protestant Evangelical Church in Timor,
Indonesia
Barnes, Mr Michael, yml, Uniting Church in Australia
Bartholomeos, Metropolitan, mo, Ecumenical Patriarchate of
Constantinople
Barus, Mr Missi, ml, Karo Batak Protestant Church, Indonesia
Baumer, Rev. Martha A., fo, United Church of Christ, USA
Bautista, Mr Liberato, yml, United Methodist Church, USA
Beaumonte, Ms Phyllis E., fl, National Baptist Convention, Inc., USA
Becker, Oberkirchenrat Henje, mo, Evangelical Church in Germany, FRG
Becker Rev. Horst, mo, Evengelical Church in Germany, FRG
Behrend, Bishop Wilbur, mo, Moravian Church in America (Northern
Province)
Bekhit, Ms Neima, fl, Coptic Evangelical Church, Synod of the Nile,
Egypt
Bena-Silu, M., ml, Church of Jesus Christ on Earth by the Prophet Simon
Kimbangu, Zaire
Bender, Mr Christopher, yml, Ecumenical Patriarchate of Constantinople/USA
Benecchi, Rev. Valdo, mo, Evangelical Methodist Church in Italy
Bertrand, Rev. Michel, mo, Reformed Church of France
Bet, Ms Elis, fl, Church of the Province of Kenya
Bettenhausen, Dr Elizabeth, fl, Lutheran Church in America
Bhandare, Most Rev. Dr R.S., mo, Church of North India
Bichkov, Rev. Alexei, mo, Union of Evangelical Christian Baptists of
USSR
Bingham, Rev. Dr Walter, mo, Christian Church (Disciples of Christ), USA
Binhammer, Rev. Dr Robert J., mo, Lutheran Church in America/Canada
Blakebrough-Fairbairn, Ms Adele, yfl, Baptist Union of Great Britain and
Ireland
Blazier, Ms Lynette E., yfl, American Baptist Churches in the USA
Blocher Smeltzer, Ms Mary, fl, Church of the Brethren, USA
Boayen, Rev. Boonratna, mo, Church of Christ in Thailand
Bobrova, Ms Nina, fl, Russian Orthodox Church
Boer, Rev. Bert, mo, Netherlands Reformed Church
Borgen, Bishop Ole E., mo, United Methodist Church/Norway
Borges, Ms Eloah M.P., yfl, Methodist Church in Brazil
Borovoy, Prof. Prot. Vitaly, mo, Russian Orthodox Church/Switzerland
Bos, Dr Jone, ml, Netherlands Reformed Church
Bottoman, Rev. Adolphus, mo, Presbyterian Church of Africa
Bouchard, Rev. Giorgio, mo, Waldensian Church, Italy
Bowles, Mr William R., ml, Evangelical Lutheran Church in Southern
Africa
Bozabalian, Bishop Nerses, mo, Armenian Apostolic Church
(Etchmiadzin), USSR

Bradley, Mr Edgar G., ml, Church of the Province of New Zealand
Branch, Mr Keith, yml, Church of the Province of the West Indies/
   Guyana
Briggs, Mr John, ml, Baptist Union of Great Britain and Ireland
Britten, Ms Elizabeth, fl, Anglican Church of Australia
Brown, Rev. Neville C., mo, Moravian Church, Eastern West Indies
   Province
Brown, Mr Beu Charles, yml, Church of the Province of Melanesia
Browne, Archbishop George D., mo, Church of the Province of West
   Africa/Liberia
Bruce, Dr Beverlee, ml, African Methodist Episcopal Church, USA
Brueggemann, Rev. Heinrich, mo, Evangelical Church in Germany, FRG
Bryce, Rt Rev. J., mo, Church of the Province of New Zealand/Fiji
Buevski, Mr A.S., ml, Russian Orthodox Church
Buku, Mr Joel, ml, Church of the Province of Kenya
Bullimore, Chancellor John, ml, Church of England
Burua, Rev. Albert, mo, United Church in Papua New Guinea and the
   Solomon Islands
Busch, Prof. Rev. Roland, mo, Uniting Church in Australia
Buschlueter, Ms Ursula, fl, Federation of the Old Catholic Church in the GDR

Cabreza, Ms Ella, fl, Philippine Independent Church
Calmer, Mr Rob, ml, Netherlands Reformed Church
Campbell, Rev. Dr Robert, mo, American Baptist Churches in the USA
Capo, Rev. Enrique, mo, Spanish Evangelical Church
Carranza-Gomez, Rev. Sergio, mo, Episcopal Church/Mexico
Carson, Rev. Leon, ml, American Methodist Episcopal Zion Church, USA
Carter, Ms Aiko Y., fl, United Church of Christ of Japan
Carter, Dr Lawrence, mo, National Baptist Convention, Inc., USA
Carvalho, Bishop Emilio de, mo, United Methodist Church/Angola
Casalis de Pury, Ms Tessa, fl, Church of the Province of Central Africa/
   Zambia
Castro, Bishop George F., mo, Evangelical Methodist Church in the
   Philippines
Catlin, Rev. Anna, fo, Uniting Church in Australia
Charles, Rev. Nelson, mo, Methodist Church of Sierra Leone
Chernobrivtseva, Sister Natalia, yfl, Russian Orthodox Church
Chivarov, Prof. Archpriest Nicolai, mo, Bulgarian Orthodox Church
Cho, Rev. Seung Hyuk, mo, Korean Methodist Church
Christiansen, Ms Ellen Juhl, fl, Church of Denmark
Christiansen, Rev. Ole, mo, Church of Denmark
Christiansen, Rt Rev. Henrik, mo, Church of Denmark
Christie-Johnston, Rev. Hamish, mo, Uniting Church in Australia
Christopher, Rt Rev., mo, Serbian Orthodox Church/USA
Chrysostomos, Metropolitan, mo, Ecumenical Patriarchate of
   Constantinople/Turkey
Chrysostomos, Metropolitan, mo, Church of Greece
Clarke, Mr Raymond, ml, United Reformed Church, UK

Cole, Ms Kara L.N., fl, Friends United Meeting, USA
Coles, The Very Rev. Dr D.J., mo, Church of the Province of New
    Zealand
Concha Ulloa, Rev. Nicolas, mo, Pentecostal Church of Chile
Cooper, Ms Rosco, fl, National Baptist Convention, Inc., USA
Cooper, Dr Rosco, ml, National Baptist Convention, Inc. USA
Cortez Washington, Ms Zelda, fl, Christian Methodist Episcopal Church, USA
Cortner, Ms Marydel, fl, Episcopal Church, USA
Corvalan Vasquez, Dr Oscar, ml, Pentecostal Church of Chile
Cragg, Rev. Dr D., mo, Methodist Church of Southern Africa
Crist, Ms Dollie, fl, United Methodist Church, USA
Crow, Rev. Dr Paul, mo, Christian Church (Disciples of Christ), USA
Crumley, Bishop James R., mo, Lutheran Church in America
Crutchfield, Rev. Kim, mo, International Evangelical Church, USA
Cruz, Most Rev. Abdia S.R. de la, mo, Philippine Independent Church
Cuffie, Ms Daphne, fl, Church of the Province of the West Indies/Trinidad
Currens, Rev. Dr Gerald E., mo, Lutheran Church in America
Cuthbert, Rev. Robert W.M., mo, Moravian Church in Jamaica
Cuthbert, Rev. Raymond A., ymo, Christian Church, Disciples of Christ,
    Canada

Dalla, Rev., yfo, Evangelical Lutheran Church of Iceland
Danilo, Rt Rev., mo, Serbian Orthodox Church, Yugoslavia
Darmoutomo, Mr Prayudi, ml, Indonesian Christian Church
Das, Prof. Dr Vincent A., ml, Church of Pakistan
David, Archbishop, mo, Georgian Orthodox Church, USSR
David, Ms Annie, fl, Malankara Orthodox Syrian Church, India
David, Ms Susy, fl, Mar Thoma Syrian Church of Malabar, India
De Gruchy, Prof. Dr John, mo, United Congregational Church of
    Southern Africa
Dean, Ms Katherine, fl, Presbyterian Church (USA)
Dede, Mr Johannes, ml, Evangelical Church in Germany, FRG
Dehne, Ms Margot, fl, Federation of the Evangelical Churches in the GDR
Dejanov, Rev. Miroslav, mo, Serbian Orthodox Church/Canada
Denson Jr, Rev. Porter, mo, National Baptist Convention, Inc., USA
Denton, Mr J.G., ml, Anglican Church of Australia
Deschamps, Rev. Guy, mo, United Church of Canada
Desroches, Mr Rosny, ml, Methodist Church in the Caribbean and the
    Americas/Haiti
Diangienda-Kuntina, His Eminence, mo, Church of Jesus Christ on Earth
    by the Prophet Simon Kimbangu, Zaire
Diangienda-Muete Luhemba, Ms, fl, Church of Jesus Christ on Earth by
    the Prophet Simon Kimbangu, Zaire
Diba, Sister Marina, yfl, Russian Orthodox Church
Ditlhage, Mr J.M.B., ml, Evangelical Lutheran Church in Southern Africa
Doll, Rev. Ulrike, yfo, Federation of the Evangelical Churches in the
    GDR
Doom, Mr John, ml, Evangelical Church of French Polynesia

Dornemann, Dr William E., ml, Episcopal Church, USA
Dorotej, Metropolitan D., mo, Orthodox Church in the CSSR,
  Czechoslovakia
Douglas, Ms Barbara, yfl, United Church in Canada
Downes, Rev. Stanley E., mo, Methodist Church in India
Dragas, Very Rev. Geroge, mo, Ecumenical Patriarchate of
  Constantinople/UK
Duarte, Mr Carlos, yml, Evangelical Church of the River Plate, Argentina
Duchrow, Rev. Dr Ulrich, mo, Evangelical Church in Germany, FRG
Duku, Dr Oliver, ml, Province of the Episcopal Church of the Sudan
Duplessis, Rev. David, mo, International Evangelical Church, USA

Ebertova, Rev. Dr Anezka, fo, Czechoslovak Hussite Church
Ekstrom, Ms Christina, fl, Church of Sweden
Elisabeth, Sister, fl, Reformed Church of France
Elmquist, Ms Marie, yfl, Mission Covenant Church of Sweden
Elonda, Rev. Dr Efefe, mo, Church of Christ in Zaire (Community of
  Disciples)
Emilianos His Eminence, mo, Ecumenical Patriarchate of Constantinople/
  Switzerland
Eneme, Ms Grace, fl, Presbyterian Church in Cameroon
Engelen, Dr O.E., ml, Evangelical Church of Sangihe Talaud, Indonesia
Englezakis, Dr Benedictos, ml, Church of Cyprus
Epifanie, Bishop, mo, Romanian Orthodox Church
Espino, Rev. Fr Cornish, mo, Philippine Independent Church
Essamuah, Rt Rev. Samuel, mo, Methodist Church, Ghana
Etchells, Ms Ruth, fl, Church of England
Euphrasia, Mother, fl, Romanian Orthodox Church
Eyre, Rev. Charles, mo, Methodist Church in Ireland

Faa'alo, Rev. Puafitu, ymo, Tuvalu Church
Faatauoloa, Ms Sauiluma, fl, Congregational Christian Church, West Samoa
Fabiny, Rev. Tamas, ymo, Lutheran Church in Hungary
Fakhoury, Ms Ina May, fl, American Baptist Churches in the USA
Familusi, Mr Michael, ml, Methodist Church, Nigeria
Fang, Bishop C.N., mo, Methodist Church in Malaysia
Farah El-Khoury, Ms Mahat, fl, Greek Orthodox Patriarchate of Antioch
  and All the East/Syria
Farah, Archdeacon Rafic, mo, Episcopal Church in Jerusalem
Farantos, Prof. Megas, ml, Church of Greece
Fassinou, Ms Marguerite, fl, Protestant Methodist Church in the People's
  Republic of Benin
Faulk, Dr I. Carlton, ml, Christian Methodist Episcopal Church, USA
Fernando, Dr J.N.O., ml, Church of Ceylon
Ferrer de Diaz, Ms Perla, fl, Evangelical Methodist Church of Argentina
Fiehland, Ms Astrid, yfl, Evangelical Church of Germany, FRG
Filippini, Ms Mabel, fl, Evangelical Methodist Church of Argentina
Finlay, Rev. Chris, mo, Baptist Union of New Zealand

Fischer, Rev. Jacques, mo, Evangelical Lutheran Church of France
Fischer Ms Nicole, fl, Swiss Protestant Church Federation
Flax, Ms Patricia, yfl, Church of the Province of the West Indies/Antigua
Flor, Judge Florentino A., ml, Philippine Independent Church
Forrester, Rev. Prof. Duncan, mo, Church of Scotland
Francis, Ms S., yfl, United Reformed Church in the United Kingdom
Frei, Pastor Dr Hans, mo, Old Catholic Church of Switzerland
Freiday, Mr Dean, ml, Friends General Conference, USA
Frempong, Rev. Isaac, mo, Presbyterian Church of Ghana
Fritz, Rev. Gerhard, mo, Evangelical Church in Germany, FRG
Fuchs, Ms Erika, fl, Evangelical Church of the Augsburg and Helvetic
  Confession, Austria

Gagua, Mr Boris, yml, Georgian Orthodox Church, USSR
Galbraith, Ms Jane, yfl, Church of Ireland
Galinski, Rev. Theophan, ymo, Russian Orthodox Church
Galitis, Prof. George, ml, Greek Orthodox Patriarchate of Jerusalem
Gardner, Ms Ursula A.M., yfl, Church of the Province of Central Africa/
  Zimbabwe
Garima, Bishop Dr, mo, Ethiopian Orthodox Church
Garkusha, Ms Valentina, fl, Union of Evangelical Baptists of USSR
Garlov, Mr Martin, yml, Church of Sweden
Garve, Mr Christian, ml, Moravian Church, GDR
Gasche, Ms Susanne, yfl, Evangelical Church in Germany, FRG
Gathuka Ngumi, Mr George, ml, African Christian Church and Schools,
  Kenya
Gatwa, Mr T., yml, Presbyterian Church of Rwanda
Gcabashe, Ms Virginia, fl, Methodist Church of Southern Africa
Geiser, Rev. Daniel, mo, Mennonite Church, FRG
George, Sister Chechamma, fl, Church of South India
Getaneh Bogale, Ato, ml, Ethiopian Orthodox Church
Geus-Nederlof, Ms Elisabeth de, fl, Netherlands Reformed Church
Gibran, Bishop Gabriel, mo, Greek Orthodox Patriarchate of Antioch and
  All the East
Gidada, Dr Solomon, ml, Ethiopian Evangelical Church Mekane Yesus
Gilbert, Dr Helga, fl, Evangelical Church in Germany, FRG
Gilson, Ms Mary, fl, Methodist Church, UK
Ginting-Suka, Rev. Anggapen, mo, Karo Batak Protestant Church,
  Indonesia
Glitz, Mr Arno, ml, Evangelical Church of Lutheran Confession in Brazil
Glushik, Mr G., yml, Russian Orthodox Church
Golemon, Mr Larry, yml, Presbyterian Church (USA)
Gorski, Rev. William E., mo, Evangelical Lutheran Church in Chile
Gqubule, Rev. Dr Simon, mo, Methodist Church of Southern Africa
Graewe, Dr W.D., ml, Federation of the Evangelical Churches in the GDR
Grant, Ms Helen, yfl, Methodist Church of New Zealand
Green, Rev. Bernard, mo, Baptist Union of Great Britain and Ireland

Gregorios, Metropolitan Paulos Mar, mo, Orthodox Syrian Church of the East, India
Grigoriy, Archimandrite J. Stefano, mo, Bulgarian Orthodox Church
Grindrod, Most Rev. John, mo, Anglican Church of Australia
Grohs, Dr Gerhard, ml, Evangelical Church in Germany, FRG
Gudmestad, Ms Fern, fl, American Lutheran Church
Guerra Quezada, Ms Rosa, fl, Pentecostal Church of Chile
Gunasekera, Ms D., yfl, Methodist Church in Sri Lanka
Gundiaev, Archpriest N., mo, Russian Orthodox Church

Haarbeck, Rev. Dr Ako, mo, Evangelical Church of Germany, FRG
Habgood, Rt Rev. John, mo, Church of England
Habib, Rev. Dr Samuel, mo, Coptic Evangelical Church in Egypt
Haddad, Ms Frieda, fl, Greek Orthodox Patriarchate of Antioch and All the East/Lebanon
Haessig, Ms Elisabeth, fl, Evangelical Church of the Augsburg, Confession of Alsace and Lorraine, France
Hagesaether, Ms Gunnhild, fl, Church of Norway
Haggart, Most Rev. Alastair, mo, Scottish Episcopal Church
Halim, Ms Inge, yfl, Indonesian Christian Church
Hallewas, Rev. C.F.G. Eddy, mo, Evangelical Lutheran Church in the Netherlands
Hamalian, Prof. Arpi, fl, Armenian Apostolic Church (Cilicia)/Canada
Hannon, Rev. Canon Brian, mo, Church of Ireland
Hark, Rev. Edgar, mo, Estonian Evangelical Lutheran Church, USSR
Harmon, Ms Janice, fl, American Lutheran Church
Havea, Rev. Dr Sione 'Amanaki, mo, Free Wesleyan Church of Tonga
Havea, Ms Maata, fl, Free Wesleyan Church of Tonga
Havemeyer, Ms Eugenie A., fl, Episcopal Church, USA
Held, Rev. Dr Heinz J., mo, Evangelical Church in Germany, FRG
Hempel, Bishop Johannes, mo, Federation of the Evangelical Churches in the GDR
Hempfling, Rev. Helen, yfo, Christian Church (Disciples of Christ) USA
Henderson, Ms Jennifer, yfl, Presbyterian Church (USA)
Henley, Ms Marion, fl, National Council of Community Churches, USA
Henry, Rev. Harry Y., mo, Protestant Methodist Church in the People's Republic of Benin
Hepburn, Ms Anne, fl, Church of Scotland
Herbst, Ms Ursula, fl, Federation of the Evangelical Churches in the GDR
Hernandez B., Rt Rev. Ulises, mo, Methodist Church of Mexico
Hlavac, Rev. Dr Josef, mo, Evangelical Church of Czech Brethren
Hoggard, Bishop J. Clinton, mo, African Methodist Episcopal Zion Church, USA
Hoiore, Ms Celine, yfl, Evangelical Church of French Polynesia
Holloway, Mr John M., yml, Episcopal Church, USA
Holmes, Ms Kathleen, fl, National Council of Community Churches, USA
Homely, Mr Gerson, yml, Evangelical Lutheran Church in Tanzania

Hook, Ms Anya, yfl, Church of the Province of New Zealand
Hoover, Ms Theressa, fl, United Methodist Church, USA
Hovsepian, Archbishop Vatche, mo, Armenian Apostolic Orthodox
    Church (Etchmiadzin)/USA
Hoyt, Jr., Dr Thomas, mo, Christian Methodist Episcopal Church, USA
Hromanik, Rev. Michal, mo, Reformed Christian Church in Slovakia,
    Czechoslovakia
Hubancev, Mr Anthony, ml, Bulgarian Orthodox Church
Hustad, Rev. Jack, mo, American Lutheran Church
Huston, Rev. Dr Robert, mo, United Methodist Church, USA
Hutchison, Ms Margaret, fl, Church of England
Huttunen, Mr Heiki, yml, Orthodox Church of Finland

Iacovos, Archbishop, mo, Ecumenical Patriarchate of Constantinople/USA
Ibrahim, Archbishop Gregorios Y., mo, Syrian Orthodox Patriarchate of
    Antioch and All the East
Ieriko, Rt Rev. Siaosi, mo, Congregational Christian Church in Samoa
Ikedji, Pastor Kesenge, mo, Church of Christ in Zaire (Community of
    Disciples)
Imasogie, Rev. Dr Osadolor, mo, Nigerian Baptist Convention
In 't Veld, Rev. Alida Anje, fo, Remonstrant Brotherhood, Netherlands
Ingelstam, Ms Margareta, fl, Mission Covenant Church of Sweden
Iofi, Rev. Faafouina, mo, Congregational Christian Church in Samoa
Ionita, Father Viorel, mo, Romanian Orthodox Church
Iordanova, Ms Raina Lyubenova, fl, Bulgarian Orthodox Church
Irshad, Mr Kenneth, yml, United Presbyterian Church of Pakistan
Isteero, Rev. Albert, mo, Coptic Evangelical Church-Snyod of the Nile,
    Egypt
Iwanow, Ms Irena, yfl, Orthodox Church in Poland

Jacobson, Rev. S.T., mo, Evangelical Lutheran Church of Canada
Jaeger, Superintendent Joachim, mo, Federation of the Evangelical
    Churches in the GDR
James, Ms S.W., fl, Church of Pakistan
Jarjour, Ms Rose, yfl, National Evangelical Synod of Syria and Lebanon
Jefferson, Rev. Canon Ruth, fo, Anglican Church of Canada
Jelks, Mr Randal, yml, Presbyterian Church (USA)
Jeremia, Rt Rev., mo, Polish Orthodox Autocephalic Church
Jernsletten, Mr Nils, ml, Church of Norway
Jesudasen, Most Rev. I., mo, Church of South India
Jimenez, Rev. Kathleen, fo, Presbyterian Church (USA)
Jivi, Prof. Aurel, ml, Romanian Orthodox Church
John of Helsinki, Metropolitan, mo, Orthodox Church of Finland
Johnson, Rev. Dr Ronald, mo, Lutheran Church in America
Johnson, Rev. Louis, mo, Progressive National Baptist Convention USA
Johnston,, Ms Heather, fl, Presbyterian Church in Canada
Jones, Rev. William, mo, Progressive National Baptist Convention, USA
Jones, Rev. Glyn T., mo, Presbyterian Church of Wales

Jones, Rev. Derwyn M., mo, Union of Welsh Independents
Jones, Rev. MacCharles, mo, National Baptist Convention, USA
Jonge, Pastor Johann de, mo, United Protestant Church of Belgium
Jornod, Rev. Jean Pierre, mo, Swiss Protestant Church Federation
Julkiree, Ms Boonmee, fl, Church of Christ in Thailand

Kabaza, Mr Z., ml, Church of Uganda
Kaddu, Ms Joyce, fl, Church of Uganda
Kaessmann, Ms Margot, yfl, Evangelical Church in Germany, FRG
Kaldy, Bishop Dr Zoltan, mo, Lutheran Church in Hungary
Kalemkerian, Ms Louise, fl, Armenian Apostolic Church (Etchmiadzin)/
    USA
Kalinik of Vratsa, Metropolitan, mo, Bulgarian Orthodox Church
Kangsen, Rt Rev. J., mo, Presbyterian Church in Cameroon
Karefa Smart, Rev. Dr Rena, fo, African Methodist Episcopal Zion
    Church, USA
Karjian, Rev. Hovhannes, mo, Union of Armenian Evangelical Churches
    in the Near East, Lebanon
Karpenko, Mr A., yml, Russian Orthodox Church
Katsuno, Ms Linda, fl, United Church of Canada
Kauma, Rt Rev. Misaeri, mo, Church of Uganda
Kawabata, Mr Junshiro, ml, United Church of Christ in Japan
Kayuwa, Mr Mike, ml, Church of Christ in Zaire (Community of Light)
Kayuwa, Patriarch Tshibumbu W.K., mo, Church of Christ in Zaire
    (Community of Light)
Kerepia, Ms Anne, fl, United Church of Papua New Guinea and the
    Solomon Islands
Kerry, Mr Jonathan, yml, Methodist Church, UK
Keshishian, Bishop Aram, mo, Armenian Apostolic Church (Cilicia),
    Lebanon
Khamis, Bishop Mar Aprim, mo, Apostolic Catholic Assyrian Church of
    the East/USA
Khoza, Ms Mavis, fl, Presbyterian Church of Africa, South Africa
Khumalo, Rev. Samson, mo, Presbyterian Church of Africa, South Africa
Kim, Rev. Dr Hyung-Tae, mo, Presbyterian Church of Korea
Kim, Dr Yong-Bock, ml, Presbyterian Church of Korea
Kim, Rev. Choon Young, mo, Korean Methodist Church
Kim, Rev. Kwan Suk, mo, Presbyterian Church in the Republic of Korea
Kingston, Ms Gillian, fl, Methodist Church in Ireland
Kiourekian, Father Tiran, mo, Armenian Apostolic Church, USSR
Kirill, Archbishop, mo, Russian Orthodox Church
Kiselev, Priest Sergei, mo, Russian Orthodox Church/Switzerland
Kishkovsky, Very Rev. Leonid, mo, Orthodox Church in America
Kiss, Rev. Dr Igor, mo, Slovak Evangelical Church of the Augsburg
    Confession in the CSSR, Czechoslovakia
Kitagawa, Rev. John E., mo, Episcopal Church, USA
Kivambe, Dr David, ml, Evangelical Lutheran Church in Tanzania

Klein, Prof. Dr Christoph, mo, Evangelical Church of the Augsburg Confession in the Socialist Republic of Romania
Klempa, Rev. Dr William, mo, Presbyterian Church in Canada
Knall, Bishop Dieter, mo, Evangelical Church of the Augsburg and Helvetic Confession, Austria
Knoblauch, Rev. Bruno, mo, Evangelical Church of the River Plate
Koch, Dr Karel, ml, Netherlands Reformed Church
Kocsis, Prof. Dr Elemer, mo, Reformed Church in Hungary
Koev, Prof. Totiu, ml, Bulgarian Orthodox Church
Koguapa Ngiringli, Mr, yml, Church of the Province of Burundi, Rwanda and Zaire
Kohli, Dr Karl, ml, Swiss Protestant Church Federation
Kojima, Ms A., yfl, Episcopal Church in the USA
Kok, Dr Justice Govaert C., ml, Old Catholic Church of the Netherlands
Kok-Frimer Larsen, Ms Grete, fl, Old Catholic Church of Austria/ Netherlands
Kolowa, Rt Rev. S., mo, Evangelical Lutheran Church in Tanzania
Kominami, Rev. J.S., mo, Anglican Episcopal Church in Japan
Komla Dzobo, Rt Rev. Noah, mo, Evangelical Presbyterian Church, Ghana
Konidaris, Prof. Gerasimos, ml, Church of Greece
Konie, Ms G., fl, United Church of Zambia
Koob, Ms Kathryn, fl, American Lutheran Church
Korban, Bishop Eli, mo, Greek Orthodox Patriarchate of Antioch and All the East
Korhammer, Dr Rita, fl, Evangelical Church in Germany, FRG
Kossen, Rev. Prof. H.B., mo, General Mennonite Society, Netherlands
Kotto, Pastor Jean, mo, Evangelical Church of Cameroon
Koulouris, Mr Antonios, ml, Greek Evangelical Church
Kovach, Rt Rev. Attila, mo, Reformed Church in Hungary
Kovalchuk, Rt Rev. Archpriest Feodor, mo, Russian Orthodox Church
Kovalevich, Sister Maria, fl, Russian Orthodox Church
Kowalski, Bishop Stanislaw, mo, Old Mariavite Church in Poland
Kravchenko, Archpriest A., mo, Russian Orthodox Church
Kroneberg, Rev. Johannes, mo, Moravian Church in the Western Cape Province, South Africa
Kruse, Mr Max, ml, Church of Denmark
Kruse, Bishop Martin, mo, Evangelical Church in Germany, FRG
Kruyswijk, Rev. Dr A., mo, Reformed Churches in the Netherlands
Kucharczyk, Ms Connie, fl, Orthodox Church in America
Kuerti, Rt Rev. Laszlo, mo, Reformed Church in Hungary
Kumar, Mr Uttam, ml, United Evangelical Lutheran Church in India
Kurian, Rev. Fr George, mo, Orthodox Syrian Church, India
Kutjame, Rev. Salmon, mo, Evangelical Christian Church in Halmahera, Indonesia
Kuusk, Rev. Carl, ymo, Church of England

Laczkovszki, Rev. Janos, mo, Baptist Union of Hungary
Ladokun, Ms Yemi, fl, Nigerian Baptist Convention

Lah, Ms Oknah Kim, fl, Korean Methodist Church
Laham, Mr Albert, ml, Greek Orthodox Patriarchate of Antioch and All
   the East/Switzerland
Lande, Mr Frederick, ml, Toraja Church, Indonesia
Landwehr, Dr Arthur, mo, United Methodist Church, USA
Larsson, Ms Birgitta, fl, Church of Sweden
Lawson, Rev. James M., mo, United Methodist Church, USA
Leb, Dr Ioan-Vasile, ml, Romanian Orthodox Church
Lee, Rev. Ching Chee, fo, Church of Christ in China, Hong Kong
   Council
Lee, Ms Tae Young, fl, Korean Methodist Church
Lee, Ms Irene, yfl, United Church of Canada
Lee, Ms Yon-Ok, fl, Presbyterian Church of Korea
Lee, Mr Dae Soo, yml, Presbyterian Church in the Republic of Korea
Lehtio, Dr Pirkko, fl, Church of Finland
Leinbach, Mr Clarence, ml, Moravian Church in America, Southern
   Province
Leland, Rev. Robert, mo, Christian Church (Disciples of Christ), Canada
Lemopulo, Mr George, yml, Ecumenical Patriarchate of Constantinople/
   Switzerland
Lengyel, Prof. Dr Lorand, mo, Evangelical Synodal Presbyterial Church
   of the Augsburg Confession in the Socialist Republic of Romania
Lennemyr-Frykman, Ms Yvonne, yfl, Church of Sweden
Lethunya, Ms E.S., fl, Lesotho Evangelical Church
Lewis, Mr Michael, ml, United Church of Canada
Libbey, Rev. Scott S., mo, United Church of Christ, USA
Lidell, Rev. Elisabeth, fo, Church of Denmark
Lindberg, Rev. Dr Lars, mo, Mission Covenant Church of Sweden
Linn, Rev. Gerhard, mo, Federation of the Evangelical Churches in the
   GDR
Linz, Ms Johanna, fl, Evangelical Church in Germany, FRG
Lislerud, Rt Rev. Gunnar, mo, Church of Norway
Lodberg, Mr Peter, yml, Church of Denmark
Lohse, Bishop E., mo, Evangelical Church in Germany, FRG
Lomindet, Ms Grace, yfl, Province of the Episcopal Church of the Sudan
Lønning, Rt Rev. Per, mo, Church of Norway
Loswyk, Rev. Edgar, mo, Moravian Church of Surinam
Lourens, Rev. William J., mo, Church of the Province of South Africa
Love, Dr Janice, fl, United Methodist Church, USA
Ludwig, Mr Marvin, ml, United Church of Christ, USA
Lumbantobing, Rt Rev. Dr A., mo, Christian Protestant Church in
   Indonesia
Lumenta, Ms E., fl, Protestant Church in Indonesia
Lumenta, Rev. D.J., mo, Protestant Church in Indonesia
Lumentut, Rev. Augustina, fo, Christian Church in Central Sulawesi,
   Indonesia
Lusis, Rt Rev. Arnold, mo, Evangelical Lutheran Church of Latvia, USSR
Luvanda, Ms Jeneth, fl, Evangelical Lutheran Church in Tanzania

Luzayamo-Nsualu, Ms, yfl, Church of Jesus Christ on Earth by the Prophet Simon Kimbangu, Zaire

Macauley, Mr John, yml, Methodist Church of Sierra Leone
Magerstaedt, Mr Hans-Jürgen, ml, Federation of the Evangelical Churches in the GDR
Majewski, Most Rev. T.R., mo, Polish Catholic Church in Poland
Makary of Uman, Most Rev., mo, Russian Orthodox Church
Makhno, Rev. Lev, mo, Russian Orthodox Church/USA
Malcolm, Rev. Capt. A., mo, Anglican Church of Australia
Malik, Rt Rev. Alexander J., mo, Church of Pakistan
Manganti, Mr Rop, ml, Christian Church in Central Sulawesi, Indonesia
Manoogian, Archbishop Torgom, mo, Armenian Apostolic Church (Etchmiadzin)/USA
Mansanga-Masakungunua, Ms, fl, Church of Jesus Christ on Earth by the Prophet Simon Kimbangu, Zaire
Manson, Mr Thorsten, ml, Church of Sweden
Manurung, Rev. L., mo, Indonesian Christian Church
Maria, Dr Francis, ml, Antiochian Orthodox Christian Archdiocese of North America
Markos, Rt Rev. Antonius, mo, Coptic Orthodox Church/Kenya
Marsh, Ms Agnes, fl, Presbyterian Church (USA)
Martinchuk, Sister Nina, fl, Russian Orthodox Church
Massoud, Mr Emad, yml, Coptic Orthodox Church, Egypt
Matthews, Bishop Marjorie, fo, United Methodist Church, USA
Matulis, Archbishop Dr Janis, mo, Evangelical Lutheran Church of Latvia, USSR
Maximos, Bishop, mo, Ecumenical Patriarchate of Constantinople/USA
Mayland, Ms Jean, fl, Church of England
Mban, Rev. Joseph, mo, Evangelical Church of the Congo
Mbemba, Ms Veronique, fl, Evangelical Church of the Congo
Mbiya Mulumba, Rev., mo, Presbyterian Church in Zaire
McBeath, Dr William H., ml, American Baptist Churches in the USA
McCloud, Rev. J. Oscar, mo, Presbyterian Church (USA)
McClurg, Rev. Patricia, fo, Presbyterian Church (USA)
McCracken, Ms Jennifer, yfl, Anglican Church in Australia
McGregor-Lowndes, Mr Myles, yml, Uniting Church in Australia
McIndoe, Rev. John H., mo, Church of Scotland
McKinney, Dr Samuel B., ml, National Baptist Convention, Inc., USA
Mehany, Dr Makram, ml, Coptic Orthodox Church, Egypt
Mekarios, Archbishop, mo, Ethiopian Orthodox Church
Melia, Very Rev. Elie, mo, Ecumenical Patriarchate of Constantinople/France
Mesters, Rev. Eriks, mo, Evangelical Lutheran Church of Latvia, USSR
Metzger, Ms Angela Serpe, fl, Lutheran Church in America
Michalko, Generalbischof Prof. Bishop Jan, mo, Slovak Evangelical Church of the Augsburg Confession the CSSR, Czechoslovakia
Michio, Mr Sano, yml, United Church of Christ in Japan
Mihing Dani, Ms Kartina, fl, Kalimantan Evangelical Church, Indonesia

Miko, Rev. Eugen J., mo, Reformed Christian Church in Slovakia, Czechoslovakia
Milker, Ms Friderike, fl, Federation of the Evangelical Churches in the GDR
Misang, Mr Jobson, yml, United Church in Papua New Guinea and the Solomon Islands
Mitchell, Mr Timothy P., ml, National Baptist Convention, Inc., USA
Mitsides, Dr Andreas, ml, Orthodox Church of Cyprus
Moabi, Ms Pinky, yfl, Church of the Province of South Africa
Moffett, Ms Marilyn, fl, Christian Church (Disciples of Christ), USA
Momo Kingue, Ms Marie, fl, Evangelical Church of Cameroon
Mooi, Rev. Dr R.J., mo, Netherlands Reformed Church
Morgan, Rev. George P., mo, Presbyterian Church (USA)
Morgans, Ms Norah, fl, United Reformed Church, UK
Mortimore, Rev. Wilfred J., mo, Moravian Church, UK
Morton, Ms Gillian, fl, Church of Scotland
Mosford, Ms S., yfl, Church in Wales
Mota, Rev. Jorge Cesar, mo, Latin American Reformed Church, Brazil
Motel, Rev. Hans-Beat, mo, European Continental Province of the Moravian Church-Western District, FRG
Moukouyou-Kimbouala, Prof. Michel, ml, Evangelical Church of the Congo
Muchena, Ms Olivia, fl, United Methodist Church/Zimbabwe
Mueller, Ms Katharina, yfl, Evangelical Church in Germany, FRG
Mueller, Ms Christine, yfl, Federation of the Evangelical Churches in the GDR
Muindi, Rev. Bernard, mo, Presbyterian Church of East Africa
Mukwenda, Rev. Mubita, mo, United Church of Zambia
Mulder, Dr Edwin G., mo, Reformed Church in America
Munthe, Rev. Armencius, mo, Simalungun Protestant Christian Church, Indonesia
Musoko, Ms C.L., fl, Presbyterian Church in Cameroon
Muston, Bishop Gerald, mo, Anglican Church of Australia
Mwakasege, Rev. Shadrack, mo, Moravian Church of Tanzania
Mweresa Kivuli, Rev. John, ymo, African Israel Church Nineveh, Kenya
Mya Han, Ven. Andrew, mo, Church of the Province of Burma

Nababan, Rev. Dr S.A.E., mo, Batak Protestant Christian Church, Indonesia
Nabulivou, Rev. Inoke, mo, Methodist Church of Fiji
Nag, Bishop Jacob, mo, United Evangelical Lutheran Church in India
Nagy, Bishop Dr G., mo, Lutheran Church in Hungary
Nahas, Ms Maud, fl, Greek Orthodox Patriarchate of Antioch and All the East/Lebanon
Najm, Father Michel, mo, Greek Orthodox Patriarchate of Antioch and All the East/Lebanon
Nakamura, Ms Julie, yfl, United Church of Christ, USA
Namata, Mr Joseph, ml, Church of the Province of Tanzania

Namato, Rev. Lawrence, ymo, Apostolic Catholic Assyrian Church of the East, USA

Nang Essono, Rev. Samuel, mo, Evangelical Church of Gabon

Narzynski, Rt Rev. Janusz, mo, Evangelical Church of the Augsburg Confession in Poland

Nashed, Rev. Dr. William N., mo, Coptic Orthodox Church, Egypt

Natana, Very Rev. E., mo, Province of the Episcopal Church of the Sudan

Nathabane, Rev. S.E., mo, Lesotho Evangelical Church

Nathaniel, Rt Rev., mo, Orthodox Church in America

Natho, Rt Rev. Eberhard, mo, Federation of the Evangelical Churches in the GDR

Nazaria, Sister, fl, Romanian Orthodox Church

Nazarkin, Rev. Vladimir, mo, Russian Orthodox Church

Ndandali, His Grace Justin, mo, Church of the Province of Burundi, Rwanda and Zaire

Neff, Rev. Dr Robert, mo, Church of the Brethren, USA

Negraru, Mother Cecilia, fl, Romanian Orthodox Church

Neophyte, Archimandrite, mo, Bulgarian Orthodox Church

Newton, Rev. Dr John, mo, Methodist Church, Great Britain

Ngcobo, Rev. Samuel, mo, Reformed Presbyterian Church in Southern Africa

Ngcokovane, Rev. Cecil Mzingisi, mo, Presbyterian Church of Africa, South Africa

Ngobe, Rev. Jablani, S., mo, Evangelical Presbyterian Church in South Africa

Nibrete Abebe, Ms, yfl, Ethiopian Orthodox Church

Nichols, Bishop D. Ward, mo, African Methodist Episcopal Church, USA

Niemczyk, Prof. Jan, mo, Evangelical Church of the Augsburg Confession in Poland

Nieminski, Rt Rev. Joseph I., mo, Polish National Catholic Church

Nikitin, Rev. Augustin, mo, Russian Orthodox Church

Nikolopoulos-Titaki, Ms Dora, fl, Ecumenical Patriarchate of Constantinople/Switzerland

Nisar, Rev. Iqbal, mo, United Presbyterian Church of Pakistan

Noakes, Rt Rev. George, mo, Church in Wales

Noe, Judge James, ml, Christian Church (Disciples of Christ), USA

Nogradi, Dean Adalbert, ml, Reformed Church of Romania

Nordhaug, Ms Liv, fl, Church of Norway

Norgaard, Rev. Per, mo, Baptist Union of Denmark

Novicova, Ms T.A., fl, Russian Orthodox Church

Nthamburi, Rev. Dr Zablon, mo, Methodist Church in Kenya

Ntontolo, Rev. L.K., mo, Church of Christ in Zaire, Evangelical Community

Nugent, Dr Randolph, mo, United Methodist Church, USA

Nxasana, Ms Vuyiswa, fl, Church of the Province of South Africa

Nyomi, Rev. Setri, ymo, Evangelical Presbyterian Church, Ghana

O'Dell, Rev. James D., mo, Presbyterian Church (USA)

O'Grady, Rev. Ronald M., mo, Associated Churches of Christ in New Zealand
Obiero, Rev. Daniel O., mo, African Israel Church Nineveh, Kenya
Oduyoye, Ms Mercy, fl, Methodist Church, Nigeria
Oehler, Ms Carolyn, fl, United Methodist Church, USA
Okeke, Rev. Dr David, mo, Church of the Province of Nigeria
Okine, Ms Naomi, fl, Methodist Church, Ghana
Okullu, Bishop Henry, mo, Church of the Province of Kenya
Oleksa, Rev. Michael, mo, Orthodox Church in America
Oliveira, Rev. Orlando S. de, mo, Episcopal Church of Brazil
Olufosoye, Most Rev. Timothy, mo, Church of the Province of Nigeria
Olunloyo, Ms Elizabeth O., fl, Church of the Province of Nigeria
Orr, Ms Lesley, yfl, Church of Scotland
Osipov, Prof. A.I., ml, Russian Orthodox Church
Ouart, Mr Juergen, yml, Federation of the Evangelical Churches in the GDR
Ovsiannikov, Mr Viacheslav, ml, Russian Orthodox Church

Pajula, Konsistorialrat Kuno, mo, Estonian Evangelical Lutheran Church, USSR
Pall, Rev. Laszlo, mo, Reformed Church in Hungary
Palma, Ms Marta, fl, Pentecostal Mission Church, Chile
Pamatmat, Rt Rev. Roberto, mo, Philippine Independent Church
Panggabean-Lumbantobing, Ms Sagum, fl, Batak Christian Protestant Church, Indonesia
Panhuis, Ms Antoinette, fl, United Protestant Church of Belgium
Panke, Rev. Rita, fo, Evangelical Church of Lutheran Confession in Brazil
Pankraty, Metropolitan, mo, Bulgarian Orthodox Church
Pannell, Ms Tammy, yfl, Anglican Church of Canada
Papadopoulos, Prof. Stylianos, ml, Greek Orthodox Patriarchate of Alexandria and All Africa
Papp, Rt Rev. D.L., mo, Reformed Church of Romania
Park, Rev. Hyung Kyu, mo, Presbyterian Church in the Republic of Korea
Parthenios, H.E. Metropolitan, mo, Greek Orthodox Patriarchate of Alexandria and All Africa
Patanduk, Rev. Paulus, mo, Toraja Church, Indonesia
Patelos, Dr Constantin, ml, Greek Orthodox Patriarchate of Alexandria and All Africa
Pattiasina-Toreh, Rev. Ms C.E., fo, Protestant Church in the Moluccas, Indonesia
Payne, Rt Rev. Roland, mo, Lutheran Church of Liberia
Peck, Dr Jane Cary, fl, United Methodist Church, USA
Peers, Most Rev. Michael G., mo, Anglican Church of Canada
Pender, Mr Charles, yml, Christian Methodist Episcopal Church, USA
Pereira, Ms Nancy C., yfl, Methodist Church in Brazil
Perera, Rev. Somasiri K., mo, Methodist Church of Sri Lanka
Persson, Rt Rev. William, mo, Church of England

Persson, Mr Per Erik, ml, Church of Sweden
Pesonen, Dr Pertti, ml, Church of Finland
Petrossian, Father Yeznik, ymo, Armenian Apostolic Church
(Etchmiadzin), USSR
Petrova, Ms G. Stefanka, fl, Bulgarian Orthodox Church
Philaret of Kiev, Metropolitan, mo, Russian Orthodox Church
Philaret of Minsk, Metropolitan, mo, Russian Orthodox Church
Pilloud, Ms Claire, yfl, Swiss Protestant Church Federation
Piperov, Mr Svetoslav Georgiev, ml, Bulgarian Orthodox Church
Piske, Rev. Meinard, mo, Evangelical Lutheran Church in Brazil
Pitirim, Most Rev. mo, Russian Orthodox Church
Pitso, Ms Celina, fl, Presbyterian Church of Southern Africa
Pitts, Rev. Charles W., mo, African Methodist Episcopal Church, USA
Plou, Ms Dafne de, fl, Evangelical Methodist Church of Argentina
Pogo, Rt Rev. Ellison, mo, Church of the Province of Melanesia
Poitier, Ms Annette, fl, Methodist Church in the Caribbean and the
Americas/Bahamas
Ponomariova, Ms Olga, yfl, Russian Orthodox Church
Popescu, Prof. Emilian, ml, Romanian Orthodox Church
Popescu, Rev. Prof. Dumitru, mo, Romanian Orthodox Church
Post, Rev. Dr Avery, mo, United Church of Christ, USA
Powell, Rev. Grady W., mo, American Baptist Churches in the USA
Pravdoliubova, Ms V., yfl, Russian Orthodox Church
Premasagar, Rt Rev. Victor P., mo, Church of South India
Preus, Bishop David M., mo, American Lutheran Church
Prins, Mr Simon, yml, Methodist Church of Southern Africa
Pu, Ms Katherine, fl, Burma Baptist Convention
Purba, Ms Dongmainta, fl, Simalungun Protestant Christian Church,
Indonesia

Quam, Ms Lois, yfl, American Lutheran Church
Quiambao, Ms Ligaya N., fl, United Church of Christ in the Philippines

Radev, Mr Ivan Penev, yml, Bulgarian Orthodox Church
Radjagukguk, Mr M.H., ml, Protestant Batak Christian Church, Indonesia
Radjawane, Rev. Dr Nico, mo, Protestant Church in the Moluccas,
Indonesia
Ramambasoa, Pastor J., mo, Church of Jesus Christ in Madagascar
Ranaivojaona, Pastor R., mo, Malagasy Lutheran Church
Randell, Mr Clarence, ml, Anglican Church of Canada
Rangelov, Mr Rangel, ml, Bulgarian Orthodox Church
Ranne, Rev. Alexander, mo, Russian Orthodox Church
Ravalomanana, Ms Voasoa F., fl, Church of Jesus Christ in Madagascar
Razivelo, Ms Mariette, fl, Malagasy Lutheran Church
Reid, Mr Idris, ml, Church in the Province of the West Indies/Bahamas
Reinich, Rev. R.R., mo, Evangelical Church of the River Plate, Argentina
Richardson, Rev. Dr W. Franklyn, mo, National Baptist Convention, Inc.,
USA

Richardson, Rev. John, mo, Methodist Church of Great Britain
Ridder, Ms Lenora, fl, Reformed Church in America
Riti, Rev. Philemon, mo, United Church of Paupa New Guinea and the Solomon Islands
Rocha Souza, Mr Enilson, ml, Evangelical Pentecostal Church "Brazil for Christ"
Roeroe, Rev. Dr W.A., mo, Christian Evangelical Church in Minahasa, Indonesia
Rogestam, Ms Christina, fl, Church of Sweden
Rohrandt, Rev. Rut, fo, Evangelical Church in Germany, FRG
Romanides, Rev. Prof. John S., mo, Church of Greece
Ross, Dr Mary O., fl, National Baptist Convention, Inc., USA
Rowinski, Most Rev. Francis C., mo, Polish National Catholic Church
Rumfabe, Mr Steven, ml, Evangelical Christian Church in West Irian, Indonesia
Runcie, Most Rev. Robert, mo, Church of England
Ruokanen, Ms Katariina, yfl, Lutheran Church of Finland
Rusch, Dr William G., mo, Lutheran Church in America
Rushbrook, Ms Margaret, fl, Presbyterian Church of New Zealand
Rusibamayila, Most Rev. John, mo, Church of the Province of Tanzania
Russell, Ms Valerie, fl, United Church of Christ, USA
Russell, Most Rev. P.W.R., mo, Church of the Province of South Africa

Sabiashvili, Mr Vladimir, yml, Georgian Orthodox Church, USSR
Sabug, Mr Fructuoso T., ml, Philippine Independent Church
Sahyouni, Rev. Dr Salim, mo, National Evangelical Synod of Syria and Lebanon
Salajka, Prof. Dr Rev. Milan, mo, Czech Hussite Church
Salamate, Rev., mo, Evangelical Church of Sanghir Talaud, Indonesia
Salmon, Rev. Dr John, mo, Methodist Church of New Zealand
Salo, Rev. Simo, mo, Church of Finland
Salonga, Dr Jovito, ml, United Church of Christ in the Philippines
Sampath, Ms Dorinda, fl, Presbyterian Church in Trinidad and Grenada
Samuel, Archbishop Athanasius, mo, Syrian Orthodox Church of Antioch/ USA
Samuel, Rt Rev. John, mo, Church of Pakistan
Samuel, Bishop Karriappa, mo, Methodist Church in India
Sandner, Rev. Peter, mo, Evangelical Church in Germany, FRG
San Lone, Rev. Victor, mo, Burma Baptist Convention
Sano, Dr Roy I., mo, United Methodist Church, USA
Santram, Rev. Pritam, mo, Church of North India
Saraneva, Rev. Dr Tapio, mo, Church of Finland
Sawa, Bishop, mo, Autocephalic Orthodox Church in Poland
Sawen, Rev. Pinehas, mo, Evangelical Christian Church in West Irian, Indonesia
Schaefer, Rev. Hans, mo, Federation of the Evangelical Churches in the GDR
Schmitz-Hertzberg, Ms Kathleen, fl, Canadian Yearly Meeting of the Society of Friends

Schneider, Ms Francine, fl, Swiss Protestant Church Federation
Schuetz, Ms Inge, fl, Federation of the Evangelical Churches in the GDR
Scrimgeour, Rev. A. Douglas, mo, United Free Church of Scotland
Seah, Dr I.S., mo, Presbyterian Church in Taiwan
Seddoh, Ms Akuyo, fl, Evangelical Church of Togo
Sekaran, Mr Premkumar, yml, United Evangelical Lutheran Churches in India
Senturias, Dr Erlinda, fl, United Church of Christ in the Philippines
Sepulveda Barra, Rev. Narciso, mo, Pentecostal Mission Church, Chile
Seraphim, His Grace Bishop, mo, Orthodox Church in Japan
Sergius, Bishop, mo, Russian Orthodox Church
Serina, Bishop Mercurio M., mo, United Church of Christ in the Philippines
Shalamberidze, Archpriest Guram, mo, Georgian Orthodox Church, USSR
Shehadeh, Mr Raja, ml, Episcopal Church in Jerusalem and the Middle East
Shenouda, Ms Iris, fl, Coptic Orthodox Church, Egypt
Shing, Rev. Philip, mo, Presbyterian Church of Vanuatu
Sigurgeirsson, Rt Rev. Petur, mo, Lutheran Evangelical State Church of Iceland
Sih Pinardi, Rev., mo, East Java Christian Church, Indonesia
Sihombing, Rev. P.M., mo, Batak Protestant Christian Church, Indonesia
Silk, Ven. R.D., mo, Church of England
Silva, Ms Ruth Lopes, fl, Evangelical Pentecostal Church "Brazil for Christ"
Silva, Mr Paulo Lutero, yml, Evangelical Pentecostal Church "Brazil for Christ"
Simanungkalit, Rev. Odjak H., mo, Christian Protestant Church in Indonesia
Simauw, Rev. B., mo, Protestant Church in Western Indonesia
Simich, Prof., ml, Serbian Orthodox Church, Yugoslavia
Simon, Bishop, mo, Autochephalic Orthodox Church in Poland
Simon, Mr Josiah, yml, Church of North India
Simone, Ms Louise, fl, Armenian Apostolic Church (Etchmiadzin)/USA
Sitahal, Rt Rev. Harold, mo, Presbyterian Church in Trinidad and Grenada
Siyachitema, Rt Rev. J.V., mo, Church of the Province of Central Africa/Zimbabwe
Sloan, Mr Miguel Gary, ml, National Baptist Convention, Inc., USA
Small, Ms Sheila, yfl, American Lutheran Church
Smith, Rev. Robert F., mo, United Church of Canada
Smolik, Rev. Dr Josef, mo, Evangelical Church of Czech Brethren
Soare, Rev. Dumitru, mo, Romanian Orthodox Church
Soejana, Rev. Koernia Atje, mo, Pasundan Christian Church, Indonesia
Sonnenday, Dr Margaret, fl, United Methodist Church, USA
Soro, Rev. Ashur A., ymo, Apostolic Catholic Assyrian Church of the East/Canada
Sorokin, Rev. Prof. Vladimir, mo, Russian Orthodox Church

Sotirios, Rt Rev. Bishop, mo, Ecumenical Patriarchate of Constantinople/ Canada

Souza, Rt Rev. Neville de, mo, Church in the Province of the West Indies/ Jamaica

Sowunmi, Dr Adebisi, fl, Church of the Province of Nigeria

Stalsett, Rev. Gunnar, mo, Church of Norway

Stoeffler, Ms Erika, fl, Evangelical Church in Germany, FRG

Stoikov, Archpriest V., mo, Russian Orthodox Church

Stonawski, Rev. Vilem, mo, Silesian Evangelical Church of the Augsburg Confession, Czechoslovakia

Strauss, Rev. Dr Gerhard, mo, Evangelical Church in Germany, FRG

Stumbo, Mr John E., ml, United Methodist Church, USA

Stylianopoulos, Rev Dr Theodore, mo, Ecumenical Patriarchate of Constantinople/USA

Suleeman, Rev. C., mo, Indonesian Christian Church

Sumo, Mr Kpadeson, yml, Lutheran Church in Liberia

Supardan, Ms E. Wilandari, fl, Javanese Christian Churches, Indonesia

Supit, Dr B.A., ml, Christian Evangelical Church in Minahasa, Indonesia

Suvarsky, Archpriest Dr Jaroslav, mo, Orthodox Church of Czechoslovakia

Tabshouri, Mr Bassam, yml, Greek Orthodox Patriarchate of Antioch and All the East/Lebanon

Tadesse, Deacon Mandefiro, mo, Ethiopian Orthodox Church

Tafese Desselegn, Rev. Melake Tsehay, mo, Ethiopian Orthodox Church

Tai, Rev. Chung-Teh, mo, Presbyterian Church in Taiwan

Talbot, Bishop Frederick H., mo, African Methodist Episcopal Church, USA

Talbot, Dr Sylvia Ross, fl, African Methodist Episcopal Church, USA

Talbot, Ms Patti, yfl, Presbyterian Church in Canada

Tanasale, Ms Lenny, fl, Christian Protestant Church in the Moluccas, Indonesia

Tanielian, Rev. Anoushaven, mo, Armenian Apostolic Church, USSR

Tapper, Ms Selena, fl, Church of the Province of the West Indies/Jamaica

Tapua'i, Rev. Faatauvaa, mo, Methodist Church in Samoa

Tarasar, Ms Constance, fl, Orthodox Church in America

Taylor, Dr Myra, fl, National Baptist Convention, Inc., USA

Taylor, Rev. Edwin, mo, Methodist Church in the Caribbean and the Americas

Tedla, Ms Berhan, fl, Ethiopian Orthodox Church

Teegarden, Rev. Dr K., mo, Christian Church (Disciples of Christ), USA

Tefera, Father Melise, mo, Ethiopian Orthodox Church

Tehindrazanarivelo, Mr Emmanuel, yml, Church of Jesus Christ in Madagascar

Teinweiawe, Mr Kaoua F., ml, Evangelical Church in New Caledonia and the Loyalty Isles

Tellez, Mr Tomas, ml, Baptist Convention of Nicaragua

Terletskaya, Ms Valentina, fl, Russian Orthodox Church

Terpstra, Mr Gerrit, ml, Reformed Churches in the Netherlands

Than, Prof. Kyaw, ml, Burma Baptist Convention
Theophilus, Dr W.S., ml, Church of North India
Thidjine, Ms Henrietta, fl, Evangelical Church in New Caledonia and the Loyalty Isles
Thompson, Rev. Mary Louise, fo, African Methodist Episcopal Zion Church, USA
Thomspon, Ms Barbara, fl, United Methodist Church, USA
Thompson Gee, Ms Frances, fl, United Methodist Church, USA
Thompson, Mr William P., ml, Presbyterian Church (USA)
Thompson, Rev. L., ymo, Moravian Church in Jamaica
Thompson, Dr Gwenda, fl, Presbyterian Church of Wales
Thomson, Mr Paul, yml, Church of England
Thorogood, Rev. Bernard, mo, United Reformed Church in the UK
Tisdale, Rev. Leonora Tubbs, fo, Presbyterian Church (USA)
Tkachuk, Rev. John, mo, Orthodox Church in America
Tolen, Dr Aaron, ml, Presbyterian Church of Cameroon
Tongdonmuan, Rev. Arun, mo, Church of Christ in Thailand
Toth, Bishop Karoly, mo, Reformed Church in Hungary
Troxell, Rev. Barbara, fo, United Methodist Church, USA
Tshihamba, Dr Mukome Luendu, mo, Church of Christ in Zaire, Presbyterian Community
Tudu, Ms Elbina, fl, United Evangelical Lutheran Churches in India
Tuell, Bishop Jack, mo, United Methodist Church, USA
Twagirayesu, Rev. Michel, mo, Presbyterian Church of Rwanda

Ude, Rt Rev. Dr I.O.A., mo, Presbyterian Church of Nigeria
Ukur, Dr Fridolin, mo, Kalimantan Evangelical Church, Indonesia
Unti, Ms Kim, yfl, Lutheran Church in America
Ursache, Most Rev. Victorin, mo, Romanian Orthodox Church
Utnem, Mr Stig, ml, Church of Norway
Uwadi, Rt Rev. Rogers, mo, Methodist Church, Nigeria

Vahtang, Bishop, mo, Georgian Orthodox Church, USSR
Valcu, Mr Vergil, ml, Romanian Orthodox Church
Valent, Rev. Jan, mo, Slovak Evangelical Church of the Augsburg Confession in Yugoslavia
Varghese, Mr Thomas, yml, Malankara Orthodox Syrian Church, India
Varkey, Prof. Titus, ml, Malankara Orthodox Syrian Church, India
Varughese, Dr K.V., ml, Mar Thoma Syrian Church of Malabar, India
Vasile, Bishop, mo, Romanian Orthodox Church
Vasiliu, Dr Cezar, ml, Romanian Orthodox Church
Vassilios, Metropolitan, mo, Greek Orthodox Patriarchate of Jerusalem
Vasumathi, Ms, yfl, Church of South India
Veem, Archbishop Konrad, mo, Estonian Evangelical Lutheran Church, USSR
Veen-Schenkeveld, Rev. M.J. van der, fo, Reformed Churches in the Netherlands
Veitch, Rev. Dr James, mo, Presbyterian Church of New Zealand

Veliashvili, Ms Dodo, fl, Georgian Orthodox Church, USSR
Vercoe, Rt Rev. Whakahuihui, mo, Church of the Province of New Zealand
Vergara, Ms Priscilla, fl, Methodist Church in Mexico
Vetrov, Rev. Markell, mo, Russian Orthodox Church
Vikstrom, Archbishop Dr John, mo, Evangelical Lutheran Church of Finland
Vishnevski, Mr Paul, ml, Russian Orthodox Church
Vivian, Rev. C.T., mo, National Baptist Convention (USA)
Vladimir, Most Rev., mo, Russian Orthodox Church
Vlodek, Archpriest Petr, mo, Russian Orthodox Church/Canada
Vorlaender, Dr Dorothea, fl, Evangelical Church in Germany, FRG
Vuakatagane, Mr Emosi, ml, Methodist Church in Fiji

Wade, Ms Jinny, fl, Church of England
Wah, Ms Regina, yfl, Methodist Church in Fiji
Wanani, Rev., mo, Church of Jesus-Christ on Earth by the Prophet Simon Kimbangu, Zaire
Wanjiku Waithiru, Ms Esther, fl, Presbyterian Church of East Africa
Waters, Rev. Robert, mo, Congregational Union of Scotland
Webley, Right Rev. Stanford, mo, United Church of Jamaica and Grand Cayman
Weinbrenner, Ms Birgit, yfl, Evangelical Church in Germany, FRG
Weir, Rev. Emmette, mo, Methodist Church in the Caribbean and the Americas/Bahamas
Westphal, Ms Marthe, fl, Reformed Church of France
Westphal, Pastor Fritz, mo, Evangelical Church of the Augsburg Confession of Alsace and Lorraine
Whiterabbit, Ms Renee, yfl, American Lutheran Church
Wilckens, Bishop Ulrich, mo, Evangelical, Church in Germany, FRG
Wilke, Dr Harold H., ml, United Church of Christ, USA
Wilkie, Ms Wendie, fl, Uniting Church in Australia
Wilkins Jr, Mr Howell O., yml, United Methodist Church, USA
Williams, Mr M.J., ml, Presbyterian Church (USA)
Williams, Ms J., yfl, Church of the Province of South Africa
Wilson, Very Rev. Lois, fo, United Church of Canada
Woertel, Ms Helga, yfl, Evangelical Church in Germany, FRG
Wood, Rev. Bertrice Y., fo, United Church of Christ, USA
Wyss, Pastor Markus, mo, Swiss Protestant Church Federation

Xavier, Mr Rathinasami Moses, ml, Church of South India

Yabantu, Mr Elliot, ml, Methodist Church of Great Britain
Yao, Datuk Ping-Hua, ml, Methodist Church in Malaysia
Yong, Ven. Ping Chung, mo, Church of England
Yongui, Ms Marie Therese, fl, Presbyterian Church of Cameroon
Yoo Shin, Ms Jewell Kumchong, fl, Presbyterian Church of Korea
Yoshimoto, Ms Cecelia, yfl, Anglican Episcopal Church in Japan

Young, Jr, Dr Claude, mo, United Methodist Church, USA
Youssef Abdou, Father Dr, mo, Coptic Orthodox Church, Egypt
Ytterberg, Rev. Claes Bertil, mo, Russian Orthodox Church
Yuvenaly, Metropolitan, mo, Russian Orthodox Church

Zaru, Ms Jean, fl, Friends United Meeting/Jordan
Zelelew, Ms Shuwaye, fl, Ethiopian Orthodox Church
Zerihun, M.T. Teshoma, mo, Ethiopian Orthodox Church
Zizioulas, Prof. Dr John, ml, Ecumenical Patriarchate of Constantinople/ UK
Zoe-Obianga, Ms Rose, fl, Presbyterian Church of Cameroon
Zumach, Ms Hildegard, fl, Evangelical Church in Germany, FRG
Zurab, Deacon, mo, Georgian Orthodox Church
Zverev, Rev. Nikolai, mo, Union of Evangelical Christian Baptist of USSR
Zvereva, Ms Maria, yfl, Russian Orthodox Church

MEMBERS OF THE RETIRING CENTRAL COMMITTEE

Appel, Rev. André, mo, Evangelical Church of the Augsburg Confession of Alsace and Lorraine, France
Brouwer, Rev. Dr Arie, mo, Reformed Church in America
Comba, Ms Fernanda, fl, Waldensian Church, Italy
Engström, Principal Olle, ml, Mission Covenant Church of Sweden
Ferrari, Ms Ana B., fl, Evangelical Methodist Church of Argentina
Franke, Mr Ludwig, ml, Federation of the Evangelical Churches in the GDR
Gatu, Rev. John G., mo, Presbyterian Church of East Africa
Gopal Ratnam, Ms Daisy, fl, Church of South India
Huebner, Dr Friedrich, mo, Evangelical Church in Germany, FRG
Kang, Rev. Dr Won Yong, mo, Presbyterian Church in the Republic of Korea
Kishimoto, Rev. Yoichi, mo, United Church of Christ in Japan
Lehtonen, Rt. Rev. Dr Samuel, mo, Church of Finland
Mahlatsi, Ms Evelyn, fl, Church of the Province of South Africa
Mathews, Rt Rev. James K., mo, United Methodist Church, USA
Meyendorff, Prof. John, mo, Orthodox Church in America
Peery, Rev. Margaret Barnes, fo, Presbyterian Church (USA)
Peper, Ms Waltraut, fl, Federation of the Evangelical Churches in the GDR
Russell, Rev. Dr David, mo, Baptist Union of Great Britain and Ireland
Thomas, Dr M.M., mo, Mar Thoma Syrian Church of Malabar, India
Wallace, Rev. Robert A., mo, United Church of Canada
Webb, Ms Pauline, fl, Methodist Church, UK
Woolfolk, Dr Jean, fl, Christian Church (Disciples of Christ), USA
Youngquist, Ms Margaret, yfl, American Lutheran Church

DELEGATED REPRESENTATIVES
OF ASSOCIATE MEMBER CHURCHES

Calvo, Rev. Samuel F., mo, Evangelical Methodist Church of Costa Rica
Chung, Bishop Kao Jih, mo, Methodist Church in Singapore
Corradino, Mr Pedro A., ml, Evangelical Methodist Church in Uruguay
Fuligno, Rev. Gioile, mo, Baptist Union of Italy
Funzamo, Rev. Isaias, mo, Presbyterian Church of Mozambique
Gonzalez, Rev. Orestes, mo, Presbyterian Reformed Church in Cuba
Guevara Perez, Rev. Luis, mo, Methodist Church in Cuba
Gutierrez, Rt Rev. Isaias, mo, Methodist Church of Chile
Hollemweguer, Bishop Juan E., mo, Methodist Church of Peru
Isaac, Bishop, mo, Presbyterian Church of Portugal
Leite, Rev. Jose, mo, Presbyterian Church of Portugal
Malakar, Dr Upendra Nath, ml, Church of Bangladesh
Maluit, Rev. Thomas, mo, Presbyterian Church in the Sudan
Mamani, Rev. Pascual, mo, Evangelical Methodist Church in Bolivia
Mastra, Rev. Dr I. W. mo, Protestant Christian Church in Bali, Indonesia
Oke Esono Atugu, Rev. Samuel, mo, Reformed Church of Equatorial
   Guinea
Pietrantonio, Rev. Dr Ricardo, mo, United Evangelical Lutheran Church,
   Argentina
Sarli, Rev. Norberto Antonio, mo, Church of the Disciples of Christ,
   Argentina
Shik, Rev. Kim Kun, mo, Korean Christian Church in Japan
Soares, Rt Rev. Fernando L., mo, Lusitanian Catholic-Apostolic
   Evangelical Church, Portugal
Taibo, Bishop Ramon, mo, Spanish Reformed Episcopal Church
Thu, Rev. En-Yu, mo, Protestant Church in Sabah, Malaysia
Vaccaro, Rev. Dr Gabriel O., mo, Church of God, Argentina

DELEGATED REPRESENTATIVES OF WCC ASSOCIATE
COUNCILS AND OF OTHER ORGANIZATIONS

Ada, Rev. S.K., mo, Evangelical Community for Apostolic Action,
   France
Aharonian, Rev. Dr Hovhannes, mo, Middle East Council of Churches
Anderson, Rev. Dr Donald W., mo, Canadian Council of Churches
Bakhsh, Rt Rev. J.S., mo, National Council of Churches, Pakistan
Balslev-Olesen, Rev. Christian, mo, Ecumenical Council of Denmark
Benedyktowicz, Prof. Witold, ml, Polish Ecumenical Council
Brews, Rev. Alan, mo, Council of Churches in Namibia
Cabezas, Rev. Roger, mo, Latin American Council of Churches
Castren, Ms Inga-Brita, fl, Ecumenical Council of Finland
Chowdhury, Dr S.M., ml, National Council of Churches, Bangladesh
Cunha, Rev. Ireneu, mo, Portuguese Council of Christian Churches

Dartey, Mr David Asante, ml, Christian Council of Ghana
Davies, Rev. Noel A., mo, Council of Churches for Wales
Davis, Rev. Edmund, mo, Jamaica Council of Churches
De Boer, Rev. John C., mo, Joint Strategy and Action Committee, USA
Dutton, Rev. Denis C., mo, Council of Churches of Malaysia
Ehlert, Rev. Heinz, mo, Latin American Council of Churches
Epting, Rev. Ruth, fo, Swiss Missionary Council
Fiolet, Rev. Dr Herman, mo, Council of Churches in the Netherlands
Fjaerstedt, Rev. Dr Biorn, mo, Swedish Missionary Council
Gape, Mr C.M., ml, Botswana Christian Council
Gutierrez, Bishop Sinforiano, mo, Church of Free Pentecostal Missions, Chile
Habib, Mr Gabriel, ml, Middle East Council of Churches
Hamilton, Mr James, ml, National Council of the Churches of Christ in the USA
Hao, Rev. Dr Yap Kim, mo, Christian Conference of Asia
Heyward, Rt Rev. Oliver S., mo, Australian Council of Churches
Illangasinghe, Rev. Kumara, mo, National Christian Council of Sri Lanka
Kim, Rev. So Young, mo, National Council of Churches in Korea
Kirton, Rev. Allen, mo, Caribbean Conference of Churches
Klein, Dr L. Werner, mo, Council of Christian Churches in the Federal Republic of Germany and West Berlin
Kodjo, Rev. Peter, mo, All Africa Conference of Churches
Kramp, Rev. Flemming, mo, Danish Missionary Council
Kuchera, Rev. Murombedzi, mo, Zimbabwe Christian Council
Kwok, Rev. Nai Wang, mo, Hong Kong Christian Council
Lehmann-Habeck, Rev. Dr Martin, mo, Protestant Association for World Mission within the Federal Republic of Germany and West Berlin
Macleod, Rev. Angus H., mo, National Council of Churches, New Zealand
Mafi, Rev. Seluipepeli, mo, Tonga National Council of Churches
Makambe, Rev., mo, Zambia Christian Council
Massey, Rev. A., South African Council of Churches
Mercado, Rev. Laverne D., mo, National Council of Churches in the Philippines
Mkhabela, Bishop, mo, Council of Swaziland Churches
Moffat, Ms Jeanne, fl, Canadian Council of Churches
Morgan, Rev. Philip, mo, British Council of Churches
Nabetari, Rev. B., mo, Pacific Conference of Churches
Ndungane, Rev. W., mo, South African Council of Churches
Park, Rev. Sang Jung, mo, Christian Conference of Asia
Paul, Rev. Cyril, mo, Christian Council of Trinidad and Tobago
Rafransoa, Rev. Maxime V., mo, All Africa Conference of Churches
Randall, Dr Claire, fl, National Council of the Churches of Christ in the USA
Ratefy, Rev. M. Daniel, mo, Christian Council of Madagascar
Renner, Rev. Eustace Lloyd, mo, United Christian Council, Sierra Leone

Schmidt-Lauber, Prof. Dr Hans-Christoph, mo, Ecumenical Council of
Churches in Austria
Shoji, Rev. Tsutomu, mo, National Christian Council of Japan
Siebert, Rev. Gerard, mo, Netherlands Missionary Council
Stenstroem, Rev. Lars B., mo, Swedish Ecumenical Council
Thews, Rev. Dieter G., mo, Federation of Evangelical Churches of
Uruguay
Thorne, Rev. John Francis, mo, Council for World Mission, UK
Trautmann, Rev. Frederic, mo, Protestant Department for Mission and
International Relations, France
Tutu, Bishop Desmond, mo, South African Council of Churches
Wilkie, Rev. James L., mo, Conference for World Mission, UK
Williams, Rev. Dr Glen Garfield, mo, Conference of European Churches
Winkelmann, Rev. Kurt, mo, Ecumenical Liaison Committee for Mission
in the GDR
Wirakotan, Dr J.H., mo, Council of Churches in Indonesia
Zachariah, Mr Mathai, ml, National Council of Churches in India

DELEGATED REPRESENTATIVES
OF ECUMENICAL ORGANIZATIONS

Amirtham, Ms Lily, fl, Frontier Internship in Mission
Andreis, Mr Sergio, ml, International Christian Youth Exchange
Bengtzon, Deaconess Inga, fo, Diakonia
Bronkema, Rev. Frederick, mo, Ecumenical Development Cooperative
Society
Brunger, Mr Harry, ml, World Alliance of YMCA's
Florin, Rev. Dr Hans, mo, World Association for Christian
Communication
Franco, Rev. Juan A., mo, World Student Christian Federation
Fueter, Rev. Paul, mo, United Bible Societies
Merz, M.H., ml, Uniapac (International Christian Union of Business
Executives)
Mirejovsky, Rev. Dr Lubomir, mo, Christian Peace Conference
Solomon, Ms Shanti, fl, International Committee/Fellowship of the Least
Coin
Sovik, Ms Ruth, fl, World Young Women's Christian Association
Wagner, Ms Dorothy, fl, World Day of Prayer
Wirmark, Mr Bo, ml, International Fellowship of Reconciliation

DELEGATED REPRESENTATIVES
OF CHRISTIAN WORLD COMMUNIONS

Beach, Dr Bert, mo, General Conference of Seventh Day Adventists
Boesak, Rev. Dr Allan, mo, World Alliance of Reformed Churches

Byfield, Ms Hazel, fl, Disciples Ecumenical Consultative Council
Cannon, Bishop William R., mo, World Methodist Council
Hale, Dr Joe, ml, World Methodist Council
Held, Ms Christa, fl, Lutheran World Federation
Keanie, Commissioner Victor C., mo, Salvation Army
Mau Jr, Rev. Carl H., mo, Lutheran World Federation
Miller, Mr Lawrence, ml, Friends World Committee for Consultation
Peachey, Rev. Urbane, mo, Mennonite World Conference
Perret, Rev. Dr E.J., mo, World Alliance of Reformed Churches
Schrotenboer, Rev. Dr Paul G., mo, Reformed Ecumenical Synod
Van Culin, Rev. Dr Samuel, mo, Anglican Consultative Council

DELEGATED OBSERVERS

Arevalo, Father Catalino, mo, Roman Catholic Church/Philippines
Bortnowska (not present), Ms Halina, fl, Roman Catholic Church/Poland
Bouwen, Father Frans, mo, Roman Catholic Church/Belgium
Caetano, Rev. José Domingos, mo, Pentecostal Mission Church, Angola
Carney, Most Rev. James F., mo, Roman Catholic Church/Canada
Chemi, Ms Daw, fl, Methodist Church, Upper Burma
Christensen, Dr Marshall K., ml, Church of God, USA
Delaney (for Bortnowska), Sister Joan, fl, Roman Catholic Church/USA
Domingos, Rev. Alexandre Luiz, mo, United Evangelical Church, Angola
Engebretson, Dr Milton B., mo, Evangelical Covenant Church, USA
Finau, Bishop Patelisio, mo, Roman Catholic Church/Tonga
Francisco, Rev. Julio, mo, Evangelical Congregational Church of Angola
Hacault, Most Rev. Antoine, mo, Roman Catholic Church/Canada
Hotchkin, Rev. John F., mo, Roman Catholic Church/USA
Hsiao, Dr Andrew Keh-Hsieh, mo, Evangelical Lutheran Church, Hong
   Kong
Kehler, Rev. Larry, mo, Conference of Mennonites, Canada
Lanne, Dom Emmanuel, mo, Roman Catholic Church/Belgium
Meeking, Msgr Basil, mo, Roman Catholic Church/Vatican
Motte, Sister Mary, fl, Roman Catholic Church/USA
Murphy, Msgr Dennis, mo, Roman Catholic Church/Canada
Mutiso-Mbinda, Father John, mo, Roman Catholic Church/Kenya
Porcile Santiso, Ms Maria Teresa, fl, Roman Catholic Church/Uraguay
Ramaholimihaso, Ms Madeleine, fl, Roman Catholic Church/Madagascar
Redford, Father John, mo Roman Catholic Church/UK
Rossano, Msgr Pietro, mo, Roman Catholic Church/Vatican
Scheele, Rev. Paul-Werner, mo, Roman Catholic Church/FRG
Schotte,, Rev. Jan, mo, Roman Catholic Church/Vatican
Smucker, Prof. Donovan E., mo, General Conference of Mennonite
   Churches, Canada
Stapleton, Most Rev. Asram L., mo, Spiritual Baptist Council, Trinidad
Stransky, Father Thomas, mo, Roman Catholic Church/USA

Tillard, Rev. Prof. Jean, mo, Roman Catholic Church/Canada
Yoder, Rev. Dr John Howard, mo, Mennonite Church, USA
Zwaanstra, Dr Henry, ml, Christian Reformed Church, USA

OBSERVERS

Adair, Dr Thelma, fl, Church Women United, USA
Adegbola, Rev. Dr Adeolu, mo, Association of Christian Lay Centres in
   Africa
Alesana, Rev. Enoka L., mo, Congregational Christian Church in
   American Samoa
Bangga, Mr Rodney W., yml, Church of Christ (Disciples) Vanuatu
Bastian, Dr Rainward, ml, German Institute for Medical Mission, FRG
Beaumont, Mr Jacques, mo, UNICEF
Becher, Rev. Werner, mo, International Committee on Pastoral Care and
   Counselling
Bellecourt, Mr Vernon, ml, International Indian Treaty Council, USA
Bleakley, Rt Hon. David W., ml, Irish Council of Churches
Bois, Pastor Roby, mo, Cimade, France
Braybrooke, Rev. M., mo, World Congress of Faiths
Brown, Mr Itshag, ml, UN High Commissioner for Refugees
Choo, Rev. Dr Prof. Chai-Yong, mo, North East Asia Association of
   Theological Schools
Chretien, Rev. Pierre, mo, French Protestant Federation
Dumbo, Rev. Abilio, mo, Apostolic Church in Angola
Frieling, Rev. Dr Reinhard, mo, Evangelical Working Group on
   Confessions, FRG
Gesner, Rev. Dr Lloyd, mo, Coordinating Committee on Theological
   Education in Canada
Godoy Sobrinho, Rev. Antonio de, mo, Independent Presbyterian Church
   of Brazil
Gullick, Ms Etta, fl, Isle of Man Council of Churches, UK
Hahn, Rev. Hans-Otto, mo, Diaconal Work of the Evangelical Church
   in Germany/Bread for the World
Haraszti, Dr Alexander, mo, Billy Graham Evangelistic Association
Harvey, Rev. T.J., mo, Caritas International
Hellberg, Dr Hakan, ml, World Heath Organization
Hickel, Rev. Giselher, mo, Ecumenical Youth Council in Europe
Hirata, Rev. Satoshi, mo, Association of Christian Institutes for Social
   Concern in Asia
Holden, Rev. Peter, mo, Ecumenical Coalition on Third World Tourism
Houtepen, Dr Anton, W.I., ml, Interuniversity Institute for Missiological
   and Ecumenical Research, Netherlands
Jack, Rev. Homer A., mo, World Conference on Religion for Peace
Janda, Rev. Clement, mo, Sudan Council of Churches
Jones, Mr Edward K., ml, First Church of Christ, Scientist

Kalu, Prof. Ogbu Uke, ml, Conference of African Theological Institutes
Kekumba, Rev. Dr Yemba, mo, Kinshasa Faculty of Protestant Theology, Zaire
Kim, Ms Eunice, fl, Asian Church Women's Conference
Kirst, Prof. Nelson, mo, Association of Evangelical Theological Seminaries of Brazil
Lange, Rev. William, mo, National Association of Congregational Christian Churches of the USA
Launikari, Rev. Jaakko, mo, Churches' Committee on Migrant Workers
Lawton, Rev. J.K., mo, International Christian Federation for the Prevention of Alcoholism and Drug Addiction
Lee, Dr Allan W., mo, World Convention of Churches of Christ
Lenders, Rev. Marc, mo, Ecumenical Commission for Church and Society in the European Community
Leonard, Brother, mo, Taizé Community, France
Leroux, Mr Roland, ml, International Confederation of Christian Family Movements
Linnenbrink, Landessuperintendent Dr G., mo, Diaconal Work of the Evangelical Church in Germany, FRG
Lubbe, Rev. G.J.A., mo, Reformed Church in Africa
Lucal, S.J., Rev. John, mo, International Labour Organization
Mahlalela, Rev. I.D., mo, Christian Council of Churches, Mozambique
Maus, Rev. Marianne, fo, Ecumenical Forum of European Christian Women
Mazamisa, Rev. L., mo, Broederkring South Africa
McMaster, Ms Belle Miller, fl, Churches Human Rights Programme, USA
Mendez, Rev. Hector, mo, Latin American Union for Ecumenical Youth
Mitchell, Rev. Robert, mo, Young Life International
Moede, Rev. Gerald F., mo, Consultation on Church Union
Nilsson, Rev. Kjell O., mo, Nordic Ecumenical Institute
Noffsinger, Dr Thomas L, mo, Reorganized Church of Jesus Christ of Latter Day Saints
Ntoni Nzinga, Rev. Daniel, mo, Angola Council of Churches
Nzo, Rev. Alfred, mo, African National Congress
Ondeng', Mr Richard O., ml, National Christian Council of Kenya
Painemal, Mr Melillan, ml, World Council of Indigenous Peoples
Pardoe, Mr David, ml, League of Red Cross Societies
Peachey, Rev. Urbaine, mo, Mennonite Central Committee
Phailbus, Dr Mira, fl, Asian Women's Institute
Picken, Ms Margo, fl, Amnesty International
Reblin, Rev. Dr Klaus, mo, German Evangelical Kirchentag
Reeves, Rev. Gene, mo, Unitarian Universalist Association, International
Reinoso, Rev. Luis F., mo, Evangelical Latin American Commission on Christian Education
Rodrigues, Rev. Alvaro, mo, Evangelical Baptist Church in Angola
Saracco, Mr J. Norberto, mo, Association of Seminaries and Theological Institutes, Argentina

Schober, Rev. Dr Theodor, mo, International Association for Inner Mission and Diaconal Service
Schoneveld, Rev. Dr Coos, mo, International Council of Christians and Jews
Shauri, Rev. S.A., mo, Christian Council of Tanzania
Shejavali, Rev. Abisai, mo, Lutheran Church in Namibia
Shogreen, Mr Andy, ml, Moravian Church, Nicaragua
Simpfendoerfer, Prof. Werner, mo, Ecumenical Association of Academies and Laity Centres in Europe
Spencer, Rev. Robert, mo, North American Retreat Directors Association
Takenaka, Mr Masao, ml, Asian Association of Christian Art
Thu, Rev. En-Yu, mo, Basler Mission Church in Malaysia
Traaen, Rev. Carl H., mo, Ecumenical Council in Norway
Tuwere, Rev. Ilaitia Sevati, mo, Fiji Council of Churches
Vander Stelt, Dr John C., ml, International Council for the Promotion of Christian Higher Education
Verstraelen, Dr Frans J., ml, International Association for Mission Studies
Viczian, Rev. Janos, mo, Council of Free Churches in Hungary
Wa'Ahero, Mr Francis, ml, Solomon Islands Christian Association
Warneck, Rev. Wilfried, mo, Church and Peace, FRG
Wilson, Rev. H.S., mo, Board of Theological Education, Serampore College, India
Wilson, Rt Rev. Cornelius, mo, Episcopal Church in Costa Rica
Winckler, Dr., ml, Evangelical Church of Schaumburg-Lippe, FRG
Wright, Rev. Canon Kenyon E., mo, Scottish Churches Council
Yeow, Rev. Dr Choo Lak, mo, Association for Theological Education in South East Asia
Youngblood, Rev. Dr Robert L., mo, World Evangelical Fellowship
Zimmermann, Rev. Jean, mo, European Evangelical Alliance

GUESTS

Barot, Ms Madeleine, fl, Reformed Church of France
Barrow, Dame R. Nita, fl, The Methodist Church in the Caribbean and the Americas
Brash, Very Rev. Alan, mo, The Presbyterian Church of New Zealand
Bührig, Dr Marga, fl, Swiss Reformed Church
Duprey, Father Pierre, mo, Roman Catholic Church
Espy, Rev. Dr Edwin, mo, American Baptist Churches
Gnanatilake, Ven. Tissa, mo, Buddhist
Goswami, Shri Shrivatsa, mo, Hindu
Hambidge, Most Rev. Douglas, mo, Anglican Church of Canada
Henderson, Ms Mary D., fl, Christian Church (Disciples of Christ), USA
Keil, Rev. Herbert J., mo, Evangelical Lutheran Church of Canada, Western Region
King, Ms Coretta Scott

Kouwenberg, Rev. H.J.H., mo, Synod of British Columbia, Canada
Legaré, Archbishop Henri, mo, Roman Catholic Church
Lough, Rev. Franklin, mo, Vancouver Council of Christian Churches, Canada
Macdonald, Rt Rev. Dr Clarke, *mo*, United Church of Canada
Maeda, Ms Frances, fl, Presbyterian Church (USA)
Makhulu, Most Rev. W.P.K., mo, Church of the Province of Central Africa
Nambiar, Dr Sita, fl, Hindu
Nezu, Mr Masuo, ml, Buddhist
Nigh, Rev. Ross, mo, Mennonite Central Committee
Pearlson, Rabbi Jordan, mo, Jewish
Polster, Ms Betty, fl, Canadian Yearly Meeting, Religious Society of Friends
Rambachan, Dr Anant Anand, ml, Hindu
Rea, Lt Col. Willard, mo, Salvation Army, British Columbia South, Canada
Saab, Dr Hassan, ml, Muslim
Shakirov, Shaykh Yusuf Khan, mo, Muslim
Singh, Dr Gopal, ml, Sikh
Sivaraksa, Dr Sulak, ml, Buddhist
Sjoberg, Bishop Donald W., mo, Lutheran Church of America, Canada Section
Smith, Dr John Coventry, ml, Presbyterian Church (USA)
Solomon, Mr Art, ml, Traditional religions
Somerville, Archbishop David, mo, Anglican Church of Canada
Talbi, Prof. Mohamed, ml, Muslim
Tanenbaum, Rabbi Marc, mo, Jewish
Theodosios, Metropolitan, mo, Orthodox Church in America
Vanier, Mr Jean, ml, Roman Catholic Church
Wing Ming, Abbess, fo, Buddhist

ADVISERS

Anastasios, Bishop, mo, Church of Greece
Andriamanjato, Ms Rahntavololona, fl, Church of Jesus Christ in Madagascar
Bayiga, Rev. Dr Alfred, mo, Presbyterian Church of Cameroon
Boesak, Rev. Dr Allan, mo, Dutch Reformed Mission Church in South Africa
Boseto, Rt Rev. Leslie, mo, United Church in Papua New Guinea and the Solomon Islands
Buthelezi, Bishop Manas, mo, Evangelical Lutheran Church in Southern Africa
Caldicott, Dr Helen, fl, Australia
Chappuis, Rev. Prof. Jean Marc, mo, Swiss Protestant Church Federation

Chungara, Ms Domitila de, fl, Roman Catholic Church
Cook, Mr Guillermo, ml, Association of Bible Churches in Costa Rica
Costas, Rev. Dr Orlando, mo, American Baptist Churches in the USA
Dahlen, Ambassador Olle, ml, Mission Covenant Church of Sweden
Deschner, Rev. Prof. John, mo, United Methodist Church, USA
Dilger, Ms Marie, fl, Evangelical Church in Germany, FRG
Dolphyne, Dr Florence, fl, Methodist Church, Ghana
Dos Santos, Mr Jose, J. C. B., ml, Roman Catholic Church
Doss, Ms Leila, fl, Coptic Orthodox Church, Egypt
Evangeline, Sister, fl, Reformed Church of France
Falcke, Probst Dr Heino, mo, Federation of the Evangelical Churches in
   the GDR
Francis, Dr John M., ml, Church of Scotland
Geraisy, Dr Sami, ml, Greek-Orthodox Patriarchate of Jerusalem
Geyer, Dr Alan, mo, United Methodist Church, USA
Gibble, Rev. Lamar, mo, Church of the Brethren, USA
Gitari, Rt Rev. David M., mo, Church of the Province of Kenya
Gnanadason, Ms Aruna, fl, Church of South India
Goeldner, Dr Horst, ml, Evangelical Church in Germany, FRG
Green, Prof. Reginald H., ml, Church of the Province of Tanzania
Harakas, Rev. Dr Stanley, mo, Greek Orthodox Archdiocese in North
   and South America
Huszti, Rev. Prof. Kalman, mo, Reformed Church in Hungary
Hutchins-Felder, Ms Annette, fl, United Methodist Church, USA
Jeyasingh, Ms Shobhana, fl, Church of South India
Johnson, Mr E. M., ml, Church of North India
Kaan, Rev. Dr Fred, mo, United Reformed Church, UK
Kalu, Ms Wilhelmina, fl, Presbyterian Church of Nigeria
Keju, Ms Darlene, fl, United Church of Christ/Marshall Islands
Kizhakkethalakkal, Prof. Tharakan, ml, Malankara Orthodox Syrian
   Church, India
Knapp, Ms Ruth Elizabeth, fl, United Church of Christ, USA
Kuzmic, Rev. Dr Peter, mo, Christ's Pentecostal Church, Yugoslavia
Lee, Ms Oo Chung, fl, Presbyterian Church in the Republic of Korea
Loh, Rev. I–To, mo, Presbyterian Church in Taiwan
Malaba, Dr Nkongola Kalala, ml, Church of Jesus Christ on Earth by the
   Prophet Simon Kimbangu, Zaire
Matsikenyiri, Mr Patrick, ml, United Methodist Church/Zimbabwe
Matthews, Prof. Robert, ml, Anglican Church of Canada
Mba, Dr Peter O., ml
McDonald, Rev. David, mo, United Church of Canada
Mendoza-Hernandez, Dr Rolando, ml, Roman Catholic Church
Micks, Prof. Marianne, fl, Episcopal Church , USA
Mills, Rev. Dr Howard, mo, United Church of Canada
Mulder, Rev. Dr Kirk, C., mo, Reformed Churches in the Netherlands
Niles, Dr Preman, ml, Prebyterian Church, Sri Lanka
Ninan, Rev. Dr A. George, mo, Church of North India
Nipkow, Prof. Karl-Ernst, ml, Evangelical Church in Germany, FRG

Nissiotis, Prof. Nikos, ml, Church of Greece
Nyoni, Ms Sithembiso, fl, Churches of Christ/Zimbabwe
Oka, Ms Yukiko, fl, Roman Catholic Church
Oporia-Ekwaro, Ms Micheline, fl, Church of Jesus Christ in Madagascar
Owens, Ms Virginia Stem, fl, Presbyterian Church (USA)
Papaderos, Dr Alexandros, ml, Ecumenical Patriarchate
Paprocki, Rev. Prof. Henryk, mo, Autocephalic Orthodox Church of Poland
Parajon, Dr Gustavo A., ml, Baptist Convention of Nicaragua
Penttila, Ms Pirkko, yfl, Orthodox Church of Finland
Poulton, Rev. Canon John, mo, Church of England
Pronk, Dr Jan, ml, Netherlands Reformed Church
Ramalho, Prof. Dr Jether Pereira, ml, Brazil Congregational Church
Robert, Brother, mo, Reformed Church of France
Robinson, Rev. Dr Gnana, mo, Church of South India
Robinson, Mr Rod, ml, Anglican Church of Canada
Saint-Victor, Ms Rosalind, fl, Roman Catholic Church
Schwob-Sturm, Dr Erika S., fl, Swiss Protestant Church Federation
Scott, Dr Waldron, ml, Presbyterian Church (USA)
Shik, Mr Oh Jae, ml, Presbyterian Church in the Republic of Korea
Simpfendoerfer, Prof. Werner, mo, Evangelical Church in Germany, FRG
Sölle, Dr Dorothee, fl, Evangelical Church in Germany, FRG
Sosa, Rev. Pablo, mo, Evangelical Methodist Church of Argentina
Soward, Mr Reginald H., ml, Anglican Church of Canada
Stendahl, Rev. Prof. Krister, mo, Lutheran Church in America
Stephens, Rev. Barbara, fo, Associated Churches of Christ in New Zealand
Styer, Mr James B., ml, General Conference of Mennonites, USA
Tamez, Prof. Elsa, fl, Methodist Church of Costa Rica
Tanner, Ms Mary, fl, Church of England
Traber, Rev. Dr Michael, mo, Roman Catholic
Trautwein, Dr Dieter, mo, Evangelical Church in Germany, FRG
Villa-Vicencio, Rev. Dr Charles, mo, South Africa
Wakira, Rev. Wakaine, mo, Evangelical Church of New Caledonia

STEWARDS

Adegbola, Mr Akinyemi, yml, Methodist Church, Nigeria
Alvarez, Mr Jaime, yml, Evangelical Lutheran Church of Columbia
Appiah, Ms Vesta, yfl, Methodist Church, Ghana
Artus-Martinelli, Ms Elena, yfl, Waldensian Church, Italy
Ashok Rufus, Mr Edward, yml, Church of South India
Audet, Mr Jean-Marc, yml, Roman Catholic Church
Baker, Ms Dianne, yfl, Canada
Bales, Ms Christine, yfl, United Church of Canada
Ball, Rev. James Michael, ymo, United Church of Canada
Baransanankiye, Mr Justin, yml, Protestant Church of Burundi
Barnes, Mr Burton, yml, Church of the Province of the West Indies

Barnett, Ms Joyce, yfl, Anglican Church of Canada
Bould, Mr Graham, yml, UK
Boyce, Ms Jane, yfl, Church of England
Brewer, Ms Martha, yfl, United Methodist Church, USA
Brown, Mr Scott, yml, Evangelical Lutheran Church of Canada
Brown, Mr Stephen, yml, United Reformed Church in the United
  Kingdom
Budworth, Mr Trevor, yml, United Church of Canada
Cardy, Mr Glynn, yml, Church of the Province of New Zealand
Casco Gonzalez, Mr Miguel, yml, El Salvador
Chan, Mr Kim-Kwong, yml, United Church of Canada
Chang, Ms Helen, yfl, United Methodist Church, USA
Chinniah, Mr Samuel, yml, Methodist Church of Sri Lanka
Daniel, Ms Lakshimi K., yfl, Church of South India
Davidson, Ms Carolyn, yfl, Presbyterian Church in Canada
Der Boghossian, Ms Kayane, yfl, Armenian Orthodox Church, Lebanon
Devashayam, Mr Bernard, yml, Methodist Church in India
Ducharme, Mr Douglas, yml, Presbyterian Church in Canada
Epistola, Mr Gideonmi G., yml, Evangelical Methodist Church in the
  Philippines
Evans, Mr Paul, yml, United Church of Canada
Farah, Ms Lina, yfl, Syria
Farrell, Mr Jackson, ml, Methodist
Fields, Rev. D. Kim, yfo, USA
Figueroa, Mr Francisco A., yml, Roman Catholic Church
Finau, Mr Tuiniua, yml, Church of the Province of New Zealand
Fournier, Ms Lucie, yfl, Roman Catholic Church
Gear, Ms Janet, yfl, United Church of Canada
Gear, Ms Alison, yfl, United Church of Canada
Gille, Ms Barbara, yfl, Federation of Evangelical Churches in the GDR
Gillette, Mr Bruce Philip, yml, Presbyterian Church (USA)
Girgis, Dr Gamal, yml, Coptic Orthodox Church, Egypt
Goepfert, Ms Esther, yfl, Evangelical Church in Germany, FRG
Goodwin, Ms Margaret, yfl, United Church of Canada
Gray, Mr Miguel, yml, "Mont Zion" Baptist Church, Costa Rica
Groot, Ms Kim, yfl, Uniting Church in Australia
Gunasekera, Ms Nelun, yfl, Church of Ceylon
Harding, Mr Scott, yml, Anglican Church of Canada
Hevita, Rev. Jonathan, mo, Evangelical Lutheran Church, Namibia
Hoekstra, Ms Deborah, yfl, United Church of Canada
Holband, Mr Urwin, yml, Surinam
Holdo, Mr Per, yml, Church of Norway
Hughes, Mr Rob, yml, Canada
Itoh Usui, Ms Noriko, yfl, United Church of Christ in Japan
Jarjour, Mr Basem N., yml, Syria
Jordan, Mr Roberto, yml, Presbyterian Church, Argentina
Karan, Ms Margaret, yfl, Methodist Church in Fiji
Karsay, Rev. Eszter, yfo, Reformed Church in Hungary

Keen, Ms Connie, yfl, United Methodist Church, USA
Kenny, Ms Cheryl, yfl, Church of the Province of Southern Africa
Keul, Ms Heidi, yfl, Lutheran Church of America
Kimuengi Massamba, Mr Ronsara, yml, Church of Christ in Zaire, Evangelical Community
Kofler, Mr Gerhard, yml, Roman Catholic Church
Kristoffersson, Ms Laila, yfl, Mission Covenant Church of Sweden
Kroker, Mr Kevin, yml, Lutheran Church in America
Lai Sum, Mr David, yml, Burma Baptist Convention
Lam, Ms Wai Kun Susan, yfl, The China Congregational Church/Church of Christ in China
Litster, Ms Lorna, yfl, Presbyterian Church in Canada
Lock, Mr Henri M., yml, United Church of Canada
Luza, Ms Rebeca, fl, Methodist Church of Peru
MacGregor, Rev. Hugh, ymo, United Church of Canada
Mackenzie, Ms Fiona, yfl, Religious Society of Friends
MacNeill, Ms Karen, yfl, United Church of Canada
Mahfud, Mr Ibrahim, yml, Orthodox Antiochian Church, Lebanon
Makal, Mr Skawomir, yml, Polish Autocephalic Orthodox Church
Mang, Ms Shannon, yfl, United Church of Canada
Marasigan, Ms Marielle, yfl, United Church of Christ in the Philippines
Martiskainen, Ms Rutta, yfl, Orthodox Church of Finland
Mbaki Banona, Ms Pascaline, yfl, Roman Catholic Church
McCarty, Ms Merritt, yfl, Episcopal Church, USA
McMillan, Ms Catherine, yfl, Presbyterian Church (USA)
Mendis, Mr Nirmal, yml, Church of Ceylon
Mills, Ms Cindy, yfl, United Church of Canada
Mitsui, Ms Evelyn, yfl, United Church of Canada
Moguel, Ms Juanita, yfl, Anglican Church in Belize
Monsalvo, Mr Ruben Eduardo, yml, Evangelical Methodist Church in Argentina
Mpofu, Rev. Menson, ymo, United Church of Christ, Zimbabwe
Mquqo, Ms Celesticia, fl, Church of the Province of South Africa
Naduitavuki, Mr Viliame, yml, Methodist Church in Fiji
Nasr, Ms Rima, yfl, Greek Catholic Church, Lebanon
Neves, Ms Amelia, yfl, Methodist Church in Brazil
Nichol, Ms Wendy, yfl, Uniting Church of Australia
Njiraini, Ms Njeri, yfl, Presbyterian Church of East Africa
Noel, Ms Esther M., yfl, Church of North India
Novotny, Mr Jaroslav, yml, Bohemian Brethren, Austria
Opitz, Mr Ernst, ml, Federation of the Evangelical Churches in the GDR
Paul, Mr Samuel, yml, Bangladesh Baptist Sangha
Paul, Mr Suresh, ml, Church of South India
Pedroso Mateus, Rev. Prof. Odair, ymo, Independent Presbyterian Church of Brazil
Pedrus, Mr Poden, yml, United Churches of Christ, Ponape
Pengelley, Ms Jenny, yfl, Anglican Church of Australia
Penton, Ms Idania, fl, Salvation Army, Cuba

Pfister, Mr Walter H., yml, Evangelical Reformed Church in Switzerland
Poulsen, Ms Kirsten, yfl, Church of Denmark
Purba, Mr Eddy E., yml, Batak Protestant Christian Church, Indonesia
Putnam, Mr Brad, yml, United Church of Canada
Rahaingosoa, Ms Odette, yfl, Church of Jesus Christ in Madagascar
Rakotoarisoa, Mr Mamy, yml, Church of Jesus Christ in Madagascar
Reeve, Mr Ted, yml, United Church of Canada
Roukema, Ms Annemarie, fl, Netherlands
Rumsey, Ms Suzanne, yfl, Anglican Church of Canada
Ruppert, Ms Marie Helene, yfl, Reformed Church of France
Sadek Mikhail, Mr Elhamy S., yml, Coptic Evangelical Church, Egypt
Sander, Mr Herwig, yml, Evangelical Church in Germany, FRG
Sanderson, Ms Debbie, yfl, Anglican Church of Canada
Santos, Ms Catalina, yfl, Independent Church of Ecuador
Sarapung, Ms Elga, Y. A., yfl, Indonesia
Sarli, Ms Mariam I., yfl, Evangelical Church (Disciples of Christ),
    Argentina
Schmale, Mr Matthias, yml, Evangelical Church in Germany, FRG
Selasie, Mr A.Y.W., yml, Ethiopian Orthodox Church
Sension, Mr Michael, yml, American Baptist Churches
Seunarine, Ms Christine, yfl, United Church of Canada
Shastri, Rev. Hermen, mo, Methodist Church of Malaysia
Sheil, Ms Karen, yfl, Church of Ireland
Shirahata, Mr Joao Takao, yml, Episcopal Church of Brazil
Shoo, Mr Fredrick O., yml, Evangelical Lutheran Church in Tanzania
Sigalet, Mr Phillip, yml, Lutheran Church of Canada
Sinaga, Ms Gloria Sahala H., yfl, Punguan Christian Batak Church,
    Indonesia
Soederberg, Mr Johannes, yml, Church of Sweden
Soga, Ms Joanne, yfl, United Church of Canada
Spanu, Mr Pietro, yml, Union of Protestant Baptist Churches of Italy
Srisang, Ms Ying, yfl, Church of Christ in Thailand
Stephenson, Mr Randall, yml, Canada
Stokes, Ms Jane, yfl, Religious Society of Friends, Vancouver Monthly
    Meeting, Canada
Surjadinata, Ms Debra, yfl, United Church of Canada
Tauvela, Ms Tina, yfl, Methodist Church in Samoa
Thomas, Mr Oral, yml, Antigua
Thorsteinsson, Mr Petur, yml, Evangelical Lutheran Church of Iceland
Tok, Mr Choe Chae, yml, Presbyterian Church of Korea
Udoh, Mr Emmanuel W., yml, Presbyterian Church of Nigeria
Uregei, Ms Emelie-Nanna, yfl, Evangelical Church in New Caledonia and
    the Loyalty Isles
Vries, Ms Greteke de, yfl, Netherlands
Vychopen, Mr Pavel, ml, Fraternal Unity of Baptists in Czechoslovakia
Waffenschmidt, Ms Annette, yfl, Evangelical Church in Germany, FRG
Walker, Ms Violet, yfl, Sierra Leone
Walker, Ms Allison, yfl, Anglican Church of Canada

Warn, Ms Kathryn, yfl, Lutheran Church in America
Warren, Ms Jennifer, yfl, United Church of Canada
Wee, Ms Deborah, yfl, American Lutheran Church
Wheeler, Mr Dana, yml, American Lutheran Church
Wiefel, Ms Katharina, yfl, Federal Republic of Germany
Wilson, Ms Amaryllis, yfl, Moravian Church, Nicaragua
Wood, Ms Barbara, yfl, Canada
Woratz, Dr Christine, yfl, Federation of the Evangelical Churches in the GDR
Yacoub, Ms Manal, H., yfl, Coptic Orthodox Church, Egypt
Young, Ms Aileen, yfl, Church of Scotland
Zakhary, Ms Magda Amin, yfl, Coptic Orthodox Church, Egypt
Zakhem, Mr Riyad, yml, Greek Orthodox Patriarchate of Antioch and All the East, Syria
Zuniga, Ms Ruth, yfl, Pentecostal Church of Costa Rica

DELEGATION STAFF

Barr, Rev. Martha, fo, American Baptist Churches
Coenen, Dr Lothar, mo, Evangelical Church in Germany, FRG
Herrbruck, Rev. Maria, fo, Federation of the Evangelical Churches in the GDR
Hill, Rev. Christopher, mo, Church of England
Norgren, Rev. William A., mo, Episcopal Church, USA

VANCOUVER PLANNING COMMITTEE

Anderson, Ms Daphne
Atkinson, Ms Judith
Bauming, Ms Julie
Bazett, Ms Barbara
Cameron, Ms Susan
Clague, Ms Barbara
George, Ms Gloria
George, Mr Len
Graham, Ms Mary
Harding, Ms Shirley
Hobbs, Dr Gerald
Ingham, Mr Michael
Jeffries, Ms Alice
Lee, Ms Elizabeth
Lythgoe, Mr Len
Lythgoe, Ms June
Martin, Dr James P.
Miller, Ms Nancy
Moir, Ms Ann
Morawski, Ms Ann
Petznik, Mr Armen
Prior, Mr Jim
Pritchard, Ms Jocelyn
Ptolemy-Stam, Ms Karen
Thompson, Rev. Carol
Wallace-Deering, Ms Kathleen

WCC STAFF

Abrecht, Rev. Dr Paul, mo, American Baptist Convention
Amirtham, Dr Samuel, mo, Church of South India
Appiah, Ms Evelyn, fl, Methodist Church, Ghana
Ariarajah, Rev. S. Wesley, mo, Methodist Church in Sri Lanka
Arx, Ms Denise von, fl, Roman Catholic Church
Aschwanden, Ms Barbara, fl, Roman Catholic Church
Assaad, Ms Marie B., fl, Coptic Orthodox Church, Egypt
Baker, Ms Brita Maja, fl, Church of England
Barkat, Prof. Dr Anwar, ml, Church of Pakistan
Becker, Rev. Dr Ulrich, mo, Evangelical Church in Germany, FRG
Beek, Mr Huibert van, ml, Netherlands Reformed Church
Beffa, Mr Pierre, ml, Roman Catholic Church
Beguin-Austin, Ms Midge, fl, Christian Church (Disciples of Christ) USA
Bel, Ms Floryse, fl, Swiss Reformed Church
Bent, Rev. Dr Ans J. van der, mo, United Church of Christ, USA
Benz, Ms Hilde, fl, Roman Catholic Church
Bischof, Ms Margareta, fl, Roman Catholic Church
Blanc, Rev. Jacques, mo, Reformed Church of France
Bluck, Rev. John, mo, Church of the Province of New Zealand
Boerma, Rev. Dr Conrad, mo, Reformed Church in the Netherlands
Botros, Ms Brigitta, yfl, Swiss Reformed Church
Bouwen, Mr Frans, ml, Netherlands Reformed Church
Bredow, Ms Suzanne, fl, Evangelical Church in Germany, FRG
Bria, Prof. Ion, mo, Romanian Orthodox Church
Bridston, Rev. Dr Keith, mo, American Lutheran Church
Brockdorff, Mr Niels, ml, Church of Denmark
Brockway, Rev. Allan, mo, United Methodist Church, USA
Burrows, Ms Auriol, fl, United Reformed Church in the UK
Buss, Rev. Theo, mo, Swiss Protestant Church Federation
Cabral, Ms Cecilia, fl, Roman Catholic Church
Cambitsis, Ms Joan, fl, Church of England
Carlez–Tolra, Ms M.V., fl, Roman Catholic Church
Cashmore, Ms Gwen, fl, Church of England
Castro, Rev. Emilio, mo, Methodist Church of Uruguay
Chaperon, Ms Danielle, fl, Roman Catholic Church
Chapman, Ms Eileen, fl, Church of Scotland
Chiarinotti, Ms Patricia, yfl, Roman Catholic Church
Christ, Ms Margrit, fl, Swiss Reformed Church
Ciobotea, Dr Dan-Ilie, ml, Romanian Orthodox Church
Clark, Ms Nancy, fl, Lutheran Church in America
Coates, Rev. Anthony J., mo, United Reformed Church, UK
Coïdan, Mr Patrick, ml, Protestant Church of the Canton of Geneva, Switzerland
Constant, Ms Brigitte, fl, Evangelical Church in Germany, FRG
Corelli, Ms Evelyne, yfl, Roman Catholic Church
Courvoisier, Ms Maryse, fl, Reformed Church of France

Crawford, Rev. Janet, fo, Church of the Province of New Zealand
Cudre-Mauroux, Mr Gilbert, ml, Roman Catholic Church
David, Rev. Kenith A., mo, Church of England
Davies, Mr Trevor, ml, Church of England
Delaraye, Ms Pilar, fl, Roman Catholic Church
Doench, Ms Rosemarie, fl, Evangelical Church in Germany, FRG
Dominguez, Mr Michael A., ml, Christian Churches (Disciples of Christ), USA
Dorris, Mr Thomas, ml, Association of Evangelical Lutheran Churches, USA
Drimmelen, Mr Rob van, ml, Reformed Churches of the Netherlands
Duinen, Ms Corrie van, yfl, Netherlands Reformed Church
Durand, Ms Andrée, fl, Swiss Reformed Church
Fenn, Ms Nirmala, fl, Church of South India
Freidig, Ms Marlise, fl, Swiss Reformed Church
Friedli, Ms Shelagh, fl, Church of England
Fung, Mr Raymond, ml, Hong Kong Baptist Church
Garcia, Ms Ana de, fl, Lutheran Diocese of Costa Rica and Panama
Gehler, Ms Marie Louise, fl, Roman Catholic Church
Gendre, Ms Marie-Christine, fl, Swiss Reformed Church
Gerber, Ms Tamara, fl, Church of England
Gjerding, Mr Uffe, ml, Evangelical Lutheran Church of Denmark
Gouel, Ms Elisabeth, fl, Seventh Day Adventists
Graaf, Mr Herman de, ml, Swiss Reformed Church
Green, Ms Rosemary, fl, United Reformed Church, UK
Gregoriades, Ms Gisela, fl, Evangelical Church in Germany, FRG
Gurney, Mr Robin, ml, Methodist Church, UK
Haller, Ms Erna, fl, Swiss Reformed Church
Harper, Rev. Charles R., mo, Presbyterian Church (USA)
Haworth, Ms Joan, fl, Roman Catholic Church
Hemmann, Ms Kathrin, fl, Roman Catholic Church
Hertz, Dr Karl, mo, Lutheran Church in America
Hoogevest, Ms Geertruida van, fl, Netherlands Reformed Church
Hoppe, Ms Anneliese, fl, Evangelical Church in Germany, FRG
Hsu, Mr Victor, ml, Church of Scotland
Hudson, Mr Harald, ml, United Methodist Church, USA
Hutter, Ms Emma, fl, Roman Catholic Church
Isaac, Mr Samuel, ml, Church of South India
Jacques, Mr Andre, ml, Reformed Church of France
Jennings, Ms Jean, fl, Church of England
Jones, Mr William, ml, Episcopal Church, USA
Kaiser, Ms Helga, fl, Evangelical Church in Germany, FRG
Kerkhoff, Ms Cornelia, fl, Roman Catholic Church
Kilchenmann, Ms Rosemarie, fl, Evangelical Methodist Church of Switzerland
Kilem Mbila, Mr Daniel, ml, Presbyterian Church of Cameroon
Kingma, Dr Stuart, ml, Christian Reformed Church, USA

Kinnamon, Rev. Dr Michael, mo, Christian Church (Disciples of Christ), USA

Kinsler, Rev. Dr Ross, mo, Presbyterian Church (USA)

Kobia, Rev. Samuel, mo, Methodist Church in Kenya

Koch, Dr Margret, fl, Roman Catholic Church

Kok, Mr Jan H., ml, Reformed Churches in the Netherlands

Kolb, Ms Ingeborg, fl, Evangelical Church in Germany, FRG

Koshy, Mr Ninan, ml, Church of South India

Lazareth, Rev. Dr William, mo, Lutheran Church in America

Leclère, Ms Catherine, fl, Roman Catholic Church

Link, Rev. Dr Hans-Georg, mo, Evangelical Church in Germany, FRG

Mahaniah, Dr Kimpianga, ml, Church of Christ in Zaire, Evangelical Community

Maro, Mr Nicholas, ml, Evangelical Lutheran Church of Tanzania

Masamba, Rev. Dr Ma Mpolo, mo, Church of Christ in Zaire, Baptist Community

May, Ms Lena de, yfl, Church of Sweden

McClellan, Ms Monique, fl, Presbyterian Church (USA)

McNulty, Ms Joyce, fl, Church of England

Moreillon, Ms Madeleine, fl, Swiss Reformed Church

Müller, Ms Anne Rose, fl, Swiss Reformed Church

Nielsen, Dr Carl F., ml, Lutheran Church in America

Nyffenegger, Mr Bernard, ml, Swiss Reformed Church

Padolina, Ms Priscilla, fl, United Methodist Church, USA

Park, Dr Kyung Seo, ml, Presbyterian Church in the Republic of Korea

Pascual, Ms Maria Julia, fl, Roman Catholic Church

Pasztor, Mr Janos, yml, Reformed Church of Hungary

Peiro, Rev. Angel, mo, Disciples of Christ, Argentina

Perkins, Rev. William, mo, Episcopal Church, USA

Pesaro, Ms Irene, fl, Netherlands Reformed Church

Pettingell, Rev. Hugh, mo, Church of England

Philpot, Rev. David, mo, Church of Scotland

Pottier, Ms Francoise, fl, Swiss Reformed Church

Quillet, Ms Anne, fl, Swiss Reformed Church

Quiquerez, Ms Irene, fl, Roman Catholic Church

Raiser, Dr Konrad, mo, Evangelical Church in Germany, FRG

Ram, Dr Eric, ml, Church of North India

Ray, Ms Sheila, fl, Church of England

Reilly, Ms Joan, fl, Church of Scotland

Reuschle, Mr Helmut, ml, Evangelical Church in Germany, FRG

Reuver, Ms Caroline, fl, Roman Catholic Church

Rollman, Ms Helga, fl, Evangelical Church in Germany, FRG

Ross, Ms Dawn M., fl, Presbyterian Church in Canada

Rubeiz, Mr Ghassan, ml, Greek Orthodox Patriarchate of Antioch and All the East

Ruiz, Ms Francoise, fl, Roman Catholic Church

Sabev, Prof. Todor, ml, Bulgarian Orthodox Church

Saravia, Ms Elizabeth, fl, Assembly of God, Chile

Sbeghen, Ms Renate, fl, Evangelical Church in Germany, FRG
Schmidt, Rev. Wolfgang, mo, Evangelical Church in Germany, FRG
Sintado, Rev. Carlos, mo, Evangelical Methodist Church of Argentina
Skiller, Ms Thelma, fl, Uniting Church in Australia
Skov, Ms Edel, fl, Church of Denmark
Smith, Ms Audrey, fl, Church of England
Solms, Mr Friedhelm, ml, Evangelical Church in Germany, FRG
Speek Droog, Ms Ula, yfl, Netherlands Reformed Church
Srisang, Dr Koson, ml, Church of Christ in Thailand
Stalschus, Ms Christa, fl, Evangelical Church in Germany, FRG
Stober, Mr Reginald, ml, Anglican Church Sierra Leone
Stromberg, Ms Jean, fl, Presbyterian Church (USA)
Stunt, Ms Heather, fl, Church of England
Swai, Mr Lalashowi, ml, Evangelical Lutheran Church in Tanzania
Sweemer, Dr Cecile de, fl, Presbyterian Church (USA)
Taylor, Dr John, ml, Methodist Church, UK
Tevi, Ms Lorine, fl, Methodist Church in Fiji
Thomas, Mr T.K., ml, Mar Thoma Church, India
Toerner, Ms Denise, fl, Church of Sweden
Traitler, Dr Reinhild, fl, Evangelical Church of the Augsburg and Helvetic
  Confession, Austria
Tsetsis, Father George, mo, Ecumenical Patriarchate, Constantinople
Turnbull, Mr Archie, ml, Church of Scotland
Van Elderen, Mr Marlin, ml, Christian Reformed Church, USA
Vaz, Ms Veronica, fl, Roman Catholic Church
Walder, Ms Evelyne, fl, Swiss Reformed Church
Wall, Ms Melita, fl, Mennonite Church of Paraguay
Wartenberg, Rev. Bärbel von, fo, Evangelical Church in Germany, FRG
Weber, Rev. Dr Hans-Ruedi, mo, Swiss Protestant Church Federation
Weingartner, Mr Erich, ml, Lutheran Church America (Canada Section)
Wiehe, Ms Malena, fl, Evangelical Church in Germany, FRG
Wieser, Rev. Dr Thomas, mo, Presbyterian Church (USA)
Williams, Mr Peter, ml, Church of Denmark
Williamson, Ms Anne, fl, Church of Scotland
Zellweger, Mr Marcel, ml, Swiss Reformed Church
Zierl, Ms Ursula, fl, Evangelical Church in Germany, FRG

COOPTED STAFF

Abraham, Rev. K.C., mo, Church of South India
Arai, Rev. Tosh, mo
Aycinena-Derugin, Ms Bosalinda, fl
Barreiro, Dr Julio, ml
Bates, Ms Robertson, fl, Anglican Church of Canada
Beaume, Rev. Gilbert, mo
Beaupère, Father René, mo, Roman Catholic Church

Bell, Mr William, ml
Belyavsky Mr Dmitri, ml, Russian Orthodox Church
Benes, Ms Dorothea, fl,
Berryman, Rev. Richard J., mo, Anglican Church of Canada
Best, Mr Bruce, ml, Uniting Church in Australia
Binder, Mr Thomas, ml
Bingle, Dr Richard J., ml, Methodist Church of Great Britain
Birchmeier, Rev. Heinz, mo,
Bird, Ms Pamela, fl, Anglican Church of Canada
Blancy, Rev. Alain, mo
Booth, Ms Maria, fl
Booth, Rev. Rodney, mo, United Church of Canada
Bowman, Ms Diana, fl
Brennan, Ms Bonnie, fl, Roman Catholic Church
Brisbin, Rev. Dr Frank, mo, United Church of Canada
Brown, Father McBeath, mo
Brown, Rev. Dr Stuart, mo
Cabrera, Mr Sandy, ml
Campbell, Rev. Joan, fo, Christian Church (Disciplesof Christ), USA
Cann, Rev. Roger, mo, Baptist Federation of Canada
Catchings, Ms Rose, fl, United Methodist Church, USA
Ceccon, Mr Claudius, ml
Cervantes Ramirez, Ms Rosa, fl
Chernykh, Ms Natalia, fl, Russian Orthodox Church
Chimelli, Ms Claire, fl
Chipenda, Rev. Jose, mo
Chisholm, Mr., ml
Coleman, Ms Elisabeth, fl
Combette, Ms Sarah, yfl
Conrad, Ms Wendy, fl
Conway, Mr Martin, ml
Cullot, Ms Martine, fl
Dalabira, Ms Helen, fl
De Raco, Mr Alexjandro, ml
Delmonte, Ms Elisabeth, fl
Demont, Ms Christiane, fl
Deruguine, Ms Tanya, fl
Dewire, Rev. Dr Norman Edward, mo, United Methodist Church, USA
Drewes-Siebel, Ms Renate, fl
Drimmelen, Ms Jenny van, fl
Dufour, Mr Daniel, ml
Eakin, Ms Joann, fl
Eckmann, Mr Mark, ml
Epps, Rev. Dwain C., mo, Presbyterian Church (USA)
Ernst, Ms Erika, fl
Evdokimoff, Ms Tomoko, fl
Faerber, Mr Robert, ml
Fiaferana, Mr Alfer, ml

Fischer, Mr Jean, ml
Flemington, Mr Peter, ml, United Church of Canada
Frey, Mr Albert, yml
Friedberg, Ms Ilse, fl
Gallego, Ms Angela, fl
Gassmann, Rev. Dr Günther, mo, Evangelical Church in Germany, FRG
Gassmann, Ms Ursula, fl
Gautier, Mr Gerard, ml, United Church of Canada
Geense, Rev. Dr Adriaan, mo, Netherlands Reformed Church
Georgiadis, Ms Maria Teresa, fl
Ghmakov, Mr Sergey, ml, Russian Orthodox Church
Gill, Rev. David, mo, Uniting Church of Australia
Ginglas-Poulet, Ms Roswitha, fl
Goertz, Rev. Marc, mo
Goodwin, Rev. G. Douglas, ymo, Presbyterian Church in Canada
Gordeev, Mr Serguei G., ml, Russian Orthodox Church
Gosling, Rev. Dr David, mo, Church of England
Goureev, Mr Slava, ml, Russian Orthodox Church
Gubern, Mr Santiago, ml
Harrand, Ms Odile, fl
Hertzberg, Ms Eva von, fl, Evangelical Church in Germany, FRG
Hes, Mr Jan, ml
Hodginkson, Rev. Douglas, mo, Anglican Church of Canada
Hoffmann, Rev. Dr Gerhard, mo, Evangelical Church in Germany, FRG
Honegger, Rev. André, mo, Reformed Church of France
Hourst, Mr Michel, ml
Howell, Mr Leon, ml
Huggel, Mr Felix, ml
Irizarry, Prof. Sara, fl
Jameson, Mr Vic, ml, Presbyterian Church (USA)
Jonas, Ms Ingrid, fl
Jonson, Rev. Dr Jonas, mo, Church of Sweden
Jorgenson, Dr Larry, ml, Roman Catholic Church
Kahle, Rev. Dr Roger, mo, Association of Evangelical Lutheran Churches, USA
Kamikamica, Ms Esiteri, fl
Kingston, Mr Fred, ml
Kock, Ms Elisabeth, fl
Koutepov, Mr Pavel, ml, Russian Orthodox Church
Krylov, Mr Igor, ml, Russian Orthodox Church
Lacombe, Ms Martine, fl
Lambertz, Ms Renate, fl
Lancaster, Rev. Lewis H., mo, Presbyterian Church (USA)
Lasserre, Ms Nelly, fl, Swiss Reformed Church
Lebbe, Ms Karin, fl
Lee-McInnes, Ms Silvia, fl
Lefevere, Ms Patricia, fl
Lema, Dr Anza, ml, Evangelical Lutheran Church in Tanzania

Lenz, Mr Gerhard, ml, Evangelical Church in Germany, FRG
Lescaze, Ms Marie Claire, fl, Protestant Church of the Canton of Geneva, Switzerland
Leventi, Ms Anna, fl
Lewis, Rev. David, mo, United Reformed Church, UK
Liljeholm, Mr Theodore E., ml
Lindquist, Rev. Prof. Martti, mo, Evangelical Lutheran Church in Finland
Lodwick, Mr Philip, yml, Presbyterian Church (USA)
Lodwick, Rev. Dr Robert C., mo, Presbyterian Church (USA)
Lorenz, Mr Günter, ml, Federation of the Evangelical Churches in the GDR
Lowis, Ms Andrea von, fl
Lucke, Rev. Hartmut, mo
Makhnev, Mr Vailiy V., ml, Russian Orthodox Church
Marquet, Rev. Claudette, fo, French Protestant Federation
Mavrocordopoulo, Mr Nicolas, ml
McCullum, Mr Hugh, ml
Mear, Ms Christine, fl
Meister, Rev. J.W. Gregg, mo, Presbyterian Church (USA)
Mely, Ms Josiane, fl
Mitsui, Rev. Tad, mo, United Church of Canada
Müller-Römheld, Dr Walter, ml, Evangelical Church in Germany, FRG
Musa, Mr Ghigeon, yml, Ethiopian Evangelical Church Mekane Yesus
Nechaev, Mr Leonid, ml, Russian Orthodox Church
Nelson, Mr Jim, ml, Lutheran Church of America
Nomura, Mr Yushi, ml, United Church of Christ in Japan
Northam, Ms Inge, fl, Evangelical Church of Germany, FRG
Nossova, Ms Zinaida, fl, Russian Orthodox Church
Nottingham, Rev. William, mo
O'Reilly, Ms Veronica, fl, Roman Catholic Church
Odell, Mr Luis E., ml
Odier, Rev. Charles, mo, United Church in Canada
Okwenje, Ms Elizabeth, fl
Olds, Ms Grace, fl
Oporia Ekwaro, Mr James, ml
Orlov, Mr Ilia, ml, Baptist Union, USSR
Pater, Ms Margaret, fl, The Methodist Church, UK
Pazos, Ms Luz, fl
Perkins, Ms Anna-Brita, fl, Episcopal Church, USA
Philibert, Ms Janine, fl
Phipps, Ms Sharon, fl, United Church of Canada
Pignot, Mr Pascal, ml
Pirri-Simonian, Ms Teny, fl, Armenian Catholicossate of Cilicia, Lebanon
Pobee, Prof. John Samuel, ml, Anglican Church, Ghana
Prideaux, Rev. Brian, mo, Anglican Church of Canada
Ptolemy, Ms Kathleen, fl
Puls, Sister Joan, fl
Raiser, Dr Elizabeth, fl, Evangelical Church in Germany, FRG

Rice, Rev. Dr Ronald B., mo, Presbyterian Church (USA)
Richter, Ms Dorothee M., fl
Richterich, Ms Amita, fl
Rouzsky, Mr Eugene, ml, Baptist Union, USSR
Samartha, Rev. Dr S.J., mo, Church of South India
Santa Ana, Ms Violaine de, fl, Evangelical Methodist Church in Uruguay
Santa Ana, Rev. Julio de, mo, Evangelical Methodist Church in Uruguay
Santisteban, Ms Annie, yfl
Scanlon, Ms Alayne, fl, United Church of Canada
Schindler, Ms Micheline, fl
Schmidt, Mr Ernst, ml
Shore, Ms Edith B., fl
Sicardi, Mr Anibal, ml, Evangelical Methodist Church of Argentina
Simons-Fischer, Ms Baerbel, fl
Smith, Ms Frances S., fl, United Church of Christ, USA
Smith, Ms Rosemary, fl
Soto-Chavez, Mr Jorge, ml
Soumerkine, Mr Lev, ml, Russian Orthodox Church
Stockwell, Rev. Eugene L, mo, United Methodist Church, USA
Stratou, Ms Stavroula, fl
Strecker, Ms Renate, fl
Stritzky, Ms Dores von, fl, Evangelical Church in Germany, FRG
Tanner, Ms Anne, fl
Tatu, Ms Evelyne, fl, Roman Catholic Church
Taylor, Rev. Robert H., mo, National Council of Community Churches,
  USA
Thompson, Ms Betty A., fl, United Methodist Church, USA
Tomlin, Ms Yvonne, fl
Valente, Ms Emilia, fl
Velez-Sotomayor, Mr William, ml
Vetrano, Msgr Vicente Oscar, mo, Roman Catholic Church
Villas, Mr Ernest, ml
Vittoz, Ms Catherine, fl, Swiss Protestant Church Federation
Voskressensky, Mr Mstislav, ml, Russian Orthodox Church
Walther, Ms Saskia, fl
Washington, Mr Alonza, ml, Presbyterian Church (USA)
Wegener-Fueter, Ms Hildburg, fl
Welsh, Dr Robert, ml, Christian Church (Disciples of Christ), USA
Wieser, Dr Marguerite, fl
Wik, Mr Boris, ml, Russian Orthodox Church
Williamson, Dr Roger, ml, Methodist Church, UK
Wilson, Rev. Frederick, mo, Presbyterian Church (USA)
Woods, Mr Donnie, ml, Presbyterian Church (USA)
Wright, Rev. William A., mo
Yvars, Ms Sofia, fl
Ziegler, Ms Harriet, fl, Church of the Brethren, USA

XII. CONSTITUTION AND RULES OF THE WCC

CONSTITUTION

I. Basis

The World Council of Churches is a fellowship of churches which confess the Lord Jesus Christ as God and Saviour according to the scriptures and therefore seek to fulfill together their common calling to the glory of the one God, Father, Son and Holy Spirit.

II. Membership

Those churches shall be eligible for membership in the World Council of Churches which express their agreement with the Basis upon which the Council is founded and satisfy such criteria as the Assembly or the Central Committee may prescribe. Election to membership shall be by a two-thirds vote of the member churches represented at the Assembly, each member church having one vote. Any application for membership between meetings of the Assembly may be considered by the Central Committee; if the application is supported by a two-thirds vote of the members of the Committee present and voting, this action shall be communicated to the churches that are members of the World Council of Churches, and unless objection is received from more than one-third of the member churches within six months the applicant shall be declared elected.

III. Functions and purposes

The World Council of Churches is constituted for the following functions and purposes:
1) to call the churches to the goal of visible unity in one faith and in one eucharistic fellowship expressed in worship and in common life in Christ, and to advance towards that unity in order that the world may believe;
2) to facilitate the common witness of the churches in each place and in all places;
3) to support the churches in their worldwide missionary and evangelistic task;
4) to express the common concern of the churches in the service of human need, the breaking down of barriers between people, and the promotion of one human family in justice and peace;
5) to foster the renewal of the churches in unity, worship, mission and service;

6) to establish and maintain relations with national councils and regional conferences of churches, world confessional bodies and other ecumenical organizations;
7) to carry on the work of the world movements for Faith and Order and Life and Work and of the International Missionary Council and the World Council on Christian Education.

IV. Authority

The World Council shall offer counsel and provide opportunity for united action in matters of common interest.

It may take action on behalf of constituent churches only in such matters as one or more of them may commit to it and only on behalf of such churches.

The World Council shall not legislate for the churches; nor shall it act for them in any manner except as indicated above or as may hereafter be specified by the constituent churches.

V. Organization

The World Council shall discharge its functions through: an Assembly, a Central Committee, an Executive Committee, and other subordinate bodies as may be established.

1. The Assembly

a) The Assembly shall be the supreme legislative body governing the World Council and shall ordinarily meet at seven year intervals.
b) The Assembly shall be composed of official representatives of the member churches, known as delegates, elected by the member churches.
c) The Assembly shall have the following functions:
   1) to elect the President or Presidents of the World Council;
   2) to elect not more than 145 members of the Central Committee from among the delegates which the member churches have elected to the Assembly;
   3) to determine the policies of the World Council and to review programmes undertaken to implement policies previously adopted;
   4) to delegate to the Central Committee specific functions, except to amend this Constitution and to allocate the membership of the Central Committee granted by this Constitution to the Assembly exclusively.

2. The Central Committee

a) The Central Committee shall be responsible for implementing the policies adopted by the Assembly and shall exercise the functions of the Assembly itself delegated to it by the Assembly between its meetings, except its power to amend this Constitution and to allocate or alter the allocation of the membership of the Central Committee.
b) The Central Committee shall be composed of the President or Presidents of the World Council and not more than 150 members.
   1) Not more than 145 members shall be elected by the Assembly from among the delegates which the member churches have elected to the

Assembly. Such members shall be distributed among the member churches by the Assembly giving due regard to the size of the churches and confessions represented in the Council, the number of churches of each confession which are members of the Council, reasonable geographical and cultural balance, and adequate representation of the major interests of the Council.

2) Not more than 5 members shall be coopted by the Central Committee at its first meeting from among the representatives which the associate member churches have elected to the Assembly.

3) A vacancy in the membership of the Central Committee, occurring between meetings of the Assembly, shall be filled by the Central Committee itself after consultation with the church of which the person previously occupying the position was a member.

c) The Central Committee shall have, in addition to the general powers set out in (a) above, the following powers:

1) to coopt not more than 5 members of the Central Committee from among the representatives which the associate member churches have elected to the Assembly;

2) to elect its Moderator and Vice-Moderator or Vice-Moderators from among the members of the Central Committee;

3) to elect the Executive Committee from among the members of the Central Committee;

4) to elect Committees and Boards and to approve the election or appointment of Working Groups and Commissions;

5) within the policies adopted by the Assembly, to approve programmes and determine priorities among them and to review and supervise their execution;

6) to adopt the budget of the World Council and secure its financial support;

7) to elect the General Secretary and to elect or appoint or to make provision for the election or appointment of all members of the staff of the World Council;

8) to plan for the meetings of the Assembly, making provision for the conduct of its business, for worship and study, and for common Christian commitment. The Central Committee shall determine the number of delegates to the Assembly and allocate them among the member churches giving due regard to the size of the churches and confessions represented in the Council; the number of churches of each confession which are members of the Council; reasonable geographical and cultural balance; the desired distribution among church officials, parish ministers and lay persons; among men, women and young people; and participation by persons whose special knowledge and experience will be needed;

9) to delegate specific functions to the Executive Committee or to other bodies or persons.

3. Rules

The Assembly or the Central Committee may adopt and amend Rules not inconsistent with this Constitution for the conduct of the business of the World Council.

4. By-Laws

The Assembly or the Central Committee may adopt and amend By-Laws not inconsistent with this Constitution for the functioning of its Committees, Boards, Working Groups and Commissions.

5. Quorum

A quorum for the conduct of any business by the Assembly or the Central Committee shall be one-half of its membership.

VI. Other ecumenical Christian organizations

1. Such world confessional bodies and such world ecumenical organizations as may be designated by the Central Committee may be invited to send non-voting representatives to the Assembly and to the Central Committee, in such numbers as the Central Committee shall determine.

2. Such national councils and regional conferences of churches, other Christian councils and missionary councils as may be designated by the Central Committee may be invited to send non-voting representatives to the Assembly and to the Central Committee, in such numbers as the Central Committee shall determine.

VII. Amendments

The Constitution may be amended by a two-thirds vote of the delegates to the Assembly present and voting, provided that the proposed amendment shall have been reviewed by the Central Committee, and notice of it sent to the member churches not less than six months before the meeting of the Assembly. The Central Committee itself, as well as the member churches, shall have the right to propose such amendment.

RULES

I. Membership of the Council

Members of the Council are those churches which, having constituted the Council or having been admitted to membership, continue in membership. The term "church" as used in this article includes an association, convention or federation of autonomous churches. A group of churches within a country or region may determine to participate in the World Council of Churches as one church. The General Secretary shall maintain the official list of member churches noting any special arrangement accepted by the Assembly or Central Committee.

The following rules shall pertain to membership.

1. Application

A church which wishes to become a member of the World Council of Churches shall apply in writing to the General Secretary.

2. Processing

The General Secretary shall submit all such applications to the Central Committee (see Art. II of the Constitution) together with such information as he or she considers necessary to enable the Assembly or the Central Committee to make a decision on the application.

3. Criteria

In addition to expressing agreement with the Basis upon which the Council is founded (Art. I of the Constitution), an applicant must satisfy the following criteria to be eligible for membership:
a) A church must be able to take the decision to apply for membership without obtaining the permission of any other body or person.
b) A church must produce evidence of sustained independent life and organization.
c) A church must recognize the essential interdependence of the churches, particularly those of the same confession, and must practise constructive ecumenical relations with other churches within its country or region.
d) A church must ordinarily have at least 25,000 members.

4. Associate membership

A church otherwise eligible, which would be denied membership solely under Rule I.3(d) may be elected to associate membership in the same manner as member churches are elected. A church applying for associate membership must ordinarily have at least 10,000 members. An associate member church may participate in all activities of the Council; its representatives to the Assembly shall have the right to speak but not to vote. Associate member churches shall be listed separately on the official list maintained by the General Secretary.

5. Consultation

Before admitting a church to membership or associate membership, the appropriate world confessional body or bodies and national council or regional conference of churches shall be consulted.

6. Resignation

A church which desires to resign its membership in the Council can do so at any time. A church which has resigned but desires to rejoin the Council must again apply for membership.

II. Presidium
1. The Assembly shall elect one or more Presidents, but the number of Presidents shall not exceed seven.
2. The term of office of a President shall end at the adjournment of the next Assembly following his or her election.
3. A President who has been elected by the Assembly shall be ineligible for immediate re-election when his or her term of office ends.
4. The President or Presidents shall be ex officio members of the Central Committee and of the Executive Committee.

5. Should a vacancy occur in the Presidium between Assemblies, the Central Committee may elect a President to fill the unexpired term.

III. The Assembly

1. *Composition of the Assembly*

a) *Persons with the right to speak and to vote*
   The Assembly shall be composed of official representatives of the member churches, known as delegates, elected by the member churches, with the right to speak and with the sole rights to vote and to propose and second motions and amendments.

   1) The Central Committee shall determine the number of delegates to the Assembly well in advance of its meeting.
   2) The Central Committee shall determine the percentage of the delegates, not less than 85 per cent, who shall be both nominated and elected by the member churches. Each member church shall be entitled to a minimum of one delegate. The Central Committee shall allocate the other delegates in this part among the member churches giving due regard to the size of the churches and confessions represented in the Council, and the number of churches of each confession which are members of the Council, and reasonable geographical and cultural balance. The Central Committee shall recommend the proper distribution within delegations among church officials, parish ministers and lay persons; and among men, women and young people. The Central Committee may make provision for the election by the member churches of alternate delegates who shall serve only in place of such delegates who are unable to attend meetings of the Assembly.
   3) The remaining delegates, not more than 15 per cent, shall be elected by certain member churches upon nomination of the Central Committee as follows:
      1. If the Moderator or any Vice-Moderator of the Central Committee is not elected a delegate within the provisions of paragraph (2) above, the Central Committee shall nominate such officer to the member church of which such officer is a member. Paragraphs 5 and 6 below apply to such nominees.
      2. The Central Committee shall determine the categories of additional delegates necessary to achieve balance in respect of:
         a) the varied sizes of churches and confessions;
         b) the historical significance, future potential or geographical location and cultural background of particular churches, as well as the special importance of united churches;
         c) the presence of persons whose special knowledge and experience will be necessary to the Assembly;
         d) proportions of women, youth, lay persons and local pastors.
      3. The Central Committee shall invite the member churches to propose the names of persons in the categories so determined whom the churches would be willing to elect, if nominated by the Central Committee.

4. The Central Committee shall nominate particular individuals from the list so compiled to the member church of which each individual is a member.

5. If that member church elects the said nominee, he or she shall become an additional delegate of that member church.

6. The member churches shall not elect alternate delegates for such delegates.

Member churches are encouraged to consult regionally in the selection of the delegates described in paragraphs (2) and (3) above, provided that every delegate is elected by the church of which he or she is a member in accordance with its own procedures.

b) *Persons with the right to speak but not to vote*
In addition to the delegates, who alone have the right to vote, the following categories of persons may attend meetings of the Assembly with the right to speak:

1) *Presidents and Officers*: Any President or Presidents of the Council or Moderator or Vice-Moderator or Vice-Moderators of the Central Committee who have not been elected delegates by their churches.

2) *Members of the retiring Central Committee*: Any members of the retiring Central Committee who have not been elected delegates by their churches.

3) *Representatives of Associate Member Churches*: Each associate member church may elect one representative.

4) *Advisers*: The Central Committee may invite a small number of persons who have a special contribution to make to the deliberations of the Assembly or who have participated in the activities of the World Council. Before an invitation is extended to an adviser who is a member of a member church, that church shall be consulted.

5) *Delegated Representatives*: The Central Committee may invite persons officially designated as Delegated Representatives by organizations with which the World Council maintains relationship.

6) *Delegated Observers*: The Central Committee may invite persons officially designated as Delegated Observers by non-member churches.

c) *Persons without the right to speak or to vote*
The Central Committee may invite to attend the meetings of the Assembly without the right to speak or to vote:

1) *Observers*: Persons identified with organizations with which the World Council maintains relationship which are not represented by Delegated Representatives or with non-member churches which are not represented by Delegated Observers.

2) *Guests*: Persons named individually.

2. *Presiding Officers and Committees*

a) At the first business session of the Assembly the Central Committee shall present its proposals for the moderatorship of the Assembly and for the membership of the Business Committee of the Assembly and make any other proposals, including the appointment of other commit-

tees, their membership and functions, for the conduct of the business of the Assembly as it sees fit.
b) At the first or second business session, additional nominations for membership of any committee may be made in writing for any six concurring delegates.
c) Election shall be by ballot unless the Assembly shall otherwise determine.

3. Agenda

The agenda of the Assembly shall be proposed by the Central Committee to the first business session of the Assembly. Any delegate may move to amend the agenda by including an item or items of new business or by proposing any other change, which he or she may have previously proposed to the Central Committee or to the Business Committee after its election. New business or any change may be proposed by the Business Committee under Rule III.5 (b) or by a delegate under Rule XIV.7.

4. Nominations Committee of the Assembly

a) At an early session of the Assembly, the Assembly shall elect a Nominations Committee, on which there shall be appropriate confessional, cultural, and geographical representation of the membership of the Assembly and representation of the major interests of the World Council.
b) The Nominations Committee in consultation with the officers of the World Council and the Executive Committee shall make nominations for the following:
   1) the President or Presidents of the World Council of Churches;
   2) not more than 145 members of the Central Committee from among the delegates which the member churches have elected to the Assembly.
c) In making nominations, the Nominations Committee shall have regard to the following principles:
   1) the personal qualifications of the individual for the task for which he or she is to be nominated;
   2) fair and adequate confessional representation;
   3) fair and adequate geographical and cultural representation;
   4) fair and adequate representation of the major interests of the World Council.
   The Nominations Committee shall satisfy itself as to the general acceptability of the nominations to the churches to which the nominees belong.
   Not more than seven persons from any one member church shall be nominated as member of the Central Committee.
   The Nominations Committee shall secure adequate representation of lay persons – men, women and young people – so far as the composition of the Assembly makes this possible.
d) The Nominations Committee shall present its nominations to the Assembly. Additional nominations may be made by any six delegates concurring in writing, provided that each such nominee shall be proposed in opposition to a particular nominee of the Nominations Committee.

e) Election shall be by ballot unless the Assembly shall otherwise determine.

5. *Business Committee of the Assembly*

a) The Business Committee of the Assembly shall consist of the Moderator and Vice-Moderator or Vice-Moderators of the Central Committee, the General Secretary, the Presidents of the Council, the Moderators of sections and committees (who may appoint substitutes), and ten delegates who are not members of the outgoing Central Committee, who shall be elected in accordance with Rule III.2.

b) The Business Committee shall:

1) coordinate the day-to-day business of the Assembly and may make proposals for rearrangement, modification, addition, deletion or substitution of items included on the agenda. Any such proposal shall be presented to the Assembly at the earliest convenient time by a member of the Business Committee with reasons for the proposed change. After opportunity for debate on the proposal, the Moderator shall put the following question to the Assembly: Shall the Assembly approve the proposal of the Business Committee? A majority of the delegates present and voting shall determine the question;

2) consider any item of business or change in the agenda proposed by a delegate under Rule XIV.7;

3) determine whether the Assembly sits in general, business or deliberative session as defined in Rule XIV;

4) receive information from and review the reports of other committees in order to consider how best the Assembly can act on them.

6. *Other committees of the Assembly*

a) Any other committee of the Assembly shall consist of such members and shall have such powers and duties as are proposed by the Central Committee at the first business session or by the Business Committee after its election and accepted by the Assembly.

b) Any such committee shall, unless the Assembly otherwise directs, inform the Business Committee about its work and shall make its report or recommendations to the Assembly.

IV.   Central Committee

1. *Membership*

a) The Central Committee shall consist of the President or Presidents of the World Council together with not more than 145 members elected by the Assembly and not more than five members coopted by the Central Committee (see Constitution, Art. V. 2 (b)).

b) Any member church, not already represented, may send one representative to the meetings of the Central Committee. Such a representative shall have the right to speak but not to vote.

c) If a regularly elected member of the Central Committee is unable to attend a meeting, the church to which the absent member belongs shall have the right to send a substitute, provided that the substitute is ordinarily resident in the country where the absent member resides. Such a substitute shall have the right to speak and to vote. If a member, or his or her substitute, is absent without excuse for two consecutive meetings, the position shall be declared vacant, and the Central Committee shall fill the vacancy according to the provisions of Article V. 2 (b) (3) of the Constitution.

d) Moderators and Vice-Moderators of Committees and Boards who are not members of the Central Committee may attend meetings of the Central Committee and shall have the right to speak but not to vote.

e) Advisers for the Central Committee may be appointed by the Executive Committee after consultation with the churches of which they are members. They shall have the right to speak but not to vote.

f) Members of the staff of the World Council appointed by the Central Committee as specified under Rule VIII.3 shall have the right to attend the sessions of the Central Committee unless on any occasion the Central Committee shall otherwise determine. When present they shall have the right to speak but not to vote.

g) The newly elected Central Committee shall be convened by the General Secretary during or immediately after the meeting of the Assembly.

2. *Officers*

a) The Central Committee shall elect from among its members a Moderator and a Vice-Moderator or Vice-Moderators to serve for such periods as it shall determine.

b) The General Secretary of the World Council of Churches shall be ex officio secretary of the Central Committee.

3. *Nominations Committee of the Central Committee*

a) The Central Committee shall elect a Nominations Committee which shall:
1) nominate for possible cooption as members of the Central Committee not more than five persons from among the representatives which the associate member churches have elected to the Assembly;
2) nominate persons from among the members of the Central Committee for the offices of Moderator and Vice-Moderator or Vice-Moderators of the Central Committee;
3) nominate a person for the office of President to fill the unexpired term should a vacancy occur in the Presidium between Assemblies;
4) nominate members of the Executive Committee of the Central Committee;
5) nominate members of Committees and Boards and where appropriate their Moderators;
6) make recommendations regarding the approval of the election of members of Commissions and Working Groups;
7) make recommendations regarding the election of persons proposed for staff positions under Rule VIII.3.
   In making nominations as provided for by (1) to (5) above the Nominations Committee of the Central Committee shall have regard

to principles set out in Rule III.4(c), and in applying principles 2, 3 and 4 to the nomination of members of Committees and Boards, shall consider the representative character of the combined membership of all such committees. Any member of the Central Committee may make additional nominations, provided that each such nominee shall be proposed in opposition to a particular nominee of the Nominations Committee.

b) Election shall be by ballot unless the Committee shall otherwise determine.

4. Meetings

a) The Central Committee shall ordinarily meet once every year. The Executive Committee may call an extraordinary meeting of the Central Committee whenever it deems such a meeting desirable and shall do so upon the request in writing of one-third or more of the members of the Central Committee.

b) The General Secretary shall take all possible steps to ensure that there be adequate representation present from each of the main confessions and from the main geographical areas of the membership of the World Council of Churches and of the major interests of the World Council

c) The Central Committee shall determine the date and place of its own meetings and of the meetings of the Assembly.

5. Functions

In exercising the powers set forth in the Constitution the Central Committee shall have the following specific functions:

a) In the conduct of its business, the Central Committee shall elect the following committees:

1) Finance Committee (a standing committee);
2) Nominations Committee (appointed at each meeting);
3) Reference Committee or Committees (appointed as needed at each meeting to advise the Central Committee on any other questions arising which call for special consideration or action by the Central Committee, except that recommendations from Committees of the Programme Units may be considered by the Central Committee without prior consideration by a Reference Committee).

b) It shall adopt the budget of the Council.

c) It shall deal with matters referred to it by member churches.

d) It shall organize Programme Units and Specialized Units and regional offices or representations as may be necessary to carry out the work of the World Council of Churches. It shall elect a Committee for each Programme Unit, a Board for each Specialized Unit, and approve the election or appointment of a Commission or a Working Group for each Sub-Unit of the Programme Units and receive reports from them at each of its meetings. It shall determine the general policy to be followed in the work of each Programme Unit, each Specialized Unit, and the Department of Finance and Central Services.

e) It shall report to the Assembly the actions it has taken during its period of office and shall not be discharged until its report has been received.

V. Executive Committee

1. Membership

a) The Executive Committee shall consist or the President or Presidents of the World Council ex officio and the Moderator and Vice-Moderator or Vice-Moderators of the Central Committee ex officio and of not less than fourteen nor more than sixteen other members of the Central Committee. Substitutes shall not be permitted to attend in place of elected members.

b) The Central Committee shall elect an Executive Committee at each of its meetings. Elected members of the Executive committee shall hold office until the next meeting of the Central Committee and shall be eligible for re-election.

c) The Moderator of the Central Committee shall also be the Moderator of the Executive Committee.

d) The General Secretary of the World Council of Churches shall be ex officio the secretary of the Executive Committee.

e) The officers may invite other persons to attend a meeting of the Executive Committee for consultation, always having in mind the need of preserving a due balance of the confessions and of the geographical areas and cultural backgrounds, and of the major interests of the World Council.

2. Functions

a) The Executive Committee shall be accountable to the Central Committee.

b) Between meetings of the Central Committee, the Executive Committee shall carry out decisions of the Central Committee and implement policies adopted by it. The Executive Committee shall not make decisions on policy except in those matters specifically delegated to the Executive Committee by the Central Committee and in circumstances of special emergency when it may take provisional decisions. The Executive Committee's power to make public statements is limited and defined in Rule IX.5.

c) The Executive Committee may make provisional appointments to those staff positions specified in Rule VIII.3 subject to confirmation by the Central Committee.

d) The Executive Committee shall supervize the operation of the budget and may, if necessary, impose limitations on expenditures.

VI. Programme Units, Specialized Units and Departments

1. There shall be three Programme Units:

Programe Unit I	:	Faith and Witness
Programme Unit II	:	Justice and Service
Programe Unit III	:	Education and Renewal

The Central Committee shall determine the size and composition of the Committee for each Programme Unit (so that at least two-thirds of the members of each Programme Unit Committee are also members of the Central Committee) and elect the members of each Committee and its Moderator. Each Committee shall propose, for consideration by the Central Committee, by-laws for the conduct of the work of the Programme Unit, including a statement of the aim and functions of the Unit, a description of the Sub-Units into which the Unit will be divided, if any, and the allocation of functions among them, provision for a Working Group or Commission related to each Sub-Unit, and such other materials as it deems desirable.

2. There shall be two Specialized Units:
a) Library
b) Ecumenical Institute, including its Graduate School.

The Central Committee shall determine the size and composition of the Board for each Specialized Unit and elect the members of each Board. Each Board may propose for consideration by the Central Committee by-laws for the conduct of the work of the Specialized Unit.

3. There shall be a Department of Finance and Central Services and a Department of Communication. The Central Committee shall determine the size and composition of the Committee for the Department of Communication and shall elect the members of it.

VII.   Finance Committee of the Central Committee

1. The Finance Committee of the Central Committee shall consist of not less than nine members, including:
a) a Moderator, who shall be a member of the Executive Committee;
b) five members, who shall be members of the Central Committee, two of whom shall also be members of the Executive Committee;
c) three members, one of whom shall be designated by each Programme Unit Committee from the membership of said Committee. Each Programme Unit Committee may designate an alternate who may attend if his or her principal is unable to be present.

2. The Committee shall have the following responsibilities and duties:
a) To present to the Central Committee:
   1) in respect of the expired calendar year, an account of income and expenditure of all operations of the World Council of Churches and the balance sheet of the World Council of Churches at the end of that year and its recommendation, based on review of the report of the auditors, regarding approval and granting of discharge in respect of the accounts of the World Council of Churches for the completed period;
   2) in respect of the current year, a review of all financial operations;
   3) in respect of the succeeding calendar year, a budget covering all activities of the World Council of Churches and its recommendations regarding the approval of that budget in the light of its judgment as to the adequacy of the provisions made for the expenditure involved

in the proposed programme of activities and the adequacy of reasonably foreseeable income to finance the budget; and

4) in respect of the year next following the succeeding calendar year a provisional budget prepared on a similar basis together with recommendations thereon as in (3) above.

b) To consider and make recommendations to the Central Committee on all financial questions concerning the affairs of the World Council of Churches, such as:

1) the appointment of the auditor or auditors who shall be appointed annually by the Central Committee and shall be eligible for reappointment;
2) accounting procedures;
3) investment policy and procedures;
4) the basis of calculation of contributions from member churches;
5) procedures and methods of raising funds.

VIII. Staff

1. The Central Committee shall elect or appoint or provide for the election or appointment of persons of special competence to conduct the continuing operations of the World Council. These persons collectively constitute the staff.

2. The General Secretary shall be elected by the Central Committee. He or she is the chief executive officer of the World Council. As such he or she is the head of the staff. When the position of General Secretary becomes vacant, the Executive Committee shall appoint an acting General Secretary.

3. In addition to the General Secretary, the Central Committee shall itself elect one or more Deputy General Secretaries, and one or more Assistant General Secretaries.

4. The Staff Executive Group shall consist of the General Secretary, the Deputy General Secretary or Secretaries, the Assistant General Secretary or Secretaries, the Directors of the Sub-Units, Departments and the Ecumenical Institute, and other staff members invited by the General Secretary. Care shall be taken that there is confessional, cultural and geographical balance in this group and that women and junior staff members are adequately represented. Additional places shall be available if needed to achieve balance. The possible need for rotation of the members who do not serve ex officio shall be examined at least annually, and in any event following each meeting of the Central Committee. The General Secretary shall be Moderator of the Staff Executive Group; in his or her absence a Deputy General Secretary shall act as Moderator. The Staff Executive Group shall advise the General Secretary on the implementation of policy established by the Central and Executive Committees and may, with his or her approval, establish regular and ad hoc coordinating groups for particular programme activities under the moderatorship of the General Secretary or of a person appointed by him or her.

5. The normal terms of appointment for the General Secretary and for the Deputy and Assistant General Secretaries shall be five years. Unless some other period is stated in the resolution making the appointment, the

first term of office for all other staff appointed by the Executive or Central Committee shall normally be four years from the date of the appointment. All appointments shall be reviewed one year before their expiration.

Retirement shall be at sixty-five for both men and women or not later than the end of the year in which a staff member reaches the age of sixty-eight.

IX. Public statements

1. In the performance of its functions, the Council through its Assembly or through its Central Committee, may publish statements upon any situation or issue with which the Council or its constituent churches may be confronted.

2. While such statements may have great significance and influence as the expression of the judgment or concern of so widely representative a Christian body, yet their authority will consist only in the weight which they carry by their own truth and wisdom and the publishing of such statements shall not be held to imply that the World Council as such has, or can have, any constitutional authority over the constituent churches or right to speak for them.

3. Any Programme Unit or Sub-Unit may recommend statements to the Assembly or to the Central Committee for its consideration and action.

4. A Programme Unit or Sub-Unit may publish any statement which has been approved by the Assembly or the Central Committee. When, in the judgment of a Programme Unit or Sub-Unit, a statement should be issued before such approval can be obtained, the Unit or Sub-Unit concerned may do so provided the statement relates to matters within its own field of concern and action, has received the approval of the Moderator of the Central Committee and the General Secretary, and the Programme Unit or Sub-Unit makes clear that neither the World Council of Churches nor any of its member churches is committed by the statement.

5. Between meetings of the Central Committee, when in their judgment the situation requires, a statement may be issued, provided that such statements are not contrary to the established policy of the Council, by:

1) the Executive Committee when meeting apart from the sessions of the Central Committee; or
2) the Moderator and Vice-Moderator or Vice-Moderators of the Central Committee and the General Secretary acting together; or
3) the Moderator of the Central Committee or the General Secretary on his or her own authority respectively.

X. Associate Councils

1. Any national Christian council, national council of churches or national ecumenical council, established for purposes of ecumenical fellowship and activity, may be recognized by the Central Committee as an associate council, provided:

a) The applicant council, knowing the Basis upon which the World Council is founded, expresses its desire to cooperate with the World Council towards the achievement of one or more of the functions and purposes of this Council; and

b) the member churches of the World Council in the area have been consulted prior to the action.

2. Each associate council:

a) shall be invited to send a Delegated Representative to the Assembly;

b) may, at the discretion of the Central Committee, be invited to send an adviser to meetings of the Central Committee; and

c) shall be provided with copies of all general communications sent to all member churches of the World Council of Churches.

3. In addition to communicating directly with its member churches, the World Council shall inform each associate council regarding important ecumenical developments and consult it regarding proposed World Council programmes in its country.

XI. Regional conferences

1. The World Council recognizes regional conferences of churches as essential partners in the ecumenical enterprise.

2. Such regional conferences as may be designated by the Central Committee:

a) shall be invited to send a Delegated Representative to the Assembly;

b) shall be invited to send an adviser to meetings of the Central Committee; and

c) shall be provided with copies of all general communications sent to all member churches of the World Council of Churches.

3. In addition to communicating directly with its member churches, the World Council shall inform each of these regional conferences regarding important ecumenical developments and consult it regarding proposed World Council programmes in its region.

XII. World Confessional Bodies

Such World Confessional Bodies as may be designated by the Central Committee shall be invited to send delegated representatives to the Assembly and advisers to meetings of the Central Committee and the World Council will take steps to develop cooperative working relationships with them.

XIII. Legal provisions

1. The duration of the Council is unlimited.

2. The legal headquarters of the Council shall be at Grand-Saconnex, Geneva, Switzerland. It is registered in Geneva as an association according to Art. 60ff. of the Swiss Civil Code. Regional offices may be organized in different parts of the world by decision of the Central Committee.

3. The World Council of Churches is legally represented by its Executive Committee or by such persons as may be empowered by the Executive Committee to represent it.

4. The World Council shall be legally bound by the joint signatures of two of the following persons: the President or Presidents, the Moderator and Vice-Moderator or Vice-Moderators of the Central Committee, the General Secretary, the Deputy General Secretaries and the Assistant General Secretaries. Any two of the above-named persons shall have power to authorize other persons, chosen by them, to act jointly or single on behalf of the World Council of Churches in fields circumscribed in the power of attorney.

5. The Council shall obtain the means necessary for the pursuance of its work from the contributions of its member churches and from donations or bequests.

6. The Council shall not pursue commercial functions but it shall have the right to act as an agency of interchurch aid and to publish literature in connection with its aims. It is not entitled to distribute any surplus income by way of profit or bonus among its members.

7. Members of the governing bodies of the Council or of the Assembly shall have no personal liability with regard to the obligations or commitments of the Council. The commitments entered upon by the Council are guaranteed solely by its own assets.

XIV. Rules of debate

1. Categories of session

The Assembly shall sit either in general sessions (see Rule XIV.4), in business session (see Rule XIV.5), or in deliberative session (see Rule XIV.6). The Business Committee shall determine the category of session appropriate to the matters to be considered.

2. Presiding officers

The presiding officers shall be proposed by the Central Committee at the first business session and by the Business Committee after its election.
a) In general session one of the Presidents or the Moderator of the Central Committee shall preside.
b) In business session the Moderator or a Vice-Moderator of the Central Committee or some other member of the Central Committee shall preside.
c) In deliberative session one of the Presidents, the Moderator or a Vice-Moderator of the Central Committee or a delegate shall preside.

3. Formal responsibilities of the Moderator

The Moderator shall announce the opening, suspension or adjournment of the Assembly, and shall announce at the beginning of every session, and at any point where the category changes, that the Assembly is in general or business or deliberative session.

4. General session

The Assembly shall sit in general session for ceremonial occasions, public acts of witness and formal addresses. Only matters proposed by the Central

Committee or by the Business Committee after its election shall be considered.

5. *Business session*

The Assembly shall sit in business session when any of the following types of business are to be considered: adoption of the agenda presented by the Central Committee, any proposal for change in the agenda, nominations, elections, proposals with reference to the structure, organization, budget or programme of the World Council of Churches, or any other business requiring action by the Assembly, except as provided in paragraphs 4 and 6 of this Rule.

The Rules of Debate applicable to a business session are:

a) *Moderator*

The Moderator shall seek to achieve the orderly and responsible despatch of business. He or she shall seek so far as possible to give fair and reasonable opportunity for differing views to be expressed. He or she shall ensure good order and the observance of the appropriate Rules of Debate and shall seek to ensure relevance and prevent repetition. To those ends the Moderator may request a speaker to move to another point or cease speaking. The Moderator shall grant the right to speak and determine the order of speakers. His or her decision is final in all matters except as to his or her decision on a point of order under paragraph (u) below or his or her announcement as to the sense of the meeting on an issue, under paragraph (l) below or as to the result of voting under paragraphs (n) and (o) below.

b) *Speaking*

Any person desiring to speak shall stand in his or her place and speak only when granted the right to do so by the Moderator. The speaker shall state his or her name and church, and address his or her remarks to the Moderator. A delegate may speak only to propose or second a motion or amendment, to engage in the debate or to state a point of order or procedure, and any other speaker only to engage in debate or to state a point of procedure. Any speaker may give notice of his or her desire to speak to the Moderator, and the Moderator shall have regard to such notice, but the Moderator remains free to grant the right to speak and determine the order of speakers under paragraph (a) of this Rule.

c) *Proposing a motion*

A delegate who desires to propose any motion arising from business on the agenda shall state it orally and, except in the case of a privileged motion or motion under paragraphs (j) or (k) of this Rule, shall furnish a written copy to the Moderator. A delegate who desires to propose an item of new business shall follow the procedure set out in Rule XIV.7.

d) *Seconding a motion*

A motion shall not be considered by the Assembly until it is seconded by a delegate. When a motion has been seconded it may not be withdrawn except with the general consent of the delegates present and voting. If general consent is given for withdrawal any delegate may then require the motion to be put in his or her own name.

e) *Debate*
When a motion has been seconded, the debate upon it shall be opened by the delegate who proposed the motion. That delegate may speak for not more than five minutes. That speech shall be followed by a delegate speaking in opposition to the motion who may speak for not more than five minutes. After that the speakers shall alternate as far as the nature of the business allows between those who favour and those who oppose the motion. Each may speak for not more than five minutes. When the debate is closed, the delegate who proposed the motion may reply, but shall speak for not more than three minutes. No other speaker may speak more than once on the motion.

f) *Amendment*
Any delegate may propose an amendment to a motion in the same manner as a motion. Paragraphs (c), (d) and (e) of this Rule shall apply to an amendment as they apply to a motion. The debate on an amendment shall be limited to the amendment. The proposer of the motion shall be given the opportunity to speak in the debate on an amendment. The Moderator shall rule out of order and not receive an amendment which is substantially the negative of the motion being debated.

g) *Amendment to an amendment*
Any delegate may propose an amendment to an amendment in the same manner as an amendment, but the Moderator shall rule out of order and not receive an amendment to an amendment to an amendment. Paragraphs (c), (d), (e) and (f) of this Rule shall apply to an amendment to an amendment as they apply to an amendment.

h) *Debate and voting on amendments*
The debate and vote shall be first upon the amendment to the amendment then upon the amendment, and finally upon the motion. When an amendment to an amendment or an amendment has been voted upon, an additional amendment to the amendment or an amendment may be proposed, but the Moderator shall rule out of order and not receive an amendment to an amendment or an amendment substantially to the same effect as one already voted upon.

i) *Rights of Moderator to take part in a debate*
The Moderator shall not propose a motion or amendment or participate in debate without handing over his or her duties to another presiding officer and shall not, after that, preside again until that matter of business has been decided.

j) *Privileged motions*
Any delegate who has not previously spoken on a motion or amendment may move at any time, but not so as to interrupt a speaker, one of the following privileged motions, which shall take precedence over pending

business, and shall have priority in the order listed, the motion with the highest priority being listed first:

1) *To recess or to adjourn*
   If the Assembly decides to recess or adjourn, the matter pending at recess or adjournment shall be taken up when the Assembly reconvenes, unless there is an "order of the day" at that time, in which event the matter pending at recess or adjournment shall be taken up at the conclusion of the "order of the day" or at such time as the Business Committee proposes.

2) *That the question not be put*
   If the Assembly agrees that the question shall not be put, it shall pass to the next business without taking a vote or decision.

3) *To postpone indefinitely*
   When a matter has been postponed indefinitely, it may not be taken up again at the entire meeting of the Assembly, except with the consent of two-thirds of the delegates present and voting.

4) *To postpone to a time specified*
   When a matter is postponed to a time specified, it becomes the "order of the day" for that time and takes precedence over all other business.

5) *To refer to a committee*
   When a matter is referred to a committee, the committee shall report on it during the meeting of the Assembly unless the Assembly itself directs otherwise.

   Once a privileged motion has been seconded, a vote on it shall be taken immediately without debate.

k) *Motion to close debate*
   Any delegate may propose a motion to close debate at any time but not so as to interrupt another speaker. If seconded, a vote shall be taken immediately without debate on the following question: Shall debate on the pending motion (or amendment) be closed? If two-thirds of the delegates present and voting agree, a vote shall be taken immediately without further debate on the pending motion (or amendment). After the vote on a pending amendment to an amendment, or on a pending amendment, the debate shall continue on the amendment or on the main motion as the case may be. A further motion to close debate can be made on any business then pending. If a motion to close debate is proposed and seconded on the main motion, before the vote is taken on that motion, the Assembly shall be informed of the names of delegates wishing to speak and any amendments remaining and the Moderator may ask the members of the Assembly for a show of hands of any wishing to speak.

l) *Sense of the meeting*
   The Moderator shall seek to understand the sense of the meeting on a pending matter and may announce it without taking a vote. Any delegate may challenge the Moderator's decision on the sense of the meeting, and the Moderator may then either put the matter to the vote under paragraph

(n) below or allow further discussion and again announce the sense of the meeting.

m) *Moderator to put question*
The Moderator shall put each matter not otherwise decided to a vote.

n) *Voting – by show of hands*
At the end of a debate, the Moderator shall read the motion or amendment and shall seek to ensure that delegates understand the matter upon which the vote is to be taken. Voting shall ordinarily be by show of hands. The Moderator shall first ask those in favour to vote; then those opposing; then those who abstain from voting. The Moderator shall then announce the result.

o) *Voting – by count or secret written ballot*
If the Moderator is in doubt, or for any other reason decides to do so, or if any delegate demands it, a vote on the matter shall be taken immediately by count on a show of hands or by standing. The Moderator may appoint tellers to count those voting and abstaining. Any delegate may propose that the Assembly vote on any matter by secret written ballot, and if seconded and a majority of the delegates present and voting agree, a secret written ballot shall be taken. The Moderator shall announce the result of any count or secret written ballot.

p) *Results of voting*
A majority of the delegates present and voting shall determine any matter unless a higher proportion is required by the Constitution or these Rules. If the vote results in a tie, the matter shall be regarded as defeated. The number of those abstaining from voting however numerous shall have no effect on the result of the vote.

q) *Voting by Moderator*
Any Moderator entitled to vote, may vote in a secret written ballot, or any vote by show of hands or standing, or may vote if the vote results in a tie, but in no case shall he or she vote more than once.

r) *Reconsideration*
Any two delegates who previously voted with the majority on any matter which has been voted upon may request the Business Committee to propose to the Assembly that that matter be reconsidered. The Business Committee may agree with or refuse that request, but if they refuse, those delegates may follow the procedure set out in Rule XIV.7, except that a matter shall not be reconsidered unless two-thirds of the delegates present and voting concur in the reconsideration.

s) *Dissent and abstention*
Any delegate voting with the minority or abstaining may have his or her name recorded.

t) *Point of order or procedure*
Any delegate may raise a point of order or procedure and may, if necessary, interrupt another delegate to do so. As a point of order, a

delegate may only assert that the procedure being followed is not in accordance with these Rules. As a point of procedure, a speaker may only ask for clarification of the pending matter.

u) *Appeal on Moderator's decision*

Any delegate may appeal the decision of the Moderator concerning a point of order, as defined in paragraph (t). If such an appeal is made the Moderator shall put the following question to the Assembly without further debate: Shall the Assembly concur in the decision of the Moderator? A majority of the delegates present and voting shall determine the appeal.

v) *Time limits*

The Moderator may, at his or her discretion, allow extra time to any speaker if the Moderator believes that injustice may be done to a member through difficulty of language or translation, or for any other reason, or because of the complexity of the matter under debate.

6. *Deliberative session*

The Assembly shall sit in deliberative session when the matters before it are of such a theological or general policy nature that detailed amendment is impracticable. Reports of sections shall be discussed in deliberative session. Any committee or other body reporting may recommend to the Business Committee that its report be considered in deliberative session.

The Rules of Debate applicable to a deliberative session are the same as those for a business session, except that the following additional rules shall apply:

a) *Motions permitted*

In addition to privileged motions or the motion to close debate, under paragraphs 5(j) and (k), the only motions which may be proposed regarding matters to be considered in a deliberative session are:

1) to approve the substance of the report and commend it to the churches for study and appropriate action;

2) to refer to the body reporting with instructions to consider whether a new or different emphasis or emphases shall be incorporated in the report;

3) to instruct the body reporting to provide, in consultation with the Business Committee, for an open hearing on the report before reporting again.

b) *Matters concerning ecclesiological self-understanding*

Where a matter being raised is considered by a member to go against the ecclesiological self-understanding of his or her church, he or she may request that it not be put to the vote. The Moderator will in such a case seek the advice of the Business Committee or the Executive Committee in consultation with this member and other members of the same church or confession present at the session. If there is consensus that the matter does in fact go against the ecclesiological self-understanding of the member, the Moderator will announce that the matter be dealt with in deliberative session without vote. The materials and minutes of the discussion will be sent to the churches for their study and comment.

c) *Speaking*

Any person presenting a report may also speak in the debate for purposes of clarification or explanation if the Moderator allows him or her to do so.

7. *New business or change in the agenda*

When any delegate desires to have an item of business included on, or any change in, the agenda and the Central Committee or Business Committee after its election has after consideration not agreed to its acceptance, he or she may inform the Moderator in writing. The Moderator shall at a convenient time read the item of business or proposed change and a member of the Business Committee shall explain the reasons for its refusal. The delegate may then give the reasons for its acceptance. The Moderator shall then without further debate put the following question to the Assembly: Shall the Assembly accept this item of business/proposal? A majority of the delegates present and voting shall determine the question. If the Assembly votes in favour of the acceptance of the item of business or change, the Business Committee shall make proposals as soon as possible for the inclusion of the item of business or for the change, in the agenda.

8. *Languages* .

The working languages in use in the World Council of Churches are English, French, German, Russian and Spanish. The General Secretary shall make reasonable effort to provide interpretation from any one of those languages into the others. A speaker may speak in another language only if he or she provides for interpretation into one of the working languages. The General Secretary shall provide all possible assistance to any speaker requiring an interpreter.

9. *Suspension of rules*

Any delegate may propose that any Rule of Debate may be suspended. If seconded, the rule shall be suspended only by vote of two-thirds of the delegates present and voting.

10. *Central Committee*

The Central Committee shall sit in business session, unless it decides to sit in general or deliberateive session, and shall follow the appropriate Rules of Debate for that category of session as are applied in the Assembly, except insofar as the Central Committee may decide otherwise.

XV. Amendments

Amendments to these Rules may be moved at any session of the Assembly or at any session of the Central Committee by any member and may be adopted by a two-thirds majority of those present and voting, except that no alteration in Rules I, IV and XV shall come into effect until it has been confirmed by the Assembly. Notice of a proposal to make any such amendment shall be given in writing at least twenty-four hours before the session of the Assembly or Central Committee at which it is to be moved.

ACKNOWLEDGMENTS

The World Council of Churches expresses thanks to the hundreds of volunteers and organizations who gave so generously of their time and resources and without whom the Assembly would not have been possible. Special thanks are due to:
- the Canadian National Coordinating Committee and the Canadian churches
- the members of the Vancouver Planning Committee
- the University of British Columbia, and particularly the Conference Centre and the catering services
- the Vancouver School of Theology
- the Lutheran Campus Centre
- St Andrew's Hall
- Presbyterian Church (USA)
- Knox United Church, Vancouver
- Broadcasting Committee, BC Conference, United Church of Canada
- Loomis Courier Service and Loomis Moving and Storage
- Apple (Canada)
- Barbecon Incorporated
- British Columbia Telephone Co.
- Campbell Sharp, chartered accountants
- Peterson, Stark and Fowler, lawyers
- Benwell Atkins Ltd., printers
- the United Church Observer and the Canadian Churchman
- the Canadian Conference of Catholic Bishops

INDEX

aboriginal peoples 1, 15, 23, 41, 89, 141, 150, 164
abortion 69
accredited visitors 7
advisers 7
Afghanistan 161 ff.
Africa 105
ageing 56, 59, 66, 70
Albania 130
alcoholism 67, 70
Amsterdam 1948 44, 114
Amsterdam Public Hearing on Nuclear Weapons and Disarmament (1981) 75, 135, 137
Angola 154
apartheid 84 ff., 152 ff.
apostolic creed 35, 45, 48
arms
– conventional 75
– increase in 3, 75
– nuclear 75, 85, 134, 154
– race 3, 25, 39, 78, 84, 131
– reduction 24, 76 ff.
art exhibitions 16
Asia 105
Assembly Committees
– Business 15, 130
– Credentials 14
– Finance 14, 113, 128
– Message 15
– Nominations 14, 123 ff.
– Policy Reference I 14, 113 ff., 115, 117, 122, 123
– Policy Reference II 14, 130 ff., 138, 144, 147, 151, 161, 162, 163
– Press and Broadcasting 15
– Programme Guidelines viii, 14, 117, 127 ff.
– Vancouver Planning 7, 15, 16
– Worship 15
Assembly work book 129
associate councils 7

Bantustan 153, 155
baptism 36, 44, 54
Belize 158 ff.
baptism–eucharist–ministry
– document 2, 12, 43, 44, 45, 46, 47, 49, 59, 101, 115, 118, 146
– liturgy 10, 43, 52
– official response to 46
– process of reception 43, 45, 46, 47, 48, 50, 101, 123
– study guide 47
Bible study 13, 89, 101
biomedical technology 69

campus ministry 93, 98, 101
Canadian involvement 10, 15, 16
Cantate Domino 9
Canvas 17
Caribbean 105, 158, 159
caste 86, 89, 130
catechetical programmes 101
Central America 86, 89, 156 ff.
Central Committees
– 1975 6, 63
– 1976 30, 129
– 1977 141
– 1980 63, 144, 150
– 1981 115, 116, 123, 124
– 1982 75, 123, 124, 141
– 1983 6, 7, 15, 18, 31, 123 ff., 126
children 35, 36, 37, 52, 56, 59, 60, 87
Christian education 93, 95, 98

Christian Medical Commission   64
Christian World Communions   7,
    14, 51, 122 ff.
Church and Society   77, 81, 114
churches responding to racism in the
    1980s   87
classism   49, 86, 88, 89
clusters   13, 27, 113
colonialism   32, 73
Commission on Inter-church Aid,
    Refugee and World Service   166
Commission of the Churches on
    International Affairs   162, 165 ff.
Commission on the Churches' Par-
    ticipation in Development   98
Commission on World Mission and
    Evangelism   114, 120
commitment
− act of   22
− to ecumenical vision   2
− to God's purpose   viii
− to justice and peace   38
− to mission and evangelism   2
"common witness"   119, 137
"credible Christian communica-
    tion"   110
communication   103 ff., 109, 132
Communication Department   108
community-building   33, 63, 93,
    94, 98, 105
community of confessing and learn-
    ing   viii
community of women and men in
    the church (see also:
    Sheffield)   43, 49, 68, 70, 88
congregation(al)   93, 113
− education   93, 95 ff.
− learning   100
conscientious objection   see: non-
    violence
coopted staff   7
Costa Rica   156 ff.
covenant   6, 89
− of life   156
creation
− God's purpose for   viii, 54

− future of   78, 137
crime against humanity   136, 138
culture
− and gospel   32 ff.
− in ecumenical communica-
    tion   109
Cyprus   162

death, forces of   3, 72
delegates   7
delegated observers   7
delegated representatives   7
destabilization   154, 155
deterrence   73, 75 ff., 136
development education   94, 98 ff.
diakonia   35, 62, 69
dialogue   23, 40, 117
− guidelines on   42
− with people of other faiths   26,
    39, 40, 41, 114, 120, 150
− with world of science   77 ff., 93
disability (see also: persons with
    disabilities)   66 ff., 70, 93
disarmament   75 ff., 134 ff.
− world disarmament cam-
    paign   134
disappearances   141
discrimination   26, 27, 52, 55, 83,
    85
drug abuse   67, 70

economy   84, 132
− economic disorder   140
− new international economic or-
    der   3, 26, 38, 55
− world economic order   74, 77,
    84, 86
ecology   68, 78, 97, 101
ecumenical
− Church Loan Fund (ECLOF)   69
− Development Cooperative So-
    ciety (EDCS)   69, 83, 91
− education   101, 121
− memory   18
− organizations   7, 14
− Prayer Cycle   99

– review vii, 10, 117
– sharing of resources 63, 64, 101
– social engagement 18, 120
– team visits 5, 58, 101, 110, 114, 116, 117
– vision 2, 120
educational programmes 68, 80, 90 ff., 93, 95, 97, 99, 100 ff.
education and renewal 30
elitism 54
El Salvador 156 ff.
"empty hands" 63
environment 36, 64
ethics 66, 69, 78, 80
– bio-ethics 80
– political 91
– of war and peace 72, 75
Ethiopia 130
eucharist 25, 26, 36, 43, 44, 54, 62, 85
– participation of children in 100
– participation of persons with disabilities in 100
Europe 87
euthanasia 69
evangelicals (open letter) 17
Evanston 1954 44, 112
exploitation 37, 78
extrajudicial detention and executions 85, 141, 152

Faith and Order 43, 47, 113 ff., 119 ff.
– conferences 51, 114, 115
faith, science and the future (conference on) 77, 114
family (see also: parent) 35, 68, 93 ff.
fellowship
– conciliar 44, 46, 52, 94, 112 ff.
– eucharistic 43, 49
film festival 16
finance (see also: Assembly committees) 113, 128
food
– disorder 144 ff.

– mismanagement of resources 144
– as political weapon 145
– production 145
forum on bilateral conversations 122, 123
fuel crisis 81

generation gap 56
genetic engineering 69, 80, 81
genocide 85, 165
gospel 32, 33
– and culture 42
– tradition of the 46
– witnessing to the 34, 44
· governments, appeals to 143, 160
grassroots involvement 26
Guatemala 156 ff.
guests 7

health care programmes 65 ff.
Helsinki Final Act 143
Hiroshima 11, 131
homelands 87, 153
homeless 38
Honduras 156 ff.
human rights 38, 83, 88, 91, 99 ff., 132, 134
– categories 139 ff.
– statement on 138 ff.
– WCC Advisory Group on 143
– WCC Programme on 143
– violations of 73 ff., 86, 88, 105, 131, 148, 158, 165, 166, 167
homosexuality 54, 69
hungry, hunger 2, 23, 26, 38, 54, 131, 144

idolatry 66, 84
illiteracy 52, 54
"images of life" 14, 21
immigration 87
injustice 3, 37, 83, 103, 131
– economic 73
– social 26
International Monetary Fund 147

interpreters 7
investment 90, 91
Israeli-Palestinian conflict 148
Issue Groups 14, 15, 18, 30, 43, 52,
    62, 72, 83, 93, 103, 113, 127

jelly babies 36
Jerusalem 150
John Paul II 8, 118
Joint Consultative Group 120
Joint Working Group 14, 117 ff.,
    119, 121
justice 34, 64, 65, 73 ff.
justice and peace (see also: peace and
    justice) viii, 3, 11, 13, 17, 19, 24,
    97, 102
– need for 49
– struggle for 49, 72 ff., 94
– covenant for 89
justice and security 133, 134
justice and human dignity 83 ff.,
    137
just, participatory and sustainable
    society 30, 78, 84, 90

Korea 86

land owners 145
land rights 87 ff.
"land rights of indigenous
    peoples" 141
language 35, 93 ff., 96, 99 ff., 109
lay, laity 7, 52, 55, 58, 101
Lebanon 148, 149
Lesotho 167
life-style 38, 63, 98, 100
liturgical education 93, 95
Lutheran World Federation 122

martyrs, martyrdom 35, 39, 89
mass media 88, 103 ff., 106
materialism 24
Melbourne conference 39, 42, 114

member churches (see also: relation-
    ships) 5, 108, 112, 115 ff.

– appeals and recommendations
    to 40, 41, 57 ff., 75, 132 ff.,
    136 ff., 143, 146 ff., 149 ff., 154 ff.,
    164
Message (Assembly) viii, 1-4, 15,
    27, 28
Middle East 147, 150
migrants 100, 142
militarism, militarization 25, 37,
    72 ff., 88, 89, 133, 141, 154, 166
military 1, 54, 77
minorities 34, 67, 100, 106
mission and evangelism viii, 2
– "an ecumenical affirmation" 41
mission 6, 38, 39, 62
missionary
– era 32
– expansion 39
– movement 33
modernization 33
monastic vows 25
Montreal 1963 44, 46
moratorium 81

Nairobi 1975 vii, 5, 6, 14, 30, 44,
    48, 63, 64, 83, 84, 88, 93, 112,
    116, 118, 122, 138, 144, 150, 151
Namibia 153, 155
national security doctrine 2, 65,
    73, 74, 84, 85, 87, 88, 133, 141,
    166
national councils of churches 51,
    108, 120
NATO 134
natural resources 145
networks 91, 101
New Delhi 1961 44
new religious movements 41
new world information and com-
    munication order 106
Nicaragua 156, 158
Nicene Creed 48
non-proliferation treaty 76, 134
nuclear (see also: deterrence)
– deployment 76, 130
– doctrines 75

– first use 76, 136
– free zone 135, 163
– moratorium 76
– testing 36, 76, 163
– war 3, 24, 27, 72, 131

observers 7
"Opening Eyes and Ears" 109 .
oppression 37, 54, 83, 86, 90, 110, 131
ordained ministry
– of homosexuals 54
– of persons with disabilities 60, 70
– of women 52, 70
Orthodox churches 27, 58, 116, 122, 124, 125, 126

Pacific 84, 105, 135, 163 ff.
Palestine Liberation Organization 149
Panama 156 ff.
panel 25
parent 68, 70, 95
participants Assembly (categories) 6–8
participation 27, 35 ff., 45, 47, 52 ff., 65 ff., 104
– peoples' 57, 60, 65, 86, 94, 96, 106
pastoral ministry 67 ff., 72, 77
peace movements 18, 27, 68, 72 ff., 77, 86
peace and justice (see also: justice and peace) 3, 16, 44, 100 ff., 132 ff., 137
peaceful resolution of conflicts 132, 134
people's movements 54, 57, 60, 86, 91
persons with disabilities 37, 52, 57, 60, 97, 100, 105
Philippines 166
plenary sessions 13, 15, 18, 19, 21
Ploughshares 16
poverty, poor 26, 37, 39, 83

power 27, 52, 54, 74, 85 ff., 113
prayer 25, 89
pre-Assembly events 16
President (Honorary) WCC 8, 125
presidium WCC 6, 15, 124, 125
press 7, 8, 15, 17
priesthood of all believers 54
Programme to Combat Racism 18, 87, 91, 166
programme concentration areas 30, 113, 127 ff.
programme hearings 14, 127
public statements 129 ff.
publications WCC 116
racism 37, 55, 57, 73, 85 ff., 89, 132, 151 ff., 167
– classism, sexism 49
reconciliation 27, 49
refugees 1, 56, 90, 100, 131, 142, 155, 158, 162
regional
– meetings 15
– councils of churches 42, 51
relationships
– among churches 41, 45, 46, 48, 50 ff., 63 ff., 115 ff.
– bilateral 43, 48, 51, 64
– with Roman Catholic Church 14 (see also: Joint Consultative Group, Joint Working Group), 120
religious fanaticism 141, 148
religious liberty 84, 130, 142
renewal 6, 43, 49, 50, 64, 113, 117, 119
repentance 37, 38
reports
– from Clusters 113
– General Secretary vii, 13, 112 ff.
– from Issue Groups 19, 30, 31
– Moderator Central Committee vii, 13, 112, 113 ff.
resource sharing system 69
righteousness 132
Roman Catholic Church 14, 27, 117, 119 ff.

Salvation Army   115, 116
science and technology   3, 23, 28,
    55, 74, 77 ff., 80, 84, 88 ff.
Secretariat for Promoting Christian
    Unity   9, 118, 122
sects   36
servanthood of ministry   114
service   6, 96, 100
sexism   49, 73, 86 ff., 89
sharing
– power   3
– resources   63, 64, 69, 101
– responsibility   84
Sheffield conference   49, 50, 88,
    114
sick, illness   2, 23, 26, 38
sign
– church as   43
– of new creation   45
Small Groups   13, 21, 27, 113
Sodepax   120
solidarity with poor, oppressed,
    marginalized   2, 34, 54, 64, 90
South(ern) Africa   85, 86, 87,
    151 ff., 155
South Korea   130
Sri Lanka   166
staff WCC   7, 17, 101, 116
– coopted   7
statements on public issues   14, 19,
    129 ff.
stewardship   22, 64, 137
sub-themes   2, 3, 21 ff.
survival
– struggle for   1
– threats to   77 ff., 131, 132
SWAPO   154

Tamil community   167
tent   12, 110
technology   33, 72, 78 ff., 85
– of food production   145
– new forms of   79
test ban treaty   76, 136
testimonies   18
theme   vii, 21, 75, 104

theology   viii, 110, 117
tobacco   67, 70
Toronto declaration   115
torture   88, 90, 141, 152
totem pole   15
"towards the common expression
    of the apostolic faith today"   48
training (see also: educational
    programmes)   68, 101
translators   7
transnational
– corporations   57, 65, 79, 86, 90,
    105, 145
– systems   84
two per cent appeal   69, 91
Turkey   162 ff.

unemployment   84, 90, 100, 142
united and uniting churches   116,
    122, 123, 127
United Nations
– charter   134
– Commission on Human
    Rights   164 ff.
– Declaration on the Elimination of
    All Forms of Intolerance and Dis-
    crimination Based on Religion or
    Belief   142
– General Secretary   156, 161
– International Covenant on Civil
    and Political Rights   140
– International Covenant on
    Economic, Social and Cultural
    Rights   139
– International Year of Peace
    1986   134
– Organization   74, 77
– Security Council   134, 148, 155
– Universal Declaration of Human
    Rights   139
unity   viii, 21, 25 ff.
– criteria for   119
– for all God's people   132
– of the Church   44 ff.
– of the Church and unity of the
    human community   26, 30, 43

– of the Church and renewal of the human community 49, 50
– and renewal of the Church 43, 50
– and mission 6
– "in each place and in all places" 123
Uppsala 1968 26, 44
USA 74, 76, 87, 89, 130, 157 ff., 161, 166
USSR 74, 76, 130, 134, 161 ff.

violence 3, 87, 90
– culture of 84
– non- 72, 77, 130
visitors 16

war (see also: arms, disarmament, nuclear) 24, 27, 36
Warsaw Treaty Organization 134
wealth 24, 27, 38, 39, 65
Well 16
witness 21, 39, 43, 45, 52
– Christian 31, 40
– common 118, 119, 120, 137
– diversity in 119
– WCC 17

women 7, 16, 33, 37, 41, 52, 55 ff., 58, 87, 124
– in theological education 93
– leadership by 18, 136
– networks 55
– oppression of 88
– ordination of 52, 58
– Orthodox 58
World Council of Churches 18, 51, 52, 57, 79, 99, 108, 110, 112 ff., 114 ff., 129, 131, 139, 144, 161, 166
– Constitution and Rules 6, 30, 43, 118
– criticism of 10, 17, 117
– recommendations to (see also: member churches, recommendations to) 37, 143, 162, 164
World Association for Christian Communication 110
working languages 8
worship 3, 9, 10 ff., 12, 15, 18, 21, 25, 27, 34, 35, 41, 43, 45, 70, 89, 95 ff., 100, 110, 137

youth, young people 7, 16, 27, 33, 35, 41, 52, 56, 58, 124, 127, 136

Biblical references

Gen. 1:26-28 84
Gen. 3:5 84
Lev. 25 146
Ps. 9:12, 18 157
Ps. 76:10 73
Isa. 58:6-12 25
Ezek. 7:10 85
Matt. 5:23-26 27
Matt. 17:1-8 11
Matt. 18:3-4 36
Matt. 19:14 36
Matt. 25:30 ff. 38
Matt. 25:35, 42 146
Matt. 28:20 85
Luke 7:22 37

Luke 16:19-31 39
Luke 18:2-5 85
John 6:1-4 146
John 6:35 146
John 12:24 2
John 17:21 52
John 19:11 85
Acts 2:5-12 104
Acts 4:34 39
Rom. 6:9 ff. 49
Rom. 13:1-2 85
1 Cor. 11:26 34
2 Cor. 8:9 38
Gal. 3:27-28 49
Eph. 1:9-19 84

Eph. 2:14 72
Eph. 2:14-16 152
Col. 1:18-20 52
Col. 2:9-10 84
Heb. 1:1 104
Heb. 1:3 104
James 5:1-3 39
James 5:4-6 39
1 Peter 2:4-10 112
1 Peter 2:21 49
1 Peter 4:6 49
1 John 1 10
1 John 1:1 104
Rev. 11:11 85
Rev. 12:11 84